*ASPECTS
OF THE
HISTORY
OF
ENGLISH*

A page from the Prologue of Chaucer's Canterbury Tales *from Harleian Ms. 7334, British Museum, leaf I,* A.D. *1400–1425. (Photocopied from* Autotype Specimens of the Chief Chaucer MSS., *Johnson Reprint Corporation, 1967.)*

JOHN C. McLAUGHLIN

The University of Iowa

ASPECTS OF THE HISTORY OF ENGLISH

HOLT, RINEHART AND WINSTON, INC.

New York · Chicago · San Francisco · Atlanta · Dallas
Montreal · Toronto · London · Sydney

For Ernest and Gladys

Acknowledgments

For permission to reproduce material for this book, the author wishes to thank The Indiana University Press, The University of Illinois Press, The University of Chicago Press, The University of Michigan Press, The M.I.T. Press, The Ronald Press, Rosenkilde and Bagger, Harcourt, Brace & World, the New Directions Publishing Corporation, J. M. Dent & Sons, Mouton & Co., the Johnson Reprint Corporation, The Pierpont Morgan Library, Det Kongelige Bibliotek, and Göteborgs Universitetsbibliotek.

I wish to express my sincere appreciation to Professor Samuel R. Levin for his scrupulous reading of the manuscript, his many useful suggestions and corrections, and his kind words.

Finally, I wish to thank my colleagues at the University of Iowa, Professors Robert R. Howren, Larry W. Martin, John C. McGalliard, and Robert S. Wachal for their advice and encouragement, and a host of patient and indulgent students.

Preface

> *"History has many cunning passages, contrived corridors*
> *And issues . . . ."*
>
> T. S. Eliot, GERONTION

Where does the history of a language begin? The obvious answer, "At the beginning," is really no answer at all; it only leads to the question, "Where does the beginning begin?" Like an epic, the history of a language must begin somewhere in the middle. And from that middle, wherever it may be, one works forward and backward, or backward and forward, or backward and forward at the same time (to the extent that this is possible). Generally speaking, we work forward on the basis of what we know, or think we know; we work backward on the basis of what we can guess at, or intuit, or conjure up.

Where does the history of the English language begin? We *could* say that it begins with the earliest extant Old English documents. And it might be our arbitrary decision to say that we will begin our history with these. But clearly our earliest documents do not represent the beginnings of English, but only some middle point in its history. Since writing tends to be conservative, it is not even safe to say that the language of such documents is representative of the period in which they were written.

We *could* say that the beginning of English is marked by certain characteristics of phonological change that eventually distinguished Old English from such other West Germanic languages as Old High German, Old Frisian, and Old Saxon. But we might still wish to ask, "What was the nature of those changes, and how does one account for them?" Or, "What changed into what?" And, "What about those language features that Old English held in common with other Germanic languages? Are they not in some important sense *English* features? Should we not know something about their history?"

Or we might ask, "What do we mean by English?" Do we mean that set of phonological, grammatical, and semantic structures with which we are more or less familiar today? If this is what we mean, then perhaps a history of English should begin toward the end of the seventeenth century. Certainly the structures of Modern English have little in common with those of Old English. But then, we find that the language of Shakespeare is what it is because of what happened to it in the fifteenth century, and the fourteenth, and the thirteenth, and so on. And what happened to it during those centuries is its history.

What we will say here is that the search for the beginnings of English is an unrewarding enterprise. It is always difficult to talk about beginnings in any serious way; it is much easier to talk about evolution. So we are back where we began—we will begin our account of the history of English somewhere in the middle.

The language history of a literate people may be discussed in terms of the extralinguistic factors—migrations, invasions, political and social upheavals, technical developments, educational reforms—that have influenced the scope and direction of change. But such factors will tell us little, if anything, about the structure of the linguistic systems and subsystems that constitute the language. If one wishes to know about the *language,* then it is the *language* that he will have to study. By whatever means at his disposal—written records, spelling practices, comparisons with other languages, meter and sound patterns in poetry, puns, comments on the language by contemporary observers— the historical linguist attempts to reconstruct the structure of language systems at some critical stage in their development. A comparison of the shapes of these systems between developmental stages will reveal the nature of linguistic change.

This is a very difficult task—far beyond the capacities of a single individual, no matter how generously endowed. To discover relevant documents, assign dates, restore and decipher handwriting, compare one text with another, assess and emend scribal errors, construct dictionaries, grammars, phonologies, and concordances, to reevaluate data in accordance with changing theories of language—all of these are tasks to which generations of scholars have devoted their professional lives. And faced with a millennium of the shifting shapes and shadows of linguistic features, that have been illumined by several hundred years of scholarly inquiry, the beginning student of English language history may well recall the words of Eliot with which this preface began. Confounding the problems of "cunning passages" and "contrived corridors" is the fact that the study of language in any of its aspects is a highly technical matter requiring some understanding of the linguistic discipline. It is a sad but true fact of life that the student who undertakes to study the history of a language without the necessary linguistic sophistication learns very little about the history of that language. To be sure, he may learn a good deal about the cultural milieu within which that history unfolds. But the two are quite different and ought not to be confused. It is necessary, then, that the student achieve some minimum control over the notions of linguistic theory and methodolgy before the facts of language change will have any meaning for him.

The present text is not written for the linguistics student. It is written for the student of English literature who decides, or for whom it is decided, that his pursuit of an understanding of literature, of whatever period, will be advanced by some technical understanding of the structure of English. Pedagogically, the effort is in two directions: (1) to explain something about linguistics so that the student may understand something about English language history; (2) to explain certain features of English language history so that he may understand something more about linguistics.

No one who attempts a history of English does so without an acute awareness of the great scholarly achievements that have made the writing of it possible. In the face of these, his own contribution seems very insignificant indeed. There is little in this book that can lay claim to originality. And there is much that has been omitted. The decision to include this fact and to omit that one is sometimes difficult to make, and more often than not quite arbitrary. If there has been one overriding criterion, it is "how much detail is necessary to make clear to the novice the nature of linguistic investigation, the structure of English at various crucial periods in its history, and the outlines of the direction of change?"

The professional linguist will find much to quarrel with in this book—not without justification. But the book has not been written for him. The treatment of phonological change as a phenomenon divorced from the grammatical component of the language will not be well received by certain schools of linguistic theory. I make only this defense, that any attempt to specify rules for phonological change in a grammatical subcomponent and in terms of an acoustic feature matrix would place unreasonable demands on the linguistically unsophisticated student. Further, the author is quite aware that the simple generative model that underlies the chapter on grammatical change is archaic. I make no apologies for it; whatever form had been chosen would have been archaic by the time this book is published. Nothing is said in the book about suprasegmental feature systems. Despite attempts by some scholars to specify such systems for various stages of English history, the fact remains that these specifications are based on little more than fertile imagination. The fact also remains that even attempts to specify the suprasegmental feature system for just one Modern English dialect leave a great deal to be desired. I avoid the problem by deliberately ignoring it. Much more can be and certainly needs to be done by way of incorporating the processes of semantic change into a general grammatical model. Here we do little more than pose some of the problems that plague discussion of semantic change, and make a few suggestions as to how one might proceed.

Although much is left undone, perhaps there is some reason to think that the book fulfills its primary purpose: to give the student of English literature some precise linguistic knowledge of the history of his language.

J. C. M.

Iowa City, Iowa
November 1969

Contents

4. *Grammatical Change*   *133*

5. *Grammatical Change Continued*   *235*

6. *Semantic Change*   *271*

ASPECTS OF THE HISTORY OF ENGLISH

1. Introduction

1.10 A Middle English Specimen

The year 1385 marks almost the exact midpoint of the historical period of English with which this book will be concerned. In that year, an Englishman named John Trevisa was at work on an English translation of a history of the world called the *Polichronicon*. This history had originally been written in Latin by Ranulphus Higden who brought his work to the year 1342. Trevisa translated Higden's history rather freely, adding to it here and there, and extending it to the year 1387. Our particular interest lies in a short passage, original with Trevisa, which contains a number of interesting remarks on the different languages and the varieties of English spoken in Britain at the time of writing. As a matter of fact, this is perhaps one of the earliest observations we have on the state of English in the country. From a careful look at both what Trevisa has to say and the characteristics of the English in which he says it, we can learn a great deal about the history of the English language. Although the text will appear strange to you, it will be perfectly obvious that it is in English and not some other language.

1

Chapter LIX. On the Languages of the Inhabitants

As hyt ys yknowe houȝ meny maner people buþ in þis ylond, þer buþ also
of so meny people longages and tonges; noþeles Walschmen and Scottes,
þat buþ noȝt ymelled wiþ oþer nacions, holdeþ wel nyȝ here furste longage
and speche, bote ȝef Scottes þat were som tyme confederat and wonade wiþ
þe Pictes drawe somwhat after here speche. Bote þe Flemmynges, þat   *5*
woneþ in þe west syde of Wales, habbeþ yleft here strange speche and
spekeþ Saxonlych ynow. Also Englysch men, þey hy hadde fram þe
bygynnyng þre maner speche, souþeron, norþeron, and myddel speche, in
þe myddel of þe lond, as hy come of þre maner people of Germania, noþeles,
by commyxstion and mellyng furst wiþ Danes and afterward wiþ Normans,   *10*
in menye þe contray longage ys apeyred, and som useþ strange wlaffyng,
chyteryng, harryng and garryng, grisbittyng. þis apeyryng of þe burþtonge
ys bycause of twey þinges. On ys, for chyldren in scole, aȝenes þe usage and
manere of al oþer nacions, buþ compelled for to leve here oune longage and
for to construe here lessons and here þinges a Freynsch, and habbeþ suþthe   *15*
þe Normans come furst into Engelond. Also gentilmen children buþ ytauȝt
for to speke Freynsch fram tyme þat a buþ yrokked in here cradel, and
conneþ speke and playe wiþ a child hys brouch; and uplondysch men wol
lykne hamsylf to gentilmen, and fondeþ wiþ gret bysynes for to speke
Freynsch for to be more ytold of.   *20*

þys manere was moche yused tofore þe furste moreyn, and ys seþthe
somdel ychaunged. For Johan Cornwal, a mayster of gramere, chayngede
þe lore in gramerscole and construccion of Freynsch into Englysch; and
Richard Pencrych lurnede þat manere techyng of hym, and oþer men of
Pencrych, so þat now, þe ȝer of oure Lord a þousond þre hondred foure   *25*
score and fyve, of þe secunde Kyng Richard after þe conquest nyne, in al
þe gramerscoles of Engelond children leveþ Frensch and construeþ and
lurneþ an Englysch, and habbeþ þerby avauntage in on syde and desavaun-
tage yn anoþer. Here avauntage ys, þat a lurneþ here gramer yn lasse tyme
þan children wer ywoned to do; disavauntage ys, þat now children of   *30*
gramerscole conneþ no more Frensch þan can here lift heele, and þat ys
harm for ham and a scholle passe þe se and travayle in strange londes, and
in meny caas also. Also gentilmen habbeþ now moche yleft for to teche here
children Frensch.

Hyt semeþ a gret wonder hou Englysch, þat ys þe burþtonge of Englysch   *35*
men and here oune longage and tonge, ys so dyvers of soun in þis ylond; and
þe longage of Normandy ys comlyng of anoþer lond, and haþ on maner
soun among al men þat spekeþ hyt aryȝt in Engelond. Noþeles, þer ys as
meny dyvers maner Frensch yn þe rem of Fraunce as ys dyvers manere Englysch in þe rem of Engelond. Also, of þe forseyde Saxon tonge, þat ys deled   *40*
a þre and ys abyde scarslych wiþ feaw uplondysch men, and ys gret wondur;
for men of þe est wiþ men of þe west, as hyt were undur þe same party of
hevene, acordeþ more in sounyng of speche þan men of þe norþ wiþ men of

þe souþ. þerfore hyt ys þat Mercii, þat buþ men of myddel Engelond, as hyt
were parteners of þe endes, understondeþ betre þe syde longages, norþeron   *45*
and souþeron, þan norþeron and souþeron understondeþ eyþer oþer. Al þe
longage of þe Norþhumbres, and specialych at ȝork, ys so scharp, slyttyng
and frotyng and unschape, þat we souþeron men may þat longage unneþe
understonde. Y trowe þat þat ys bycause þat a buþ nyȝ to strange men and
aliens þat spekeþ strangelych, and also bycause þat þe kynges of Engelond   *50*
wonep alwey fer fram þat contray; for a buþ more yturnd to þe souþ contray, and ȝef a goþ to þe norþ contray a goþ wiþ gret help and strenghe. þe
cause why a buþ more in þe souþ contray þan in þe norþ may be betre cornlond, more people, more noble cytes, and more profytable havenes.

With the text before us, let us consider some of the problems it offers a
speaker of Modern English who is unfamiliar with English of the fourteenth
century.

THE ORTHOGRAPHY

Since we are dealing here with the written language we should perhaps
begin our investigation with a look at the spelling system which Trevisa employs. We note immediately that a great many words are spelled exactly as
they are in Modern English writing: *as, people, also, were, after,* and so on.
What other words do you find spelled as we would expect them to be
in Modern English?

A little imagination will enable you to add a great many more words to
your first list of familiar items. For example, what sound or sounds do you
think Trevisa is representing by his use of the symbol þ in such words as þ*is,*
þ*at,* þe, *wi*þ*?* How would this sound be represented in Modern English spelling? Respell all the words in the text in which þ occurs, converting this symbol
to its Modern English counterpart. How many additional familiar words can
you now add to your original list? It should also be perfectly clear to you that
Trevisa uses the symbol *y* where Modern English spelling demands *i*. What
spellings do you find in the text that fall into this category? Can you find
words in the text in which *y* would *not* be replaced by *i* in Modern English
spelling? What would it be replaced by?

Somewhat more difficult to interpret than either þ or *y* in the text is the
symbol ȝ called a *yogh*. In those written dialects of Middle English in which
this symbol occurs it represents at least two, and sometimes three, quite
different sounds, depending upon the position and environment in which it
occurs. Two of these sounds occur in Modern English, but spelled differently;
one of them no longer occurs in *standard* Modern English dialects. How

would you respell the words *ytauȝt* (1. 16) and *ȝork* (1. 47) in Modern English? What *sound* does *yogh* represent in the first word? in the second? Respell in Modern English the words *noȝt* (1. 3), *ȝer* (1. 25), *aryȝt* (1. 38), and *nyȝ* (11. 3, 49).

A great many words you will already have guessed at correctly although their spellings may differ slightly from what we would expect in Modern English. For instance, how does Trevisa spell these words: *speech, speak, three, leave, great, deal, teaching, seems, east, heaven?* At some time or other in reading poetry you may have come across an outmoded variant of the word *enough,* namely *enow.* Can you find in Trevisa an earlier variant spelling of this form? Given the fact that the Middle English form *-lych* has descended from an earlier Old English *lic* meaning "like," "alike," "similar," what can you conclude about the original meaning of such Modern English adverbs and adjectives as *hardly, softly, easily, friendly, lovely, weakly,* and so on?

Consider now another problem. The following third person singular pronouns all begin with the letter *h: he, his, him, himself, her, hers, herself.* (Notice also the second word in the text, *hyt,* which would be *it* in Modern English.) What guesses can you make about the meaning and the modern form of these words in the text: *here* (1. 5), *hy* (1. 7), *hy* (1. 9), *here* (1. 15), *hamsylf* (1. 19), *ham* (1. 32)? In this connection you will have observed that Trevisa mentions an important *external* fact that bears on the development of English, namely the mingling of the English and the Danes in Britain. It is, indeed, just this mingling that accounts for the fact that Modern English has *th-* forms in the third person plural pronouns: *they, their, theirs, them, themselves.* The Old English plurals all began, as did the singulars, with *h-;* our *th-*forms were all borrowed from the Danes during the time that they had settlements in England beginning at the end of the ninth century. With this information in hand, can you make any judgment about the extent of Danish influence in the area in which Trevisa lived?

While we are on the subject of pronouns we might consider one other point. In Shakespeare's play *King Henry the Fifth* there occurs the following conversation between some characters in a tavern in Eastcheap. The subject of the conversation is Sir John Falstaff who has just died:

NYM.   They say he cried out of sack.
HOSTESS.   Ay, that 'a did.
BARDOLPH.   And of women.
HOSTESS.   Nay, that 'a did not.
BOY.   Yes, that 'a did, and said they were devils incarnate.
HOSTESS.   'A could never abide carnation; 'twas a colour he never lik'd.

(II, iii, 29–36.)

The question is, what is this form *'a?* As you may guess, it represents the occurrence of the third person singular masculine subject pronoun in unstressed position. This form was not uncommon two centuries earlier in some written dialects of Middle English. How many instances of it do you find in Trevisa? What number of the pronoun does it represent here?

We will now do a little linguistic detective work. The form *houʒ* (1. 1) is Modern English *how; now* (1. 25) is Modern English *now; ynow* (1. 7) has a later variant *enow* and is standard Modern English *enough.* Further, we have noted the fact that ʒ sometimes replaced the spelling combination *gh,* representing one kind of sound, and sometimes indicated a sound otherwise represented by *y.* Now, look up in a good collegiate dictionary the *etymology* (that is, the earliest recorded form) of each of these words. For our particular problem you will need to know one additional fact; namely, that rather early in the Middle English period the symbol *u* was replaced under certain conditions by the combination *ou,* as a result of French scribal tradition. Thus, very early Middle English would have *hus* for Modern English *house,* while later Middle English would have *hous.* Having found the words in question in your dictionary, can you account for the spelling *ynow* in our text? If you cannot, perhaps it will help if you compare the standard pronunciations of Modern English *enough* and *dough* and their etymologies, or the standard pronunciation of Modern *plow* and its spelling variant *plough.* Regarding *enough* and *dough,* what sound is represented by *gh* in each? Is the final sound in their *etymons* (forms from which they derive) represented by the same Old English symbol? What *different* developments does it seem that this final sound must have had? Now having answered these questions, can you account for the spelling *houʒ?* Would you expect to find the symbol ʒ in this word? If not, why not? How, then, does it come to be there? Can you think of any reason why a rather naive writer of English, perhaps a foreigner not very familiar with English spelling, might spell the word *bite* as *bight?* or *kite* as *kight?* Your answer to this question will help you to explain the occurrence of ʒ in *houʒ.*

THE LEXICAL ITEMS

At this point you have learned a good deal about the written forms of words in Trevisa's text, and with a few good guesses here and there you can probably make quite good sense out of the passage. For the interpretation of certain words, however, you will need some additional direction. And for most of these a good modern dictionary will suffice. Look up the *derivation* (origin, source, or descent) of the words *meddle* and *pell-mell.* Can you now interpret Trevisa's word *ymelled* (1. 3)? You will find in your dictionary a word *won* marked as being archaic. What does it mean? Do you find its counterpart in our text? Look up the derivation of the Modern English word *impair*. From what language does it come? Did some form of the word occur in Middle English? Does a form of it occur in Trevisa? Notice the word *grisbittyng* (1. 12). If it were to occur in Modern English it would be *gristbiting*. What, then, do you think it means?

Look up the noun *deal* in your dictionary. Notice its etymology and its early meaning which is now obsolete in standard English. Does this help you to interpret Trevisa's *somdel* (1. 22)? In Modern English the auxiliary *can* means "to be able to." Can you find an earlier meaning for it in the dictionary? With this earlier meaning in mind, how might you interpret the phrase "conneþ no more Frensch þan can here lift heele"? In Modern English, again, we sometimes make use of a form *-ling* to derive certain nouns of a particular kind; for example, *gosling* from *goose*, and such others as *duckling*, *hireling*, *youngling*, and *foundling*. What seems to be the meaning of *-ling* in these words? Is it the same in all cases? Can you suggest a meaning for *comlyng*?

There are now very few words left in the passage that you do not know; perhaps only these: *þey* "though," *menye* "in general," *suþthe/seþthe* "since," *fondeþ* "try," *moreyn* (look up Modern English *murrain*), *unneþe* "hardly, scarcely," *wlaffyng* "stammering," *chyteryng* "chattering," *harryng* "snarling," *garryng* "roaring," *slyttyng* "piercing," *frotyng* "harsh sounding."

THE GRAMMAR

Although the vocabularly of the text may now be quite clear to you, certain of the grammatical forms and constructions may remain puzzling. For example, early Middle English had a form ʒe prefixed to verb stems as one marker of the past participle of the verb. By the fourteenth century in some dialects this form ʒe had been reduced to *i* or *y*. How many instances of this past participle marker can you find in Trevisa? Consider another grammatical form. In standard Modern English we are accustomed to seeing a linking or auxiliary verb with a shape *be(-)* only as an infinitive, "I want to *be* there"; a present participle, "The house is being painted"; a past participle, "The house has been painted"; an imperative, "Be good, now"; and, more rarely, a subjunctive. "If this be treason, make the most of it." A slight acquaintance with certain dialectal forms of English will, however, convince you that this has not always been, nor is even now, the case. Among some speakers of the language such an utterance as, "They *be* two very good horses," would be quite natural. Falstaff remarks to Prince Hal, ". . . let men say we *be* men of good government." In the Middle English period of our text the *be* shape of the auxiliary and linking verb could be conjugated in all persons and numbers of the present tense, depending upon the dialect of the speaker. Thus:

singular	*plural*
1. be	1., 2., 3. ben, beþ, bes
2. bist (best) bes	
3. biþ (beþ), bes	

In most dialects of England in the fourteenth century, the vowel of this verb was represented by *e* as above; however, in some, because the quality of the vowel had developed differently, it was represented differently. How many occurrences of the verb do you find in Trevisa and how is the vowel represented? Does the linking-auxiliary verb have more than one *stem* shape (by "stem shape" here we mean the combination of consonant and vowel symbols that form the basic part of a word)?

We may note two or three additional grammatical formations that distinguish Trevisa's language from ours. The form *tofore* (1. 21) has given way entirely to *before* in the standard language although both occurred in Old and Middle English. Is the form *caas* (1. 33) singular or plural? What would it be in Modern English? Note the forms *Mercii* (1. 44) and *Norþhumbres* (1. 47). What would these be in Modern English? In Modern English the standard form for the third person plural reflexive pronoun is *themselves.* This is an example of grammatical *redundancy;* that is to say, plurality is marked in two ways: by the form *them* and by the *s* added to the form *selve.* You will notice that such redundancy does not occur in Trevisa where we find the form *hamsylf* (1. 19). As a matter of fact, it was not until a little more than a century later that the form *-selves* began to appear.

Not only do we find that the grammatical structure of words in Trevisa's English is somewhat different from what we would expect in Modern English, but we may also note that the ways in which words combine with each other further distinguish fourteenth century English from Modern English. For example, do you think the phrase "houȝ meny maner people" (1. 1) would be an acceptable grammatical construction in Modern English? If not, why not? What changes would have to be made in order to make it acceptable? Notice the use of *for to* in the two phrases "compelled for to leve" (1. 14) and "for to be more ytold of" (1. 20). Is the use the same in both? If not, how does one differ from the other? At times the definite article does not appear before nouns in situations in which Modern English would demand it: "fram tyme þat a buþ yrokked in here cradel" (1. 17), rather than "from *the* time that." Where else would Modern English require the insertion of a definite article? How do the following constructions differ from their Modern English equivalents: "þat ys bycause þat a buþ nyȝ to strange men" (l. 49), "also bycause þat þe kynges of Engelond" (l. 50), and "þe cause why a buþ more in þe souþ" (ll. 52–53)?

Other arrangements of words and constructions appear strange to the modern reader. Note, for instance, "þer buþ also of so meny people longages and tonges" (ll. 1–2), where we should perhaps say something like, "there are also (different) languages and dialects for so many (diverse) people." Or, "of þe secunde Kyng Richard after þe conquest nyne" (l. 26), which we would write, "after the conquest, the ninth year of King Richard the Second's reign," or "after the conquest, the ninth year of the second King Richard's reign." Consider the phrase "a child hys brouch" (l. 18). What is the modern equivalent? Can you explain the relationship between the Middle English and the Modern English construction?

SEMANTIC CHANGE

[handwritten: Leile no-one but you.]

We have had occasion to take note of certain words in the text that have since been lost to standard Modern English or that survive only as archaisms. We should be aware of the fact that not all words in Trevisa's text which look familiar had the same significance in the fourteenth century that they have today. The combination "bote ȝef" (l. 4) must be interpreted somewhat differently from modern *but if*. Here it must be taken to mean "except." What examples of the use of *but* meaning "except" can you cite in Modern English? In Trevisa, the adjective *confederat* (l. 4) means "associated with." In what kinds of expressions would you use *confederate* today? Would you be apt to use it as Trevisa does? Notice the expression "drawe somwhat after" (l. 5). In such a context what Modern English expression would you use? Look up the words *busy, business,* and *busyness* in your dictionary. What meaning would you attach to *bysynes* (l. 19) in Trevisa's text? In the phrase "lurnede þat maner techynge of hym" (l. 24), what preposition might you substitute for *of?* Notice the difference in the meaning of the *and's* in Middle English illustrated by the following: ". . . *and* þat ys harm for ham *and* a scholle passe þe se *and* travayle in strange londes. . . ." (ll. 31–32). What other conjunction might one substitute in Modern English for the second *and* here? What conjunction would you be inclined to substitute for the *and* in line 21?

In the phrase "chayngede þe lore in gramerscole and construccion of Freynsch into English" (ll. 22–23), both the words *lore* and *construccion* are of some interest. You are undoubtedly familiar with both, but would you be likely to use them in the context in which each appears here? How might you use the word *lore?* What word or words might you use in place of it in Trevisa's context? What does the verb *construe* mean? How would you form a noun from this verb? What, then, does *construccion* mean here?

THE SOUNDS

Thus far we have considered *some* of the differences and similarities that exist between Trevisa's *written* language and the *written* language of Modern English—differences and similarities in spelling, in various kinds of grammatical constructions, and in vocabulary and meaning. But we should keep in mind the fact that the most significant characteristic of language communication is speech, and that most writing is by and large (although not entirely) a way of representing speech. It is of considerable importance, then, that we give some attention to the *sound* of Trevisa's language. But here we encounter certain difficulties for the reason that any very useful discussion of speech sounds at once involves us in a consideration of the physical mechanisms for speech production and in the rather specialized terminology for referring to these mechanisms. In a later chapter of this book we will consider the nature and function of the physical apparatus involved in speech, and present some of the terms generally needed to refer to various aspects of the speech act. And in that chapter we will represent and describe the sounds that characterize one of the prevailing dialects of late Middle English.

EXERCISES

Having now worked out most of the linguistic problems of the text, you will have learned a good deal about the state of English in the fourteenth century. In addition, you will have learned quite a few facts about the *external* history of the language (that is, about the *nonlinguistic* influences that helped to shape the development of the language). See, for example, what answers you can give to the following questions on the basis of the information provided by Trevisa.

1. How many different peoples are mentioned as inhabiting, or having inhabited, the British Isles, and who are they?
2. Can you make a guess as to which of these were the earliest dwellers in Britain?
3. Where did the "Englysch men" come from? *Germany*
4. English, then, must be closely related to what European language? *German*
5. What peoples came to Britain after the English, and in what order? *Danes Normans*
6. What language did the Normans speak? *French*

7. How many different varieties or dialects of English does Trevisa mention as being spoken in England at the time of his writing?
8. What parts of England, according to Trevisa, show the greatest dialect diversity?
9. In what part of England did the Mercians live? In what part the Northumbrians? From what part is Trevisa himself?
10. What reasons does Trevisa give for the sharp, piercing, harsh, and unpleasant speech of the Northumbrians?
11. When Trevisa says that the Northumbrians live near to "strange men and aliens þat spekeþ strangelych," to whom is he referring?
12. Why do you think the kings of England, when they went to the north country, went "wiþ gret help and strengthe"? What might this have to do with dialect differences between north and south?
13. Of what importance do you think the location of the king's residence might have been to the development of the language and of dialectal differences between different regions of the country? (Think of this question in terms of the kinds of activities that are likely to take place in and about a king's court, and how these activities might affect the language.)
14. Trevisa notes the differences in speech between the urban and rural populations of his day. What differences in the mode of life between these two might contribute to some differences in speech? Can you think of urban areas in the United States or elsewhere in which the speech of the inhabitants is in some way distinct from those who live in outlying districts?
15. Would you say that Trevisa was a city dweller? How would you characterize his attitude toward the speech of "uplondysch" men? Do you know people whose manner of speaking English seems harsh and unpleasant to you? Or just strange?
16. How does Trevisa account for the "impairment" of the native tongue?
17. What varieties of Modern English speech are you familiar with? (Keep in mind that differences in the manner of speaking or writing a language can be the result of social as well as geographical conditions.) Would you say that any of these varieties carried with them greater social or political prestige than some others? In what ways might you characterize an individual by his manner of speaking English?
18. Does Trevisa seem to think that it is a good idea for a student to learn French in school? What arguments might *you* use to convince a fellow student of the value of learning a second language?

1.20   An Old English Specimen

Despite its divergences in spelling, sound, and grammar from standard dialects of Modern English, Trevisa's text is quite obviously English. The passage that we will now consider looks much less like English. This is from an earlier stage of the language, Old English. Again, this specimen was originally written in Latin by the Old English historian and scholar Bede (673–735) who spent most of his life and did most of his writing in a monastery at Jarrow, in the north of England. The Latin work was titled *Historia Ecclesiastica Gentis Anglorum*, the *Ecclesiastical History of the English People*, and was completed in the year 731. Some hundred and fifty years later Alfred, King of the West Saxons, presumably had Bede's monumental work translated into Old English for the edification of his people. It is from this translation that the following passage dealing with victories of the Britons over the Saxon invaders is taken, and the language, therefore, is that of the southwestern part of England during the latter part of the ninth century, about five hundred years before Trevisa.

And þa æfter ðon þe se here wæs ham hweorfende ond hi hæfdon ut amærde ond tostencte þa bigengan þysses ealondes, ða ongunnon hi sticcemælum mod ond mægen niman; ond forðeodan of þam diglum stowum þe hi ær on behydde wæron, ond ealre anmodre geðafunge heofonrices fultumes him wæron biddende, þæt hi oð forwyrd æghwær 5 fordiligade ne wæron. Wæs on ða tid heora heretoga ond latteow Ambrosius haten, oðre naman Aurelianus. Se wæs god man ond gemetfæst, Romanisces cynnes man. On þyses mannes tid mod ond mægen Bryttas onfengon; ond he hi to gefeohte forðgecygde ond him sige gehet; ond hi eac on þam gefeohte þurh Godes fultum sige onfengon. Ond þa of ðære tide hwilum 10 Bryttas, hwilum eft Seaxan sige geslogan oð ðæt ger ymbsetes þære Beadonescan dune, þa hi mycel wæll on Angelcynne geslogan, ymb feower ond feowertig wintra Angelcynnes cyme on Breotone.

And then in view of the fact that the army was home turning and they had out driven and expelled the inhabitants of this island, then began they 15 little by little heart and courage to take; and forth went from the secret places which they before in hidden were, and all with unanimous consent heaven kingdom's aid for themselves were asking, that they as far as destruction everywhere destroyed not might be. Was at that time their general and leader Ambrosius called, other name Aurelianus. He was good man and 20 even-tempered, of the Roman kind man. In this man's time heart and courage Britons took; and he them to battle exhorted and them victory promised; and they moreover in the battle through God's help victory took. And then from that time sometimes Britons, sometimes again Saxons victory won by fighting until that year of the siege around Badon mountain, 25 when they great slaughter on the Angle kind made about four and forty of winters of the Angle kind's coming on Britain.

THE VOCABULARY

Certainly, the form of the language here looks far stranger and is more difficult to understand than Trevisa's English. Indeed, except for a few words here and there such as *æfter, ond, wæs, ealondes, of, him, man,* the text hardly looks like English at all. In actual fact, however, there are more resemblances between the vocabulary of the text and that of Modern English than appear in a superficial examination. For example, you may not realize that the word *here* "army" is related to Modern English *harry* meaning "to raid, pillage, torment"; from *mod* we get Modern English *mood; anmodre* literally means "with one (an) mind (mod)," thus "unanimous"; *ær* is a slightly different form of the poetic *ere;* Old English *rice* meant "kingdom," "nation," "power," "rule," and as an adjective "strong," "mighty," "great"; by association also "wealthy," "rich." *Rice,* then, is the Old English parent of Modern English *rich.* From the stem of the word *cynnes* comes Modern English *kin,* and from the infinitive form of the verb *geslogan,* which is *slean,* comes Modern English *slay.* Notice the phrase "of þam diglum stowum" translated "from the secret places." What Modern English verb derives from *stowum?*

Despite the number of relationships one might uncover between the Old English and Modern English forms, there still remains a large number of Old English words in this text that have no Modern English counterparts. In general, these words have been lost to the language and have been replaced by words borrowed from other languages. In the translation, we have replaced the following:

here	by	army
amærde	by	driven
tostencte	by	expelled
bigengan	by	inhabitants
mægen	by	courage
niman	by	take
diglum	by	secret
geðafunge	by	consent
fultumes	by	aid/help
forwyrd	by	destruction
heretoga	by	general
forðgecygde	by	exhorted
sige	by	victory
gehet	by	promised

Look up the derivation of the words in the right-hand column in your dictionary. On the basis of this very limited list, what language or languages would seem to have made important contributions to the vocabulary of English?

The Grammar

As important as this matter of vocabulary loss and replacement may be to our understanding of the history of English, of considerably greater significance are certain grammatical patterns found in Old English but not in Modern English. We can make this statement because it is quite clear that a language is a kind of *code,* a system of signals that tells us how to *interpret* the vocabulary items in relation to their parts and to each other. In order to understand the meaning of an utterance we must understand the code of the language that orders these relationships. The meaning of an utterance is not a matter of simple addition, of taking the meaning of one word, adding this to a second, adding the sum of these two to a third, and so on. To convince yourself of this you need only to recall your own experience in learning a foreign language. In translating from German, French, Spanish, or Latin into English, you may often have known the meaning of every word, but still not have understood the meaning of the whole, simply because you did not fully understand the code or system of signals that defined the relationships between the words in the text. Vocabulary loss and replacement, then, rarely have any effect on the *code* of a language.

Let us consider a few of the ways in which the grammatical patterns of Old English differed from those of Modern English. Notice the following phrases:

1. se here	the army
2. þa bigengan	the inhabitants
3. of þam diglum stowum	from the secret places
4. on þam gefeohte	in the battle

We wish to call attention to the fact that the Old English form which we translate as Modern English "the" has different shapes that signal differences in grammatical function. Considering the translation, how does the grammatical function of 1 differ from that of 2? How do these two differ from 3 and 4? What element is common to each of the words in þam *diglum stowum?* You will notice not only that the form of the word which we translate "the" changes in order to signal a change in the grammatical function of the phrase in which it occurs, but also that in this particular phrase it contains an element common to the other two words in the phrase. In other words, there is a form of the word that signals singular "subject," a form that signals "object plural," and a form that signals something like "location." Furthermore, there is a certain kind of *agreement* between the form of the article, the form of the adjective, and the form of the noun. These are two grammatical patterns that are characteristic of Old English but not of Modern English. A similar example is to be found in the phrases *þysses ealondes* "of this island," and *þyses mannes tid* "this man's time" or "the time of this man." In Modern English the form of the word *this* does not signal the grammatical function of the phrase in which it occurs; it makes no difference to the form of the word whether it occurs in a subject phrase, "This boy ran home," an object phrase, "I saw this boy in the field," or an "of" construction, "I saw the mother of this boy." In standard Modern English the form of *this* changes only to signal plurality.

In the case of *diglum stowum* the common element *-um* indicates not only grammatical function in the sentence but plurality as well. Unlike Modern English, the grammatical form of the adjective agrees with that of the noun it modifies. Another case of agreement between adjective and noun occurs in the phrase *anmodre geðafunge,* but here there are some complications: *geðafunge* belongs to a class of "feminine" nouns, as distinct from "masculine" or "neuter" nouns. Such a classification of nouns is quite common in many of the world's languages, and has nothing to do with the sex of that to which a noun refers. For example, the word for "hand" in French is a feminine noun *la main,* while the word for "foot" is masculine *le pied.* In Latin, the word for "hand," *manus,* is feminine; the word for "lake," *lacus,* is masculine; while the word for "knee," *genū,* is neuter. Such languages are said to have *grammatical gender* in contrast with languages like Modern English which have *natural gender.* Old English, then, had grammatical gender. The final *-e* of *geðafunge* signals the grammatical function and the number, singular. The adjective *anmodre* contains a grammatical signal *-re* that indicates three things: (1) grammatical function, (2) gender (feminine), and (3) number (singular). No adjective in Modern English functions in this way.

We find in the text two verbal forms, the present participles *hweorfende* and *biddende.* The infinitive forms of these verbs are *hweorfan* and *biddan.* What is the signal for the present participle? How does it differ from that in Modern English? Notice the infinitive form *niman,* "to take." Considering all three of these verbs, what is the signal for the infinitive? How is the infinitive signaled in Modern English? The past participles *amærde, tostencte,* and *fordiligade* have as their infinitive forms *amæran, tostencan,* and *fordiligian.* What is the signal for the past participle? Does this appear to bear any relationship to the way in which Modern English signals its past participle?

The verbs *forðgecygde* and *gehet* are both in the past tense; their infinitive forms are *forðgecygan* and *gehaten.* In Modern English we may distinguish verb classes according to the way in which each forms its past tense and past participle. For instance, a very large class add an *-ed* (with various pronunciations) to the verb stem to form both the past tense and the past participle.

Verbs in this class are sometimes referred to as "regular," sometimes as "weak." Another very much smaller class forms the past and past participle by changing the *vowel* of the stem, as in *sing/sang/sung; begin/began/begun.* Such verbs are often (erroneously) called "irregular," sometimes "strong." To which of these classes would you say the Old English verbs in question belong?

Having looked at some of the ways in which word forms in Old English signal grammatical relationships between one word and another, and the difference between these word forms and those to be found in Modern English, let us consider briefly the ways in which words in Old English may be combined into larger grammatical units. You will notice immediately from the translation that the *word order* is quite unlike Modern English: *Se here wæs ham hweorfende* 'the army was home turning,' *hi hæfdon ut amærde* 'they had out driven,' *ða ongunnon hi sticcemælum mod ond mægen niman* 'then began they little by little heart and courage to take,' *þe hi ær on behydde wæron* 'which they before in hidden were!' What other examples of Old English word order do you find that would sound strange to Modern English ears? Rewrite the translation making your revision as much like Modern English as possible. As you are doing this, the point often made by students of Old English may occur to you, namely that the *order* of arrangement of words in an Old English sentence is somewhat less important than the order of arrangement in Modern English sentences; and further, that the *forms* of words in Old English are more important in the grammatical code of the language than are the forms of words in Modern English.

For the most part this estimate of Old English is true. There are times, however, when the word forms of Old English do not tell us quite as much as we would like to know about the grammatical function of a form or set of forms, and we are forced to look to the word order for help. (Since word order is not as fixed in Old English as it is in Modern English, this too may fail us and we are left with a problem in interpretation.) In the sentence *On þyses mannes tid mod ond mægen Bryttas onfengon,* the forms *mod* and *mægen* may signal either subject or object. Further, the form *Bryttas,* too, may indicate either subject or object. The form *onfengon* signals plural, past tense. In Old English we can find examples of both the order *subject-object-verb* and *object-subject-verb.* This means that we can translate the phrase either 'The Britons took heart and courage' or 'heart and courage seized the Britons.' However we translate it, there is very little difference in meaning; the ambiguity is syntactic and not semantic. (Perhaps we need to remark that the second Modern English rendering is also syntactically ambiguous.)

In a later chapter we will consider the structure of Old English in greater detail. Here, we have tried only to illustrate *some* of the kinds of differences between Old and Modern English. Again, because of the technical difficulties involved in discussing the sound system, we will reserve that discussion until later.

1.30   Early Modern English Specimens

Now that we have considered specimens of the language from late Middle English and from Old English, let us look at two that will bring us back to more familiar ground. The first is taken from the works of William Caxton, the first English printer, and is, as he tells us, from a book on chivalry translated from French. The date is about 1484, just a century after the writing of Trevisa. This is an example of very early Modern English.

Here endeth the book of thordre of chyualry, which book is translated
oute of Frensshe in to Englysshe at a requeste of a gentyl and noble esquyer
by me, William Caxton, dwellynge in Westmynstre besyde London, in the
most best wyse that god hath suffred me, and accordynge to the copye that
the sayd squyer delyuered to me; whiche book is not requysyte to euery   *5*
comyn man to have, but to noble gentylmen, that by their vertu extende to
come and entre in to the noble ordre of chyualry, the whiche in these late
dayes hath ben used accordyng to this booke here to fore wreton but for-
geten and thexcersytees of chyualry not vsed, honoured, ne exercysed, as hit
hath ben in auncyent tyme, at whiche tyme the noble actes of the knyghtes   *10*
of Englond that vsed chyualry were renomed thurgh the vnyuersal world, as
for to speke to fore thyncarnacion of Jhesu Cryste, where were there euer
ony lyke to Brenius and Belynus, that from the grete Brytayne, now called
Englond, vnto Rome and ferre beyonde conquered many royammes and
londes, whos noble actes remayne in thold hystoryes of the Romayns; and   *15*
syth the incarnacion of oure lord byhold that noble kyng of Brytayne, Kyng
Arthur, with al the noble knyȝtes of the round table, whos noble actes and
noble chyualry of his knyghtes occupye soo many large volumes, that is a
world or as a thyng incredyble to byleue.

O, ye knyghtes of Englond, where is the custome and vsage of noble   *20*
chyualry that was vsed in the dayes? What do ye now but go to the baynes
and playe atte dyse? And some not wel aduysed vse not honest and good
rule agegn alle ordre of knyghthode. Leue this! Leue it, and rede the noble
volumes of Saynt Graal, of Lancelot, of Galaad, of Trystram, of Perseforest,
of Percyval, of Gawyn, and many mo! Ther scalle ye see manhode, curtosye,   *25*
and gentylnesse.

Allas, what doo ye, but slepe and take ease, and ar al disordered fro
chyualry! I wold demaunde a question, yf I shold not displease, how many

knyghtes ben ther now in Englond that haue thuse and thexercyse of a
knyghte; that is to wete that he knoweth his hors, and hys hors hym, that is
to saye he beynge redy at a poynt to haue al thyng that longeth to a knyght: *30*
an hors that is accordyng and broken after his hand, his armures and
harnays mete and syttyng, and so forth et cetera. I suppose, and a due serche
shold be made, ther shold be many founden that lacke, the more pyte is.

We have said that this is an example of very early *Modern English.* The
question is, what makes it an example of early Modern English rather than
of late Middle English? For a number of reasons that we will not go into here,
we cannot answer this question fully. But we can at least make a beginning by
comparing Caxton's writing with Trevisa's on the one hand and with Modern
English on the other. Try rewriting the Caxton selection in your own English,
staying as close to the original as possible by making only those changes that
are necessitated by the grammatical, mechanical, and stylistic requirements
of Modern English prose.

Having written out your own modern version of Caxton, it will have occurred to you that you did this with almost no help, whereas had you been
asked to do this with the Trevisa text you may well have had considerable
difficulty. How do you account for the fact that, apart from some strange
phraseology here and there, Caxton's text is much easier for you to read than
Trevisa's? In formulating your answer, consider such matters as spelling,
vocabularly, word forms, and word order. In the same terms, consider the
kinds of differences that are apparent between Caxton's English and standard
Modern English. What differences still remain in spelling? In verb forms? In
the use of the definite and indefinite articles? In the use of prepositions (for
example, would we be likely to refer to a horse "broken after his hand"?) In
the use of the relatives *which* and *that?* In the use of adjective forms? Consider these sentences: (1) "What do ye now. . . ." and (2) "Some not wel
aduysed vse not honest and good rule. . . ." How do these differ grammatically
from their modern counterparts? What use of an English verb form important to Modern English structure has yet to be developed? After you have
compared the texts and answered the questions posed above, you can perhaps
formulate your own answer to the question of why Caxton's English is
considered early Modern English rather than late Middle English.

For our second example of early Modern English writing we turn to a very
short letter written almost a hundred years after Caxton's work on chivalry.
This letter was written by one Sir John Harington, a notable scholar, poet,
courtier, soldier, and translator, born probably in Hartfordshire about 1561.
He wrote the letter when he was still a very young student at Eaton, no more
than ten or eleven years old.

Althoughe good Mistres Penn my longe silence maie make you suppose
that I ame unmyndefull both of yow and also of your benefites yet trulye it is
nothinge so. For I have often tymes since my commynge to Eaton purposed
to wryte to you and now at the lengthe I have founde leysure to wryte theis
letters whiche thoughe they be rude and unworthie of your sighte yet I truste   *5*
you will accepte them as comminge from an humble and lovynge mynde.
Many thinges you have at many tymes bestowed one me more I knowe then
I can requyte but not more suerlye then I willingely beare in minde and
entend alwaye hereafter to shew my selfe thankefull for. You promised that
you woulde send me a letter when I was withe you laste: and I woulde gladly   *10*
se it that I mighte have occasione to wryt to you agayne. I wulde verie glad-
lye here that Master Penn were in good healthe. Thus wishinge you with
Master Penn great helthe and longe life I take my leave of you this 19 day of
May anno 1571.

youres to commaunde
Jhon Harringeton

Apart from the matter of spelling, which has still to be standardized, and
what may seem to us a rather precocious formality of style, the language here
is certainly not very far from what might be used by a modern young man
away from home, writing to a young lady of his acquaintance. To be sure,
there are a few strange phrases: "it is *nothing* so," "I have . . . *purposed* to
wryte to you," "at *the* lengthe," "that Master Penn *were* in good healthe."
Nevertheless, there is little question but what the vocabulary and the grammatical structure is perfectly clear to a Modern English speaker.

1.40   Conclusion

In this introductory chapter we have considered specimens of *written* English
from three historical periods: the Middle English of Trevisa, the Old English
of Alfred's time, and two examples of early Modern English from Caxton and
Harington. It must be emphasized very strongly that we do not *know* what
the *spoken* English of these three periods was like. We can only make educated
guesses. Furthermore, our specimens are examples of the written English of
well-educated men. Imagine, if you will, that sometime during the next five
hundred years most of the books written in English in the twentieth century
and all of the recordings of twentieth-century English speech were destroyed.
In the year 2500, an English teacher wishing to explain to his students what
the English language was like during the first half of the twentieth-century
presents them with a copy of the memoirs of Sir Winston Churchill. As flatter-
ing as such a view of twentieth-century English language might be, how erro-

neous it would be to assume that this was the kind of English used by all English speaking contemporaries! Even though we are in a somewhat better position to comment on the nature of earlier stages of English than the twenty-sixth-century teacher would be, there is much that we do not know, nor ever will know, about the structure of spoken Old, Middle, and early Modern English.

1.50   Special Linguistic Terms

yogh	agreement
etymology	grammatical gender
etymon	natural gender
derivation	weak verbs
stem	strong verbs
grammatical redundancy	word order
reflex	grammatical code

1.60   Exercises

1. You will find below five short examples of English, each representing one of the three stages of the language that we have discussed. Identify the stage illustrated by each one and present evidence from spelling, grammatical structure, and vocabulary for your decision in each case. Suggest a possible date for each.

   a. Maistres Alyce, in my most harty wise I recommend me to you; and whereas I am enfourmed by my son Heron of the losse of our barnes and of our neighbours also, with all the corn that was therein, albeit (saving God's pleasure) it is gret pitie of so much good corne lost, yet sith it hath liked hym to sende us such a chaunce, we must and are bounden, not only to be content, but also to be glad of his visitacion. He sente us all that we have loste: and, sith he hath by such a chaunce taken it away againe, his pleasure be fulfilled.

   b. Brytons wonede furst in þis ylond þe ȝer of Helg þe preost eyȝtetene; of Silvius Posthumus, King of Latyns, enlevene; after þe takyng of Troye þre and fourty ȝere; tofore þe buldynge of Rome foure hondred and two and thryty. Hy come hyder and tok here cours from Armoryc þat now ys þe oþer Brytayn; hy huld long tyme þe souþ contrays of þe ylond. Hyt byful afterward in Vespasian hys tyme, Duk of Rome, þat þe Pictes out of Scitia schipede into occean, and were ydryue aboute wiþ þe wynde and entrede into þe norþ costes of Irlond, and fond þer Scottes and prayede for to have a place to wony ynne, and myȝte non gete; for Yrlond, as Scottes seyde, myȝte noȝt susteyne boþe people.

   c. To prey Grenefeld to send me feythfully word, by wrytyn, who Clement Paston hath do his dever in lernyng. And if he hathe nought do well, nor wyll nought amend, prey hym that he wyll trewly belassch hym, tyl he wyll amend; and so ded the laste maystr, and the best that ever he had, att Caumbrege. And sey Grenefeld that if he wyll take up on hym to brynge hym in to good rewyll and lernyng, that I may verily know he doth hys dever, I wyll geve hym 'x' marcs for hys labor, for I had lever he wer fayr beryed than lost for defaute.

   d. Breoton ist garsecges ealond, ðæt was iu geara Albion haten: is geseted betwyh norðdæle and westdæle, Germanie ond Gallie ond Hispanie þam mestum delum Europe myccle fæce ongegen. Þæt is norð ehta hund mila lang, ond tu hund mila brad. Hit hafað fram suðdæle þa mægþe ongean, þe mon hateþ Gallia Bellica. Hit is welig þis ealond on wæstmum ond treowum misenlicra cynna; ond hit is gescræpe on læswe sceapa ond neata; ond on sumum stowum wingeardas growaþ.

   e. We redeth i þe holi godspelle of todai þat ure Lord Jesu Crist yede one time into ane ssipe and hise diciples mid him into þe see. And so hi were in þo ssipe, so aros a great tempeste of winde; and ure Lord was ileid him don to slepe ine þo ssipe er þane þis tempeste aroos. Hise diciples hedde gret drede of þise tempeste, so awakede hine and seiden to him, 'Lord, save us; for he perisset.' And ha wiste wel þet hine hadde nocht gode beleave ine him, þo seide to hem, 'wat dret yu, folk of litle beliave?'

2. What comments might you make on the following constructions found in the preceding passages, and how would you interpret them?

   a.   "it hath liked hym"

   b.   (1.) "þe ȝer of Helg þe preost eyȝtetene"
          (2.) "in Vespasian hys tyme"
          (3.) "were ydryue aboute"

   c.   (1.) "And sey Grenefeld"
          (2.) "for I had lever"

   d.   (1.) "is geseted"
          (2.) "þam mæstum delum"

   e.   (1.) "And so hi were . . . so aros"
          (2.) "and ure Lord was ileid him don to slepe"

2. The external history

Introduction

As is the case with most languages, the external history of English is very complex. A full account of the impact that the cultural, economic, social, and political growth of England and America, and of those other countries in which English is spoken either as a first or as a second language, has had on the development of the English language would fill a very large volume. In this chapter we will present a sketch of only those facts of external history that account for some of the more obvious aspects of the development of our language.

Before we proceed with the historical periods of English, however, it will be useful to have a brief look at its prehistory. We will do a little exercise in comparative historical linguistics. Examine the chart below. Each column represents a distinct language.

Chart 1

Modern English	1	2	3	4	5	6
father	abbat	pitr	vater	gūr	fæder	pere
five	amɨst	panca	fünf	diyič	fīf	cinq
who	man	kas	wer	ngah	hwā	qui
mother	ɨnnat	mātr	mutter	man	mōdor	mere

On the basis of your examination, which *one* of the *numbered* languages looks most like Modern English? Which *two numbered* languages seem to be most closely related to each other? What reasons can you give for your answer? Do these both seem related to Modern English? Are there any other numbered languages that seem related either to Modern English or to the first two numbered languages you selected? Give reasons for your answer. Are there any languages in the chart that seem *not* to be related either to Modern English or to any of the other languages? Which one(s)? Now look at Chart 2:

Chart 2

Modern English	1	2	3	4	5	6
brother	niican (older)	brat	phrater	wondɨm	fratello	brathair
door	to	dver(e)	thura	bər	porta	dorus
red	akai (is red)	ruda	eruthros	k'ay	rosso	ruath

In Chart 2, which of the words for "brother" seems most like the Modern English word? Which of the words for "door"? Which of the words for "red"? Which seem not at all related? Are you doubtful about any of the numbered languages? Which ones?

If you have examined the words in each chart carefully, you have probably come to the following conclusions. Regarding Chart 1, language 5 seems most closely related to Modern English; languages 3 and 5 seem closely related to each other, and both to Modern English; you may have guessed that languages 2 and 6 are both related to each other and to Modern English (especially on the basis of the words for "father" and "mother"); and languages 1 and 4 are quite unrelated to Modern English, to each other, and to the other numbered languages. Language 5 is Old English; language 3 is Modern German; language 2 is Sanskrit (the classical language of India); language 6 is Modern French; language 1 is Amharic (a Semitic language spoken in Ethiopia); language 4 is Nuer (a Nilotic language spoken in the Southern Sudan). Modern English, then, seems to be closely related to Modern German, and also, though less obviously, to Sanskrit and Modern French.

Regarding Chart 2, the word *brathair* in language 6 looks most like the Modern English form; also in language 6, the word *dorus* may have seemed to you most nearly akin to "door"; as far as the word for "red" is concerned, it is perhaps a toss up whether *ruath* in 6 or *ruda* in 2 is closer to Modern English. Languages 2 and 6 seem most closely related to Modern English; 1 and 4 show no relation to English; and you may have thought 3 and 5 doubtful. Language 6 is a Celtic language; language 2 is Russian; 3 is classical Greek; 5 is Italian; 1 is Japanese; and 4 is again Amharic.

Let us look now at some of the *correspondences* that appear in the two charts. In Chart 1, the correspondences between Old English (5) and German (3) are very close. Old English *f* in *fæder* corresponds to German *v*, *æ* to *a*, *d* to *t*, and *er* to *er*. In the word in question, the sound represented by Old English *f* was very much like that represented by the German *v*; the Old English sound represented by *æ* was different from, yet similar to, the sound represented by the German *a*; Old English *d* and German *t* are different only in the fact that the first is articulated with voicing, the second without voicing. In the word for "five," the chief difference is that the *n* that is retained in the German form (and also in the Sanskrit and French forms) has been lost in the Old English form. As a result of this loss, the vowel in Old English has been lengthened (such lengthening often being referred to as *compensatory lengthening*). The German and Old English words for "who" seem quite different, but the words for "mother" are again similar. The chief difference is in the quality and length of the first vowel, and in the voiced and voiceless character of the *d* and *t*. Incidentally, how has the spelling of Old English *fæder* and *mōdor* changed? What changes in the *sound* of the medial consonant do these spelling changes represent?

The correspondences of Sanskrit (2) and French (6) to each other, to German and Old English, and to Modern English are not quite so clear. They are the most evident in the word for "mother," where the *m*'s and *r*'s occur in all five related forms, the vowels correspond (but in a very intricate way), and the dental consonants (the *t*, *d*, and *th* sounds) correspond in four of the languages, but not in French. What has happened to this consonant in French? Note that it is also missing in the French word for "father." Do you know the French word for "brother"? If not, what is the literal meaning of the word *friar*? From what language does it come? Did the word at some earlier stage contain a *t*? In what language? What are the words for "father" and "mother" in this language? Do these contain a *medial dental t* sound?

In the word for "father," the problem for late eighteenth- and early nineteenth-century linguists was in recognizing the fact that a *regular correspondence* existed between the initial *f* sound of Germanic languages and the initial *p* sound that occurred in corresponding forms in other languages, and thereby concluding that all of these languages must be related. In Chart I, Sanskrit has an initial *p* sound in the word for "father," as does French from Latin *pater,* where the Germanic languages have an *f* sound. Note that Sanskrit also has a *p* sound in the word for "five." Classical Greek has *p* in *pater,* while the word in Persian is *pidar.* With what Modern English words derived from Germanic languages do the following words derived from Greek and Latin correspond: *Pedal, plume, peril, pecuniary, pyre, piscatorial, nepotism?* You should, of course, consult your dictionary.

The French form meaning "five" has neither an initial *f* nor a *p* sound. The initial sound represented by *c* is the result of a rather special development within the *Italic* group of languages, of which Latin is the most prominent representative. The Latin form is *quinque.* The Greek form, however, retains the *p* sound in *pɛntɛ* (see *pentegon, pentameter, Pentateuch, Pentecost,* and so on). As we have noted, the Sanskrit, French, and Modern German forms for "five" all retain an *n* sound. Further, the Sanskrit and French forms both contain for their third consonant a *k* sound. We need not dwell on the word for "who" except to say that the sounds in the Modern English, the Sanskrit, German, Old English, and French forms do in fact correspond to each other and that their various developments have been carefully plotted by comparative linguists.

In Chart 2, point out the correspondences that you observe between the Modern English forms and those of the related numbered languages. (NOTE: The Italian word meaning "door" comes from a Latin word that is related to Modern English *ford,* not *door.* Compare English *port* and *portal* and note the *p-f* correspondence.)

Certain facts about the backgrounds of English should have emerged from this exercise. English belongs to the *Germanic branch of languages.* This branch is usually subdivided into three geographically denominated groups: *West Germanic* (to which English, Modern German, Dutch, Flemish, and Frisian belong); *North Germanic* (to which Modern Danish, Swedish, Norwegian, and Icelandic belong); and *East Germanic* (of which there is no modern *reflex,* but which affords us the earliest written records in any Germanic language, the *Gothic* Scriptures translated by Wulfila in the fourth century).

The Germanic languages are themselves related to a number of other large language families: to the *Indian* languages, which derive from Sanskrit; to the *Romance* languages, which derive from Latin, itself a member of an older *Italic* group of languages; to the *Slavic* languages, of which Russian is one modern representative; to the *Celtic* languages, of which Old Irish is one member; and to the *Hellenic* languages, to which Greek belongs. We may add that other related languages are Tocharian, once spoken in Central Asia from the seventh to the tenth centuries, and Illyrian and Phrygian, both presumably spoken at a very early date in the Mediterranean area.

All of these languages and groups of languages, and in addition all languages derived from them, are said to belong to the *Indo-European* language family, and to have derived from a *proto-language* that students of language call *proto-Indo-European.* There are no written records of this language; it is called a *reconstructed* language. By a careful examination and comparison of the linguistic forms that exist in the earliest written records of those related languages thought to be derived from this common parent, scholars have been able to reconstruct with a fair degree of accuracy a great many of the forms of proto-Indo-European. Furthermore, a variety of evidence suggests that proto-Indo-European was probably spoken in east-central Europe some time before 2500 B.C. By dates ranging from 2000 B.C. to a few centuries before Christ, a great many of its speakers had gradually migrated, for various reasons, as far to the southeast as Persia, as far to the west as the British Isles, as far to the south as the Italian peninsula, and as far to the north as the Scandinavian peninsula.

We noted that the other languages represented in the charts, Amharic, Nuer, and Japanese, showed no relationship to each other nor to any of the Indo-European languages. Amharic belongs to the *Semitic* branch of what is sometimes called the *Afro-Asiatic* language family. It is closely related to Hebrew and Arabic. Nuer belongs to the *Nilotic* branch of a larger family called the *Chari-Nile,* and is spoken by a relatively small number of cattle-raising people in parts of the southern Sudan and southwestern Ethiopia. Japanese, along with Ryukyu, belongs to still a different language family, called, after its most prominent member, Japanese.

What we have tried to do in this exercise is to orient Modern English in terms of the other large groups of languages to which it is related. The details of the relationships that hold among members of the Indo-European language family are very complex indeed, and are of considerable linguistic interest. They will not, however, claim our attention in this book.

2.10   In the Beginning

If you should look at a map of England containing the designations of regions, cities, towns, villages, rivers, streams, hills, and valleys, you would find such names as these: *Kent, Devon, Cornwall, Lichfield, York, Thames,*

Avon, Dover, Bredon, Bryn Mawr, Pendle, Duncombe, Torhill, Huntspill, and *Brockhall.* These *place-names* are Celtic or contain Celtic elements; they are very old names, and testify to the early presence of the Celts in England. It is impossible to say just when the Celts crossed the channel from Europe and began taking up residence in various parts of the British Isles, but they must have begun to arrive shortly after the beginning of the Bronze Age in England —not long after 2000 B.C. There are two Celtic language groups, the *Goidelic* or *Gaelic* Celts, and the *Cymric* or *Brythonic* (Brittanic) Celts. The language of the former group is represented by *Irish, Scotch,* and *Manx* (on the Isle of Man), that of the latter by *Welsh, Cornish,* and *Breton.*

The Celts inhabited England more or less undisturbed by outside influence until in the summer of 55 B.C. Julius Caesar, who had just completed his conquest of Gaul, decided to invade the southeast coast. His first attempt was not a huge success. He had considerable difficulty effecting a landing, and was able to make little headway against the spirited defense of the inhabitants. He returned to Gaul with little but wounded pride to show for his efforts. The following summer, somewhat better prepared, he made a second attempt that was considerably more successful. He established himself in the southeast, defeated the Celts in a number of encounters, and exacted from their chiefs tribute, which in fact was never paid. Having accomplished this much, he again returned to Gaul and the Celts were left to their own devices for almost another hundred years.

In 43 A.D., the Emperor Claudius began the actual conquest of the island, and within three years his armies had subjugated most of the Celtic tribes in the central and southeastern regions. The Romans never extended their control very far into the mountains of Wales or Scotland, but for more than three hundred years the central and southern regions were under their rule and influence. They built numerous roads, several cities, and more than a hundred towns. Their cities and towns contained Roman houses, baths, and temples, and here and there one could find a theater. Roman habits of life, Roman dress, ornaments, utensils, pottery, and glassware were introduced into the island, as was Christianity. There seems to be no question but that many of the Celts, especially those who for administrative reasons were thrown most closely into contact with their Roman masters, adopted many of their cultural traits.

Upwards of six hundred Latin words adopted by the Celts during the period of Roman occupation have been identified. But so far as we are able to tell, few of these words were passed on by the Celts to their later Germanic conquerors, those who brought with them the language that developed ultimately into Modern English. To be sure, these Germanic invaders borrowed a few Latin words from the Celts. The form *caster* and its doublet *chester,* deriving from Latin *castra* "camp," appears in many familiar English place names: *Chester, Colchester, Dorchester, Gloucester, Worcester, Lancaster,* and the like. The word *wīc* "village," in such names as *Harwich* and *Berwick,* is from Latin *vīcus,* and was probably borrowed from the Celts. There are a few others, but on the whole the Latin influence on English stemming from the Roman invasion of Britain was very slight indeed.

The Roman occupation of Britain lasted until the first years of the fifth century. It is generally thought that the last of the Roman legions had been withdrawn from the island by about 410 A.D. The Celts again held sway, but not without difficulty. Without Roman arms and fighting men to aid them they were hard put to defend themselves from attack by the Picts and Scots in the north. It is reported that Vortigern, a Celtic chieftan, invited the Jutes, a Germanic tribe from the Continent, to assist him in driving off those savage fighters in exchange for the island of Thanet in southeast England. (This tract of land is cut off from the mainland by the arms of the Stour River.)

Bede and his translator report the coming of the Angles, the Saxons, and the Jutes in this way:

þa wæs ymb feower hund wintra ond nigon ond feowertig fram ures Drihtnes menniscynsse, þæt Martianus casere rice onfeng ond VII gear hæfde. Se wæs syxta eac feowertigum fram Agusto þam casere. þa Angelþeod ond Seaxna wæs geladod fram þam foresprecenan cyninge, ond on Breotone com on þrim myclum scypum; ond on eastdæle þyses ealondes　　　5 eardungstowe onfeng þurh ðæs ylcan cyninges bebod, þe hi hider geladode, þæt hi sceoldan for heora eðle compian ond feohtan. Ond hi sona compedon wið heora gewinnan, þe hi oft ær norðan onhergedon; ond Seaxan þa sige geslogan. þa sendan hi ham ærenddracan ond heton secgan þysses landes wæstmbærnysse, ond Brytta yrgþo. Ond hi þa sona hider sendon maran　　10 sciphere strengran wihgena; ond wæs unoferswiðendlic weorud, þa hi togædere geþeodde wæron. Ond him Bryttas sealdan ond geafan eardungstowe betwih him þæt hi for sibbe ond for hælo heora eðles campodon ond wunnon wið heora feondum, ond hi him andlyfne ond are forgeafen for heora gewinne. Comon hi of þrim folcum ðam strangestan　　15 Germanie, þæt of Seaxum ond of Angle ond of Geatum. Of Geata fruman syndon Cantware, ond Wihtsætan; þæt is seo ðeod þe Wiht þæt ealond oneardað. Of Seaxum, þæt is of ðam lande þe mon hateð Ealdseaxan, coman Eastseaxan ond Suðseaxan ond Westseaxan. And of Engle coman Eastengle ond Middelengle ond Myrce ond eall Norðhembra cynn; is þæt land ðe　　20 Angulus is nemned, betwyh Geatum ond Seaxum; is sæd of þære tide þe hi ðanon gewiton oð to dæge, þæt hit weste wunige.

Then it was about four hundred of winters and nine and forty from our Lord's incarnation, that Martianus Emperor the kingdom seized and 7 years held. He was sixth and forty from Augustus the Emperor. Then the Angle people and people of the Saxons was invited by the aforementioned king [Vortigern], and into Britain came in three great ships; and in the east part of this island dwelling place took up at that same king's request, who them hither invited, that they should for their own territory contend and fight. And they soon contended with their enemies, whom they often before from the north over ran; and the Saxons then the victory won by fighting. Then sent they home messengers and told [them] to tell of this land the fertility, and the Briton's cowardice. And they then soon hither sent a greater naval fleet stronger of warriors; and it was an invincible host, when they together united were. And them the Britons gave and bestowed a dwelling place among them on condition that they for peace and for welfare of their native land fought and strove against their enemies, and they them substance and property gave for their struggle. Came they from three peoples the boldest of Germany, those of the Saxons and of the Angles and of the Geats [Jutes]. Concerning the Geats in the beginning they are in Kent, and the Isle of Wight; that is the people who that Wight island dwell in. From the Saxons, that is from the land which people call Old Saxon, come the East Saxons, and the South Saxons and the West Saxons. And from the Angles come the East Angles and Middle Angles and Mercians and all the Northumbrian folk; is that land the Angulus [land of the Angles] is called, between the Geats and the Saxons; it is said from that time when they hence departed until today, that it waste remains.

Bede's account of the Germanic invasion of Britain is much more extensive than this, but we have quoted the part that most interests us here. Scholars are not in complete agreement as to the precise continental homeland of the three Germanic tribes mentioned by Bede. The traditional notion is that the Jutes came from the northern part of the Danish peninsula (Jutland), the Angles from the southern part, and the Saxons from an area south and west of the Angles between the Ems and the Elbe rivers. Whatever their exact point of origin, the important thing for us to realize is that these people did not suddenly appear out of the blue, fully established in their respective regions of Britain. During the fourth century, while the island was still under Roman rule, raiding parties of Saxons attacked the southeast coast with some frequency, and these attacks were serious enough to cause the Romans concern. Apparently, however, the Jutes were the first to come in numbers, perhaps with Franks from the lower Rhine and Frisians, and establish themselves permanently in the southeast, in what has since been called Kent. Somewhat later, and throughout the fifth century, the Saxons came, settling, as Bede tells us, in Sussex (South Saxon), Wessex (West Saxon), Essex (East Saxon),

FIRTH OF FORTH

NORTHUMBRIA

● Edinburgh

● Lindisfarne

ROMAN WALL
● Jarrow

SOLWAY FIRTH

● Whitby

R. Ribble

● York

Mouth of the
HUMBER RIVER

R. Mersey
R. Dee

THE WASH

MERCIA
●
Lichfield

(NORTH FOLK)

EAST ANGLIA

WELSH MOUNTAINS

DYKE (c. 784)

MIDDLE ANGLIA

(SOUTH FOLK)

ESSEX
(EAST SAXONS)

Mouth of the
THAMES RIVER

Severn River

London ● Canterbury ●

WESSEX
(WEST SAXONS)

KENT
(JUTES)

ISLE OF
THANET

SUSSEX
(SOUTH SAXONS)

WEST WALES

JUTES

● Cornwall

ANGLO-SAXON HEPTARCHY

29

and Middlesex (Middle Saxon). The Anglians had begun settlements in East
Anglia by the end of the fifth century and in 547 established an Anglian
kingdom north of the Humber River.

Although we know relatively little about the contact between the Celts and
their Germanic conquerors, we should not suppose that the invaders went
unresisted. Where Celtic settlements were sparse the Germans undoubtedly
had an easy time of it, but in more densely populated areas, as in what was
to become West Saxon territory, resistance to the Germanic host was very
stubborn indeed. If the legendary King Arthur was in fact, as some people
believe, modeled after an actual Celtic chieftan, he must have made life very
difficult for the invaders. Be that as it may, the Celts were ultimately driven
into the west to find their refuge in Cornwall and in the rugged mountains of
Wales.

These, then, were the Germanic tribes that brought our language to
England. In the course of time, tribal groupings occurred in various parts
of the island and small kingdoms were established. Seven of these, Northumbria, Mercia, East Anglia, Kent, Sussex, Essex, and Wessex were referred
to as the *Anglo-Saxon Heptarchy*. These seven were not, however, equal in
political power and influence. At different times, various of these kingdoms
gained the supremacy over the others. During the seventh century Northumbria appears to have been the most prominent in politics and in learning,
while the eighth century saw the rise of Mercia to a position of considerable
influence. And it was from Wessex that Alfred the Great, noted for his military prowess and extensive learning, came in the second half of the ninth
century (871–899).

For the most part we tend to speak of Old English, or Anglo-Saxon, as if
it had been spoken in just the same way throughout the island. This is no
more correct than it would be to assume that all speakers of Modern English
speak in just the same way. No doubt you have already concluded that because different parts of Britain were settled by different Germanic tribes from
different parts of the European continent, different varieties of Old English
were being spoken and written in England. Unfortunately, the evidence for
dialect diversity is rather scanty since the only extensive body of texts to be
preserved is in the West Saxon dialect. Nevertheless, on the basis of that much
of the language from other sections of the country preserved in charters,
inscriptions, Bible translations, and brief scraps of verse, students of the
language distinguish four main dialects of Old English: *Northumbrian,
Mercian, Kentish,* and *West Saxon.* Because Northumbrian and Mercian
show certain linguistic features not characteristic of the other two, they are
sometimes lumped together under the term *Anglian.* Ultimately, it was the
dialect spoken in East Anglia that made the greatest contribution to what
was to become Modern Standard British English.

OLD ENGLISH LITERATURE

Since Old English literature is almost the sole basis for our knowledge of the language, we should make some comment about it. Most of the manuscripts containing both Old English prose and poetry date from the tenth or the early eleventh century (although a few are perhaps a century or so earlier), so that the language we are dealing with is not that of the fifth-century invaders, but is a very late Old English. The fact that we have many of these manuscripts at all is probably due to the extensive reform movement in the church during the tenth century—the Benedictine Reform—which aimed not only at revitalizing the practice of Christian morals among the clergy and the people, but also at the establishment of schools and the encouragement of learning. As a result of this encouragement, monasteries again became, as they had been in the past, centers of literary activity where new works were produced for the enlightenment of the people, and old manuscripts both in Old English and in Latin were recopied and preserved for posterity. Of course, we have no very precise notion of just how much Old English literature has been lost to us.

But much of Old English literature, especially the poetry, is considerably older than the tenth century. The customs of war and peace and the values of life reflected in the great poetry are those of a society that by the tenth century had ceased to exist. There is no question but that a large portion of the essential material of many Old English poems came to England with the Germanic invaders as a part of their cultural heritage and was passed on from generation to generation by oral transmission. It is quite apparent that the Christianizing of the island from the end of the sixth century had a certain impact on the poetry of an older period. In many instances we find Christian ideals imposed on a text that obviously antedates the coming of Christianity to England. On the other hand, the reverse is also true; that is, the values and world view of a pagan North Germanic society are to be found in works of a fundamentally Christian character. The great English epic *Beowulf* is the poem most people think of in connection with the Old English period. The form in which it is preserved to us in writing is of a very late Old English date, but the central actions of its three main divisions, the fundamental character of its actors, and the nature of the many episodes that play on and about the central action giving it depth and breadth, are all a part of an oral literary tradition that had its roots on the European continent. What makes it a great poem is the genius with which the English poet has used his language and shaped his material into a highly sophisticated work of art.

While *Beowulf* is certainly the longest (3182 lines) and most impressive of the Old English poems, the native tradition of Germanic verse in England

HPÆT PELARDE

na ingeap dagum þeod cyninga þrym gefrunon hu ða
æþelingaſ ellen fre medon. oft ſcyld ſcefing ſceaþen þreacum
monegũ mægþum meodo ſecla of teah egſode eorl ſyððan
æreſt peaſð rea ſceaft funden he þæſ frofre gebad peox
under þolenum þeorð myndum þah oð þ him æghþyle þare
ymb ſictendra ofer hron rade ſcolde goban gyldan þpæſ god
cyning. ðæm eafera pæſ æfter cenned geong ingeardum þone
god ſend folce tofrofre fyren ðearfe ongeat þhie ærðrug
on aldor . . . . aſe lange hpile him þæſ lif frea puldreſ
pealdend porold are forgeaf. beopulf pæſ breme blæð
pide ſprang ſcyldeſ eafera ſcede landum in. Spa ſceal
gode ge pyrcean fromum feohgif tum onpæðer þine
þhine on ylde eft gepumgen pil geſiþaſ þonne pig cume.
leode ge læſten lof dædũ ſceal inmægþa gehpære
mange þeon. him ðaſcyld gepat toge ſcæp hpile
hpor fe þan onfrean pære hi hyne þa æcbæron tobru
meſ farode ſpæſe geſiþaſ Spa he ſelfa bæd þenden
porðum peold pine ſcyldinga leof land fruma lange
ahte þær æchyðe ſtoð hrimgeð ſtefna iſig 7 utc fuſ
æþelingeſ fær. aledon þaleofne þeoden beaga
bryttan onbearm ſcipeſ merne be mæſte þær pær
pær

Opening lines of *Beowulf.* (*Photocopied from the Thorkelin Transcripts, Edited by Kemp Malone, in* Early English Manuscripts in Facsimile, *Rosenkilde and Bagger, Copenhagen, 1951. Reproduced by permission.*)

produced a great many poems that, though much shorter, rival it in poetic artistry and sophistication of thought. Frequently these are elegies—poems of lament for the changeable quality of life, for glorious days long past, for the loneliness and isolation of a man in this world, for the hardship and danger that everywhere beset him, for the loss of friends and king. Some are patriotic in nature, celebrating the virtues of steadfastness, and boldness, and unflinching loyalty in the face both of victory and defeat. Other poems are Christian in content and in the outlook on the world that they present. Some are based on stories from the Old and New Testaments, some deal with legends of early Christian saints, some with the lives of the apostles. Many of the poems are devotional and didactic in character, designed to teach Christian doctrine and virtues.

Due in large part to the concern for learning that characterized much of the reign of Alfred the Great, Old English developed a literary prose at a much earlier date than did the majority of Continental languages. This prose consisted for the most part of translations from Latin into Old English, done either by Alfred himself or by scholars under his direction, of works on theology, history, and philosophy. Bede's work, the *Ecclesiastical History of the English People,* was translated into English at Alfred's insistence. He must be credited with having been responsible for the rise of an English prose tradition which successive ages of English and American writers have inherited, and to which each has made its own special contributions.

CHRISTIANIZATION

Now that we have provided the English language with a habitation and a name, that is, placed it in its proper linguistic and social-historical context, we can consider some of the historical events and social attitudes that tended to shape its development during succeeding centuries.

If you were to look in your dictionary for the etymologies of the following list of words, you would discover that they are all derived from Latin: *abbot, altar, angel, anthem, candle, canon, cleric, disciple, hymn, litany, mass, organ, pope, priest, psalter, shrine, relic, temple.* To what social institution do these words refer? What, then, do you think was the occasion of their introduction into English? The answers to these questions are perhaps too obvious. The words refer to the Christian Church and its practices, and the occasion was the Christianizing of Britain. In 597 A.D. a mission from Rome headed by Augustine (later St. Augustine) arrived in the kingdom of Kent ruled over by King Aethelberht and his Christian queen, Bertha. Bertha had come from the nation of Franks on the European continent where she had been brought up as a Christian. This circumstance had much to do with the success of Augustine's mission. Shortly after his arrival, Aethelberht was himself baptized, and by the time of Augustine's death seven years later the whole kingdom of Kent had been converted. The little chapel in Kent-wara-byrig (Canterbury) that Aethelberht had built for his Christian wife became, and has remained, the center of Christianity in England.

The Christianizing of England was not accomplished over night, but it went on apace during the seventh century. Northumbria was converted by a separate operation begun in 635 A.D. by the monk Aidan from the Scottish monastery of Iona. Wherever the missionaries went they appear to have been well received and to have attracted a large following. However it was, England had been almost entirely converted to Christianity by the beginning of the eighth century, and as a result a considerable number of Latin words generally associated with the Church had been adopted by the English.

We have mentioned the Benedictine Reform in connection with the preservation of Old English manuscripts. The revival of learning and of a more spiritual existence that was occasioned by this reform was largely influenced by three men: Dunstan, Archbishop of Canterbury (d. 988), Athelwold, Bishop of Winchester (d. 984), and Oswald, Bishop of Worcester and Archbishop of York (d. 992). Under their leadership, more and more English churchmen developed the ability to read and write Latin. With the increase in facility in Latin came an increased knowledge of and interest in Latin works, not only on Christian theology, but also on history, philosophy, and natural science. Ideas new to the English were introduced, as were the Latin terms needed to express them: *anti-Christ, apostle, cell, cloister, creed, demon, idol, sabbath, history, term, title, cucumber, ginger, cedar, cypress, fig, cancer, paralysis, camel, tiger, scorpion.*

Old English scholars modified their vocabulary in another way, by using native terms to express new ideas. Thus, Latin *patriarch* became Old English *heah fæder* (high father); *prophet* became *witega* (wise one); saint became *halga* (holy one); *baptize* was rendered by the Old English verb *fullian* (to consecrate), and *baptism* by the noun *fulluht*. *Scriptures* became *gewritu* (that which was written); *Judgment Day* became *Doomsday;* and *evangelium* became *god spell* (modern *gospel*).

In spite of the fact, then, that the Roman occupation of Britain had almost no impact on the English language, the language of the invaders did in fact contribute markedly to the vocabulary of Old English through other channels, in particular the Christianization of the English people during the seventh century and the Benedictine Reform of the tenth.

SCANDINAVIAN INVASIONS

Before leaving the Old English period, we must consider a series of events that contributed much to the development of English society and to its language. We refer here to the Scandinavian invasions of Britain that began as intermittent raids along the coast by small but efficient bands of Northmen about 787 A.D., and culminated in the seizure of the English throne by the Dane Svein in 1014. Svein was followed to the throne almost immediately by his son Cnut, king of Denmark and conqueror of Norway, who ruled until 1042. This period of almost three centuries is often referred to as the *Viking Age*. The sea-roving Vikings established a kingdom in Russia, colonized parts of the British Isles, established settlements in the Faroe Islands, along the Normandy coast of France, sailed westward to Iceland and the New World, and south and east through the Straits of Gibralter and on into the Mediterranean. Some of the Vikings were Swedes, some Norwegian, and some Danes, but they were all North Germanic people who spoke much the same language and whose social and cultural patterns of behavior were very much alike. Furthermore, these North Germans were close relatives of the West Germans who had already settled England.

By the second half of the ninth century the Danish invaders had captured not only the culturally important city of York, but almost the whole of East Anglia as well. They then turned their attention to Wessex. Attacks began shortly before Alfred's accession to the West Saxon throne, and fighting between Saxons and Danes was bitter indeed. For seven years the tide of battle rose and fell, now favoring Alfred and his Saxons, now the Danes. Finally, on the verge of total defeat, Alfred made a surprise attack on the Danish army under Guthrum at a place in Wiltshire called Edington, and won an overwhelming victory. In this same year (878), Alfred and Guthrum signed the Treaty of Wedmore. In accordance with this treaty the Danes withdrew from Wessex, but were allowed to maintain their settlements in the eastern part of Britain under their own government. This territory came to be known as the *Dane-law*.

Unfortunately, at least for the English, the Treaty of Wedmore proved to be no very permanent solution to the Danish problem. Hostilities between Saxons and Danes continued to break out during most of the tenth century, with the English taking the offensive more and more and extending their control over much of the eastern and northern sections of the country. However, in 991 a fleet of ninety-three ships under Olaf Tryggvason entered the Thames River, and Danish warriors defeated the East Saxons under Byrhtnoth in the battle of Maldon, made famous in one of the most moving

FIRTH OF FORTH

• Edinburgh

• Lindisfarne

STRATHCLYDE

ENGLISH NORTHUMBRIA

GALLOWAY

SOLWAY FIRTH

CUMBERLAND WESTMORELAND

• Durham

• Whitby

DANISH NORTHUMBRIA

LANCASHIRE

THE HUMBER

D A N E – L A W

Lincoln •

THE WASH

DANISH MERCIA

• Nottingham

EAST ANGLIA

Cambridge •

SOUTH WALES

ENGLISH MERCIA

London •

THE THAMES

• Wedmore

Glastonbury •

Winchester •

DEVON

W E S S E X

WELSH CORNWALL

THE DANE–LAW
Districts settled by Norse or Danes

of Old English heroic poems. This Scandinavian victory paved the way for even more extensive invasions. The city of London was forced to pay tribute in order to pacify the marauding Norsemen now led by both Olaf, who had become king of Norway, and Svein, king of Denmark. It was not until 1042 that an English king again ruled the country.

Linguistic Influence

In our discussion of the Celts we noted the importance of place names as indicators of the extent to which the influence of a given language on a particular region may have been felt. The Danish word for "town" was *by*, a form that survives in the fossilized word *by-law*, "town-law." We also find it occurring in the names of over six hundred English towns and villages: *Derby, Whitby, Grimsby, Moresby, Rugby, Farnesby,* and the like. The Scandinavian word *thorp* meant "village," thus *Linthorpe, Bishopsthorpe, Gawthorpe.* The word *thwaite* referred to an isolated piece of land, thus *Applethwaite, Braithwaite, Langthwaite,* and *Satterthwaite.* Further, the patronymic *-son* in such personal names as *Adamson, Johnson, Paterson, Stevenson,* and *Richardson* is of Scandinavian rather than Old English origin.

But the influence of Scandinavian on Old English went far beyond the simple matter of place and personal names. Consider the first four stanzas of a poem written in the eighteenth century by Robert Burns. Doubtless you are familiar with it.

To a Mouse (1785)

Wee, sleekit, cow'rin', tim'rous beastie,
O what a panic's in thy breastie!
Thou need na start awa sae hasty,
    Wi' *bickering* brattle!
I wad be laith to rin an' chase thee
    Wi' murd'ring pattle!

I'm truly sorry man's dominion
Has broken nature's social union,
An' justifies that ill opinion
    Which makes thee startle
At me, thy poor earth-born companion,
An' fellow-mortal!

I doubt na, whiles, but thou may thieve;
What then? poor beastie, thou *maun* live?
A daimen-icker in a *thrave*
      'S a sma' request:
I'll get a blessin' wi' the *lave,*
      And never miss 't!

Thy wee bit housie, too, in ruin!
Its silly wa's the win's are strewin':
And naething, now to *big* a new ane,
      O' *foggage* green!
An' bleak December's winds ensuin'
      Baith snell an' keen!

As you know, Burns was writing a Scots dialect, a dialect of the north of Britain, a dialect that was in fact much influenced by Scandinavian settlers. As a result, it contains a fairly large number of Scandinavian borrowings, illustrated here by the italicized words.

Another northern poem, but of a much earlier date, the late fourteenth-century "Bruce" by Barbour, illustrates even more impressively the extent of Scandinavian borrowing. The poem is much too long to quote here, but we will point out some of its Scandinavian vocabulary.

As King Robert of Bruce is being pursued by John of Lorn we learn that he is "wery, forswat, and *will* of *wayn*." The italicized Scandinavian phrase means "despairing of hope." Speaking of a saying he has heard, Robert says:

Bot I haf herd oftsiþys say,
þat quha endlong a wattir ay
wald wayd a bowdraucht, he suld *ger*
bath þe *sleuth*hund and his ledar
tyne þe *sleuth* men *gert* him *ta.*

But I have heard it oft times said
that who along a water over
would wade a bow draught, he shall make
both the sleuthhound and his leader
lose the track men made him take.

As he is being chased:

Bat þe sleuthhund maid stynting þar,
And *waveryt* lang tyme to and *fra*
þat he na certane *gat* couth ga.

But the tracking hound made a stopping there,
And wavered a long time to and fro
That he no certain way could go.

Somewhat later the Bruce meets three would-be slayers who do not recognize him at first, but then:

> þai persavit be his spekying,
> And his *effer,* he wes þe kyng
> And changit contenanss and *lat,*
> And held nocht in þe first estat,
> For þai war fayis to þe kyng,
> And thoucht to cum into *scowking*
> And duell with him quhill þat þai saw
> þar tyme, and bryng hym þan of daw.

> They perceived by his speaking,
> And his behavior, he was the king,
> And changed their countenance and manner,
> And held not in the first state (original condition)
> For they were foes to the king,
> And thought to come into a treacherous position
> And dwell with him until that they saw
> Their opportunity, and bring him then from day (out of life).

A number of the Scandinavian items to which we have called attention will be unfamiliar to you since most of these are not preserved in most standard English dialects. One of the reasons for this is that British Standard arose from a Middle English dialect that was less exposed to Scandinavian influence than were those of the north and north-Midland counties. Investigation of these latter dialects indicates that even today they preserve a large number of Scandinavian words that elsewhere have been lost.

On the other hand, a great many Scandinavian loan words have found a permanent place in the standard language. In some cases the Scandinavian and Old English words exist side by side to express related notions; thus, Old English *whole, from, to, craft, ridge, hide, sick* beside Scandinavian *hale, fro, till, skill, rick, skin, ill.* Note that although the ideas expressed by the corresponding items in each list are related, they are not the same. *Whole* has a much broader meaning than *hale,* which occurs almost exclusively in the formula *hale and hearty.* Similarly, occurrences of *fro* are limited to the expression *to and fro.* How would you state the differences in meaning between *craft* and *skill, hide* and *skin,* and *sick* and *ill*?

It is often the case that etymologically related words in both languages survive in the standard language, but with different meanings. Compare, for example, Old English *shirt, ditch, shin,* and *ridge,* with Scandinavian *skirt, dike, skin,* and *rick.* It may also be that Scandinavian influence helped to differentiate both the form and meaning of the pair *shatter–scatter.*

At times the meaning of an Old English word is taken over by a borrowed word, while the Old English word is retained with a different meaning. Old English *feþer* meant "wing"; but when this meaning was taken over by the Scandinavian form *wing, feþer* developed a physiologically related, but different, meaning. In like fashion, the meaning of Old English *rinde*, "bark," was expressed by the borrowed form *bark*. The Scandinavian word is now used exclusively in reference to trees, while the Old English word generally refers to the hard, outside covering of certain fruits and vegetables (but see *bacon rind*). Scandinavian *cut* has assumed the general meaning once expressed by Old English *ceorfan*, Modern English *carve*, used now in a special sense of cutting.

In some instances a Scandinavian form has completely, or almost completely, replaced an Old English form, at least in the standard language. For example, Scandinavian *sky* has ousted Old English *wolcen*, surviving as *welkin* in some poetic expressions. Scandinavian *window* (wind-eye) has replaced Old English *eagþyrel* (eye-hole), and *take* has replaced *niman*. Scandinavian *cast* has replaced Old English *weorpan*, but now exists with rather specialized meanings alongside the Old English derivative *throw*. What differences in usage can you cite for *cast* and *throw?* Other indications of Scandinavian influence are *kettle* for Old English *chettle*, *get* for *yet*, *gate* for *yate*, *egg* for *eye*, *weak* for *wake*.

We have no difficulty in finding Old English derivatives that have won out over their Scandinavian counterparts in the standard language: Old English *church* over Scandinavian *kirk;* Old English *bridge* over Scandinavian *brig; fish* over *fisk; ashes* over *askes; true* over *trig.*

In Chapter 1 we referred to the fact that Scandinavian forms for the third person plural pronoun had gradually replaced the native forms. This replacement occurred at different times in different regions of England. The earliest Middle English records show that in the northern dialects *þai* (*þei*), *þaim* (*þam*), and *þair* (*þeir*) had replaced Old English *hi(e)*, *heom*, and *heore* at a very early date. These forms gradually spread from the north into all Middle English dialects, moving from areas in close proximity to those showing heavy Scandinavian influence to those more remote from such influence. You will recall that Trevisa, a southerner, uses only the Old English forms of these pronouns. Furthermore, not all three of the forms were necessarily adopted at the same time. Notice these lines from Chaucer's General Prologue to the *Canterbury Tales*, written just a few years after Trevisa's translation but in a different dialect:

And specially, from every shires ende
Of Engelond, to Caunterbury *they* wend,
The holy, blisful martir for to seke
That *hem* hath holpen whan that *they* were seeke.

And these:

> So hadde I spoken with *hem* everichon
> That I was of *hir* felaweshipe anon.

Chaucer's southeast Midlands dialect has not by this time, at least for literary purposes, adopted the Scandinavian forms for the third person plural object and possessive pronouns. However, by 1500 the so-called *th* forms were being used by writers in all parts of the country, although the Old English forms continued to exist, and still exist, along side them.

Aside from these pronominal forms and a few minor grammatical features, the chief contribution of the Scandinavian invaders was to the vocabulary of English. It is perhaps worth noting here that the situation that led to the considerable influx of Scandinavian words into English was unlike any other that has affected our vocabulary before or since. One of the important factors in the development of English has been its facility for borrowing words, from whatever source, to suit its needs. But in only this particular instance has it been the case that the ordinary English farmer, laborer, peasant—what you will—has borrowed extensively from a foreign element as the result of so complete a cultural intermingling. Unlike the extensive French and Latin borrowings of a later period, which were primarily aristocratic and academic, the Scandinavian borrowings pertained to the affairs of everyday life, as words like *kettle, egg, weak, bark, sky, wing, skin, skill, give, get,* and *anger* indicate. We are not suggesting that English does not as a rule borrow words that refer to common things and events. Of course it does, as such items as *garage, rodeo, moccasin, chop suey, cole slaw,* and *pizza* testify. We mean only that the circumstances in which the borrowing took place were quite unique.

You will recall Trevisa's complaint that "... by commyxstion and mellyng furst wiþ Danes and afterward wiþ Normans, in menye þe contray longage ys apeyred," and that "... chyldern in scole, aзenes þe usage and manere of al oþer nacions, buþ compelled for to leve here oune longage and for to construe here lessons and here þinges a freynsch, and habbeþ suþthe þe Normans come furst into Engelond." Trevisa notes the impact of two historical events on the development of English, the coming of the Danes, and of the Normans. We have commented on the first of these, and will now turn our attention to the second.

2.20 The Norman Invasion

Trevisa makes a point that is of considerable importance to our understanding of what happened to English under the Normans. He says that school children are compelled to learn their lessons in French and *have* since the arrival of the Normans in England. Remember that he is writing in 1385 and that the Normans under William came to the British Isles from French Normandy in 1066. In short, for three centuries much of the literate activity of England was carried on in the French language, not in English.

Imagine that the United States were suddenly to be subjected to a foreign power whose people spoke language X. All government officials from the President down to the mayors of all major cities were replaced by representatives of this foreign power who spoke only language X, as were all executives of the major business institutions in the country. English was replaced as the language of instruction in all schools and colleges by language X. Foreign troops were stationed over the length and breadth of the land; church services were conducted in the new language; all major news publications, popular magazines, and professional journals were printed in it; TV and radio broadcasts were made in it; most plays, movie scripts, novels, poetry, and other forms of language art were written in it. And imagine that this situation persisted for three centuries! What do you think would be the effect on English?

Of course, we cannot say for certain what the effect would be because of the great many intangible and unpredictable factors involved in such a situation, but we can make some reasonably safe generalizations. For one thing, as the nation lost its prestige as a world power, so would its language. People of the United States would be considered politically, and perhaps culturally, inferior, and their language no longer important in the conduct of national or international affairs. People over the globe who now learn English as a second language because of its significance as a world language would abandon it in favor of language X. As a result, English would lose much of the vitality and richness of expression that now characterizes it.

Because English would no longer be taught in the schools, it might very well undergo rather remarkable changes both in its sounds and in its grammatical patterns. For it is well known that the formal instruction in one's language tends to inhibit language change, tends to stress conservatism and standardization, and tends to regard innovation as undesirable. We can be specific here. In English we have certain sets of verb forms sometimes referred to as "irregular" verbs: *swim/swam/swum; run/ran/run; sing/sang/sung; bite/bit/bitten;* and the like. As you well know, the acceptable standard forms of these verbs are carefully taught in the schools. But suppose they were not taught. A considerable number of English-speaking people already use such expressions as "He's just went to the store," "I swum the river yesterday," "He run the 100 in 9.2," "I've never drove a car before," or "She's already tooken the money." A five-year-old boy remarks, "I swimmed in the pool yesterday." Without the pressures exerted by formal learning and standards of social acceptability, one suspects that the patterns of usage of such verb forms would change rapidly throughout the English-speaking community.

With some assurance, we might predict that during these three centuries *dialect diversity* would increase in the United States. We are all aware that distinct varieties of English are now spoken in different parts of the country, and even those of us without much formal linguistic training can properly identify some of these. We can distinguish a speaker from Atlanta, Georgia, from one from Chicago, Illinois, and both of these from a resident of the Bronx. Nevertheless, our great physical and social mobility plus the tendency toward standardization of language patterns both in the schools and in the communication media leads to a reduction of this dialect diversity. The hypothetical political situation we have just described would have the effect of removing from the scene some of the forces that have contributed to the standardization of English usage. Both spoken and written English would be used only in *local* situations to carry on the every day affairs of the community. Thus, the political situation would act as a barrier, isolating the use of English and restricting it to regional and communal communication. The language mannerisms that now characterize different regions of the country would be allowed to pursue their own courses unhampered by external pressures to conformity. After three centuries, a person from Chicago might find it virtually impossible to communicate in English speech with someone from Atlanta.

Clearly, we cannot draw a valid analogy between the hypothetical situation just described and the effects of the Norman invasion on English. The worlds of the eleventh and the twentieth centuries are so vastly different that attempts at comparison are generally futile and unrewarding. What we have tried to do is to suggest the magnitude of the disruption that must have taken place in English society as a result of this invasion. We do not know, nor can we even guess, how the English language would have developed had it been left to its own devices. We only know how it did develop under French influence. Let us consider, then, some of the more obvious results of this influence.

THE ASCENDENCY OF FRENCH

William the Conqueror was a Norman who spoke Norman French. His claim to the English throne rested in part on the fact that he was a second cousin of England's king, Edward the Confessor, and in part on the fact that Harold, who was elected king after Edward's death in January 1066, had once been captured by William and had sworn not to oppose his succession to the English throne. When Harold was elected king, William invaded the south coast with a very large army drawn not only from France but from other European countries as well. After defeating Harold at the Battle of Hastings as a result of a ruse and a lucky chance, and after burning and pillaging the southeast coast of England, he was crowned king of England on Christmas Day, 1066.

During the next four years William succeeded in destroying most of the Old English nobility in a series of campaigns to subjugate the whole country. Important positions in the King's court and government were filled by William's Normans who also confiscated many of the great estates formerly owned by English nobility. English churchmen who had been responsible not only for the conduct of ecclesiastical affairs but also for the maintenance and development of the great centers of learning were replaced by French bishops, archbishops, abbots, and monks. The literature produced for the upper social and political classes was written in French, not in English.

There was little reason for William and his immediate successors to learn English. They had brought with them their own Norman French culture, and for generations political and economic concerns tied them more closely to the Continent than to England. From the time of William until the reign of Edward IV (1461–1483) only one king of England, Henry I (1100–1135), took an English wife. Perhaps you are familiar with the scene in Shakespeare's *Henry the Fifth* (1413–1422) in which Henry woos Katharine, daughter of the French King Charles:

K. HEN. Fair Katharine, and most fair,
Will you vouchsafe to teach a soldier terms
Such as will enter at a lady's ear
And plead his love-suit to her gentle heart?

KATH. Your Majesty shall mock at me; I cannot
Speak your England.

K. HEN. O fair Katharine, if you will love
me soundly with your French heart, I will
be glad to hear you confess it brokenly
with your English tongue. Do you like me, Kate?

KATH. *Pardonnez-moi,* I cannot tell wat is
"like me."

K. HEN. An Angel is like you, Kate, and you
are like an angel.

KATH. *Que dit-il? Que je suis semblable a
les anges?*

ALICE. *Qui, vraiment, sauf votre grace,
ainsi dit-il.*

K. HEN. I said so, dear Katharine; and I
must not blush to affirm it.

KATH. *O bon Dieu! les langues des hommes
sont pleines de tromperies.*

K. HEN.   What says she, fair one? That the tongues
of men are full of deceits?

ALICE.   *Oui,* dat de tongues of de mans is be
full of deceits: dat is de Princess.

(Act V. ii. 99–123)

And so goes Henry's courtship. Love, of course, surmounts all obstacles, including language barriers, and Henry and Katharine are eventually wed.

One should not infer that during this period of French influence none of the English kings and their nobility bothered to learn English. Certainly some of them did, as did many of the French churchmen. And certainly some of them learned English out of a sense of obligation to their constituents, whoever these might have been. But whatever the reasons for learning it, they were not very pressing.

On the other hand, among the upper and middle classes of native Englishmen considerable prestige was attached to one's ability to speak French. After all, French was the language in which the affairs of the country were conducted; it was also, together with Latin, the language of refinement and culture. A native Englishman who spoke and understood French well must have been looked up to by his fellows, and must have been in a better position for social and political advancement than those who knew no French. Recall Trevisa's words as late as the end of the fourteenth century: "... and uplondysch men wol lykne hamsylf to gentilmen, and fondeþ wiþ gret bysynes for to speke freynsch for to be more ytold of." Among English knights a knowledge of French seems to have been expected; in the trading centers of the country English middle class business men spoke French; the stewards, bailiffs, and reves whose duty it was to manage the great estates must have conducted much of their business in French.

To summarize, with the coming of the Normans we find that French becomes the official language of England, and because of the long continued political and social ties which the English Court thereafter maintained with the Continent, it remains the official and socially accepted language for several centuries. Some of the ruling class know English, and certainly many of the Norman French lower classes—those who come to England as soldiers and retainers of the Norman Barons, and who remain to take up their livelihoods in close contact with the English people. The use of French by a large number of the native English upper and middle classes becomes quite common. Another historian, Robert of Gloucester, writing at the turn of the thirteenth century, puts the matter this way:

þus com, lo, Engelond into Normandies hond;
And þe Normans ne couþe speke þo bote hor owe speche,

And speke French as hii dude at hom, and hor children
  dude also teche;
So þat heie men of þis lond þat of hor blod come
Holdeþ alle þulke speche þat hii of hom nome;
Vor bote a man conne French me telleþ of him lute.
Ac lowe men holdeþ to Engliss, and to hor owe speche ʒute.
Ich wene þer ne beþ in al þe world contreyes none
  þat ne holdeþ to hor owe speche, bote Engelond one.
Ac wel men wot vor to sonne boþe wel it is
Vor þe more þat a mon can þe more wurþe he is.

Thus came, lo, England into Normandy's hand;
And the Normans didn't know how to speak then but their own speech,
And spoke French as they did at home, and their children
  did also teach;
So that high men of this land that from their blood came
Hold all the same speech that they from them took;
For except a man know French men count of him little.
But low men hold to English and to their own speech yet.
I think there are not in all the world countries none
That do not hold to their own speech, except England only.
But surely men know (that) for to know both it is well
For the more that a man knows the more worth he is.

RESTORATION OF ENGLISH

In some ways the very conditions that led during the twelfth century to the replacement of English by French as the prestige language of England served to reestablish English as the national language during the thirteenth and fourteenth centuries. For one thing, Normandy was lost to England in 1204 in the reign of King John. Norman French barons residing in England were given the choice by the French King Philip either of giving up their holdings in France and remaining in England or returning to France as subjects of the French king. This policy served to sever once and for all many of the close ties, economic, social, and political, between England and the Continent. By 1250 there was little reason for members of the English nobility to consider themselves anything but English. Furthermore, a new flood of Frenchmen into England, mainly administrators and churchmen, during the reign of John and continuing apace in the reign of Henry III, was strongly resented by Englishmen, both those of native and of Norman descent. A feeling of English nationalism was being reborn, and with this rebirth an increased concern for the use of English as a mark of the true Englishman.

Abuse of power by the "foreign" intruders in matters of church and state resulted in an opposition coalition of baronial and middle classes which in 1258 wrested from Henry III a document called the Provisions of Oxford. This document guaranteed certain political rights to the baronial class. Indicative of the Normans' newfound sense of English nationalism is the fact that the leader of this coalition was Simon de Montfort, himself a Norman. Of even greater importance for our concerns is the fact that these provisions were set forth in an *English* proclamation (along side French and Latin versions), the first public document to be written in the English language in almost two hundred years.

Another indication of the fact that English was now beginning to supplant French as the first language of the land is the number of manuals for learning French that appeared in the homes of the English nobility during the thirteenth century. The language learning situation that must have obtained in these homes is interesting. English children, even those of Norman descent, were learning English as their native tongue and French as a second language from manuals. In other words, their "book learned" language was French and from French grammars they learned about grammar in general. This situation was not unlike that which has plagued the English-speaking school boy for centuries, namely, the application of Latin rules of grammar to the study of English. But as Trevisa points out, by his time children no longer learn their grammar from French books, but they now learn it from English grammars. The fact that English books are now being used in the schools is a very significant measure of the extent to which the prestige of English had increased during the fourteenth century.

We noted above the disaffection that occurred between the Norman French in England and the Norman French on the Continent as a result of the loss of Normandy under King John. From 1337 until 1453 a series of power struggles known as the Hundred Years' War took place between the kings of England and the kings of France, each attempting to obtain political domination over the other. These intermittent outbreaks of hostility served to unite England and to infuse noble and commoner alike with a fervant nationalism. There were great victories for the English at Crecy (1346), at Poitiers (1356), and again at Agincourt (1415) where the English under the spirited leadership of the young King Henry V won the day against great odds. But the English met their match in the little Maid of Orleans, Joan of Arc, and by the middle of the fifteenth century their invasions of French soil had ceased.

Whatever the other effects of this long, drawn-out struggle were, one was that it left no doubts about who was a Frenchman and who an Englishman. French was the language of the enemy, English the language of the patriot; and this fact went far in encouraging the reestablishment of English as the national language and the gradual disuse of French.

The French Influence

By the time English had again come into its own as the language of Englishmen, its aspect had changed greatly from what it had been in the ninth and tenth centuries. Certain changes, of course, were well under way before the arrival of the Normans. As we suggested earlier, language varieties, whether regional or social, will pursue their individual courses more rapidly when pressures to conform to some intraregional or intrasocial standard have been removed. Innovations in pronunciation, spelling, grammatical structure, and vocabulary will be much less inhibited. With the coming of Norman French as the language of the culturally and politically superior classes, English was left to develop however it might with little interference of a formal nature. Changes in certain of the grammatical patterns of the language which had begun before 1066 went on at a rapid pace simply because no one of any great importance was interested in arresting these changes. In addition, tendencies toward a greater and greater differentiation among regional dialects were accelerated, probably for the reason that those who had the greatest need to communicate between one region of the country and another would have done so in French. In regard to such changes French influence was more indirect than direct.

Direct French influence can be seen in the English spelling system. In the passage from Trevisa, the *ou* and *ow* spellings of the vowels in native English words, *hou, ynow, souþeron, oune, þousond, now* (as also Modern English *house, mouse, town, found,* and the like) are the result of Norman scribal practice (see the spelling of the French borrowing *soun,* "sound"). The *u* spelling in *buþ, furste, burþtonge, suþthe, lurneþ,* was also introduced by Norman scribes. This particular spelling practice led indirectly to another which is also apparent in Trevisa's writing. At an earlier time the words cited directly above had, in this dialect, been spelled with a *y*. With the change in spelling habits, *y* came to be used in place of *i* in certain positions. Thus we have *hyt, ys, tyme, Inglysch, bygynnyng, nyne,* and so on. Another spelling innovation borrowed from the French can be seen in the word *conquest* (l. 26). This is, of course, a borrowed word and contains the letters *qu* used by the Normans to represent the combined sounds /kw/. But in England this spelling of these sounds was not limited to French borrowings, but was transferred to native English words as well: *queen* (Old English *cwen*), *quick* (Old English *cwicu*), *quake* (Old English *cwacian*), *quench* (Old English *cwencan*), *quell* (Old English *cwellan*). The use of the letter *o* for *u*, especially before *n*'s and *m*'s was another innovation of the Norman scribes. The word *tonge* in Trevisa comes from Old English *tunge;* but in a Middle English manuscript the *u* and the *n* combination would look something like this: ⅋. The change of spelling from *u* to *o* helped to reduce this kind of writing confusion. Our modern spelling *tongue* is the result of a somewhat later French influence in which the letter *u* followed the letter *g* in order to indicate a "hard" rather than a "soft" *g* sound: *tongue, ague, plague, guide, guard, guess, guilt, rogue,* and so on.

But by far the most significant contribution that this long period of French influence made to English was in terms of vocabulary. Notice, for instance, the number of French borrowings that Trevisa uses: *maner, people, longages, nacions, confederat, strange, commyxstion, apeyred, usage, compelled, construe, lessons, gentil-, brouch, moreyn, chaunged, mayster, gramere, conquest, construccion, avauntage, travayle, cass, dyvers, soun, rem, party, acordeþ, parteners, special-, -cause, aliens, contray, cytes, noble, profytable.* Notice too, that the borrowed words are nouns, verbs, and adjectives, and that they tend to refer to rather specialized areas of human activity rather than to every day things and events. For instance, we find political reference in *nacion, rem, aliens, cytes, people, confederat, party;* educational in *lessons, mayster, gramere, construe, cause, construccion;* social in *noble* and *gentil;* ornamental in *brouch;* and trade in *profytable, parteners, travayle.* Chaucer's debt to French is readily apparent in the italicized words of the first 18 lines of his General Prologue.

Whan that *Aprill* with his shoures soote
The droghte of *March* hath *perced* to the roote
And bathed every *veyne* in swich *licour*
Of which *vertu engendred* is the *flour,*
Whan *Zephirus* eek with his sweete breeth
Inspired hath in every holt and heeth
The *tendre* croppes, and the yonge sonne
Hath in the Ram his half cours yronne,
And smale foweles maken *melodye*
That slepen al the nyght with open eye,
So priketh hem *Nature* in hir *corages,*
Than longen folk to goon on *pilgrymages,*
And *palmeres* for to *seken straunge* strondes,
To ferne halwes couthe in sondry londes,
And *specially,* from every shires ende
Of Engelond, to Caunterbury they wende,
The holy blisful *martir* for to seke
That hem hath holpen whan that they were seeke.

There are a total of 128 words in this excerpt, 20 of which (or about 16 percent) are of French origin. This seems a rather small percentage; however, if we remove from the total number all those words whose function is primarily grammatical, that is, the auxiliaries, prepositions, conjunctions, articles, pronouns, and intensifiers, we find that there are 42 of what are sometimes called *full* words: nouns, verbs, adjectives, and adverbs. When we now consider that 20 of these (or almost 50 percent) are French loans, the extent of French influence on Chaucer's vocabulary looks more impressive.

During the Middle English period, that is, from about the middle of the eleventh until the beginning of the fifteenth centuries, approximately ten thousand French words were adopted by Englishmen. According to tables first drawn up by Otto Jespersen and later modified by A. C. Baugh, the greatest influx of French words came during the hundred and fifty years between 1250 and 1400. It was during these years that English was being reestablished as the national language. As greater demands were placed on English to express concepts hitherto expressed only in French, the more numerous became the French borrowings.

Unlike the Scandinavian borrowings, French loans have to do especially with the activities of an aristocratic society. The word *government* itself is French as is much of the vocabulary associated with its practice: *crown, state, reign, sovereign, power, minister, council, chancellor, authority,* and *parliament. Feudalism* came to England with the Normans as did *fief, feudal, vassal, liege, prince, peer, duke, baron.* It was the aristocracy that chiefly concerned itself with military affairs: *war, peace, arms, armor, lance, banner, buckler, cutlass, assault, siege, officer, lieutenant, sergeant, soldier, troops, navy, challenge, enemy, spy, danger, escape, guard, prison;* with legal matters: *judge, just, justice, court, suit, sue, plaintiff, defendant, accuse, attorney, crime, damage, heritage, property, real estate, penalty, injury;* with ecclesiastical matters: *service, trinity, chant, saviour, virgin, friar, orison, sacrifice, charity, covet, pity, mercy, feast, virtue, vice, conscience, grace;* with hunting: *chase, leash, falcon, quarry, scent, track, brace, forest, park, pheasant, quail, squirrel, kennel;* with fashion and food: *apparel, habit, gown, robe, garment, cape, cloak, collar, veil, chemise, lace, embroidery, kerchief, garter, adorn, satin, fur, sable, ermine, jewel, ornament, ivory, enamel, ruby, pearl, diamond, dinner, supper, appetite, taste, nourish, sustenance, venison, sausage, gravy, poultry, cream, sugar, salad, olive, spice, clove, herb, goblet, plate, saucer, curtain, couch, chair, cushion, towel, parlor, closet, pantry, recreation, leisure, chess, conversation;* with art and learning: *art, beauty, colour, image, design, paint, music, melody, sculpture, cathedral, palace, mansion, ceiling, tower, choir, column, poet, rime, romance, story, title, preface, chapter, paper, pen, study, noun, verb, clause, physician, surgeon, malady, pain, ague, gout, jaundice, leper, plague, anatomy, remedy, poison, pleurisy.*

Perhaps nowhere is the use of French vocabulary so noticeable in Middle English as in the English romances of the fourteenth century, themselves modeled after continental French romances. These are generally very long poems concerned with knightly adventure, chivalry, courtly love, magic, tournaments, battles, feasting, hunting, and gaming, and often religious quests. As you can see, their very subject matter would demand the use of a great many borrowed terms. The selections below are taken from one of the finest poems of this type, "Sir Gawayne and the Grene Kny3t." Although many of the elements that have gone into its composition are indeed "romantic," the poem is much more than *just* a romance. In the first selection we see Sir Gawain as he is about to set out on the adventure that constitutes the central action of the poem:

He dowelle3 þer al þat day, and *dresse3* on þe morn,
Aske3 erly hys *arme3,* and alle were þay bro3t.
Fyrst a *tule tapit* ty3t ouer þe flet,
And miche wat3 þe gyld gere þat glent þeralofte;
þe stif mon steppe3 þeron, and þe stel hondele3,
Dubbed in a *dublet* of a dere *tars,*
And syþen a crafty *capados,* closed aloft,
þat wyth a bry3t *blaunner* was bounden withinne.
þenne set þay þe *sabatoun3* vpon þe segge fote3,
His lege3 lapped in stel with luflych *greue3,*
With *polayne3* piched þerto, *policed* ful clene,
aboute his kne3 knaged wyth knote3 of golde;
Queme *quyssewes* þen, þat *coyntlych* closed
His thik þrawen þy3e3, with þwonges to *tachched;*
And syþen þe brawden bryne of bry3t stel rynge3
Vmbeweued þat wy3 vpon wlonk *stuffe,*
And wel *bornyst brace* vpon his boþe armes,
With gode *cowters* and *gay,* and gloue3 of *plate,*
And alle þe godlych gere þat hym gayn schulde
    þat tyde;
        Wyth ryche *cote-armure,*
        His gold spore3 spend with pryde,
        Gurde wyth a bront ful *sure*
        With silk *sayn* vmbe his syde.

He dwells there all that day, and dresses on the morn,
Asks early for his arms, and all were they brought.
First a rich red carpet was spread over the floor
And much was the gilt gear that glittered above it;
The sturdy man steps thereon, and the steel handles,
Dressed in a dublet of costly silk [from Turkestan]
And then a cunning hood, closed at the top,
That with a bright fur was bound within.
Then set they the steel shoes upon the man's feet,
His legs wrapped in steel with fine greaves,
With knee pieces attached thereto, polished most brightly,
About his knees tied with knots of gold;
Goodly thigh pieces then, that cleverly enclosed

His thick, brawny thighs, with thongs attached;
And then the linked mail of bright steel rings
Weaved about the man upon the glorious stuff,
And well burnished braces upon both his arms,
With good elbow pieces and fair, and gloves of plate armor,
And all the goodly gear that him profit should
   that time;
      With rich coat armor,
      His gold spurs fastened proudly
      Girt with a trusty sword
      With a silk sash at his side.

In the next, Gawain takes his ease in a castle hall preparing to dine:

A *cheyer* byfore þe *chemne,* þer charcole brenned,
Watȝ grayþed for Sir Gawan grayþely with cloþeȝ,
Whyssynes vpon *queldepoyntes* þat *koynt* wer boþe;
And þenne a mere *mantyle* watȝ on þat mon cast
Of a broun *bleeaunt, enbrauded* ful ryche
And fayre *furred* wythinne with felleȝ of þe best,
Alle of *ermyn inurnde,* his hode of þe same;
And he sete in þat settel semlych ryche,
And *achaufed* hym *chefly,* and þenne his *cher mended.*
Sone watȝ telded vp a *tabil* on *tresteȝ* ful fayre,
Clad wyth a clene cloþe þat *cler* quyt schewed,
Sanap and *salure,* and syluerin sponeȝ.
þe wyȝe wesche at his wylle, and went to his mete.
Seggeȝ hym *serued* semly innoȝe
Wyth sere sewes and sete, *sesounde* of þe best,
Double-felde, as hit falleȝ, and fele kyn fischeȝ,
Summe baken in bred, summe brad on þe gledeȝ,
Summe soþen, summe in sewe *sauered* with *spyces,*
And ay *sawes* so sleȝe þat þe segge lyked.
þe freke calde hit a *fest* ful frely and ofte
Ful hendely, quen alle þe haþeles *rehayted* hym at one
   as hende:
      'þis *penaunce* now ȝe take,
      And eft hit schal *amende.*'
      þat mon much merþe con make,
      For wyn in his hed þat wende.

A chair before the chimney, where charcoal burned,
Was prepared for Sir Gawain beautifully with cloths
Cushions and coverlets that elegant were both;
And then a comely mantle was on the man cast
Of a brown, silken fabric embroidered most richly

And fair furred within with pelts of the best,
All of ermine adorned, his hood of the same;
And he sat in that settle fittingly splendid,
And warmed himself quickly, and then his mood mended.
Soon was set up a table on trestles most fair,
Clad with a clean cloth that clear white showed,
Over cloth and salt cellar, and silver spoons.
The wight washed at his will, and went to his meat.
People served him courteously enough
With various and excellent stews, seasoned of the best,
Double fold, as was fitting, and many kinds of fish,
Some baked in bread, some broiled on the coals,
Some seethed, some in stews savored with spices,
And ever sauces so subtle that the man pleased.
The knight called it a feast most courteously and oft
Very graciously, when all the knights acclaimed him together
  as well bred:
   'This penance now you take
   And later it shall amend.'
   That man much mirth did make,
   For the wine in his head that went.

In the third scene, Gawain is approached by the beautiful wife of the lord of the castle. She asks him to talk to her about matters of courtly love, and when he seems reluctant, she chastises him lightly:

'I woled wyt at yow, wyȝe,' þat worþy þer sayde,
'And yow wrathed not þerwyth, what were þe skylle,
þat so ȝong and so ȝepe as ȝe at þis tyme,
So *cortayse,* so knyȝtyly, as ȝe ar knowen oute —
And of alle *cheualry* to chose, þe *chef* þyng *alosed*
Is þe *lel* layk of luf, þe *lettrure* of *armes;*
For to telle of þis *teuelyng* of þis trwe knyȝteȝ,
Hit is þe *tytelet* token, and *tyxt* of her werkkeȝ,
How ledes for her *lele* luf hor lyueȝ han *auntered,*
Endured for her *drury dulful* stoundeȝ,
And after *wenged* with her *walour* and *voyded* her care,
And broȝt blysse into *boure* with *bountees* hor awen —
And ȝe ar knyȝt comlokest kyd of your elde,
Your worde and your worchip walkeȝ ayquere,
And I haf seten by yourself here sere twyes,
ȝet herde I neuer of your hed helde no worde
þat euer longed to luf, lasse ne more;
And ȝe, þat ar so *cortays* and *coynt* of your hetes,
Oghe to a ȝonke þynk ȝern to schewe
And teche sum tokeneȝ of trweluf craftes.

Why! ar ȝe lewed, þat alle þe *los* weldeȝ?
Oþer elles ȝe demen me to *dille* your *dalyaunce* to
    herken?
                For schame!
        I com hider *sengel,* and sitte
        To lerne at yow sum game;
        Dos, techeȝ me of your wytte,
        Whil my lorde is fro hame.'

'I would learn from you, Sir,' that worthy there said,
'If it made you not angry, what were the reason,
That one so young and so bold as you at this time,
So courteous, so knightly, as you are renouned —
And from all chivalry chosen, the chief thing praised
Is the true sport of love, the science of arms;
For to tell of these deeds of these true knights,
It is the inscribed token, and true text of their works,
How men for their loyal love their lives have adventured,
Endured for their love doleful days,
Then avenged them with their valour and avoided their cares,
And brought bliss into bowers with virtues their own —
And you are the knight most famed of your age,
Your word and your worship walk everywhere,
And I have sat by your side here two separate times,
Yet heard I never from your head proceed any words
That ever belong to love, neither less nor more;
And you, that are so courteous and gracious in your behests,
Ought to a young thing most eagerly show
And teach some signs of true love's art.
Why! are you a peasant, who all this praise merits?
Or do you deem me too dull your dalliance to
    hear?
                For shame!
        I come hither alone, and sit
        To learn from you some sport;
        Do! teach me by your wit,
        While my lord is away from home.'

   In the first selection, to what aspects of aristocratic-chivalric life do the italicized loan words refer? To what in the second selection? To what in the third?
   It should be clear, then, that with the coming of the Normans a whole new set of social and political customs and institutions were introduced into England, and with these came the thousands of French terms needed to refer to them. We should not forget, however, that English continued to be used,

not only among the peasants but among many of the learned as well. Indeed, one of the great English poems of the thirteenth century, Layamon's *Brut,* a very long (32,241 lines) history of the founding of Britain, owes very little in its vocabulary to French influence. In works that used an extensive French vocabulary, it was often the practice of the writer to *gloss* such items with a native English word or phrase. Otto Jespersen has noted a number of examples: "*cherite,* þet is *luve* [*love*]"; "*desperaunce* [*despair*], þet is in *unhope*"; "two *manere temptaciuns*—two *kunne* [*kinds*] *vondunges*"; "*pacience,* þet is *þolemodnesse* [*mind suffering*]"; "*ignoraunce,* þet is *unwisdom* and *unwitenesse* [*unknowing*]"; "*bigamie* is *unkinde* [*unnatural*] þing, on engleis *twiewifing* [*two-wifing*]."

Our discussion of the impact of the Norman invasion on the development of English has by no means been exhaustive. However, we have considered some of its more obvious effects, and perhaps that is all we can do in a brief text. At any rate, we will move on now to take account of another external force which shaped our language—the English Renaissance.

EXERCISE

In Modern English we find a great many pairs of nearly synonymous forms: *happiness-felicity, cottage-hut, bill-beak, dress-clothe, amity-friendship, help-aid, folk-people, cordial-hearty, deep-profound, lonely-solitary, commence-begin, hide-conceal, nourish-feed, hinder-prevent, action-deed, ask-demand, power-might, wish-desire, cow-beef, mutton-sheep, veal-calf, seethe-boil, shun-avoid, likeness-similitude, conquer-win, pardon-forgive.* Select the word from each pair which seems to you more polite or refined. You will now have two separate lists. Which list contains the native English words and which the French loan words? Check the derivation of these words in the dictionary to see how right you are. Are your lists consistent? That is, does one contain *all* native English words and the other *all* French loans? Or is there some inconsistency? What does this exercise tell you about the relative social status of the native Englishman and the Norman Frenchman during early Middle English times? Are the words in each pair strictly synonymous? That is, might you use either word in precisely the same situations? If not, how do they differ?

2.30　*The Renaissance*

The French word *Renaissance* means literally "rebirth." It is a convenient label for a particular period in European history, and like many other such labels (*Dark Ages, Neoclassical period. Age of Enlightenment, Romantic Age,*

Victorian Era, Space Age, and so on) should not be taken too seriously as an adequate characterization of the period it labels. However, it is a useful term which does in fact imply many of the cultural, social, and political developments that took place in Europe and England between the thirteenth and the seventeenth centuries. Precisely when the Renaissance began, when it ended, to what extent it actually constituted a break with the medieval past, and which of its many features are to be considered most characteristic—these are questions still argued by historians.

But it is generally agreed that the Renaissance was a period that saw a revival of interest in classical antiquity, in the philosophies, arts, and religions of the Greeks and Romans; it saw the rise of a new interest in man as an individual rather than as a cipher; it saw a new spirit of exploration, not only of the geographical world, but of the psychological and spiritual world of men; it saw the development of a new sense of political and religious freedom, the growth of new art forms, the spread of education, an increased social mobility, and an improvement in channels of communication. Not the least of these was the development of a vital interest in the *vernacular* languages, in Italian, French, Spanish, German, and English, the languages spoken by the people. These new attitudes and interests had taken hold in England at least by the end of the fifteenth century, and probably before, and their effects were felt well into the seventeenth. Inevitably, many aspects of the Renaissance world modified standard English in a number of ways. It is to some of these that we will now turn our attention.

THE BEGINNINGS OF A STANDARD BRITISH DIALECT

In an earlier section of this book we mentioned the fact that it was the dialect of East Anglia (especially the Southeast Midlands) that eventually became the standard dialect of the country. There were several reasons for this, some of which are pointed out by Trevisa:

> . . . for men of þe est wiþ men of þe west, as hyt were undur þe same party of hevene, acordeþ more in sounyng of speche þan men of þe norþ wiþ men of þe souþ. þerfore hyt ys þat Mercii, þat buþ men of myddel Engelond, as hyt were parteners of þe endes, understondeþ betre þe syde longages, norþeron and souþeron, þan norþeron and souþeron understondeþ eyþer oþer.

... þe kynges of Engelond woneþ alwey fer fram þat contray [the North].
... þe cause why a buþ more in þe souþ contray þan in þe norþ may be betre
cornlond, more people, more noble cytes, and more profytable havenes.

In other words, the Southeast Midland area occupied an intermediate position between the north and the south, and its dialect shared certain features of both; its speakers could understand both Northern and Southern dialects better than Northern and Southern speakers could understand each other. Further, the seat of government, the abode of the kings of England, was in the southeast—in London. Here was the social, political, and commercial center of the land, and to it flocked not only Englishmen from the southern, western, and northern provinces, but courtiers, diplomats, artists, scholars, and teachers from all over the known world. As one might expect, the London dialect became a prestige dialect. As Trevisa points out, this region was more heavily populated, more fertile, and more readily accessible from the sea than other regions.

In addition, the Southeast Midlands was the seat of two very famous universities, Oxford and Cambridge. One might expect that they would have lent at least some of their prestige to the dialect of the area. The part played by the language of Chaucer's poetry in bringing about the adoption of a standard English is often overrated. Certainly, the popularity of his works and the imitation of his language by later poets contributed to the spread of his dialect. But there are good reasons for believing that Chaucer's poetic language was quite different from the casual language spoken by his fellow Londoners, and further that some of its features belong not to London but to an area south of London. Of greater importance to the development of standard English were the court documents, official records, and nonliterary papers of men of affairs. Finally, one can hardly overestimate the effects of printing on the spread of London English. The first English printer, William Caxton, established his press in London in 1476; and from it came a steady stream of books, both translations and original works, all printed in the Southeast Midland dialect. By the sixteenth century a standard British English had emerged that was destined to become the mark of the highly educated in almost every part of the world.

THE COMING OF AGE

It was chiefly this standard language that felt the impact of certain features of the Renaissance spirit. The very suggestion of a *standard* language recalls certain comments we have already made in this regard. Greater social

MIDDLE ENGLISH DIALECT AREAS AND SOME ILLUSTRATIVE TEXTS

NORTHERN

Barbour's *Bruce*
Cursor Mundi

NORTHWEST
MIDLAND

*Sir Gawain and
the Green Knight*

NORTH CENTRAL
WEST MIDLAND

Laȝman A

NORTHEAST
MIDLAND

Ormulum
Havelok the Dane

CENTRAL EAST
MIDLAND

SOUTHEAST
MIDLAND

Bokenam's
Lives of Saints
Chaucer

SOUTH CENTRAL
WEST MIDLAND

Ancren Riwle

SOUTHWEST
MIDLAND

Laȝman B
Trevisa

KENTISH

Kentish Homilies
Aȝenbite of Inwyt

SOUTHERN

Poema Morale
Owl and Nightingale
Proverbs of Alfred

(Adapted by permission from map 11, "Boundaries of Middle English Dialect Regions," from Moore, Meech, and Whitehall, "Middle English Dialect Characteristics and Dialect Boundaries," in Essays and Studies in English and Comparative Literature, *University of Michigan Press, 1935.)*

suspect persone ⸿ And sayde. the wele disposed man re-
membreth /but his synnes /and the euyl disposed hath
mynde/but on his vertues/It fortuned his wyf was dece-
sed in a ferre countre /and som axed him If there were
ony difference to dye in their propre lande orellis ferre from
thens/He answerd/Wherfomeuer one dye /the wepe to the
other worlde is all like ⸿ And sayde to a yong man that
wolde not lerne in his yought/If thou wolt not take peyne
to lerne thou shalt haue the peyne to be lesse ,and vncon
nyng ⸿ And sayde god loueth thoos that bee disobeissaunt
to euyl temptacion ⸿ And sayde/ good prayer is one of
the beste thinges aman may present to god/¶ if thou axe
him ony boon lete thy werkis be agreable vnto him

Dyogenes otherwyse called vgly byçause he hadde
som condicions of a dogge/and he was the wysest
man that was in his dayes .He dispraised grete
ly the worlde/and lay in a tonne/Whiche he tourned for
his auantage from the sonne/And the wynde/as it pleased hym / and therin he rested Whansomeuer the nyght fil
vpon him/ He ete Whansomeuer he was hungered/ Were it
by day or by nyght in the strete or ellis where Wythoute ony
shame therof . And was content Wyth .ij. gownes of
Wollen cloth in the yere · And so he kepth and gouuer-
ned him self til his deth . Somme axed him Why he
was called vgly / he sayde be cause I barke vpon the foo-
les and falle vpon the Wysemen . Alexandre the grete
cam vnto him of Whom he toke litle regarde . he axed him
Why he sette so litil by him / seeyng that he was so mighty a
king and hadde noo necessite/he answerd I haue noght to

First page from William Caxton's first printed book, *The Dictes and Sayengis of the Philosophres.* (*Folio 21, "Diogenes," PML 773, Reproduced by permission of The Pierpont Morgan Library.*)

mobility, increased facility of communication, higher literacy rates, wider interest in reading and in formal education, and concern for elegant expression—all these lead toward the standardization of language patterns. And standardization can in part be defined as conservatism and a certain rigidity in language usage. During the Renaissance, several principles governing the "right writing and right speaking" of English began to be developed. In other words, language usage began to be regulated in a way that it had never been before. On the other hand, the Renaissance spirit of innovation was reflected in the language by the thousands of new words that were borrowed.

We have noted the interest that men of the Renaissance took in their native tongues. Hitherto, avenues of learning had been open almost exclusively to those scholars who knew Latin and perhaps some Greek. But now men whose primary concerns were the affairs of every day life wanted to share in the "new learning." They wanted to read for themselves these new-found and exciting works of the ancients. Arguments that the vernacular languages were too vulgar and imperfect to express adequately the thoughts of the classical writers were no longer either convincing or acceptable. One of the most outspoken defenders of the use of English was Richard Mulcaster, headmaster of the Merchant Taylors' School and author of two books in English on the education of middle class children. In his *Elementarie* published in 1582, he says:

> But why not all in *English,* a tung of it self both depe in conceit, & frank in deliverie? I do not think that anie language, be it whatsoeuer, is better able to vtter all arguments, either with more pith, or greater planesse, then our *English* tung is, if the *English* vtterer be as skilfull in the matter, which he is to vtter: as the foren vtterer is, which methink I durst proue in anie most   *5* strange argument, euen mine own self, tho no great clark, but a great welwiller to my naturall cuntrie. And tho we vse & must vse manie foren terms, when we deal with such arguments, we do not anie more then the brauest tungs do and euen verie those, which crake of their cunning. The necessitie is one betwene cuntrie and cuntrie, for communicating of words,   *10* for vttering of strange matter, and the rules be limited how to square them to the vse of those which will borrow them. It is our accident which restrains our tung, and not the tung itself, which will strain with the strongest, and stretch to the furthest, for either gouernment if we were conquerers, or for cunning, if we were treasurers, not anie whit behind either the subtile *Greke*   *15* for couching close, or the statelie *Latin* for spreding far. Our tung is capable, if our peple wold be painfull.

This attitude toward English coupled with the popular demand for learning resulted during the sixteenth century in a flood of books in English: hundreds of English translations of Greek and Latin works of history, philosophy, politics, morals, bibliography, and poetry, and with these a great number of original English works inspired by the intellectual fervor of the age. And now that English was being put to such lofty purposes, attempts were made to provide it with the elegance of expression suitable to those purposes. As Mulcaster points out, in order to meet the new demands being placed on English a much more extensive vocabulary was required. Throughout the sixteenth century English writers sought to embellish and enrich their language by introducing terms not only from the classical languages, but from French, Italian, and Spanish as well. And embellish they did. Consider the following excerpt from John Bourchier's (Lord Berners) *Preface* to his translation (1523–1525) of the chronicles of Jean Froissart (1337?–1410):

What condygne graces and thankes ought men to gyue to the writers of historyes, who with their great labours, haue done so moche profyte to the humayne lyfe; they shewe, open, manifest and declare to the reder, by example of olde antyquite, what we shulde enquere, desyre, and folowe; and also, what we shulde eschewe, auoyde, and vtterly flye: for whan we (beynge vnexpert of chaūces) se, beholde, and rede the auncyent actes, gestes, and dedes, howe and with what labours, daūgers, and parylls they were gested and done, they right greatly admonest, ensigne, and teche vs howe we maye lede forthe our lyues: and farther, he that hath the perfyte knowledge of others ioye, welthe, and highe prosperite, and also trouble, sorowe, and great aduersyte, hath thexpert doctryne of all parylles. And albeit, that mortall folke are marueylously separated, both by lande and water, and right wōderously sytuate; yet are they and their actes (done perāduenture by the space of a thousande yere) cōpact togyder by thistographier, as it were, the dedes of one selfe cyte, and in one mānes lyfe: wherefore I say, that historie may well be called a diuyne prouydence; for as the celestyall bodyes aboue complecte all and at euery tyme the vniuersall worlde, the creatures therin cōteyned, and all their dedes, semblably so dothe history. Is it nat a right noble thynge for vs, by the fautes and errours of other, to amēde and erect our lyfe into better? We shulde nat seke and acquyre that other dyd; but what thyng was most best, most laudable, and worthely done, we shulde putte before our eyes to folowe. Be nat the sage counsayles of two or thre olde fathers in a cyte, towne, or coūtre, whom long age hath made wyse, dyscrete, and prudent, far more praysed, lauded, and derely loued than of the yonge menne? Howe moche more than ought hystories to be cōmended, praysed, and loued, in whom is encluded so many sage counsayls, great reasons, and hygh wisedoms of so innumerable persons, of sondry nacyons, and of euery age, and that in so long space as four or fyue hundred yere. The most profytable thyng in this worlde for the instytution of the humayne lyfe is hystorie. Ones the contynuall redyng therof maketh yonge men equall in prudence to olde men; and to olde fathers stryken in age it mynystreth experyence of thynges. More, it yeldeth priuate persons worthy of dignyte,

5

10

15

20

25

30

rule, and gouernaunce: it compelleth themperours, hygh rulers, and
gouernours to do noble dedes, to thende they may optayne immortall glory:
it exciteth, moueth, and stereth the strong hardy warriours, for the great   *35*
laude that they haue after they ben deed, promptly to go in hande with great
and harde parels, in defence of their countre: and it prohibyteth reprouable
persons to do mischeuous dedes, for feare of infamy and shame: so thus,
through the monumentes of writynge, whiche is the testymony vnto vertue,
many men haue ben moued, some to bylde cytes, some to deuyes and estab-   *40*
lisshe lawes right profitable, necessarie, and behouefull for the humayne
lyfe: some other to fynde newe artes, craftes, and sciences, very requisyte to
the vse of mākynde: but aboue all thynges, wherby mans welthe ryseth,
speciall laude and cause ought to be gyuen to historie: it is the keper of suche
thinges as haue ben vertuously done, and the wytnesse of yuell dedes: and by   *45*
the benefite of hystorie all noble, highe, and vertuous actes be immortall.
What moued the strong and ferse Hercules to enterpryse in his lyfe so many
great incōparable labours and paryls? Certaynly nought els but y for his
meryt immortalyte mought be gyuen to hym of all folke. In sēblable wyse
dyd his imytator, noble duke Theseus, and many other innumerable worthy   *50*
prīces and famouse men, whose vertues ben redemed frō oblyuion and
shyne by historie. And whereas other monumentes in processe of tyme, by
varyable chaunces, are confused and lost: the vertue of history dyffused and
spredde throughe the vnyuersall worlde, hath to her custos and kepar, it
(that is to say, tyme), whiche cōsumeth the other writynges.   *55*

There are a number of things worth noting here. One of the most striking
is the stylistic device of grouping synonyms, or near synonyms: "For whan
we (beynge vnexpert of chaūces) *se, beholde,* and *rede* the auncyent *actes,*
gestes, and *dedes,* howe, and with what *labours, daūgers,* and *paryls* they were
gested and *done,* they right greatly *admonest, ensigne,* and *teche* vs howe we
maye lede forthe our lyues." Students of English have often remarked on
the fact that it is rich in synonyms and that these reflect three different levels
of usage, *popular, literary,* and *scholarly.* The popular expression is a native
English word, the literary a French word, and the scholarly a Latin word.
Thus we find the triplets *rise-mount-ascend, fast-firm-secure, ask-question-*
interrogate, fire-flame-conflagration, in which the first item in each set is from
Old English, the second from French, and the third from Latin. John
Bourchier's stylistic practice would not be very acceptable in Modern
English prose. We would find it unnecessarily repetitive, somewhat precious,
mannered, and tiresome. But in the sixteenth century it served not only as
a way of embellishing and enriching the language, but as a way of glossing
the unfamiliar terms as well.

   We should point out here that it is not always possible to tell whether a
word is a French or Latin borrowing, since French was being enriched by

Latin in much the same way as was English, and at much the same time. A word like *act*, for instance, appears in Middle English probably from French, though quite possibly from Latin as well. In later Renaissance times its use would have been reenforced by Latin. Furthermore, words that entered English from French during Middle English times, and reflected French spelling practices and pronunciation, were often respelled during the Renaissance according to their Latin models. For the most part these later spellings have been retained. Middle English *dette, doute,* and *faute* from Norman French were respelled *debt, doubt,* and *fault* from Latin *debitum, dubitare,* and Late Latin *fallitus.* In Trevisa we noted the French loan *construccion,* later spelled *construction* from Latin *constructio-constructionis;* Trevisa's *avauntage* is Norman French from Latin *ab-ante,* but later scholars thinking the *a-* was from the Latin prefix *ad-* respelled the word *advantage.* There are instances in which the same Latin word borrowed indirectly through French and then again directly from Latin will assume two different shapes and meanings, and both will remain in the language; for example, Modern English *feat,* Middle English *fete, feete,* is from French *fait* which is itself from Latin *factum,* while Modern English *fact* is a direct borrowing from Latin.

EXERCISES

1. Examine the following sets of synonyms taken from the quotation. As far as you are able, determine from your dictionary which are native English, which are French loans, and which are Latin loans?

show	manifest	declare
eschew	flee	avoid
acts	gestes	deeds
sorrow	trouble	adversity
faults	errors	
amend	erect	
seek	acquire	
wise	prudent	discreet
praised	lauded	commended
diffused	spread	
keeper	custos	
moveth	compelleth	stirreth
abhorreth	irketh	detesteth
lifteth	extolleth	enhanceth
depresseth		thrusteth down
deeds	acts	enterprises
achieved	done	accomplished

2. How similar to each other are the modern meanings of the items in each set? Can you define and illustrate shades of difference between them? Examine carefully the contexts in which these items occur. Are any of the words used in senses that are no longer usual? If so, which ones?
3. Not all of the words that were borrowed during the Renaissance have remained in the language; some that have remained occur very infrequently; and many have since changed their meanings. According to your dictionary, what seems to be the present status of *custos, complecte, laud, behouefull, ensigne* (as a verb), *sytuate* (as an adjectival), *cōpact* (as a verb), *gested,* and *semblably?* How often have you come upon the word *condygne?*

REACTION AGAINST BORROWINGS

As one might suppose, the process of enrichment, primarily through Latin borrowings, was frowned upon by some who felt that these "learned" or "ink-horn" terms were the mark of pedants who desired more to impress their readers with their own scholarship than to inform them. This attitude is well illustrated by remarks made by Sir John Cheke in 1557 to Sir Thomas Hoby who had recently translated Castiglione's *The Courtyer,* published in 1561:

> I am of this *opinion* that our own tung shold be written cleane and *pure, unmix't* and *unmangled* with borowing of other tunges, wherin if we take not heed by tiim, ever borrowing and never *payeng,* she shall be fain to keep her house as *bankrupt.* For then doth our tung *naturallie* and *praisablie* utter her meaning, when she bouroweth no *counterfeitnes* of other tunges to *attire* her self withall, but *useth plainlie* her own, with such shift, as *nature,* craft, *experiens* and folowing of other *excellent* doth lead her unto, and if she want at ani tiim (as being *unperfight* she must) yet let her borow with suche *bashfulnes,* that it mai *appeer,* that if either the *mould* of our tung could *serve* us to *fascion* a woord of our own, or if the old *denisoned* wordes could *content* and *ease* this neede, we wold not boldly *venture* of unknowen words.

The 25 italicized words, all of which are loans, suggest how difficult it was for Sir John to take his own advice. We will have occasion to comment on this matter of "purity" in language again. Here we will only say that there have always been so-called "purists" who claim to despise mixtures of any kind, whether in art, philosophy, religion, race, language, or whatever. More often than not it turns out that such people are woefully ignorant of their own cultural heritage.

We should not, however, accuse Sir John Cheke of ignorance. His plea for moderation and good sense in the matter of borrowing was certainly justified considering the number of contemporary writers who exhibited neither. The chief characteristics of a good prose style, no matter what the language or the age, have always been clarity, precision, and simplicity. No doubt you are familiar with writers whose practice it is to use "hard" or obscure words and involved sentences rather than simple words and simple sentences merely to impress their readers or to avoid the responsibility of saying what they mean.

In an essay called "Politics and the English Language" (in *Shooting an Elephant and Other Essays,* Harcourt, Brace & World, Inc.), George Orwell parodies the "Latinized style" that he feels is gaining ground in modern English. Beside a verse from *Ecclesiastes,* plain, simple, and precise in its expression, he sets his own modern English parody:

> I returned and saw under the sun, that the race is not to the swift, nor the battle to the strong, neither yet bread to the wise, nor yet riches to men of understanding, nor yet favour to men of skill; but time and chance happeneth to them all.

> Objective considerations of contemporary phenomena compel the conclusion that success or failure in competitive activities exhibits no tendency to be commensurate with innate capacity, but that a considerable element of the unpredictable must invariably be taken into account.

In a strikingly similar way Thomas Wilson parodied the Latin embellishments of some of his sixteenth-century contemporaries in the *Art of Rhetorique* (1553). The parody is set in the form of a letter that Wilson introduces with this comment: "Some will thinke & swere it to, that there was neuer any suche thing written, well, I wil not force any man to beleue it, but I will saie thus muche, and abide by it to, the like haue been made heretofore, and praised aboue the Moone."

> Ponderyng, expendyng, and reuolutyng with my self, your ingent affabilitee, and ingenious capacitee for mundane affaires: I cannot but celebrate & extolle your magnificall dexteritee aboue all other. For how could you haue adepted suche illustrate prerogatiue, and dominicall superioritee, if the fecunditee of your ingenie had not been so fertile, and wonderfull pregnaunt. Now therfore beeyng accersited, to suche splendent renoume, & dignitee splendidious: I doubt not but you will adiuuate such poore adnichilate orphanes, as whilome ware condisciples with you, and of antique familiaritie in Lincoln shire. Among whom I beeyng a scholasticall panion, obtestate your sublimitee to extoll myne infirmitee. There is a sacerdotall dignitee in my natiue countrey, contiguate to me, where I now contemplate: which your worshipfull benignitee, could sone impetrate for me, if it would like you to extend your scedules, and collaude me in them to the right honor-

able lorde Chauncellor, or rather Archgrammarian of Englande. You knowe my literature, you knowe the pastorall promocion. I obtestate your clemencie, to inuigilate thus muche for me, accordynge to my confidence, and as you know my condigne merites, for such a compendious liuyng. But now I relinquishe to fatigate your intelligence with any more friuolous verbositie, and therfore he that rules the climates, be euer more your beautreux, your fortresse, and your bulwarke. Amen.

Dated at my Dome, or rather Masion place in Lincolneshire, the penulte of the moneth sextile. Anno Millino, Quillino, Trillino.

Per me Johannes Octo.

The amount of Latinate vocabulary in this letter makes it almost incomprehensible, even considering the fact that many of the words, like *pondering, ingenious, celebrate, extol, fertile, pregnant, antique, dignity, promotion,* are now a part of our standard vocabulary. You can imagine how difficult the interpretation of such diction would have been for a nonscholar in the sixteenth century. The letter means something like this:

> Considering your great affability and cleverness in worldly affairs, I can't help praising your adroitness above all others. For how could you have attained such an illustrious position if you hadn't been so wise. Now that you have achieved this renoun, I am sure you will help the poor orphans who were once your fellow students and old friends in Lincolnshire. Among whom, I, who was once your school mate, ask your aid. There is a benefice near where I am now studying which your honor could attain for me, if you would try, by recommending me to the right honorable lord Chancellor. You know my qualifications and you know the post. I ask your favor, to keep an eye out for me, as you know my ability and that I am worthy of such a good post. But I won't tire you any longer with this trivial matter, and so may God be your guardian. Amen.

LYLY, DONNE, AND SPENSER

The concern among men of letters that English be a suitable vehicle for artistic and scholarly expression led to the adoption of certain stylistic mannerisms, some borrowed from the great Latin stylists, not only in choice of vocabulary, but in sentence structure as well. Although today we may find some of these labored, ponderous, unduly elaborate, and at times an impediment to understanding, it is very likely that without such experimentation with style we would not have had such eminent prose stylists as Milton, Samuel Johnson, Edmund Burke, Winston Churchill, and John F. Kennedy.

The almost poetic prose of John Lyly, author of *Euphues: The Anatomy of Wit* (1578), is an extreme example. Here is a short passage:

> This young gallaunt [Euphues], of more witte then wealth, and yet more wealth then wisedome, seeing himselfe inferiour to none in pleasant conceits, though himselfe superiour to all his [in] honest conditions, insomuch that he thought himselfe so apt to all thinges that he gaue himselfe almost to nothing but practising of those things commonly which are indicent [incident] to these sharp wits, fine phrases, smooth quippes, merry tauntes [vsing] iestinge without meane, and abusing mirth without measure. As therefore the sweetest Rose hath his prickell, the finest veluet his bracke, the fairest flower his branne, so the sharpest wit hath his wanton will, and the holiest head his wicked way. And true it is that some men write and most men beleeue, that in all perfect shapes, a blemish bringeth rather a lyking euery way to the eyes, than a loathing any way to the minde.

You will notice for one thing the elaborately balanced parallelism: "of more wit then wealth—of more wealth then wisedome ... inferiour to none in pleasant conceits—superiour to all in honest conditions." What other similar constructions can you find? Note too the alliteration: *wit ... wisedome ...wealth; conceits ... conditions; fine phrases; bracke ... branne; wanton will; holiest head;* and so on. There is assonance in *vsing ... abusing; inferiour ... superiour; all thinges ... nothing; eyes ... minde.* And there is a somewhat extravagant simile: "As therefore the sweetest Rose hath his prickell ... so the sharpest wit has his wanton will. ..." Lyly attempts to make his use of the language esthetically pleasing. But, of course, he goes too far. A style that calls so much attention to itself ultimately fails. Happily, the reputation of the Renaissance as an age that produced some of the greatest English prose in our history does not rest on John Lyly. Compare his style with that of John Donne writing some forty years later:

> The bell doth toll for him that thinks it doth; and though it intermit again, yet from that minute that that occasion wrought upon him, he is united to God. Who casts not up his eye to the sun when it rises? but who takes off his eye from a comet when that breaks out? Who bends not his ear to any bell, which upon any occasion rings? but who can remove it from that bell which is passing a piece of himself out of this world? No man is an island, entire of itself; every man is a piece of the continent, a part of the main; if a clod be washed away by the sea, Europe is the less, as well as if a promontory were, as well as if a manor of thy friend's or of thine own were. Any man's death diminishes me, because I am involved in mankind. And therefore never send to know for whom the bell tolls. It tolls for thee.

Here is English prose at its best: simple, uncluttered, clear; yet stately, resonant, and moving. The desire of Renaissance scholars that English should be a noble language capable of expressing noble thoughts was not better fulfilled than in the writings of John Donne.

An interest in the English language of a somewhat different sort is reflected in the poetic diction of Edmund Spenser (1552?–1599). Spenser tried to give to his poetry a certain archaic flavor by reviving words that had gone out of use, and in some cases by coining words which had the "look" of old words. Much of his poetry is sprinkled with phrases like these:

> And *eek* [also] my name bee wyped out lykewisee
> your doleful *dreriment* [dreariness]
> and soone her *dight* [adorned]
> wel *beseene* [looked after, overseen]
> And Phoebus *gins* [begins] to shew his glorious hed
> the thing that *mote* [must] thy mind delight
> that ye would *weene* [think]
> with *joyance* [joyfulness] bring her and with jollity
> night is *nighing* [nearing] fast
> calm and *quietsome*
> *Eftsoons* [afterwards] the nymphs . . . ran all in haste
> There *whilome* [once upon a time] wont the templar knights to bide

Such diction was intended to endow his language with a kind of fresh, vigorous, rustic quality appropriate to the matter and the scenery of his poetry. Not all of these words remained strictly "poetic." To Spenser and his imitators we owe a number of words that are now part of our common language stock: *belt, dapper, forthright, glance, surly, elfin, disrobe, drizzling, grovel, gaudy, gloomy, wary, witless,* and others.

"GRAMMATICAL" PRINCIPLES

The interest which English Renaissance scholars took in the use of English led inevitably to a concern that such use be regulated according to a set of more or less justifiable principles. After all, the principles governing the use of Latin and Greek were very rigorous indeed, and were carefully taught and conscientiously practiced. If English was to take its place beside these eminent languages as a noble vehicle for noble thoughts, it too must have principles governing writing and speaking to guide those who would use it to their best advantage.

In the first place, Middle English spelling had been a mess. Here are some spellings of the adjective *fair* with its comparative and superlative forms, taken from the *Middle English Dictionary,* edited by Hans Kurath and Sherman M. Kuhn and published by the University of Michigan Press (1953): *feʒer, fæʒer, faʒʒerr, faiger, fehere, fair, fayr, faire, fayre, uayr, ueirest, veir, vair, feir, feier, feire, fœiere, farrer, feyre, ffayr, ffayre, feirore.*

Now, as historians of the language we do not complain about this spelling situation since one of our chief clues to dialect diversity in Middle English and to the nature and development of Middle English sounds is the spelling of words. It is a great advantage to us that there was no standard spelling system. Not having one, Middle English writers tended to write as they spoke. But obviously a free spelling practice of this sort is not designed to aid communication, and scholars and teachers like Richard Mulcaster were well aware of this fact. To be sure, the spelling situation in the sixteenth century was by no means so chaotic as it had been during Middle English times, but it was bad enough.

Although not the first, Mulcaster's *Elementarie,* to which we have already referred, was one of the most reasonable attempts to bring some order to English spelling practice. Mulcaster sets forth each letter of the alphabet, both capitals and small letters, discusses the sounds each represents, and indicates how each is to be used in the representation of a word. Here in part is what he has to say about the troublesome final -*e*:

> Whensoeuer e, is the last, and soundeth not, it either qualifieth som letter going before, or it is mere silent, and yet in neither kind encreaseth it the number of syllabs. I call that E, qualifying, whose absence or presence, somtime altereth the vowell, somtime the consonant going next before it. It altereth the sound of all vowells, euen quite thorough one or mo consonants as, *made, steme, eche, kinde, stripe, ore, cure, toste* sound sharp with the qualifying E in their end: whereas, *mad, stem, ech, frend, strip, or, cur, tost,* contract of *tossed* sound flat without the same E. . . . It altereth also the force of c, g, s, tho it sound not after them, as in *hence,* for that, which might sound *henk,* if anie word ended in e. in *swinge* differing from *swing,* in *vse* differing *vs.* I call that e, mere silent, which tho it neither sound, nor qualifie anie letter, yet maie it not be spared from the ends of fiue kindes of words. First of foren denisons, which ar derived from originalls ending in s, tho being not the last letter of their ending syllab, as, *case, cause, verse, diverse, repose, nose.* Secondlie of those words, which end in s. sounding like a z. and have a vowell next before the s, as the silent e, after, as *cruse, excuse, abuse, snese, wise, amase.*

He goes on to discuss the other three "kindes of words" that contain a final, silent -*e,* and considers additional rules relating to the use of *e* in the spelling system, and the various ways in which it is to be pronounced. Regarding the doubling of consonants he says this:

This is a generall note to be obserued in writing of all the consonants, that none of them is to be dubled, but where theie ar referred to diuerse syllabs, the former ending the former syllab, & the latter beginning the next, as in *bud-ding, strip-ped, buf-fetting, begin-ning,* & whereby it appeareth, that no consonant can be dubled in the end of a word, bycause there is no syllab to follow: and that therefor the dubling of the last syllab is mere ouersight. For if ye write *putt* with a duble, t, is not the syllab ended in the first *put?* and wherefor then serueth the latter, t,? Some when theie haue dubled the consonant, will put an e to it, which is to make two syllabs, where theie mean but one, as *putte:* bycause of the rule, that the dubled consonants ar referred to diuerse syllabs.

Mulcaster's rules were a considerable contribution to spelling standardization. Many of them are still taught in our schools today. His comments on the use of the final, silent -*e* as qualifying the preceding vowel sound are especially perceptive, as is his use of the terms "sharp" and "flat" in referring to vowel quality. In the two quoted passages, how many of Mulcaster's own spellings have undergone change in the course of development?

Some fifty-eight years after the appearance of the *Elementarie,* a famous seventeenth-century poet, playwright, and essayist, Ben Jonson, produced *The English Grammar,* "Made by Ben Jonson for the benefit of all Strangers out of his observation of the English Language now spoken and in use." It was Jonson's notion that with such a grammar "We free our language from the opinion of rudeness and barbarism, wherewith it is mistaken to be diseased: we shew the copy of it, and matchableness with other tongues; we ripen the wits of our own children and youth sooner by it, and advance their knowledge." Like Mulcaster, Jonson discusses the letters of the English alphabet, the sounds they represent, and their use in word formation. He also has a word to say about English accent and word formation. He comments on the parts of speech, which he equates with Latin parts of speech, on the "declensions" of nouns, the "conjugations" of verbs, on the formation of comparative and superlative degrees of the adjective, on the various kinds of pronouns, and on conjunctions. "The Second Book of the English Grammar" deals very briefly with some aspects of syntax, and presents some rules of punctuation. Here are some excerpts from his book; in the first he considers the letter *Q*:

Q

Is a letter we might very well spare in our *alphabet,* if we would but use the serviceable *k* as he should be, and restore him to the right reputation he had with our forefathers. For the English Saxons knew not this halting Q, with her waiting woman *u* after her; but exprest

quail		kuail
quest	by	kuest
quick		kuick
quill		kuill

Till custom, under the excuse of expressing enfranchised words with us, intreated her into our language, in

quality, quantity, quarrel, quintessence, & c.

And hath now given her the best of *k*'s possessions.

Of A Verb

Hitherto we have declared the whole *etymology* of *nouns;* which in easiness and shortness, is much to be preferred before the Latins and the Grecians. It remaineth with like brevity, if it may be, to prosecute the *etymology* of a *verb*. A *verb* is a word of number, which hath both *time* and *person. Time* is the difference of a verb, by the *present, past,* and *future,* or *to come.* A *verb finite* therefore hath three only *times,* and those always *imperfect.*

The first is the present; as *amo,* I love.

The second is the time *past;* as *amabam,* I loved.

The third is the *future;* as *Ama, amato:* love, love.

The other *times* both *imperfect; amem, amarem, amabo.* And also *perfect;* as *amavi, amaverim, amaveram, amavissem, amavero,* we use to express by a *syntax,* as shall be seen in the proper place.

The extent of Jonson's orientation to Latin grammar, which was not at all untypical, can be seen in his use of Latin models to illustrate the English forms. His view that a verb "hath three only *times*" shows an awareness of English structure not characteristic of many later eighteenth- or nineteenth-century English grammarians, as does his relegation of the *perfect* forms to the area of syntax. Of course, he is wrongly influenced by the Latin form *amabam,* which *is* imperfect, to consider the perfect "I loved" to be imperfect also. Furthermore, English does not have anything that can properly be termed a "future" tense. Nevertheless, considering his background, Jonson's comments on the English verb forms are an improvement over much that was to come later.

Of the Syntax of a Verb with a Verb

When two verbs meet together, whereof one is governed by the other, the latter is put in the infinite, and that with this sign *to,* coming between; as, *Good men ought* to *join together in good things.*

But *will, do, may, can, shall, dare* (when it is in transitive), *must,* and *let,* when it signifieth a sufferance, receive not the sign.
Gower:
To God no man may *be fellow.*

Jonson's book is throughout written in a lively and humorous fashion, and makes enjoyable reading even today. Although he obviously imposes his notions of Latin grammatical structure on English, he nevertheless is perceptive enough to see that Latin rules do not always work for English. His book is an important landmark in the history of English grammars, and as such deserves the attention of students of English language history. Like Mulcaster he not only recognized the necessity to standardize language usage, but also the importance to English prestige of grammatical and mechanical principles governing that usage.

THE ENGLISH DICTIONARY

One further contribution of Renaissance scholarship to the development of standard English was the English dictionary. Since Anglo-Saxon times English scholars had had available to them dictionaries of a sort. The earliest of these were word lists of less familiar Latin terms glossed in more familiar Latin. Such lists were followed by those in which the Latin term was glossed in Old English. Lists of this kind continued to be compiled throughout the Middle English period, until in 1499 Wynkyn de Worde issued the first dictionary to be printed in England, a work called the *Promptorium Parvulorum sive Clericorum.* It is important to our purposes that this work was the first to give the English word first and its Latin equivalent second.

As you might guess from our discussion of Renaissance interests, the first dictionaries of this period were foreign language dictionaries rather than native English. Palsgrave's French-English *Lesclaircissement de la Langue Francayse* appeared in 1523; Salesbury's Welsh-English dictionary in 1547; Percival's Spanish-English dictionary in 1591; and Florio's Italian-English dictionary in 1599. Cooper's great classical *Thesaurus* was produced in 1565. We have noted above the significance of and also the concern over the considerable importation of Latin words into English during the sixteenth century. And we have noted the interest of the nonscholarly reading public in the new learning of the age. But the nonscholar needed something to tell him what the unfamiliar Latin words in his English text meant. You can imagine what heavy going he would make of Sir Thomas Wilson's parody even after all the Latin terms no longer current had been removed. There was a demand, then, for a dictionary that would explain these "hard" words. This demand was met by several works that appeared during the seventeenth century: Robert Cowdrey's *Table Alphabeticall of Hard Words* (1604), John Bullokar's *English Expositor* (1616), Cokeram's *The English Dictionary: An Interpreter of Hard Words* (1623), Edward Phillips' *New World of Words* (1658), and Blount's *Glossographia* (1656).

CONCLUSION

It should be clear that one of the most notable effects of the English Renaissance on the English language was to elevate it to a position of scholarly and artistic eminence that it had never enjoyed before. As a result of the spread of education, increased interest among lay people in learning, the invention of printing, the publication of works on spelling, pronunciation, and grammar, and of dictionaries, knowledge and use of an English standard in speech and writing was becoming increasingly prevalent. Somewhere between 10,000 and 12,000 new words were added to the language during the Renaissance period, at least half of which have become a permanent part of the English word stock. By the end of the Renaissance the English language had become one of the most versatile and expressive vehicles for communicating thought and emotion the world has ever seen. It had become the language of John Donne, of William Shakespeare, and of John Milton:

> Is this the Region, this the Soil, the Clime,
> Said then the lost Arch-Angel, this the seat
> That we must change for Heav'n, this mournful gloom
> For that celestial light? Be it so, since hee
> Who now is souran can dispose and bid
> What shall be right: fardest from him is best
> Whom reason hath equall'd, force hath made supream
> Above his equals. Farewell happy Fields
> Where Joy foreuer dwells: Hail horrours, hail
> Infernal World, and thou profoundest Hell
> Receive thy new Possessor: One who brings
> A mind not to be chang's by Place or Time.
> The mind is its own place, and in itself
> Can make a Heav'n of Hell, a Hell of Heav'n.
> What matter where, if I be still the same,
> And what I should be, all but less than hee
> Whom thunder hath made greater? Here at least
> We shall be free; th' Almighty hath not built

Here for his envy, will not drive us hence:
Here we may reign secure, and in my choice
To reign is worth ambition though in Hell:
Better to reign in Hell, then serve in Heav'n.

(*Paradise Lost,* Book I, 242–63)

2.40   *The Eighteenth Century*

In the previous section we had occasion to refer to the appearance of the English dictionary. Let us begin our discussion of the eighteenth century, the Neoclassical Age, the Age of Reason, the Age of Enlightenment, with reference to another English dictionary, the prodigious effort of one man, that provided many of the principles on which modern lexicography is based. In 1748, Samuel Johnson undertook the monumental task of writing a full dictionary of English containing etymologies, definitions, and examples of usage for each entry. The *English Dictionary* was finally published in 1755 after seven years of unremitting, and financially unrewarding labor. With this dictionary Johnson published a preface that is remarkable not only for its majestic prose style and perceptive comments on the nature of language, but also for its revelation of the nature of the man and the conditions under which he worked. Here is the final paragraph from that preface:

> In this work, when it shall be found that much is omitted, let it not be forgotten that much likewise is performed; and though no book was ever spared out of tenderness to the author and the world is little solicitous to know whence proceeded the faults of that which it condemns, yet it may gratify curiosity to inform it that the *English Dictionary* was written with little assistance of the learned and without any patronage of the great; not in the soft obscurities of retirement or under the shelter of academic bowers, but amidst inconvenience and distraction, in sickness and in sorrow. It may repress the triumph of malignant criticism to observe that if our language is not here fully displayed, I have only failed in an attempt which no human powers have hitherto completed. If the lexicons of ancient tongues, now immutably fixed and comprised in a few volumes, be yet, after the toil of successive ages, inadequate and delusive; if the aggregated knowledge and cooperating diligence of the Italian academicians did not secure them from the censure of Beni [an Italian critic of the seventeenth century]; if the embodied critics of France, when fifty years had been spent upon their work, were obliged to change its economy and give their second edition another

form, I may surely be contented without the praise of perfection, which, if I could obtain in this gloom of solitude, what would it avail me? I have protracted my work till most of those whom I wished to please have sunk into the grave and success and miscarriage are empty sounds. I therefore dismiss it with frigid tranquillity, having little to fear or hope from censure or from praise.

In the face of such eloquence one can only marvel at the development of English prose style during the centuries that separate Johnson from Trevisa. But in dealing with the impact of the eighteenth century on the development of English, we are chiefly interested in Johnson's motives for writing the dictionary, and in his final assessment of those motives as they relate to the nature of language generally. Johnson comments on the state of English as he found it when he first began the work:

> I have . . . attempted a dictionary of the English language, which, while it was employed in the cultivation of every species of literature, has itself been hitherto neglected, suffered to spread under the direction of chance into wild exuberance, resigned to the tyrrany of time and fashion, and exposed to the corruption of ignorance and caprices of innovation.
>
> When I took the first survey of my undertaking, I found our speech copious without order and energetic without rules. Wherever I turned my view, there was perplexity to be disentangled and confusion to be regulated; choice was to be made out of boundless variety without any established principle of selection; adulterations were to be detected without a settled test of purity; and modes of expression to be rejected or received without the suffrages of any writers of classical reputation or acknowledged authority.

Of particular interest are the words "wild exuberance," "innovation," "order," "rules," "regulated," "principle," "purity," "classical reputation," and "acknowledged authority." For in many ways these terms define attitudes that are often thought to characterize eighteenth-century intellectuals.

The "Settled" Age

Unlike the Renaissance, which vibrated with its enthusiasm for beholding and conquering new worlds, for seeking new answers to old questions and finding new questions to be asked, which rejoiced in a newfound spiritual and intellectual vigor, the eighteenth century was a settled age, firm in its conviction that Truth at last had been found.

For the Age of Reason, all the important questions had been asked, and, for the most part, satisfactorily answered. The road to Enlightenment had been discovered and all that remained was to set up the signposts for all men of good common sense to follow. It had been pioneered by the English philosopher John Locke (1632–1704) and the philosopher-scientist Sir Isaac Newton (1642–1727). Nature was conceived to be a *system* of divine *laws* carefully *ordered* and precisely *regulated* by a *rational* intelligence. It exhibited *order, harmony,* and *beauty,* and these characteristics provided insight into the nature of the God who had created Nature. To any *reasonable* man the works of Nature gave evidence of a Divine Being, the great Mechanic who had set in motion Newton's machinelike universe. And to those who had neither ears to hear the dictates of Reason nor eyes to behold the revelation of God through Nature, God revealed Himself through the Holy Scriptures. We might say that the Age of Reason was an a-place-for-everything, and-everything-in-its-place-age. Alexander Pope expresses it this way:

> See, through this air, this ocean, and this earth
> All matter quick, and bursting into birth.
> Above, how high, progressive life may go!
> Around, how wide! how deep extend below!
> Vast chain of Being! which from God began,
> Natures ethereal, human, angel, man,
> Beast, bird, fish, insect, what no eye can see,
> No glass can reach; from Infinite to thee,
> From thee to Nothing.—On superior powers
> Were we to press, inferior might on ours:
> Or in the full creation leave a void,
> Where, one step broken, the great scale's destroyed:
> From Nature's chain whatever link you strike,
> Tenth or ten thousandth, breaks the chain alike.

. . . .

> Cease then, nor ORDER Imperfection name:
> Our proper bliss depends on what we blame.
> Know thy own point: This kind, this due degree
> Of blindness, weakness, Heaven bestows on thee.
> Submit.—In this, or any other sphere,
> Secure to be as blest as thou canst bear:
> Safe in the hand of one disposing Power,
> Or in the natal, or the mortal hour.
> All Nature is but Art, unknown to thee;
> All Chance, Direction, which thou canst not see;
> All Discord, Harmony not understood;

All partial Evil, universal Good:
And, spite of Pride, in erring Reason's spite,
One Truth is clear, WHATEVER IS, IS RIGHT:

(*An Essay on Man,* 233–46; 281–94)

In some ways, this is a comforting view of man's relationship to God and to Nature. He knows where his place is in the total scheme of things, and he knows the limitations of that place. The notion of a Great Chain of Being stretching from God's throne down to and including the simplest forms of matter provided a sense both of security and stability. This was the way things were, and it was *right* that they should be so.

"Fixing" the Language

To an age settled in such convictions, whatever manifested "wild exuberance," "corruptions of ignorance," "caprices of innovation," "adulterations," "perplexity," "confusion," and the like, was clearly distasteful. It must at once be put right, corrected, purified, regulated, and refined. It must be made to conform to certain rules which have the weight of authority behind them. Furthermore, when this has been done, the principles established and the rules laid down, change and innovation must be firmly resisted. For once the mechanism has been set running in the proper way, *any* change must be for the worse. And so it was a part of Johnson's original design not only to order and refine the use of English by providing accurate definitions of both common and uncommon words, etymologies, and abundant illustrations of usage from some of the best writers, but also to stabilize the language and inhibit change. It is a measure of his perception, however, that he came to realize the futility of this latter aim:

> Those who have been persuaded to think well of my design will require that it should fix our language and put a stop to those alterations which time and chance have hitherto been suffered to make in it without opposition. With this consequence I will confess that I flattered myself for a while, but now begin to fear that I have indulged expectation which neither reason nor experience can justify. When we see men grow old and die at a certain time one after another, from century to century, we laugh at the elixir that promises to prolong life to a thousand years; and with equal justice may the lexicographer be derided who, being able to produce no example of a nation that has preserved their words and phrases from mutability, shall imagine that his dictionary can embalm his language and secure it from corruption and decay, that it is in his power to change sublunary nature and clear the world at once from folly, vanity, and affectation.

With this hope, however, academies have been instituted to guard the avenues of their language, to retain fugitives, and repulse intruders. But their vigilance and activity have hitherto been vain; sounds are too volatile and subtile for legal restraints; to enchain syllables and to lash the wind are equally the undertakings of pride unwilling to measure its desires by its strength.

The inevitability of language change had been recognized for some time, never more clearly perhaps than by Richard Mulcaster to whom we have already referred:

I said before, that those men, which will giue anie certain direction for the writing of anie tung, or for anie thing else, which concerneth anie tung, must take some period in the tung, or else their rules will proue vnrulie. For euerie tung hath a certain ascent from the meanest to the height, and a discent again from the height to the meanest, the one in the remouing kinde, as the other was in mounting. . . . This period of mine, and these risings to mount, as the dismounting again, till decaie ensew, do giue vs to wit, that as all thinges else, which belong to man be subject to change, so the tung also is, which changeth with the most, and yet contineweth with the best.

Regardless of what rules we may make governing the use of a language, the principle of change, which Mulcaster calls *prerogatiue*, will prevail. And for him, *prerogatiue* is the very "lifeblood" of language.

But not all seventeenth- and eighteenth-century men of learning were willing to accept the principle of language change as a virtue. For many it embodied at least these two evils: first, that if the language was permitted to change with such rapidity, what was now being written would soon be unintelligible; and second, that change would just as surely lead to corruption. The poet Edmund Waller (1606–1687) expresses the first in a little poem:

But who can hope his lines should long
Last in a daily changing tongue?
While they are new, envy prevails;
And as that dies, our language fails.

Poets that lasting marble seek,
Must carve in Latin, or in Greek;
We write in sand, our language grows,
And, like the tide, our work o'erflows.

Chaucer his sense can only boast;
The glory of his numbers lost!
Years have defaced his matchless strain;
And yet he did not sing in vain.

The second evil is discussed at great length by Jonathan Swift in a letter first printed in 1712 called "A Proposal for Correcting, Improving, and Ascertaining the English Tongue," and directed to the Most Honourable Robert Earl of Oxford and Mortimer, Lord High Treasurer of Great Britain:

> My lord, I do here, in the name of all the learned and polite persons of the nation, complain to your lordship, as first minister, that our language is extremely imperfect; that its daily improvements are by no means in proportion to its daily corruptions; that the pretenders to polish and refine it have chiefly multiplied abuses and absurdities; and that in many instances it offends against every part of grammar.

Swift expresses the opinion that ". . . if it [English] were once refined to a certain standard, perhaps there might be ways found out to fix it forever, or at least till we are invaded and made a conquest by some other state. . . ." Apart from major revolutions which might upset completely the social and political state of affairs, he sees ". . . no absolute necessity why any language should be perpetually changing." Swift's lack of linguistic perception is very noticeable when he attributes "This perpetual disposition to shorten our words by retrenching the vowels" to "the barbarity of those northern nations from whom we are descended, and whose languages labour all under the same defect." The lack of heat in the northern countries, he thinks ". . . which gives a fierceness to our natures may contribute to that roughness of our language, which bears some analogy to the harsh fruit of colder countries." Swift proposes that a society of well-qualified persons be appointed as a kind of legislative body to regulate the use of English. And then:

> But what I have most at heart is, that some method should be thought on for ascertaining and fixing our language for ever, after such alterations are made in it as shall be thought requisite. For I am of the opinion, it is better a language should not be wholly perfect, then that it should be perpetually changing.

We should note that to the eighteenth century *ascertainment* meant the settling of a question once and for all. For this purpose, the age felt the need for both a dictionary and a grammar that would determine in some authoritative way how the language *should* be used. This, then, is the beginning of what has turned out to be a rather major skirmish between conflicting attitudes toward language usage, and toward the nature and function of grammars and dictionaries: *prescriptivism* based on authority, and *descriptivism* based on observation. The first is concerned with the question, "How *should* the language be used?" The second with the question, "How *is* the language used?" The first is characterized by an insistence that language usage conform to some standard of "correctness" which it is the business of both grammar and dictionary to define; the second by the notion that the responsibility of both grammar and dictionary is to record the facts of language usage, and nothing more.

These opposing attitudes did not, certainly, originate with the eighteenth century; they have an ancient and honorable history. But by the nature of the age, they were more sharply defined and the lines of battle more clearly drawn than perhaps in any previous century. In our own time the war between *prescriptivism* and *descriptivism* has been pursued with renewed vigor, especially during the last twenty-five years. See, for example, the recent controversy over the publication of *Webster's Third New International Dictionary*.

Swift's proposal that a society be formed to regulate the use of English was not the first such. Societies of learned men had existed in England as early as the sixteenth century, but these had never actually turned their attention to matters of the English language. However, after the establishment of the famous Italian Accademia della Crusca in 1582 and l'Académie française in 1635, both of which professed deep concern for the "purity" of their respective languages, the notion of an English academy became more and more popular. And it received some impetus from the founding of the Royal Society in 1662 which, though primarily oriented toward the furthering of scientific interests, did in fact set up a committee that was to consider the improvement of the language.

In 1697 Daniel Defoe in *An Essay on Projects* praised the work of the French Academy and proposed that an English academy modeled after it be established by the King of England:

> The peculiar study of the Academy of Paris has been to refine and correct their own language, which they have done to that happy degree that we see it now spoken in all the courts of Christendom as the language allowed to be most universal.

> . . . .

> And such would this be; and because I am speaking of a work which seems to be proper only for the hand of the King himself, I shall not presume to carry on this chapter to the model as I have done in other subjects. Only thus far:

> That a society be erected by the King himself, if His Majesty thought fit, and composed of none but persons of the first figure in learning; and it were to be wished our gentry were so much lovers of learning that birth might always be joined with capacity.

> The work of the society should be to encourage polite learning, to polish and refine the English tongue, and advance the so much neglected faculty of correct language, to establish purity and propriety of style, and to purge it

from all the irregular additions that ignorance and affectation have introduced; and all those innovations in speech, if I may call them such, which some dogmatic writers have the confidence to foster upon their native language, as if their authority were sufficient to make their own fancy legitimate.

The part to be played by *rule* and *authority* in the work of the society Defoe makes clear in the following statement:

> The voice of this society should be sufficient authority for the usage of words, and sufficient also to expose the innovations of other men's fancies; they should preside with a sort of judicature over the learning of the age, and have liberty to correct and censure the exorbitance of writers, especially of translators. The reputation of this society would be enough to make them the allowed judges of style and language; and no author would have the impudence to coin without their authority.

OPPOSITION TO AN ACADEMY

Although the attitude held by Defoe and Swift on matters of language usage was common in the early eighteenth century, it was by no means universal. Samuel Johnson, whose opinions were very influential, found the notion of such a regulatory body clearly repugnant: "If an academy should be established for the cultivation of our style—*which I, who can never wish to see dependence multiplied, hope the spirit of English liberty will hinder or destroy* [author's italics]—let them, instead of compiling grammars and dictionaries, endeavor with all their influence to stop the license of translators, whose idleness and ignorance, if it be suffered to proceed, will reduce us to babble a dialect of France."

Arguments against the notion of a grammar as a kind of device for legislating language usage in accordance with some mythical standard of propriety were convincingly put forth by George Campbell in his *Philosophy of Rhetoric,* first published in 1776:

> It is not the business of grammar, as some critics seem preposterously to imagine, to give law to the fashions which regulate our speech. On the contrary, from its conformity to these, and from that alone, it derives all its authority and value. For, what is the grammar of any language? It is no other than a collection of general observations methodically digested, and comprising all the modes previously and independently established, by which the significations, derivations, and combinations of words in that language are ascertained. It is of no consequence here to what courses originally

these modes or fashions owe their existence, to imitation, to reflection, to affectation, or to caprice; they no sooner obtain and become general, than they are laws of the language, and the grammarian's only business is to note, collect, and methodize them.

. . . .

Only let us rest in these as fixed principles, that use, or the custom of speaking, is the sole original standard of conversation, as far as regards the expression, and the custom of writing is the sole standard of style: that the latter comprehends the former, and something more; that to the tribunal of use, as to the supreme authority, and consequently, in every grammatical controversy, the last resort, we are entitled to appeal from the laws and the decisions of grammarians; and that this order of subordination ought never, on any account, to be reversed.

The notion of a British academy or society to regulate language usage failed not only because there were influential men of good sense who deplored it, but also because in part it was seen to have political overtones. Swift, for instance, was a Tory, and when his proposal was published many of the Whig faction assumed that the establishment of an academy under a Tory government would be intended to serve Tory interests and to further Tory prestige. Swift's letter to the Earl of Oxford was, therefore, roundly attacked by the Whigs on political grounds. John Oldmixon's *Reflections on Dr. Swift's Letter, about Refining the English Tongue* was one of the most vicious and personal of these, motivated quite clearly by political bias:

> The merriest part of the Project he has been hatching, for an *English* Academy to bring our Tongue to his pitch of Perfection, is that he has assign'd, that Task to the *Tories,* whose Wit have so distinguish'd them in all Times. If there had ever been a man among 'em who had a right Notion of Letters or Language, who had any relish of Politeness, it had been something. But as there never was one, unless it were two or three Apostate Whigs who had been bred up by the Charity of those Friends they deserted, that had any smattering of Learning, except in Pedantry . . . 'tis amazing that he shou'd be so foolish as to fancy, that Learning which always goes by the Stile of Common-wealth, would submit to the Arbitrary Government of an Ignorant and Tyrannical Faction.

AUTHORITARIANISM DIES HARD

Although the eighteenth century did not succeed in establishing an academy, controversy stirred up by its proposal served to focus the attention of learned men on the need for a good English dictionary and grammar. And despite the liberal view toward grammar taken by such men as Campbell and Joseph Priestley, the tendency was toward the authoritarian. Those who were not blessed with polite learning should be told how to pronounce, spell, and write "correctly" according to the practices of the best authorities. Lindley Murray puts it this way in the third revised edition of his *An English Grammar*, published in 1816:

> Amidst the diversity and fluctuation of sentiment, respecting the correctness of language and the true idiom of our tongue, which are so frequently found to prevail amongst writers and critics, the student will naturally wish to be directed to some authority and standard, by which his doubts may, on most if not all occasions, be removed, and the propriety of his literary compositions ascertained. This principle or standard, is *reputable, national,* and *present* use.

Murray goes on to amplify the notions of *reputable, national,* and *present* by citing passages from Campbell's *Philosophy of Rhetoric,* which had defined these at some length. For instance, *reputable* is to be understood as ". . . whatever modes of speech are authorized as good, by the writings of a great number, if not the majority, of celebrated authors." The point we wish to direct attention to, however, is the concern for an indisputable authority to which one could have recourse. Such an authority on the meaning and use of words was Dr. Johnson's *Dictionary.* Despite its obvious flaws, the age was prone to accept it, with some reservations, as an important step toward *refining* and *fixing* the language. In his section on orthography, Murray comments on such variants as *honour* and *honor, inquire* and *enquire, negotiate* and *negociate, surprise* and *surprize, complete* and *compleat.* He goes on to say:

> Some authority for deciding differences of this nature, appears to be necessary: and where can we find one of equal pretentions with Dr. Johnson's Dictionary? though a few of his decisions do not appear to be warranted by the principles of etymology and analogy, the stable foundations of his improvements.

He then quotes a contemporary scholar:

> 'As the weight of truth and reason . . . is irresistible, Dr. Johnson's Dictionary has nearly fixed the external form of our language. Indeed so convenient is it to have one acknowledged standard to recur to; so much preferable in matters of this nature, is a trifling degree of irregularity, to a continual change, and fruitless pursuit of unattainable perfection; that it is earnestly to be hoped, that no author will henceforth, on light grounds, be tempted to innovate.'

The latter part of the eighteenth century saw the production of a number of English grammars written to fill the need for authoritative rules that would prescribe the proper use of the language. Johnson himself wrote a short English grammar which met, however, with little interest. Joseph Priestley's *The Rudiments of English Grammar,* published in 1761, is notable for its exceedingly moderate views on the notion of legislating grammatical practice. And for this very reason, perhaps, did not receive the attention it deserved. Bishop Robert Lowth, best known for his studies in Old Testament literature, published in 1762 *A Short Introduction to English Grammar.* This grammar, heavily pedantic and authoritarian, was a suitable counterpart to the *English Dictionary.* In attitude and method it provided the model for succeeding generations of English grammar writers.

Both Priestley and Lowth were scholarly men writing primarily for other scholars. It remained for Lindley Murray, an ex-American lawyer who had migrated to Yorkshire after the Revolutionary War, to provide for the schools an authoritative textbook of English grammar. His *An English Grammar* is divided into four main sections: *Orthography* "... of the form and sound of the letters, the combination of letters into syllables, and syllables into words"; *Etymology* "... of the different sorts of words, their various modifications, and their derivation"; *Syntax* "... of the union and right order of words in the formation of a sentence"; and *Prosody* "... of the just pronunciation, and poetical construction of sentences." His third edition of this work also contains "Appropriate Exercises" and "A Key to the Exercises." To Murray may be attributed the somewhat pernicious method of teaching correctness by the voluminous citation of error, a method that continues to persist in a number of English grammars in present-day use.

Murray's *Grammar* went through at least fifty editions, it sold millions of copies in both England and America, and was freely imitated by scores of later grammar writers. More than any other product of the eighteenth century it was responsible for the doctrine of authority, correctness, and prescription that characterizes much English teaching in our schools and colleges today.

Summary

Ultimately, then, the effect on the development of English of eighteenth-century modes of thought was to further the determination of a standard language, and, to the extent that this was possible, to prevent change. It was further to bestow on the dictionary and the grammar an authority that was well nigh unimpeachable, and to foster methods of teaching English that have been attacked as unsound only within the past few decades. As a result of eighteenth-century grammarians, the teaching of English grammar in a vacuum to school children became almost a way of life for nineteenth- and early twentieth-century school teachers in both England and America. Fortunately, there is some evidence that this unrewarding practice is going out of style.

2.50   Conclusion

With this brief account of the impact of eighteenth-century modes of thought on the development of English we will bring to a close our discussion of the external history of English. The fact that we do so does not, of course, mean that external influence ceased after the eighteenth century. What it *does* mean is that after this century the main stream of English language development divides into a number of channels, each of which should properly be discussed in its own right. As we have seen, English has been characterized by a number of regional and social dialects since Old English times. But our principal concern here has been with the development of the prestige dialect—that of the Southeast Midlands. Now as a result of empire expansion, the English language was spread throughout the world—to North America, to India and the Far East, to Africa, to Australia and New Zealand. Each new geographical environment exerted its own particular influence, as did each new political situation and each modification in the social ecology of native English speakers.

After the eighteenth century it becomes necessary to speak of the development of American English (or, as H. L. Mencken would have it, the American Language), of Australian and Canadian English, of the characteristic intonation and rhythmic patterns of Indian English, of West African English. Each of these differs markedly from what was once the prestige dialect, Southern British Standard, or Received Standard. Each has a standard of its own, though the criteria for defining this standard may differ from one political entity to another. In recent years, as English has become the lingua franca for nonnative speakers in many of the emerging nations of the world, the question of *what* or *whose* English to teach has become more and more critical. School children in nonnative English speaking countries, especially those of Africa and the Middle East, are frequently subjected to the confusion of being taught by a speaker of Indian English in some grades, an American English speaker in others, and a British English speaker in still others. Furthermore, the American English which the children hear may be at one time Eastern New England, at another Southern, at another Northern Midwestern, and so on. Under such conditions it is very difficult to impose on a nonnative speaker a given native English pronunciation. The teacher who sets for himself such a task is almost certain to be frustrated. In many countries the solution to the problem seems increasingly to be the establishment of a standard of English pronunciation that will permit facility of communication and will be neither British nor American, but characteristic of the country in question. To a lesser extent, perhaps, much the same thing has happened to French. Thus, we may say that in a very real sense the number of English "standards" has increased during the last few decades, especially since World War II.

After the eighteenth century, then, it becomes almost meaningless to talk about the development of *standard English*. We must talk about the development of standard British English, or standard American English (of this or that variety), of the English spoken in Gibraltar or Auckland or Sydney or Ibadan or Addis Ababa. Such developments must be the concern of other books.

2.60   Special Linguistic Terms

regular correspondences	gloss
compensatory lengthening	vernacular
a proto-language	prescriptivism
a reconstructed language	descriptivism
dialect diversity	ink-horn terms

2.70   For Additional Reference

Barfield, Owen. *History in English Words.* London, 1953; Grand Rapids, 1967.

Baugh, A. C. *A History of the English Language,* 2d ed. New York, 1957.

Bennett, Henry S. *English Books and Readers—1475–1557.* Cambridge, 1952.

Bloomfield, Leonard. *Language History.* From *Language* (1933 edition) ed. Harry Hoijer. Los Angeles, 1965.

Brook, G. L. *A History of the English Language.* London, 1958.

————. *English Dialects.* London, 1963.

Bryant, Margaret M. *Modern English and Its Heritage.* 2d ed. New York, 1962.

Craigie, William A., and others. *The Scottish Tongue: A Series of Lectures on the Vernacular Language of Lowland Scotland.* London, 1924.

Green, J. R. *Short History of the English People.* 2 vols. New York, 1899.

Groom, Bernard. *A Short History of English Words.* London, 1934; repr. 1965.

Hodgkin, R. H. *History of the Anglo-Saxons*. 2 vols. 3d ed. New York, 1953.

Jespersen, Otto H. *Growth and Structure of the English Language*. 9th ed. Oxford, 1962.

Jones, R. F. *The Triumph of the English Language*. Stanford, 1953.

Krapp, George Philip. *The English Language in America*. 2 vols. 2d ed. New York, 1960.

McIntosh, Angus. *An Introduction to a Survey of Scottish Dialects*. Edinburgh, 1952.

Marckwardt, Albert H. *American English*. New York, 1958.

Mathews, M. M. *The Beginnings of American English*. Chicago, 1931.

Mencken, H. L. *The American Language*. 4th ed. and two supplements abridged, with annotations and new material, by Raven I. McDavid, Jr. New York, 1963.

Mitchell, A. G. *The Pronunciation of English in Australia*. Sydney, 1946.

Myers, L. M. *The Roots of Modern English*. Boston, 1966.

Potter, Simeon. *Our Language*. Harmondsworth, England, 1950.

Pyles, Thomas. *Words and Ways of American English*. New York, 1952.

Skeat, W. W. *English Dialects from the Eighth Century to the Present Day*. Cambridge, 1912.

Sledd, James, and Wilma R. Ebbitt. *Dictionaries and "That" Dictionary*. Chicago, 1962.

Starnes, DeWitt, and Gertrude E. Noyes. *The English Dictionary from Cawdrey to Johnson*—1604–1755. Chapel Hill, 1946.

2.80   Exercises

1. Indicate the importance to the development of English of each of the following:

St. Augustine	Richard Mulcaster
Treaty of Wedmore	*Art of Rhetorique*
Benedictine Reform	Edmund Spenser
Battle of Hastings	John Lyly
Loss of Normandy	Wynkyn de Worde
Provisions of Oxford	Samuel Johnson
William Caxton	George Campbell
Lindley Murray	

2. What external influence is reflected in the following forms:

Lancaster	dike
Chichester	skirt
Pendleton	window
Cornwall	quick
Rugby	guilt
Thorpe	doubt
	fault

3. Match the Latin borrowings in List A with the native English words in List B. What *regular phonetic correspondences* can you identify?

List A	List B
patriot *1*	*5* fee
agriculture *2*	*2* nephew
cordial *3*	*13* slippery
host *4*	*16* fish
pecuniary *5*	*16* hen
grain *6*	*3* hearty
edible *7*	*4* guest
gelatine *8*	*12* brother
tri- *9*	*7* eat
nepotism *10*	*10* father
genus *11*	*2* acre
fraternity *12*	*15* thin
lubricate *13*	*11* kin
cornet *14*	*8* cold
tenuous *15*	*9* three
canto *16*	*14* horn
piscatorial *17*	*6* corn

4. Examine carefully one of the following and report on the contribution it makes to the methods of modern lexicography. You may also wish to consult Henry S. Bennett, *English Books and Readers—1475–1557*, Cambridge, 1952 and DeWitt Starnes and Gertrude E. Noyes, *The English Dictionary from Cawdrey to Johnson—1604–1755*, Chapel Hill, 1946.

John Baret, *An Alvearie....* 1580
Robert Cawdrey, *A Table Alphabeticall....* 1604
John Bullokar, *An English Expositour.* 1616
Henry Cockeram, *The English Dictionarie or An Interpreter of Hard English Words.* 1623
Thomas Blount, *Glossographia....* 1656, 1681
Edward Phillips, *The New World of English Words.* 1658
Stephen Skinner, *Etymologicon Linguae Anglicanae....* 1671
N. Bailey, *A Universal Etymological English Dictionary.* 1721
Defoe, B. W., *A Compleat English Dictionary....* 1735
Samuel Johnson, *A Dictionary of the English Language.* 1755

5. Consider some of the ways in which the following have affected the use of English or attitudes toward the use of English in our century:

a. World Wars I and II; the Korean War; the war in Vietnam
b. The transportation industries

c. The advertising agencies
d. The development of nuclear science
e. Foreign aid
f. The Peace Corps
g. The communication media
h. Recent tendencies in the creative arts: painting, sculpture, novel, drama, poetry
i. Sports
j. Social crises and movements (black power, hippies and Yippies, the New Left, the ghettos, use of drugs, reactions against censorship, urban renewal)
k. What other cultural conditions have arisen in the United States or Great Britain that have had some impact on the way in which the English language appears to be developing?

3. Phonemic change in English

Introduction

In this chapter we are going to talk about *phones, allophones,* and *phonemes.* These terms symbolize concepts that are very important to any discussion of the sounds of a language, and the changes which these sounds may undergo in the course of time.

Let us consider first the physical nature of the speech act. When you speak you bring into play a great many different organs of the body: your diaphragm moves up and down; your rib cage pushes in and out; your lungs are alternately filled with and emptied of air; the vocal cords in the "Adam's apple" (the *larynx*) may be drawn together only partially, they may be tightly closed, or quite open and relaxed; air may pass through nose or mouth, or both; the *uvula* (the little fold of skin hanging down in back of the mouth) may vibrate; the tongue is almost constantly in motion, assuming many different shapes and positions in the mouth; the teeth, lips, and jaw are always in use during speech. In other words, the act of speaking involves a great many different and fairly complex physical movements, a number of which occur simultaneously.

Perhaps we can suggest a useful analogy to the operation of the gasoline engine. Like the vocal apparatus, the engine is composed of many different *systems:* the ignition system, the starting mechanism, the carburetor system, the fuel system, the electrical system, the piston and valve system, the cooling system, and so on. When the ignition key is turned on and the starter button pressed, most of these systems and their individual parts come to life. Each system performs its job simultaneously with other systems in the engine. We may carry the analogy a step further. The power to drive the automobile results from the ignition of gasoline in the cylinder. When the gasoline ignites, an explosion occurs. But notice that when an engine is firing properly, individual explosions occur in such rapid succession that it is virtually impossible to distinguish one from another. We hear only the seemingly uninterrupted roar of the motor. Of course, the number of explosions per second can in fact be measured by an appropriate mechanical device, considerably more sensitive than the human ear.

Much the same thing happens in speech. Perhaps you have had the experience of listening to people carry on a conversation in a foreign language, or of hearing a foreign speaker on radio or television. For the most part, it is very difficult for the untrained listener to identify individual speech sounds. Everything seems to be run together. All that one can distinguish are the stretches of speech that occur between breath intakes. And these will of course vary in length. It is not unlike listening to someone start his engine, run it a few seconds, shut it off, start it again, run it a few more seconds, shut it off, start it again, shut it off, and so on.

PHONES AND PHONEMES

Individual segments of sound occurring between breath intakes *can* be identified by an appropriate mechanism. One such mechanism is a native speaker of the language in question. Barring an abnormal amount of interference, this speaker can identify all of the speech segments that are important to his understanding. If he could not, he would not be a native speaker. The smallest segments of speech which a native speaker of a language can identify because these are important to him in the communication process are called *phonemes*. Another kind of mechanism for identifying speech sounds is the trained phonetician. Such a person has considerable training and experience in listening for, identifying, and describing the great variety of speech sounds that occur in the world's languages. Like the musician who has been trained to hear the slightest variations in pitch, the phonetician is able to identify very slight variations in speech sounds, and to describe these in terms of the movements of the speech organs. Now the smallest segments of speech which a phonetician can identify are called *phones*. The phonetician is both capable of and interested in making finer distinctions between speech sounds than is the native speaker of a language. There are other devices, both electrical and electronic, that are capable of perceiving much finer distinctions, even, than the phonetician can; but these will not concern us here.

The native speaker of a language rarely articulates a given sound twice in exactly the same way. His production of a sound may be modified by his emotional state, by his physical environment, and by the complex of surrounding sounds which he is also producing. For the most part, however, these variations will not be so great as to cause confusion for the listener. For example, in English we have a particular kind of sound that we refer to as a "p" sound. It occurs in such words as *pot, spot, top, topper, sprocket, explode,* and so forth. Each one of these "p" sounds differs in some describable way from each other "p" sound. And the differences can be accounted for by the fact that each "p" sound either occurs in a different position in the word or is in contact with a different "non-p" sound. The chances are, however, that you have never given any thought to the fact that these "p" sounds are different. As native speakers of English we are not concerned with these differences since they are not *significant* in the communication process.

To convince yourself that the "p" sounds in *pot, spot,* and *top* are different, hold a piece of paper about two inches in front of your mouth as you pronounce the three words. You will notice that when you say "pot," you release a puff of air that moves the paper in quite a noticeable way. A much smaller amount of air is released when you say "spot"; in fact, the paper may scarcely move at all with some articulations. The "p" in "top" differs from the other two in that in the speech of most people the mouth *closes* for the "p," but *does not open* again when the word is pronounced in isolation. We say that the initial "p" which occurs with a heavy puff of breath is *aspirated;* the "p" which occurs after *s* is *lightly aspirated,* or sometimes *unaspirated;* and the one that occurs at the end of a final word is *unreleased.* Try the same experiment with the "t" sound in *top, stop,* and *pot,* and with the "k" sound in *kit, skit,* and *tick.* Notice that the aspiration of the "k" sound in *kit* is less than the aspiration of the initial "p" sound, but is still evident.

Because the various "p" sounds are phonetically similar, that is, they are articulated by the speech organs in similar ways and in the same place, and because each type of "p" sound occurs in a different position in the word, we say that the "p" sounds all belong to the same class of sounds. We call such a class of sounds a *phoneme,* and we indicate that for English this is a *significant* class of sounds by placing the symbol *p* between slant lines: /p/. The word *significant* is important to our definition of a phoneme. We need to ask, "For whom is a particular class of sounds significant?" The answer is that such a class is significant to a native speaker of the language in question. And it *is* significant because it enables him to distinguish one *meaningful* form in the language from another. For example, *spill, still,* and *skill* are distinguished from each other solely by the occurrence in the first of a "p" sound, in the second of a "t" sound, and in the third of a "k" sound. We say, then, that in English these three sound types, or classes, are distinct phonemes: /p/, /t/, and /k/. The members of each of these classes are called *allophones.* Thus, we may say that the *phoneme* /p/ in English has at least three *allophones:* (1) the aspirated [pʰ] which occurs in *pot,* (2) the lightly aspirated or simple [p] which occurs in *spot,* and (3) the unreleased [p⁻] which occurs in *top.* And so also for /t/ and /k/. You will notice that to indicate *allophones* we have used square brackets [ ], whereas to indicate *phonemes* we have used slant lines / /. Writing which occurs between square brackets is called *phonetic transcription;* that which occurs between slant lines is called *phonemic transcription.*

It is very important that you understand that the primary function of phonetic writing is to represent the *actual* sounds that occur in speech, and that the function of phonemic writing is to represent *classes* of sounds. A phonetic or phonemic transcription of English differs from our conventional alphabetic writing system in that *one* symbol consistently represents *one* actual speech sound, or *one* class of speech sounds. Our conventional writing system, on the other hand, is inconsistent and multivalued. Notice in how many ways the "ee" sound is represented in the following words: *receive, believe, beet, beat, ski, Negro, Pete, lovely, people.* Furthermore, because almost all of your formal English language study has been of the written language, you will have a tendency to confuse *what we say* with *what we write.* Throughout this chapter, therefore, keep in mind that we are talking principally about the *sounds* of the language and *not* their conventional representation in English writing.

English Consonants

The sound system of English, like all other languages, is made up of *consonants* and *vowels.* A simple way of explaining the difference between these two types of sounds is to say that consonant sounds result from some *obstruction* in the stream of air as it passes from the lungs out through the mouth and/or nose (or, in some languages, *in* through the mouth and/or nose), while vowel sounds result from an unobstructed and resonated stream of air. Like many definitions, this one is an oversimplification of the actual facts of the matter, but it will serve us here. When a linguist wishes to talk about vowels and consonants he usually talks about them in terms of their *place* and *manner* of articulation. In order for you to see how this works we will

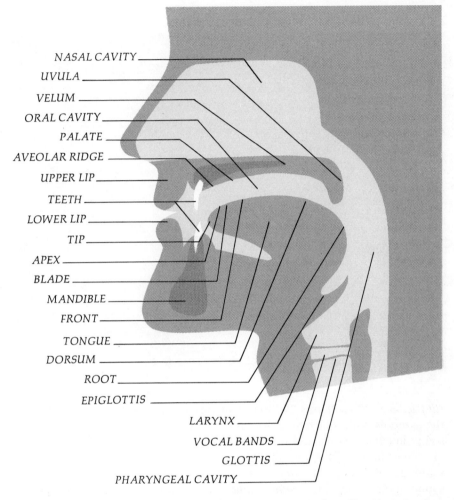

Cross section of head, showing principal speech organs. (*Adapted by permission from W. Nelson Francis,* The Structure of American English, *Copyright © 1958 The Ronald Press Company, New York.*)

refer to the following matrix chart of English consonant phonemes and to the labeled diagram of the head and throat on the facing page. The horizontal matrix indicates *place* of articulation; the vertical matrix, *manner* of articulation.

We now have an inventory of English consonants, and a fairly precise way of referring to them. Rather than talk about a "p" sound, we will talk about a *bilabial, voiceless stop;* rather than an "f" sound, a *labiodental, voiceless,*

English Consonant Phonemes

		Bilabial	Labiodental	Dental	Alveolar	Alveo-palatal	Velar	Glottal
Stops	voiceless	p			t		k	
	voiced	b			d		g	
Affricates	voiceless					č		
	voiced					ǰ		
Fricatives Slit	voiceless		f	θ				h
	voiced		v	ð				
Groove	voiceless				s	š		
	voiced				z	ž		
Lateral	voiced				l			
Nasals	voiced	m			n		ŋ	
Semivowels		w			r	y		

slit fricative; rather than a "y" sound, an *alveo-palatal, voiced semivowel.* Note the symbols with which you may not be familiar: /č/ represents the "ch" sound in *child, church,* and the "tch" in *kitchen* and *witch;* /ǰ/ represents the "j" sound in *just, June,* and the "dg" in *judges, badge,* and *ridge;* /θ/ represents the "th" sound in *think, thin,* and *path,* while /ð/ represents the "th" sound in *then, this, that, weather, father, bathe, soothe;* /š/ represents the "sh" sound in *shoe, short, shape, wash,* and in *action, election, faction, mission, tissue;* /ž/ represents the sibilant sound in *measure, leisure, azure, occasion;* /ŋ/ represents the nasal sound often spelled *ng* in such words as *sing, ring, long,* and the sound spelled *n* before *k* in *sank, tank, think, banker,* and the like. The remaining symbols are a part of our standard spelling system.

Some comment on the terms signifying *manner of articulation* is in order. By *stop* we mean that at some point in the articulatory system the air stream is completely shut off by the contact of one organ against another. By *affricate* we mean that the air stream is momentarily blocked completely, but is then released with friction sound. By *fricative* we mean that some articulatory organ impedes the air stream to the extent that friction noise occurs continuously during the process of articulation. In the case of *slit* fricatives the air passes between a narrow horizontal slit usually formed by the two lips, lower lip and upper teeth, or tongue and teeth. The term *groove* refers to the configuration of the tongue. Laterals, nasals, and semivowels are all vowel-like consonants and are sometimes classed as *resonants;* that is, like vowels their sounds are reenforced and amplified by the vibration of the walls of the oral and nasal cavities. In the lateral, the vibrating air column passes along the sides of the tongue as the front of this organ comes in contact with the alveolar ridge directly behind the upper front teeth; in the nasals, the air stream passes into the nasal cavity where it is amplified. The semivowels are so called because they function in the syllable as both vowels and consonants, as in *wow* and *yey,* where initial *w* and *y* represent consonantal features, final *w* and *y* represent vocalic features.

The tongue is a very active organ, and one of the most important articulators in the speech of any language. We sometimes refer to sounds according to the segment of the tongue that performs the articulation. For example, in English, dental and alveolar sounds are generally articulated by the *apex* of the tongue and are called *apical;* alveo-palatal sounds are articulated by the *front* of the tongue and are called *frontal;* velar sounds are articulated by the back of the tongue or *dorsum,* and are called *dorsal* (see diagram).

Because we will make frequent reference to these consonant symbols in this chapter, you should learn to use and interpret them, and to describe the articulatory features of the sounds they represent.

EXERCISES

1. Write the appropriate phonemic symbol for the *initial* consonant in each of the following words:

a. shut š̌
b. thistle θ
c. cream ǩ
d. chose č̌
e. than š̌
f. German ǰ
g. fiend ⨍

h. rich
i. cider
j. Jane
k. Thursday
l. Nancy
m. wrong
n. choir

[NOTE: Be sure you use the precise written form of the printed symbols you find on the chart.]

2. Write the appropriate phonemic symbol for the *middle* consonant in each of the following words:

a. robber
b. trucker
c. gadget
d. treasure
e. mission
f. singer
g. listen

h. feather
i. catcher
j. liquor
k. Roger
l. facial
m. raisin
n. patience

3. Write the appropriate phonemic symbol for the *final* consonant in each of the following:

a. singe
b. path
c. antique
d. dredge
e. rage
f. breathe

g. frantic
h. check
i. garage
j. strong
k. with
l. wretch

4. Write the appropriate phonemic symbol indicated by each of the following descriptions:

a. a labiodental, voiced slit fricative
b. an alveolar nasal
c. a voiceless velar stop
d. a voiced alveo-palatal affricate
e. a bilabial semivowel
f. a voiceless glottal fricative
g. a voiced dental slit fricative
h. a voiceless alveo-palatal grooved fricative
i. a voiced bilabial stop
j. a velar nasal

5. Write the appropriate articulatory description of each of the following symbols:

a. /v/
b. /t/
c. /ǰ/
d. /y/
e. /l/
f. /θ/

g. /h/
h. /š/
i. /m/
j. /r/
k. /g/
l. /ž/

ENGLISH VOWELS

When we come to speak of the English vowel system, we are faced with a more difficult situation. In fact, we cannot speak of *the* English vowel system at all, but only of English vowel *systems*. The English consonant system that we have presented is, with few exceptions, characteristic of all native English speakers regardless of dialect. What principally enables us to distinguish between one English dialect and another is the difference in the vowel systems of the dialects being compared. We will, therefore, present a kind of overall inventory of English vowels. Each vowel in this inventory occurs in *some* English dialect, but *no* dialect has all of the vowels in the inventory. Then we will illustrate by a selection from this inventory some of the vowel systems which occur.

Above, we defined the difference between consonants and vowels as being one between obstruction and nonobstruction. We need to go further and say that vowels constitute the *peaks* of *resonance* or *sonority* within an English syllable. To put it another way, the most audible part of the syllable /tat/ occurs between the two consonants. A syllable may contain more than one peak of sonority, as in some pronunciations of the word *couch* [kʰauč] in which there is strong resonance on both the [a] and the [u]. In this case we have a *complex resonance peak,* or a *complex syllabic nucleus* with the strongest resonance occurring with [a]. Such a complex peak is often called a *falling diphthong.* If the relative strengths of the peaks were reversed, the strongest occurring with [u], we would have a *rising diphthong.* Where there is only one syllabic peak, we may speak of a *simple resonance peak* or a *simple syllabic nucleus.*

Just as we presented the consonant system in terms of a matrix which indicated features of articulation, we will use a similar device to present our overall vowel inventory. For the most part, English vowels are resonated in the *oral* cavity, and their quality is determined by the shape and size of that cavity. And the shape of the cavity is determined by the shape and position of the articulating organs: the tongue, the teeth, the lips, and the jaw. Think of the oral cavity as a boxlike structure, open at both ends, containing a movable divider, and a floor that can be raised or lowered. The shape of one opening can be changed from a fairly narrow slit, to a wide-open, squarish opening, to a small round opening.

In terms of the articulating organs, the roof of the mouth is the top of the box, the jaw is the floor that can be raised or lowered, the tongue is the movable divider, and the lips determine the configuration of one opening. The

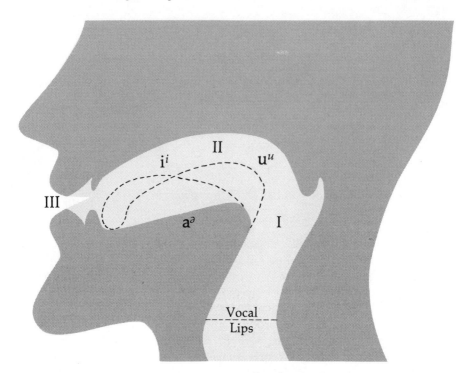

Relative tongue positions for [iⁱ], [aᵉ], and [uᵘ]. (*Adapted by permission from Ernst Pulgram,* Introduction to the Spectrography of Speech, *Mouton & Co., 1959.*)

throat is the other opening, and the front teeth, especially the uppers, may function as a kind of secondary divider. We may think of the throat as the mouth piece of a reed instrument containing the vocal lips that function like a reed. When the vocal lips are set in motion by the passage of air between them, a vibrating column of air is set up in the oral cavity. The vibrations are transmitted to the walls of the mouth in the same way that the vibrations of the column of air in a reed instrument are transmitted to the walls of the instrument. The result of this transmission, in both cases, is that the sound created by the vibrating column of air is *amplified.* A vibrating column of air, or a vibrating string, will vibrate at different speeds depending on the length and thickness of the column. Differences in the rate of vibration determine differences in pitch. Furthermore, not only will a column of air or a string vibrate as a whole, but it will also vibrate in sections of itself; and these sections will vibrate at different speeds depending upon the length of the section. The tone of the body vibrating as a whole is called the *fundamental;* the tones imposed on this fundamental by each of the vibrating sections are called *harmonics*. As the column of air passes through the oral cavity, different harmonics will be amplified depending on the size and shape of that cavity. Our divider, the tongue, tends to split the cavity into two smaller cavities which will vibrate more rapidly than the large cavity; and since the two smaller cavities will rarely be exactly the same size, they will vibrate at different rates of speed from each other. Each time the size and shape of the large cavity and those of the two smaller cavities relative to each other are changed there is a change in vowel quality.

Let us consider the shape of the mouth and the position of the articulators in reference to three fairly common English vowels: [iⁱ] in *beet,* [uᵘ] in *boot,* and [aₐ] in *father.* If you put the tip of a finger between your teeth as you pronounce each word, you will notice certain changes taking place. As you pronounce the vowel in *beet,* your tongue will be touching your finger; but as you move to *boot,* it will be withdrawn. As you go from *beet* or *boot* to *father,* your jaw will tend to drop. You will notice too that in going from *beet* to *boot,* your lips will become rounded. The diagram on the opposite page indicates the relative tongue positions for each of these three vowel sounds.

Simple vowels

Now for English we can set up the following matrix defined by tongue position, jaw height, and lip configuration:

	Front	*Central*	*Back*
High *Mid*	i /bit/ *bit* e /bet/ *bet*	ɨ /jɨst/ *just* (adv) ə /bət/ *but*	u /put/ *put* o /rod/ *road* (in older eastern New England)
Low	æ /bæt/ *bat*	a /pat/ *pot* (Northern)	ɔ /bɔt/ *bought* (Northern)
	Unrounded		*Rounded*

Exercise

In describing the vowel sounds we refer to the positions identified on the chart. Thus /i/ is a high, front, unrounded simple vowel; /ə/ is a mid, central, unrounded simple

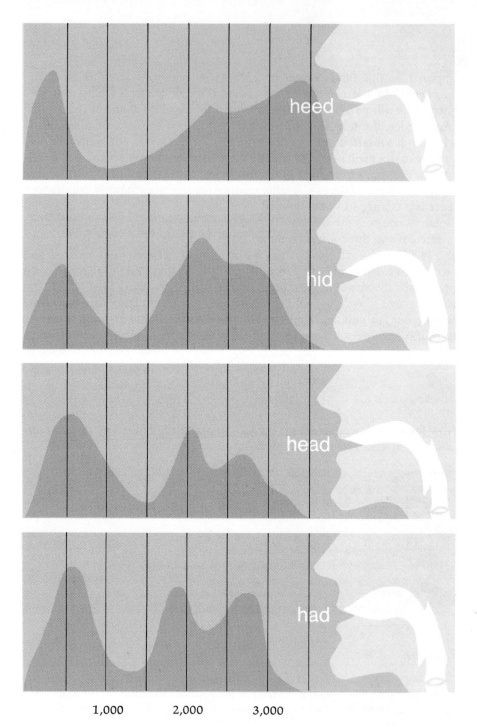

1,000   2,000   3,000

The position of the vocal organs and the spectra of the vowel sounds in the middle of the words *heed, hid, head, had, hod, hawed, hood, who'd* in Professor Peter Ladefoged's speech; based on data from x-ray photographs. (*Adapted by permission from Peter*

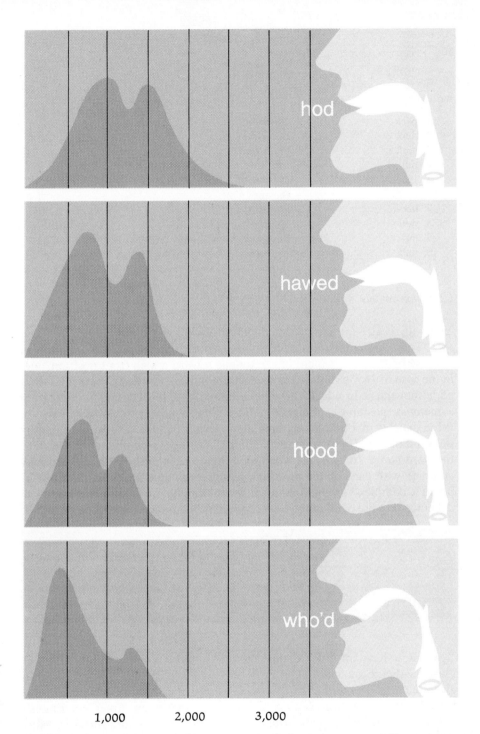

1,000   2,000   3,000

Ladefoged, Elements of Acoustic Phonetics, *copyright by the University of Chicago Press, 1962.*)

vowel; /ɔ/ is a low, back, rounded simple vowel, and so on. For the following words write the consonant and vowel phonemes according to your own pronunciation:

1. peck	11. good
2. duck	12. blood
3. look	13. head
4. pill	14. dust
5. taught	15. hot
6. pan	16. ant
7. hook	17. aunt
8. done	18. foot
9. pull	19. flood
10. said	20. gone

Complex vowels

You will recall that the consonant chart included the semivowels /y/ and /w/. These are sometimes called glides since their articulation involves, in the case of /y/ a movement of the tongue toward a high front position, and, in the case of /w/, a movement toward a high back position. There is another glide movement in which the tongue moves to a low central position from some *other* position in the mouth. This glide is perhaps most noticeable in those dialects of English that lack a *postvocalic* [r], and will be indicated by the symbol /ə/. The word *fear* in some dialects may be phonemically /fiə/, the word *mayor* /meyə/, the word *poor* /puə/. Each of these three glides may combine with each of the nine simple vowels to give an overall total of 27 possible complex vowels. Again, we should emphasize that *no single* English dialect makes use of all of these. A chart of the complex vowels looks like this:

	Front	Central	Back
High	iə, iy, iw	ɨə, ɨy, ɨw	uə, uy, uw
Mid	eə, ey, ew	əə, əy, əw	oə, oy, ow
Low	æə, æy, æw	aə, ay, aw	ɔə, ɔy, ɔw

We now have an inventory of 36 total possible vowel symbols. We will illustrate their occurrence by reference to some specific vowel systems within given dialects. The author of this book was born in Albany, New York, and brought up in western New York State. He speaks an American English dialect often called *General American, Western Reserve,* or *Northern.* Most speakers of this dialect have the following vowel system:

A. *Simple vowels*
/i/ *bit*   /u/ *put*
/e/ *bet*   /ə/ *but*
/æ/ *bat*   /a/ *hot*   /ɔ/ *bought*

B. *Complex vowels*
/iy/ *beet*   /uw/ *boot*
/ey/ *bait*   /oy/ *boy,* /ow/ *boat*
          /aə/ *calm,* /ay/ *bite,* /aw/ *bout*

There are 14 vowel phonemes in this dialect.
    In eastern New England the vowel system is somewhat different:

A. *Simple vowels*
/i/ *bit*   /u/ *put*
/e/ *bet*   /ə/ *but*   /o/ *road* (among older,
                                                          rural speakers)
/æ/ *bat*   /a/ *aunt*   /ɔ/ *hot*

B. *Complex vowels*
/iə/ *here,* /iy/ *beet*   /uə/ *poor,* /uw/ *boot*
                                              /oə/ *four,* /ow/ *boat*
/eə/ *care,* /ey/ *bait*   /ɔə/ *caught,* /ɔy/ *boil*
                            /aə/ *cart*

In this dialect there are 19 vowel phonemes.
    Still another set of vowels can be illustrated from one of the dialects of
inhabitants of Lancashire in northwestern England:

A. *Simple vowels*
/i/ *fist*   /u/ *sun, cut, run*
/e/ *friend*   /o/ *blossom*
                            /a/ *cap*

Note the lack of an /ə/ phoneme in this dialect.

B. *Complex vowels*
/iə/ *mean* (verb), /iy/ *green*   /uə/ *stone, coach,* /uw/ *fruit*
/eə/ *day* /ey/ *meat*   /oy/ *coal, goat,* /ow/ *grow*
      mane   *weave*
      fever   *head*
                    /aə/ *mine, joint, mouth*

An examination of these three English dialects tells us that dialects may be defined in terms both of their phonemic inventory and of the way in which phonemes are distributed in the forms of the language. Not only do the systems above differ in their selection of phonemes, but also in the range of occurrence of a common phoneme. This latter fact is particularly evident if we compare the American Northern dialect of western New York State with the British dialect. Both dialects have the phonemes /aə/, /ow/, and /oy/, but the words in which these are realized are different. New York has /oy/ in *joint* while Lancashire has /aə/; New York has /ow/ in *goat* while Lancashire has /oy/; New York has /ay/ in *mine,* /aw/ in *mouth,* and /oy/ in *joint,* while Lancashire has /aə/ in all three; New York has /e/ in both *dead* and *head,* while Lancashire has /iə/ in the first and /ey/ in the second.

EXERCISES

1. Write the following words in phonemic transcription according to your own pronunciation:

beat	few	bird	horse
bait	beauty	fur	hoarse
bite	beer	fir	merry
boat	bear	due	marry
boot	poor	do	dairy
bought	pour	Tuesday	tune
bout	fool	fuel	foal
fall	follow	fellow	pillow
cot	cart	caught	coat
think	bush	mush	pull
dull	full	lathe	loose
choose	lose	chose	root
roof	route	witch	which
score	scare	scar	scour
orange	horrid	log	fog
dog	hog	shirt	floor
bath	bathe	voice	noise
pleasure	leisure	measure	mesher
manage	garage	language	

2. Practice reading the following transcriptions:

jǽk ən jil went əp ðə hil to feč ə peyl əv wɔtər.
jǽk fel dawn ən browk ɨz krawn, æn jil keym təmblɨŋ æftər.

ðer wəns wəz ə felow neymd skinər
hu wəz towld ðæt iy hæd tu get θinər
ðow iy hæd ə gud dayɨt
hiy ɉɨst nevər wud tray ɨt
fɔr iy fird it mayt ruɨn ɨz dinər.

ðer wəz ə yəŋ leydi neymd hɔl
huw fel in ðə spriŋ in ðə fɔl.
twud əv bin ə sæd θiŋ
if šiyd dayd in ðə spriŋ,
bət šiy didnt, šiy dayd in ðə fɔl.

ðə sən əv ferowz dɔtər, iz ðə dɔtər əv ferowz sən.

   it iz veri impɔrtənt ðæt yuw əndərstænd ðæt ðə praymeri fəŋkšən əv
fownetɨk raytiŋ iz tu repriyzent ðiy ækšuəl sawnz ðæt əkər in spiyč, æn ðæt
ðə fəŋkšən əv fowniymɨk raytiŋ iz to repriyzent ðə klæsɨz əv sawnz ðæt əkər.
ðə sawn sistəm əv iŋliš, layk ɔl əðər læŋgwɨɉɨz, iz meyd əp əv kansənənts æn
vawlz.

3.10   Development of English Consonants

With this preliminary background out of the way, we can now look at some
of the problems of historical sound change in English. This will involve setting
up charts of the phoneme systems for different periods in English and showing how the sounds in certain Modern English words (as these are pronounced in a given dialect) developed from one historical stage to another.
Such a procedure immediately presents a number of problems. First of all
the question arises "How do we know what the phonemic systems of different
historical periods were?" In this book we can only give a somewhat unsatis-
factory answer. Extensive written records available for all stages of the language we mean to consider, plus the techniques of comparative and historical
linguistics, plus commentaries on the pronunciation of English by early
observers of the language enable us to establish at least a reasonable approximation of an English phonemic system at a given stage in English history.
One might also ask "Isn't it true that a given sound may have developed
differently in different dialects? And if this is true, will we not have to consider the way in which a particular phoneme has developed in each of the
several British and American dialects?" The answer to the first part is an
emphatic "Yes." The answer to the second is that a comprehensive treatment

of phonemic development is certainly desirable in any work that pretends to be a more or less complete history of the language, but that such comprehensiveness is beyond the scope of this book.

What we will do in the following pages will be to show certain lines of phonemic development from West Saxon Old English through the late fourteenth-century dialect of Chaucer and the early seventeenth-century dialect of Shakespeare to the Northern or General American dialect. We choose this latter dialect only because its system of vowel phonemes is fairly simple and it is spoken by a large segment of the American population.

OLD ENGLISH

Late West Saxon Old English had the following consonant phonemes:

/p/ *pipe* "pipe"	/t/ *tellan* "tell"	/č/ *ceap* "purchase, sale"	/k/ *cwic* "living"
/b/ *bacan* "to bake"	/d/ *dæg* "day"	/j/ *ecg* "edge"	/g/ *gamen* "sport, joy"
/f/ *feoht* "fight"	/θ/ *þing* "thing, creature"		/x/ *heah* "high, eminent, tall"
	/s/ *soð* "true, real"	/š/ *scip* "ship"	
/m/ *mod* "heart, mind"	/n/ *niht* "night, darkness"		
	/l/ *lufian* "to love, cherish"		
	/r/ *rap* "rope, cord"		
/w/ *wac* "weak, soft, cowardly"		/y/ *geong* "young, youthful, recent"	

You will notice certain differences between this system and the one we charted for Modern English. First, the phonemes /v/, /ð/, /z/, /ž/, and /ŋ/ are missing here. Second, the phoneme /x/ is represented rather than /h/. We will see now what changes took place to give rise to the Modern English system.

Voiced fricatives become phonemic

The Old English phonemes /f θ s/ had voiceless allophones [f θ s] in word initial and word final positions, but voiced allophones [v ð z] between vowels in open syllables. In addition, inherited from older stages of Germanic, a great many forms had "double consonants" in medial position between vowels.

In the fricative system, these double consonants were voiceless and have traditionally been interpreted as /ff θθ ss/. In the opinion of this writer, the effect of consonant doubling was to create a closed syllable, the first consonant of the pair closing off the first syllable, the second consonant beginning the second syllable, with the result that the distribution of voiceless and voiced fricative allophones described above applied here as well. We have two types of disyllabic structure: (1) $(C_1)V(V)C_2V(C_3)$ and (2) $(C_1)VC_2 + C_2V(C_3)$ in which + represents some kind of interruption feature between syllables. If C_2 of (1) is a fricative it will be voiced; the C_2's of (2), however, will both be voiceless since the first occurs in syllable final position while the second occurs in syllable initial position. Thus the Old English verb *blysian* 'to burn' is realized phonetically as [blyziɑn]; the verb *blissian* 'to be glad' is realized phonetically as [blis + siɑn]. When in early Middle English (after the lengthening of short vowels in open syllables) the interruption feature + is lost, the resulting voiceless medial fricative contrasts with the earlier voiced medial fricative; thus *blissian* [blisian] contrasts with *blysian* [blyzian]. In this way the voiced-voiceless allophones of Old English /f θ s/ split into separate phonemes, /f θ s/, /v ð z/.

Initial /v/ and /z/ resulted primarily from the adoption in Middle English of French words: *valour* 'valor,' *veel* 'veal,' *vengeaunce* 'vengeance,' *vers* 'verse,' *vois* 'voice,' *vyce* 'vice,' *zele* 'zeal,' *zodiak* 'zodiac,' *zepherus* 'zephyr,' and the like. In those areas of the North and Midlands that had been strongly influenced by the Scandinavian invasions, initial /v/ was reinforced by Old Norse forms which had initial /v/ for Old English /w/ as in *vif* 'wife,' *verð* 'worth,' *vinna* 'win,' *vængr* 'wing.'

Old English /x/

In the Old English consonant chart the phoneme /x/ represents a palato-velar *fricative*, a sound that no longer occurs in Standard British English or in American dialects, but that still occurs in some of the nonstandard dialects of England and Scotland. The allophones of this phoneme had a long and rather complicated history from Old English to early Modern English. Here we will be content to give a much simplified account of that history. In Old English this phoneme had voiceless allophones represented by the letter *h* in a number of positions: *hus* 'house,' *heorte* 'heart,' *hleapan* 'to leap,' *hnutu* 'nut,' *hræfn* 'raven,' *hreod* 'reed,' *hwa* 'who,' *hwit* 'white,' *dohtor* 'daughter,' *cniht* 'boy,' *feohtan* 'fight,' *leoht* 'light,' *sohte* 'he sought,' *pohha* 'pocket,' *crohha* 'crock,' *heah* 'high,' *ruh* 'rough,' *furh* 'furrow.'

In initial position before vowels this phoneme was undoubtedly pronounced very much like [h] in modern *house* and *heart*. In other words it was a strong, voiceless puff of breath with perhaps some slight friction. This [h] has remained in the standard language before stressed vowels, although it has frequently been lost by late Middle English times before unstressed vowels (for instance, our neuter pronoun *it* is from Old English *hit*). Some confusion regarding the pronunciation of *h* before vowels arose during the Middle English period as a result of the introduction of Norman French loan words such as *habit, hermit, herb, homage, humble, host, hotel, heir, honest, hour, haste, horrible.* The initial *h* was not pronounced in Norman French nor in educated Middle English speech. However, it was sometimes pronounced by those who were not aware of French practice. As a result, some of the forms have an initial [h] in the standard dialects of Modern English, and some do not. Among educated speakers *heir, honest,* and *hour* never have [h], *host, haste, horrible, hotel, habit* for the most part have [h], while practice seems to vary in the case of *hermit, herb, homage,* and *humble.* Some of the confusion regarding the pronunciation of initial *h* in French words was transferred to the pronunciation of *h* in native English words, so that during Middle English times an original [h] may occasionally be dropped and a nonoriginal [h] may be added. Although in many English dialects the reflex of Old English [h] does not occur, it was a distinct phoneme in Chaucer's dialect.

The Old English variant of /x/ which occurred before /r/, /l/, /n/, and /w/ is generally thought to have been a voiceless, palato-velar fricative. By Chaucer's time this sound had been lost before /r/, /l/, and /n/, though still retained before /w/ probably as [h] in the standard language. In late Middle or early Modern English this [h] was also lost, and remains absent in a number of the standard modern dialects. So *what, wheat, when, which, while* are /wət/, /wiyt/, /wen/, /wič/, and /wayl/.

Before /t/, the fricative allophone [x] spelled *h* in Old English in such words as *cniht, feohtan, leoht* (Modern English *knight, fight, light*) was retained throughout the Middle English period. In the standard dialect it was lost during the fifteenth century. However, there is considerable evidence that this sound was disappearing when it followed *back* vowels (as in *sohte* and *dohter*) as early as the thirteenth century. For example, in this century one finds the spellings *broute* and *naut* for *brought* and *naught.* In an early fourteenth-century text the *reverse* spelling *foghte* occurs for *foot.* Such a spelling is extremely important for establishing the occurrence or nonoccurrence of a given sound. What it tells us is that since the spelling *gh* no longer represented anything in the sound system of the language, it could be used, mistakenly, in words like *foot* which had *never* contained the sound formerly represented by this *gh*. In the fifteenth century we find a number of such spellings: *ought* for *out, abought* for *about, dought* for *doubt, wright* for *write, quight* for *quite, whight* for *white,* and so on. You may recall that in Chapter 1 we commented on the variant spellings *houȝ* and *hou* in Trevisa's text. The suggestion is that since ʒ no longer represented any sound in this position, it could be attached to words where etymologically it did not belong. This kind of spelling practice is sometimes called a *hyperurbanism.*

In addition to loss, the allophone [x] underwent a somewhat different change after rounded vowels. In a well-known fourteenth-century poem "King Horn," the rhyme *softe*:*dohter* occurs. This change of [x] to [f], presumably the result of lip-rounding, is more evident in the early Modern period where one finds such rhymes as *after*:*daughter,* and such spellings as *soft* for *sought, slafter* for *slaughter,* and *taft* for *taught.* These pronunciations with [f], however, were not retained in the standard language long after the eighteenth century. The [f] in *laughter* occurs in present-day English by analogy with the verb *laugh* (Old English *hliehhan*).

In final position, in such words as Old English *dah, ruh,* and *furh,* [x] (1) gradually disappeared, as in *dough,* (2) became [f], as in *rough,* or (3) developed into a vocalic, as in *furrow.* That these changes were taking place in the fourteenth century is clear from such spellings as *enow* in Trevisa, Modern English *enough* from Old English *genog, genoh,* and *þof,* Modern English *though* from Old English *ðeah* in the late fourteenth-century poem "Gawain and the Grene Knyʒt."

It is difficult to assess precisely the status of [x] in Chaucer's time. We will assume here that it *may* still have been an allophone of /h/ before /t/. It is certain that in the standard language it had ceased to be pronounced very early in the fifteenth century.

Old English /n/

The Old English phoneme /n/ had two allophones, [ŋ] before /g/ and /k/, as in *bringan* [briŋgan] "bring," *drincan* [driŋkan] "drink," *tunge* [tuŋge] "tongue"; and [n], which occurred elsewhere. As final grammatical inflections were lost during the Middle English period, the combinations [ŋk] and [ŋg] came to stand finally in a word; for instance, Old English [briŋgan] becomes Middle English [briŋg(ə)]. Final [k] in this combination was retained, while final [g] was lost, as in Modern English /siŋk/-/briŋ/. With the loss of final [g] after [ŋ], this [ŋ] stands in contrast with final [n] so that *sing-sin, sung-sun, tongue-ton* now constitute minimal pairs. [ŋ], then, is no longer an allophone of /n/, but a distinct phoneme, /ŋ/.

The problem, in Chaucer for example, is in knowing whether or not the residues of final inflectional endings have in fact been lost. These residues are normally represented in spelling by a final -*e,* and the question of the pronunciation of final -*e* in Chaucer's poetry has been raised numerous times. Those who insist that it should be pronounced base their argument on the metrical structure of the poetic line maintaining that the lines are more regularly iambic and thus (for them) more satisfying when the final -*e* is pronounced. Others argue in opposition that there is clear evidence that final -*e*'s carried no grammatical information and were retained in the spelling system solely by custom. For our particular purposes in dealing with the phonemic status of [ŋ], if final -*e* [ə] had been lost, then it is probable that final [g] following [ŋ] had also been lost, so that [ŋ] stood in phonemic contrast with [n]; otherwise, [ŋ] was still an allophone of /n/. Whether in fact we should consider [ŋ] to have achieved phonemic status in the Chaucerian dialect of the fourteenth century is uncertain. We will tend toward conservatism here and treat it in our Middle English chart as an allophone of /n/, keeping in mind, however, the fact that it was clearly a separate phoneme in the fifteenth century.

Development of /ž/

The remaining missing phoneme in our Modern English consonant chart is /ž/. In early Modern English the phonemic combinations /si/ and /ti/ in such words as *passion, malicious, partial, action* became /š/ as indicated by the spellings *conschens* 'conscience,' *partyschon* 'partition,' *commyshins* 'commissions,' *instrocshens* 'instructions,' *suspishiously* 'suspiciously,' and *condishon* 'condition.' Some of these spellings are recorded as early as the middle of the fifteenth century. In like manner, /zi/ gradually developed to /ž/ in such items as *occasion* and *division,* and came to stand in contrast with /š/ as in /əkeyžən/ *occasion* and /veykeyšən/ *vacation.* Apparently the change that has altered the pronunciation of -*dure, -ture, -sure* in *verdure, picture, measure* to /-jər/, /-čər/, /-žər/ had not taken place by Shakespeare's time. Helge Kökeritz in his book *Shakespeare's Pronunciation* cites the rhymes *departure:shorter* and *venture:enter,* the puns *departure-departer, features-faitors,* and *pasture-pastor,* and the spellings *lectors* 'lectures,' *tortering* 'torturing,' *venter* 'venture,' *tenure* 'tenor,' *tuture* 'tutor,' as evidence that in Shakespeare's dialect the change referred to had not yet occurred. But by the middle of the seventeenth century /ž/ in words like *pleasure* and *measure* was common.

MIDDLE AND EARLY MODERN ENGLISH

The inventory of consonant phonemes for the late Middle English period we will take to be these:

/p/		/t/	/č/	/k/	
/b/		/d/	/ǰ/	/g/	
/f/	/θ/	/s/	/š/		/h/
/v/	/ð/	/z/			
/m/		/n/			
		/l/			
		/r/			
/w/			/y/		

For the standard early Modern English system we need add only the two phonemes /ž/ and /ŋ/ to bring us to the consonant system that has remained fairly stable up to the present time.

This is not, of course, all there is to the development of English consonants. We pointed out earlier that one dialect may be distinguished from another not only in terms of its phoneme inventory, but also in terms of the differences in the ways a given common phoneme may be distributed between two dialects. All English dialects have an /r/ phoneme; but the phonetic realization of this phoneme is not the same in all dialects, nor is its distribution the same. Here we have touched only on the general outlines of consonant development in English, omitting a considerable number of important and interesting details.

/r/ and /l/

Two details will detain us here. In this country we often speak of the "r-less" dialects of certain areas along the eastern seaboard and in the South. What we mean is that *postvocalic* [r] in these dialects has been replaced by a central glide [ə] as in eastern New England [haəd] "hard" and [kaə] "car." In standard British English postvocalic [r] was gradually disappearing during the late Middle English period. H. C. Wyld in his *A Short History of English* cites such spellings from the fifteenth to the seventeenth century as *passell* 'parcel,' *posshene* 'portion,' *Wosseter* 'Worcester,' *Dasset* 'Dorset,' *passons* 'parsons,' *fust* 'first.' Professor Kökeritz cites these spellings from Shakespeare: *accust* 'accurst,' *gosse* 'gorse,' *depature* 'departure,' *gater* 'garter'; and the rhymes *forsworn*:*John*, *earth*:*death*. Present-day *cuss* for *curst* and *bust* for *burst* are survivals of this development. However, postvocalic [r] was retained in a great many nonstandard British dialects, and this fact accounts in part for its widespread distribution in the United States.

In the Midland and Southern British dialects [l] had already disappeared during the Middle English period in such words as Old English *ælc* 'each,' *mycel* 'much,' *swylc* 'such,' and *hwylc* 'which.' It was also disappearing in *should* and *would* when these occurred in *unstressed* positions. [l] was not original in *could* (from Old English *cuðe*), but was inserted probably on analogy with *would* and *should*. In the early Modern English period [l] was lost before *labial* consonants and /k/. The spelling *haf* 'half,' is found in the fourteenth century; later spellings have *Fakonbrige* 'Falconbridge,' *Tawbot* 'Talbot,' *stauke* 'stalk,' *behaf* 'behalf.' That [l] was retained in the *stressed* forms of *should, would,* and *could* until the eighteenth century is indicated by the rhymes, chiefly seventeenth century, *would:hold; should:behold, gold; could:behold.* But Edmund Waller rhymes *would:mud* and John Dryden, *could:good.* As a result of Latin influence [l] was restored in words that Middle English had borrowed from French without the [l]: Middle English *assaut* rewritten *assault, faute* rewritten *fault, ream* rewritten *realm, cauderon* rewritten *cauldron,* and the like.

3.20 Development of English Vowels

We now turn our attention to the development of English vowel phonemes. The following simple vowel system is assumed for the late Old English West Saxon dialect.

OLD ENGLISH SIMPLE VOWELS

	Front	*Front*	*Central*	*Back*
High	/i/ *biddan*	/y/ *cyning*		/u/ *uppe*
Mid	/e/ *settan*		/ə/ *heofon*	/o/ *botm*
Low	/æ/ *sæt*		/a/ *earm*	/ɑ/ *catt*
	Unrounded	*Rounded*	*Unrounded*	*Rounded*

The Old English verb *biddan* 'to ask, entreat, pray' and also 'to order, command, require' appears in Modern English as *bid,* presumably with little change in vowel quality. Similarly, the vowel in *settan* 'to occupy, set, put down, lay, deposit,' has undergone little change, showing up in Modern English *set.* The vowel in Old English *sæt,* third person singular past tense of *sittan* 'to sit,' must have been phonetically very close to that in Modern *sat.*

The vowel in *cyning* 'king' does not occur in the standard dialects of Modern English. As the chart indicates, *y* represents a high, front, rounded vowel. If you pronounce /i/ while your lips are rounded you will produce a close approximation to the sound in question. This sound had a variety of developments in Middle English, as you can see from some of its modern reflexes. Old English *synn* /syn/ has become Modern English *sin* /sin/; Old English *cynn* /kyn/, Modern English *kin* /kin/; Old English *cyssan* /kyssan/, Modern *kiss* /kis/; but Old English *scytel* /šytel/ has become Modern English *shuttle* /šətəl/; Old English *scyttan* /šyttan/, Modern English *shut* /šət/; further, Old English *lyft* /lyft/ has become Modern English *left* /left/; Old English *flycge* /flyǰe/, Modern English *fledge* /fleǰ/; Old English *cnyll*, Modern *knell*.

The phonemic status of the late Middle English reflex of Old English /y/ is not entirely clear; and the somewhat confusing spelling conventions of the period do not help. Certainly in many areas of the country, including London, a gradual process of *unrounding* occurred during the Middle English period. In some dialects spelling and rhyme indicate that Old English /y/ had fallen together with /e/; in some others that it had become /i/; in some that competing forms with both /e/ and /i/ existed side by side. At any rate, the sound [y] was no longer a distinct phoneme in late Middle English.

During the Middle English period reflexes of Old English /ə/, as in *heofon,* 'heaven,' had fallen together with those from Old English /e/, as in *settan;* in other words [ə] had become [ɛ], as it is in Modern English.

The traditional explanation has it that in late Old English /a/ [a] *ea* fell together with /æ/ [æ] *æ*, and that during the Middle English period this [æ] became [a] /a/ *a*. In other words the reflexes of Old English *sæt* and *earm* have the same sound in Middle English: /sat/ and /arm/. A somewhat better explanation seems to be that in late Old English [æ] and [a] no longer contrasted with each other so that there was no longer any need to differentiate them in spelling. From about the twelfth century both sounds were represented by the letter *a* which itself represented a single phoneme /a/ containing, at least in some dialects, two allophones, [æ] and [a]. In the Modern period these allophones split again into distinct phonemes /æ/ and /a/ when new contrasts, say between *hat* and *hot,* or *cat* and *cot,* began to appear. Similarly, the contrast between Old English /a/ and /α/ was also lost. In Middle English, then, the dialect with which we are concerned shows only one phoneme, /a/, where one stage of Old English had three, /æ/, /a/, and /α/.

The Old English phonemes /u/ and /o/ are retained throughout the Middle English period. The distinction, however, is sometimes obscured by the spelling system. Since in manuscript *u*'s are often hard to distinguish from *n*'s, *m*'s, and *w*'s, and because *u* could also represent /v/ in certain positions, thirteenth-century scribes adopted the practice of writing *o* instead of *u* for /u/. As a result we find competing spellings of this phoneme: *hunger-honger, yung-yong, tunge-tonge, wulf-wolf, cumen-comen*. It is this substitution that accounts for our Modern English spellings *tongue, wolf, come, love.*

MIDDLE ENGLISH SIMPLE VOWELS

The late Middle English dialect of the Southeast Midland area had, then, the following simple vowel contrasts:

$$/i/ \qquad /u/$$
$$/e/ \qquad /o/$$
$$/a/$$

OLD ENGLISH COMPLEX VOWELS

We assume the following system of complex vowels for late West Saxon Old English:

	Front	*Front*	*Central*	*Back*
High	/i•/ *bitan* "bite"	/y•/ *hydan* "hide"		/u•/ *hus* "house"
Mid	/e•/ *med* "meed, reward"		/ə•/ *deop* "deep"	/o•/ *boc* "book"
Low	/æ•/ *slæpan* "sleep"		/a•/ *hleapan* "leap"	/ɑ•/ *bat* "boat"
	Unrounded	*Rounded*	*Unrounded*	*Rounded*

[NOTE: /•/ is a phoneme of length.]

In the change from late Old to late Middle English this system underwent the following developments:

/i•/ *bitan*	>	/iy/ *bite(n)*
/e•/ *med*	>	/ey/ *mede*
/æ•/ *slæpan*	>	/eə/ *slepe(n)*
/y•/ *hydan*	>	/iy/ *hide(n)*

/ə•/ *deop*	>	/ey/ *depe*
/a•/ *hleapan*	>	/eə/ *lepe*
/ɑ•/ *bat*	>	/oə/ *bot*
/o•/ *boc*	>	/ow/ *boke*
/u•/ *hus*	>	/uw/ *hous*

In addition to the developments charted above, certain other phonological changes took place which added additional vowel phonemes to the Middle English inventory. For one thing, Old English short or simple vowels became complex in *open* syllables. (Syllables may be *checked* or *open; checked syllables end in a consonant, open syllables do not.*) Thus, Old English /alu/ *ealu* 'ale' became Middle English /aəl(ə)/; Old English /bɑkɑn/ *bacan* becomes Middle English /baəkə(n)/ *bake(n)* 'bake.' This process adds the additional phoneme /aə/ to the Middle English system.

The Middle English phoneme /ay/ developed from Old English *æg*. So *mai, day, hail* /may/, /day/, /hayl/ come from Old English *mæg, dæg, hægl.*

Middle English /aw/ developed from a number of Old English combinations, among them /ɑw/ and /ɑx/, as *clawu* becomes Middle English *clawe, clau* 'claw,' *dragan* becomes Middle English *drawe(n)* 'to draw.' Middle English /ew/ comes from Old English /a•w/ *eaw* as in *feawe* becoming *fewe* 'few.' Middle English /iw/ is in part from Old English /ə•w/ *eow,* as *breowan* 'to brew' becomes Middle English *brewe(n)* /briwə(n)/. The Middle English phoneme /oy/ was borrowed from French as in *noise, noyse* from French /nɔyse/, and *point, poynt* from French /poynt/.

MIDDLE ENGLISH COMPLEX VOWELS

Middle English had, then, at least these complex vowel phonemes:

/iy/ *bite*	/iw/ *brewe*	/uw/ *hous*
/ey/ *mede*	/ew/ *fewe*	/ow/ *boke*
/eə/ *slepe*	/oy/ *poynt*	/oə/ *bot*
/ay/ *mai*	/aə/ *bake*	/aw/ *drawe*

We might very well reduce this phonemic inventory by one since the evidence for both /ew/ and /iw/ is indeed slight.

Vocalic changes from Old to Middle English were much more complex than is suggested by the superficial view presented here. Keep in mind that we have considered only one dialect. The inventories and distributions that developed in other dialects were often quite different from this one. Further, within a given dialect a particular sound often developed differently depending upon the nature of the surrounding sounds. We will illustrate this last point with one example. In Modern English we have the pairs *wise-wisdom* /wayz/-/wizdəm/ and *house-husband* /haws/-/həzbənd/. The first word in each pair contains a complex vowel, while the same word combined with a form beginning with a consonant has a simple vowel. This situation results from the fact that in late Old English or early Middle English vowels that had been long in Old English were shortened before certain *consonant clusters*. An additional factor in the shortening of the *stem* vowel was the occurrence of a following syllable which had relatively *strong stress*. In Modern English, for instance, we have *wild* /wayld/ beside *wilderness* /wildərnis/ and *holy* /howliy/ beside *holiday* /halidey/. Although in Modern English the secondary stress on the final syllable of *wilderness* has been lost, it is still retained in *holiday*. Such factors as these played a considerable part in the development of English sounds from Old to Middle English.

3.30   The Great Sound Shift

In late Middle English times a change in the quality of both simple and complex vowels began to occur, a change that resulted in an almost total reshaping of the vowel system. This change is known as the *great sound shift* or the *Middle English vowel shift.* We do not know *why* this shift occurred. We can only trace its movements in terms of spellings, rhymes, and commentaries on English pronunciation by early grammarians, phoneticians, and lexicographers. This shift did not begin in all dialects at the same time, it did not affect them all in precisely the same way, nor did it continue in all of them for the same length of time. In some dialects there is evidence of it having begun by the end of the thirteenth century; in others, among these the dialect of the Southeast Midlands, it seems to have begun somewhat later. It is not until the eighteenth century that we find pronunciations in the standard language that are essentially like those we hear in the Received Standard Pronunciation of British English today.

For the sake of convenience and simplicity we will chart below only the beginning and end points of the vowel shift in what was to become the standard dialect. We will then discuss some of the details of the shift and some of its intermediate stages.

Simple Vowels

Late Middle English	Modern Northern American
/i/ *bit*	/i/ *bit*
/e/ *bet*	/e/ *bet*
/a/ *sat*	/æ/ *sat*
/o/ *pot*	/a/ *pot*
/u/ *cut*	/ə/ *cut*

Middle English /i/ and /e/

A few comments on some of these is necessary here. There is considerable evidence from both spelling and rhyme that among a great many speakers of the language words which had had Middle English /i/ often had /e/ between the fifteenth and the eighteenth century. One finds such spellings as *shellynges* for *shillings, fesshermen* for *fishermen, reches* for *riches, cheldren* for *children, sens* for *since, essue* for *issue;* and in the seventeenth and eighteenth centuries the rhymes *sperit:merit, prince:sense, gift:theft,* and the like. Presumably the earlier pronunciation of these words was restored on the basis of standard spellings.

Middle English /e/ had a raised allophone that occurred before alveolar and velar nasal consonants [n] and [ŋ], and this allophone fell together with the allophones of /i/. This shift accounts for the standard modern pronunciation of such words as *England* /iŋ(g)lənd/, *wing*/wiŋ/, *hinge*/hinǰ/, *string*/striŋ/ from Middle English *weng, henge, streng.* We should note that this tendency for [ɛ] to become [ɪ] in this environment is not a shift peculiarly related to the Middle English Sound Shift. In many parts of England this change had undoubtedly occurred before the end of the fourteenth century. On the whole, however, spelling evidence for it is not found until the fifteenth.

Old English /æ/

We have indicated that there is some difficulty in tracing the development of Old English /æ/. Many linguists believe that the allophones of this phoneme were retracted to [a] in Middle English, and that this sound was gradually fronted again to [æ] during the seventeenth century. There are differing opinions about this process, but we will not argue the point here. However it came about, the reflex of the Old English /æ/ phoneme was /æ/ [æ] in the eighteenth century. In Middle English, the phoneme we indicate as /a/ must have had a number of allophonic variations. One such variation occurred in the words *all, call, fall, small,* and *salt, talk, malt, bald,* and the like. Late fifteenth-century spellings as Tawbot 'Talbot,' *aull* 'all,' and *schawl* 'shall' indicate that before /l/, [a] had become [au]. This [au] later became [ɔə] or [ɔ].

MIDDLE ENGLISH /u/ AND /o/

In many regional dialects of England Middle English /o/, presumably [ɔ] or [o], was unrounded to [a] during the early Modern period. Pronunciation of some earlier [o] forms as [a] also became fashionable for a time in London English, although British Received Standard now has a slightly rounded vowel. The unrounded pronunciation is suggested by such spellings in the fifteenth century as *starme* 'storm,' *aft* 'oft,' and *last* 'lost'; *yander* 'yonder,' *hars* 'horse,' *caffen* 'coffin,' *stap* 'stop,' *swarn* 'sworn' occur in the sixteenth. The sound [a] in *hot, rock, college, top, shot* and the like is very widespread in the United States, but note the occurrence of the rounded vowel in these words especially in Eastern New England. Note, too, your own pronunciation of *lost, cost, soft, loft, frost.* What do you think accounts for the difference (if you have one) between your pronunciation of the vowels in *cost* and *cot?*

How would you write phonemically the vowels in *run, cut, bud, but, nut, summer,* on the one hand, and *put, bull, bush, full, pull, wolf,* on the other? Are they the same or different? In Middle English, both groups contained the sound represented by the phoneme /u/, but during the early Modern period this sound was unrounded to [ə]. Apparently this unrounding process affected all words that contained late Middle English or early Modern English /u/. So, for instance, we have Modern /fləd/ *flood* and /bləd/ *blood* from a Middle English /flowd/-/blowd/. But this /ow/ was raised to /uw/ and then shortened to /u/. Once the vowel in *flood* and *blood* had fallen together with allophones of /u/, it participated in the general shift of these allophones from /u/ to /ə/. It appears that among *some* speakers lip-rounding of the vowel was restored after labial consonants giving Modern /pul/, /bul/, /buš/ rather than /pəl/, /bəl/, /bəš/. Lip-rounding was not restored by other speakers in this environment so that in Modern English we also have /məd/, /bəd/, /fən/ for *mud, bud,* and *fun.*

SHAKESPEARE'S PRONUNCIATION

On Shakespeare's pronunciation of the reflexes of the Middle English simple vowels we may make the following comments. Clearly a phoneme /æ/ in such words as *act, apple, at, back, matter, ran* had been established. /e/ occurred as in Modern English *bet* and *bed* and is sometimes spelled *ea* in Shakespeare as *creadit* 'credit' and *seaventie* 'seventy' by analogy with the spelling of /e/ in *head* and *read*. Among polite society a number of forms that in both Middle and Modern English have /e/ were pronounced with /i/; thus, *blisse* 'bless,' *divell* 'devil,' *intertainment* 'entertainment,' *pibble* 'pebble,' *togither* 'together,' and the rhymes *imprinted:contented, theft:shift, well:ill, yet:sit*. Notice the standard Modern English pronunciation of *pretty*.

/i/ occurred very much as in Modern English, although there is spelling evidence for a lowered vowel in some items: *arethmaticke* 'arithmetic,' *cestern* 'cistern,' *satericall* 'satirical,' *hether* 'hither,' *thether* 'thither.'

We have commented above on the fact that the reflexes of Middle English /o/ developed differently in different dialects. There is some question as to whether or not Shakespeare himself used the unrounded vowel [a] in *hot, pot, cod,* and so on. There is evidence, from his rhymes and puns especially, that he was familiar with both rounded and unrounded reflexes. Furthermore, the unrounded type appears to have been fairly common in and around London. We find the rhymes *corn:harm, George:charge, short:heart, storms:arms*. Presumably, preconsonantal /r/ had been replaced by the glide /ə/ by this time so that the vowel nucleus in these rhyming words was probably /aə/.

How far the shift of Middle English [u] to Modern English [ə], with consequent development of the phoneme /ə/, in *cut, but, rut, bud,* and so on had proceeded by Shakespeare's time is not altogether clear. Professor Helge Kökeritz points out that "As a Warwickshire man Shakespeare must originally have pronounced [u] for ME *u*, and this is still the regular dialectal sound. . . ." (240) He goes on to say, however, that as an actor in London he probably adopted a London pronunciation which was much closer to [ə]. Spelling and rhyme evidence is not conclusive. Shakespeare does have such rhymes as *bud:good; mud:flood; blood:good, stood; bush:rush, blush; fullness: dullness; pull:dull;* and *wolf:gulf*. Superficially, these would seem to suggest the vowel [u] as in Modern standard *bush, push, full*. But it is quite possible to argue that the vowel in most of these is [ə]. Certainly, there is every reason to think that for the purpose of rhyming and punning Shakespeare would have made use of all his resources, including more than one current pronunciation.

Regarding the simple vowels, then, our conclusion must be that by the seventeenth century the basic system was very much like that of the standard English dialects today.

COMPLEX VOWELS

A look at the following chart will indicate the extent of the qualitative changes that have taken place in the complex vowel system between late Middle English and the present. Again, we take General or Northern American English as our end point.

Late Middle English	Modern Northern American
/iy/ *bite(n)*	/ay/ *bite*
/ey/ *mede*	/iy/ *meed*
/eə/ *slepe(n)*	/iy/ *sleep*
/ay/ *mai*	/ey/ *may*
/aə/ *bake(n)*	/ey/ *bake*
/aw/ *drawe(n)*	/ɔ/ or /ɔə/ *draw*
/uw/ *hous*	/aw/ *house*
/iw/ *brewe(n)*	/uw/ *brew*
/ew/ *fewe*	/uw/ *few*
/ow/ *boot*	/uw/ *boot*
/oə/ *bot*	/ow/ *boat*
/oy/ *poynt*	/ɔy/ *point*

Notice that as a result of *phonemic merger* the great vowel shift has reduced the number of vowel phonemes in the modern dialect illustrated here by four. This does not mean, of course, that *all* English dialects underwent such a reduction.

We are not simply concerned here with the fact that Middle English /iy/ appears in some Modern dialects as /ay/, and /uw/ as /aw/, and so on. We would like to know something about the stages of development in between. The following chart indicates the stage of development the complex vowels are thought to have reached by Shakespeare's time:

Late Middle English	Intermediate Stage	Shakespeare
/iy/ *bite(n)*		/ɔy/ *bite*
/ey/ *mede*	/iə/ >	/iy/ *meed*
/eə/ *slepe(n)*	/eə/ >	/ey/ *sleep*
	/ey/ >	/iy/ *sleep*

/ay/ *mai*	/eə/ >	/ey/ *may*
/aə/ *bake(n)*	/eə/ >	/ey/ *bake*
/aw/ *drawe(n)*	/ɔw/ >	/ɔə/ *draw*
/uw/ *hous*		/əw/ *house*
/iw/ *brewe(n)*		/uw/ *brew*
/ew/ *fewe*		/uw/ *few*
/ow/ *boot*	/uə/ >	/uw/ *boot*
/oə/ *bot*		/ow/ *boat*
/oy/ *poynt*		/əy/ *point*
		/ɔy/ *point*

Concerning this chart we should call attention to two points in particular. There are conflicting theories as to the development of late Middle English /eə/. We will assume that different dialects current in and around London showed different developments; that in some, Middle English /eə/ had somewhat conservatively developed only to /ey/ by the seventeenth century, while in others it had by this time become /iy/. In other words, during Shakespeare's time there were competing pronunciations of such words as *sleep*: /sleyp/ and/or /sliyp/. It is perhaps this fact that enables Shakespeare to rhyme *defeated*:*created, ease*:*case, head*:*aid, dead*:*made, sea*:*play, please*: *grace* on the one hand, and on the other *speech*:*each, speak*:*cheek, sea*:*free, please*:*knees*.

The situation regarding late Middle English /oy/ is somewhat more complicated owing to certain developments that occurred in the Middle English period itself. Suffice it to say here that again we appear to have a situation in which there were competing pronunciations. In some dialects /oy/ had become /əy/, falling together with the /əy/ from Middle English /iy/. Thus one finds Shakespeare rhyming *die*:*joy*:*annoy, exploit*:*right, joy*:*eye*:*majesty*.

MIDDLE ENGLISH /er/

One further phonological change is of considerable interest. Most native speakers of standard British or American English have [ar] or [aə] in such words as *far, star, carve, dark, barley, start, starve, parson*. Similarly, these speakers have [ar] or [aə] in *hearken, hearth, heart*, and *sergeant*. Notice, however, that most Americans have [ər] or [əə] in *clerk* and *derby*, while most speakers of British standard have [əə]. Notice, too, that while the spelling *Hartford* reflects the current pronunciation, the British spelling *Hertford* does not. Furthermore, Chaucer spells *far, carve, start, dark, parson* as *fer, kerven, stert, derk, persoun*. We have, then, a situation in which a Middle English [er] gradually developed to [ar] in some dialects. A few *ar* spellings have been noted for Middle English, some of which are as early as the thirteenth century. During the early Modern period such spellings occur much more frequently and reflect a pronunciation that became popular at Queen Elizabeth's court. At the same time, a pronunciation [ər], later [əə], was retained in some regional speech. French words introduced or reintroduced into the language during the early Modern period, and especially in the eighteenth century, tended to retain the sound [ər] or [əə].

As far as Modern English is concerned, we have in the standard dialects of American and British English words such as *far, carve, start* spelled *ar* and pronounced [ar] or [aə], but which go back to a Middle English *er* [er]; we have words such as *mercy, merchant, servant, eternal* spelled with *er* and pronounced [ər] or [əə]; and we have words such as *clerk* and *derby* spelled with *er* but pronounced [ər], [əə] in some dialects and [ar], [aə] in others.

During Shakespeare's time a great many words of the second type listed above were pronounced with [a], although this pronunciation seems to have died out in the eighteenth century. One finds such rhymes in the seventeenth century as *convert : art, desert : impart, heard : regard, serve : carve,* and the spellings *clarke* for *clerk, darth* for *dearth, marmaide* for *mermaid, starling* for *sterling.*

We have now attempted to trace in a very limited way *some* of the phonological changes which took place in the English spoken in and around London from Old English times to the present. Much has been omitted, for we have said almost nothing about the kinds of developments that took place in various regional dialects and varieties either in England or America. We have suggested here only the general direction of phonological change in the English language.

3.40   Special Linguistic Terms

phone	apical
allophone	frontal
phoneme	dorsal
aspirated	resonance peak
unreleased	sonority
phonemic transcription	falling diphthong
phonetic transcription	rising diphthong
consonant	amplification
vowel	harmonic
place and manner of articulation	reverse spelling

stop
affricate
fricative
resonant

hyperurbanism
open and closed syllable
consonant cluster
unrounding

3.50   For Additional Reference

Brunner, K. "The Old English Vowel Phonemes," *English Studies* 34:247–51, 1953.

Campbell, A. *Old English Grammar*. Oxford, 1959.

Daunt, Marjorie. "Some Notes on Old English Phonology," *Transactions of the Philological Society* 1952:48–54. London, 1953.

Dobbie, Elliot. "On Early Modern English Pronunciation." *American Speech* 33:111–15, 1958.

Dobson, Eric John. *English Pronunciation, 1500–1700*. 2 vols. Oxford, 1957.

Gleason, H. A. *An Introduction to Descriptive Linguistics*. Chapters 12–18. New York, 1955; revised ed. New York, 1961.

Heffner, Roe-Merrill Secrist. *General Phonetics*. Madison, 1949.

Hill, A. *Introduction to Linguistic Structures*. Chapters 3–6. New York, 1958.

Hockett, C. F. *A Course in Linguistics*. Chapters 2–13, 43. New York, 1958.

Jones, Daniel. *The Phoneme: Its Nature and Use*. Cambridge, 1950.

———. *An Outline of English Phonetics*. 6th ed. New York, 1940.

Kökeritz, Helge. *Shakespeare's Pronunciation*. New Haven, 1953.

McLaughlin, John C. *A Graphemic-Phonemic Study of a Middle English Manuscript*. The Hague, 1963.

Matthews, William. "Variant Pronunciations in the Seventeenth Century." *Journal of English and German Philology*. 37:189–206, 1938.

Moore, Samuel, Sanford B. Meech, and Harold Whitehall. "Middle English Dialect Characteristics and Dialect Boundaries," *Essays and Studies in English and Comparative Literature*. University of Michigan Publication, Language and Literature XIII. Ann Arbor, 1935:1–60.

Mosse, Fernand. *A Handbook of Middle English*. Trans. James A. Walker. Baltimore, 1952.

Moulton, William G. "Stops and Spirants of Early Germanic," *Language* 30:1–42, 1954.

Quirk, Randolph, and C. L. Wrenn. *An Old English Grammar*. London, 1955.

Samuels, M. L. "The Study of Old English Phonology," *Transactions of the Philological Society* 1952:15–47. London, 1953.

Sievers, Eduard. *An Old English Grammar*. Trans. and ed. by Albert S. Cook. 2d ed. Boston, 1896.

Stockwell, Robert P. "The ME 'long close' and 'long open' Vowels," *Texas Studies in Literature and Language*. 4:530–38, 1961.

Trager, G. L., and H. L. Smith, Jr. *Outline of English Structure*. (See also review by James Sledd, *Language* 31:312–35, 1955.)

Wright, Joseph, and Elizabeth Mary. *Old English Grammar.* 3d ed. London, 1925. *An Elementary Middle English Grammar.* 2d ed. Oxford, 1928. *An Elementary Historical New English Grammar.* Oxford, 1924.

Wyld, H. C. *A Short History of English.* 3d ed. London, 1927.

————. *History of Modern Colloquial English.* 3d ed. London, 1953.

Zachrisson, R. E. *Pronunciation of English Vowels, 1400–1700.* Göteborg, 1913.

3.60   Exercises

1. What phonological process accounts for the fact that the vowel nucleus of the Old English forms in the following list is *simple* while that in the parallel Modern English forms is *complex?*

Old English	Modern English
talu /tɑlu/	*tale* /teyl/
nama /nɑmɑ/	*name* /neym/
nosu /nosu/	*nose* /nowz/
æcer /æker/	*acre* /eykər/
þrotu /θrotu/	*throat* /θrowt/
sunu /sunu/	*soon* /suwn/

Can you explain the fact that the stem vowel in *nostril* and *throttle* is simple rather than complex?

2. If you were to find the following spellings in a late fifteenth-century text, what conclusions might you draw about the quality of the stressed vowel in each?

gannes 'guns'	*camyth* 'cometh'
sadanly 'suddenly'	*samersett* 'Sumerset'

3. Your collegiate dictionary cites the forms *strap–strop* and *plat–plot.* In the standard dialects these doublets are now somewhat differentiated in both meaning and pronunciation. To what effect of the Great Vowel Shift do they testify?

4. For each of the following *Modern English* words, write phonemically the stressed vowel each would have had in *Middle English;* for example, Modern English *bite* would have had the stressed vowel /iy/ in Middle English.

fat	*noon*
cut	*flock*
good	*heap*
right	*road*
write	*down*
sheep	*bush*

5. The following poetic lines have been quoted from a variety of works of sixteenth-
and seventeenth-century poets. Each quotation contains a rhyme or a set of rhymes
which would no longer be exact in Modern English. Assuming that the rhymes were
intended by the poets to be exact, or very nearly so, what would have been the pronunciation of the stressed vowels in each set of rhymes? Read the lines aloud and
then write each of the rhyme words phonemically. Try to justify as many of your
transcriptions as possible.

   a. Souring his cheeks, cries, 'fie, no more of love!
     The sun doth burn my face. I must remove.'

   b. I'll make a shadow for thee of my hairs.
     If they burn too, I'll quench them with my tears.

   c. And now she weeps, and now she fain would speak,
     And now her sobs do her intendments break.

   d. And whence from thence he struggles to be gone,
     She locks her lily fingers one in one.

   e. Melodious discord, heavenly tune harsh sounding,
     Ear's deep-sweet music, and heart's deep-sore wounding.

   f. The mellow plum doth fall, the green sticks fast,
     Or being early pluck'd is sour to taste.

   g. The thorny brambles and embracing bushes,
     As fearful of him, part; through whom he rushes.

   h. For know, my heart stands armed in mine ear
     And will not let a false sound enter there.

   i. Grief hath two tongues, and never woman yet
     Could rule them both without ten women's wit.

   j. And nuzzling in his flank, the loving swine
     Sheath'd unaware the tusk in his soft groin.

   k. With this, she falleth in the place she stood
     And stains her face with his congealed blood.

   l. To all sins past and all that are to come,
     From the creation to the general doom.

   m. Sometime her grief is dumb and hath no words;
     Sometime is mad and too much talk affords.

   n. So Priam's trust false Simon's tears doth flatter
     That he finds means to burn his Troy with water.

   o. And never he forgot in mighty Rome
     Th' adulterate both of Lucrece and her groom.

   p. Weak words, so thick come in his poor heart's aid
     That no man could distinguish what he said.

q. Lest the wise world should look into your moan
   And mock you with me after I am gone.

r. For I am sham'd by that which I bring forth,
   And so should you, to love things nothing worth.

s. Not one whose flame my heart so much as warmed,
   Or my affection put to th' smallest teen,
   Or any of my leisures ever charmed.
   Harm have I done to them, but ne'er was harmed.

t. But whether unripe years did want conceit,
   Or he refus'd to take her figured proffer,
   The tender nibbler would not touch the bait,
   But smile and jest at every gentle offer.

u. Beauty is but a vain and doubtful good;
   A shining gloss that vadeth suddenly;
   A flower that dies when first it gins to bud;

v. But when I did behold
   My sparrow dead and cold,
   No creature but that wold (would)
   Have rued upon me.

w. I think nature hath lost the mould
   Where she her shape did take,
   Or else I doubt if nature could
   So fair a creature make.

x. Then since that by thine own desart
   My songs do tell how true thou art.

y. With feigned words that were but wind
   To long delays I was assigned.

z. Lo, ladies, here (if you can use it well)
   An arbor fenced from burning fire and frost;
   A place it is where pride shall never dwell,
   Nor fortune work a maze, do she her worst.

6. The following are parallel texts of the Gospel according to St. Matthew 6:25–29. The first is from the Anglo-Saxon Gospels (c. 995); the second is from the late Middle English translation (c. 1389) of John Wycliffe; the third is from the early Modern English translation (1526) of William Tyndale. Each text is provided with an interlinear phonemicization. Study the differences among translations and practice reading aloud both the phonemic transcriptions and the standard orthography. The translation from the *Revised Standard Version* (1946) is also given for reference and comparison.

West Saxon

25. Forðam ic secge eow, ðæt ge ne sin ymbhydige eowre sawle,
    /Forθɑm ik seǰe əw, θæt ye ne si·n ymbhy·dige əwre sɑ·wle/

    hwæt ge eton; ne eowrum lichaman, mid hwam ge syn ymbscrydde.
    /hwæt ye· eton ne əwrum li·čhɑmən, mid hwɑm ye· sy·n ymbšry·dde/

    hu nys seo sawl selre ðonne mete, ɑnd eower lichama
    /hu· nys sə sɑ·wl se·lre θonne mete, ɑnd əwer li·čhɑmɑ/

    betera ðonne ðæt reaf?
    /beterɑ θonne θæt raf/

26. Behealdaþ heofonan fuglas, forðam ðe hig ne sawaþ, ne
    /behaldɑθ həfonɑn fuglɑs, forθɑm θe hi· ne sɑ·wɑθ, ne/

    hig ne ripaþ, ne hig ne gadriaþ on berne; and eower
    /hi· ne ri·pɑθ, ne hi· ne gɑdriɑθ on berne; ɑnd əwer/

    heofonlica fæder hig fet. Hu ne synt ge selran ðonne hig?
    /həfonli·kɑ fæder hi· fe·t. hu· ne synt ye· se·lrɑn θonne hi·/

27. Hwylc eower mæg soþlice geþencan ðæt he ge-eacnige ane
    /hwylč əwer mæg so·θli·ke yeθenčɑn θæt he ye-ačnige ɑ·ne/

    elne to hys anlicnesse?
    /elne to hys ɑnli·knesse/

28. And to hwi synt ge ymbhydige be reafe? Besceawiaþ æcyres
    /ɑnd to hwi· synt ye· ymbhy·dige be· ra·fe? bešawiɑθ ækyres/

    lilian, hu hig weaxaþ. Ne swincaþ hig, ne hig ne spinnaþ;
    /li·liɑn hu· hi· wɑksɑθ. ne swinkɑθ hi·, ne hi· ne spinnɑθ/

29. Ic secge eow soþlice, ðæt furðon Salomon on eallum hys
    /ik seǰe əw so·θli·ke, θæt furθon sɑlomon on ɑllum hys/

    wuldre næs oferwrigen swa swa an of ðyson.
    /wuldre næs oferwrigen swɑ· swɑ· ɑ·n of θyson/

Wycliffe

25. Therefore Y say to ʒou, that ʒe ben nat besie to ʒoure
    /ðerfowr iy say to yow, ðat yey beyn nat beziy to yowr/

    lijf, what ʒe shulen ete; othir to ʒoure body, with what
    /liyf, wat yey šulən eət oðir to yowr bodiy, wiθ wat/

    ʒe shuln be clothid. Wher ʒoure lijf is nat more than mete,
    /yey šuln bey kloəðid. wer yowr liyf iz nat moər ðan meət/

    and the body more than clothe?
    /and ðə bodiy moər ðan kloəθ/

26. Beholde ʒe the fleeʒinge foulis of the eir, for thei sowen
    /beyhoəld yey ðə fleying fuwliz ov ði eyr, for ðey sowen/

    nat, ne repyn, neither gadren in to bernys; and ʒoure

/nat, ne repin, neyðer gadren in tow berniz; and yowr/
fadir of heuen fedith hem. Wher ʒe ben nat more worthi
/fadir ov heven feydiθ hem. wer yey beyn nat moər worðiy/
than thei?
/ðan ðey/

27. Sothely who of ʒou thenkinge may putte to his stature oo cubite?
/sowθeliy how ov yow θenking may put tow hiz statyuwr ow kuwbiyt/

28. And of clothing what ben ʒe besye? Beholde ʒe the lilies
/and ov kloəðing wat beyn yey beziy? beyhoəld yey ðə liliyz/
of the feelde, how thei waxen. Thei traueilen nat,
/ov ðə feyld, huw ðey weksen. ðey traveylen nat/
nether spynnen;
/neyðer spinen/

29. Trewly I say to ʒou, for whi neither Salamon in al his glorie
/Triwliy iy say tow yow for hwiy neyðer salamon in aul hiz gloəriy/
was keverid as oon of thes.
/waz keverid az own ov ðeyz/

Tyndale
25. Therefore I saye vnto you, be not carefull for youre lyfe,
/ðeəfoə əy sæy untu yuw biə not kæəful foə yuə ləyf/
what ye shall eate, or what ye shall dryncke; nor yet for
/hwæt yiə šæl eyt (iət) oə hwæt yiə šæl driŋk; noə yit foə/
youre boddy, what rayment ye shall weare. Ys not the lyfe
/yuə bodiy, hwæt ræymənt yiə šæl weə. iz not ðə ləyf/
more worth then meate, and the boddy more off value
/moə wuəθ ðen meyt (miət) ænd ðe bodiy moə ov vælyuw/
then rayment?
/ðen ræymənt/

26. Beholde the foules of the aier, for they sowe not neder
/biyhowld ðə fəwlz ov ði æyə foə ðey sow not nedə/
reepe, nor yet cary into the barnes; and yett youre
/riəp noə yit kæriy intu ðə baənz; ænd yit yuə/
hevenly father fedeth them. Are ye not better then they?
/hevenliy faðə feydeθ (fiədeθ) ðem. æə yiə not betə ðen ðey/

27. Whiche off you though he toke tought therefore coulde
/wič ov yuw ðoə hiə tuək toət ðeəfoə kuwd (kuwld, kuld)/
put one cubit vnto his stature?
/put own (wown) kyuwbit untu hiz stætəə/

28. And why care ye then for rayment? Beholde the lyles off
/ænd wəy keə yiy ðen foə ræymənt? bihowld ðə liliyz ov/

the felde, howe thy growe. They labour not, nether spynn.
/ðə feld hɔw ðiə grow. ðey læybuə not, neyðə (niəðə) spin/

29. And yet for all that I saie vnto you, that even Solomon
/ænd yit foə ol ðæt əy sæy untu yuw, ðæt iəvən solomon/

in all his royalte was nott arayed lyke vnto one of these.
/in ol hiz royəltey wɔz not əreəd ləyk untu own (wown) ov ðiəz/

Revised Standard Version

25. Therefore I tell you, do not be anxious about your life, what you shall eat or what you shall drink, nor about your body, what you shall put on. Is not life more than food, and the body more than clothing?

26. Look at the birds of the air: they neither sow nor reap nor gather into barns, and yet your heavenly Father feeds them. Are you not of more value than they?

27. And which of you by being anxious can add one cubit to his span of life?

28. And why are you anxious about clothing? Consider the lilies of the field, how they grow; they neither toil nor spin;

29. yet I tell you, even Solomon in all his glory was not arrayed like one of these.

4. *Grammatical change*

Introduction

One way of defining a grammar of a *natural* language (as distinct from an *artificial* language like that used in mathematics, or symbolic logic, like the Morse code, or Esperanto) is to say that it is *a set of ordered rules capable of producing an infinite number of grammatical sentences and no ungrammatical sentences, and automatically assigning a description to those sentences.* No matter what our native language may be, by the time we are seven or eight years old, we are equipped with such a set of grammatical rules. Each of us acquires his own set of rules subconsciously in much the same way that he acquires other sets of rules that govern his behavior in and response to the world around him. The precise way in which this rule-formulation is accomplished, and the precise nature of these rules, is as yet not thoroughly understood. Nevertheless, rule-formulation and rule-ordering plays a key role in the learning process, and in the case of language learning this formulation and ordering is accomplished at a very early age.

When we *write a grammar of a language,* or a part of a language, we attempt to write a set of grammatical rules which will account for the sentences in that language, or a part of it, and which hopefully may be a *model of the internalized* grammar of a native speaker of that language. Furthermore, if we are writing a grammar of our own native language, we must rely for our grammatical rules on our intuition as to what constitute grammatical sentences in our language. Within a given social class, and perhaps a regional dialect, we will find a high percentage of agreement regarding the constitution of grammatical sentences, although we are sure to find *some* marginal disagreements. It may well be that we will find the highest percentage of disagreement between various class dialects, although such a statement must be made and accepted with caution. If we are writing a grammar of a language that is not native to us, we must rely on the intuition of a native speaker of that language for our information about grammatical and ungrammatical sentences. Again we will find areas of disagreement depending upon the types of informants we happen to use, the extent of their knowledge of the language, and the social class or classes to which they belong. One of the inferences to be drawn from what has just been said is that the construction of an exhaustive and totally adequate grammar for any natural language is a practical impossibility since such a grammar would require an omniscience about the grammatical structures of the language in question which none of us possesses.

Even if it were possible to write a complete grammar of a natural language, the task would be very formidable indeed. And whether or not a complete grammar would be of any use to us is open to serious question. Perhaps the best we can do for now is to write pieces of grammars that can be used for different purposes, and this is not an uninteresting or unrewarding endeavor. As we learn more and more about the operation of the human mind, our written models may approach more and more closely the grammar or set of grammars that we have developed during the process of language learning. On the other hand, grammatical models that we construct may suggest areas of mental behavior that need investigation. They may also suggest ways of dealing with problems in composition, literary analysis, historical change, dialect differentiation, and the like, that may not have occurred to us before.

A written grammar, then, to be of any value, must be a highly complex and precise instrument which "explains" how it is that we produce and interpret the sentences of a language. We will not attempt to discuss here all of the features of the kind of grammatical model that would perform the tasks we have set for it. We will, rather, demonstrate a very simple grammatical model that will be sufficient for our purposes in discussing grammatical change in English.

4.10   A Grammatical Model

In *Aspects of the Theory of Syntax* (The M.I.T. Press, 1965) Noam Chomsky describes the form of a grammar in the following way:

A grammar contains a syntactic component, a semantic component, and a phonological component. The latter two are purely interpretative; they play no part in the recursive generation of sentence structures. The syntactic component consists of a base and a transformational component. The base, in turn, consists of a categorical subcomponent and a lexicon. The base generates deep structures. A deep structure enters the semantic component and receives a semantic interpretation; it is mapped by the transformational rules into a surface structure, which is then given a phonetic interpretation by the rules of the phonological component. Thus the grammar assigns semantic interpretations to signals, this association being mediated by the recursive rules of the syntactic component (p. 141).

In the model grammar given below we are concerned only with the base and transformational components. We will have more to say about the nature of semantic interpretation in Chapter 6.

ABBREVIATIONS

S = sentence
NP = noun phrase
Aux = auxiliary
VP = verb phrase
Adv = adverb
V = verb
Pred = predicate
PP = prepositional phrase
Prep = preposition
Adj = adjective
Pred Nom = predicate nominative
Det = determiner
N = noun
No = number
Pro = pronoun
Poss = possessive
CS = complex symbol
T = tense
M = modal
Pres = present
Pas = past
Pl = plural
T_{ob} = obligatory transformation
T_{op} = optional transformation

Ca = case
nom = nominative
gen = genitive
dat = dative
acc = accusative
Ind = indicative
Sub = subjunctive
Imp = imperative
Af = affix
Dem = demonstrative

[Other abbreviations used in this chapter will be explained as they occur.]

SPECIAL SYMBOLS

$\rightarrow$ 'rewrites as' or 'is expanded into'
()   'optional'
{ }   *one and only one* of the items so enclosed *must* be selected.
/__   'in the context of'
[]   specifies categorial features in the base component; selectional features in the lexicon; in the transformation component indicates that what is written on a given line in the brackets on the left is transformed into what appears on the *same line* in the bracket on the right. (See below for illustrations.)
+   plus
−   minus
±   plus or minus
$\Rightarrow$ 'is transformed into'
=   'is equal to'
$\neq$ 'is not equal to'
$\frown$ conjoining

SPECIAL SYMBOLS ILLUSTRATED

(a) A → B$\frown$C
    'A rewrites as *B plus C*.'
(b) A → B$\frown$C(D)E

'A rewrites as *B plus C plus D plus E* or as *B plus C plus E*.' In other words, *D* is optionally selected.

(c) $A \rightarrow \begin{Bmatrix} B \\ C \\ D \end{Bmatrix}$

'A rewrites as *either B, C, or D*.'

(d) $A \rightarrow \begin{Bmatrix} B/\_X \\ C/\_Y \\ D \end{Bmatrix}$

'A rewrites as B when it occurs in the context before X, C in the context before Y, *and as* D in all *other* contexts.'

(e) $A \quad CS/\_\begin{bmatrix} B \\ C \\ D \\ E \\ X \\ Y \end{bmatrix}$

'A rewrites as a complex symbol (CS) consisting of a set of sub-categories each of which is defined by the item in brackets selected.' For example, *A* in the context of *B* may be a transitive verb; *A* in the context of *E*, a copulative verb; *A* in the context of *X*, an intransitive verb; *A* in the context of *Y*, a verb which takes an object followed by an infinitive phrase; and so on.

(f) $A \rightarrow [+B, -E, +X\_Y, \pm W]$

'A is something which is a *B*, is not an *E*, occurs in a context in which it is preceded by *X* and followed by *Y*, and may or may not be a *W*.'

(g) $\begin{bmatrix} A \\ B \\ C \\ D \end{bmatrix} X \Rightarrow \begin{bmatrix} a \\ b \\ c \\ d \end{bmatrix}$

'*A plus X* is transformed into *a*; *B plus X* is transformed into *b*; *C plus X* is transformed into *c*; *D plus X* is transformed into *d*.'

(h) $\left.\begin{array}{l} A\widehat{\ }B\widehat{\ }C\widehat{\ }D \\ \qquad C^1\widehat{\ }D^1 \end{array}\right\} \Rightarrow A\widehat{\ }B\widehat{\ }C^1\widehat{\ }D^1\widehat{\ }D$

where: $C = C^1$
$\qquad D \neq D^1$

This is one way of symbolizing the embedding of one string of elements into another. It says this: 'given two strings $ABCD$ and C^1D^1 such that $C = C^1$ and $D \neq D^1$, the latter may be embedded in the former to give ABC^1D^1D.

EXERCISES

The following is a very simple set of base and transformational rules for an abstract grammar:

1. $A \rightarrow B^\frown C$

2. $B \rightarrow (E) \begin{Bmatrix} F \\ G \end{Bmatrix} K$

3. $C \rightarrow L(M(N))$

4. $L \rightarrow \begin{Bmatrix} O/\_\_M \\ P \end{Bmatrix}$

5. $M \rightarrow \begin{Bmatrix} S \\ T(W) \end{Bmatrix}$

6. T_{ob}:

$$X^\frown O \begin{bmatrix} S \\ T \\ T^\frown W \end{bmatrix} Y \Rightarrow X \begin{bmatrix} a \\ b \\ c \end{bmatrix} Y \qquad \text{where: } X \neq W$$
$$\text{and X and Y are cover symbols}$$

We will now apply in order each rule of the base component, rewriting the symbol on the left of the arrow with the symbol or set of symbols on the right of the arrow. This process will give us a set of strings of elements called a *derivation*. Most of the rules provide options, but since each rule may be applied only once for a given derivation we can make only one choice for that derivation.

According to rule 1: $B^\frown C$
According to rule 2: $E^\frown F^\frown K^\frown C$
According to rule 3: $E^\frown F^\frown K^\frown L^\frown M$
According to rule 4: $E^\frown F^\frown K^\frown O^\frown M$
According to rule 5: $E^\frown F^\frown K^\frown O^\frown T^\frown W$

Application of rule 5 exhausts the rules of the base component, and the string of elements given at line 5 is an underlying *terminal string;* all other strings are *preterminal.* Our particular grammar would allow us to produce several different derivations and terminal strings depending upon the options chosen in the rules. For example, instead of the preceding derivation we might have produced this one:

1. $B^\frown C$
2. $E^\frown G^\frown K^\frown C$
3. $E^\frown G^\frown K^\frown L^\frown M^\frown N$
4. $E^\frown G^\frown K^\frown O^\frown M^\frown N$
5. $E^\frown G^\frown K^\frown O^\frown S^\frown N$

Rule 6 in the grammar is a transformation rule. Applying this to line 5 of the first derivation we get a *derived string:*

$$E^\frown F^\frown K^\frown c$$

and to line 5 of the second derivation:

$$E\widehat{\ }G\widehat{\ }K\widehat{\ }a\widehat{\ }N.$$

1. Construct as many different derivations as you can from the base component of the preceding grammar.
2. Which of the following strings are *terminal,* which are *nonterminal,* which are *derived,* and which are *impossible?*

    a. F⌢K⌢a⌢N
    b. E⌢G⌢K⌢L
    c. E⌢F⌢K⌢P⌢M⌢W
    d. E⌢G⌢K⌢P
    e. G⌢K⌢C
    f. E⌢F⌢K⌢L⌢N
    g. G⌢K⌢a
    h. F⌢K⌢b⌢T
    i. E⌢G⌢K⌢P⌢N
    j. F⌢K⌢O⌢T⌢W⌢N

3. Construct *three* different abstract "grammars" similar to the one we have been using. Write out three or four derivations for each one.

DIAGRAMING

We have said that a grammar automatically assigns a structural description to the set of sentences that it generates. A derivation provides a *history* of a given terminal string, showing the ordered steps by which the string has been produced. Essentially the same information can be gotten from a diagram of the string's history. The first derivation from the grammar given on page 138 may be diagramed this way:

A.

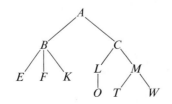

Such a diagram is called a *tree diagram* or a *phrase marker*. Since in the case of A. above it represents the structure provided by the rules of the base before the application of the transformation rule, it is also referred to as an *underlying phrase marker*. The application of rule 6 may be diagramed this way:

B.

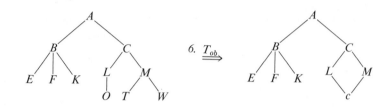

Phrase markers that result from the application of transformation rules are called *derived phrase markers*. You should notice two things about these phrase markers. First, although they illustrate the derivational history of a given string, they do not show the order in which the grammatical rules have been applied. We cannot tell from the diagram, for instance, which has been developed first, element (node) B or element (node) C; on the other hand, a derivation does give us that information. Second, the *derived phrase marker* illustrates the fact that *transformation rules tend to destroy structure*. As a result of rule 6 the elements O, T, and W have been blocked out or erased.

EXERCISE

Construct branching tree diagrams for *each* of the derivations written for exercise C. above.

DEEP AND SURFACE STRUCTURES

The grammatical rules 1–5 of the model presented on page 138 provide deep structure for any underlying terminal string derived by these rules. Rule 6 of the model provides surface structure. You will notice, however, that because of the simplicity of the model there will be a number of instances in which an underlying terminal string does not undergo the transformation of rule 6. In other words, in these instances line 5 of a derivation will represent surface structure as well as deep structure. Natural languages are much too complex to behave in this way.

An English example may be useful here. Consider the sentence

(1) A man wearing a red felt hat is getting on a bus.

Sentence (1) represents surface structure. It has, in the course of its development, undergone a number of transformations of underlying terminal strings generated by the base component. A base component will produce the following:

(2) a man is getting on a bus
(3) a man is wearing a hat
(4) a hat is red
(5) a hat is made of felt

Each of the strings (2)–(5) is given a semantic interpretation by the semantic component, and then by certain transformational operations all four are put together so as to produce (1). For example:

(6) a man (a man is wearing a hat $\left(\begin{array}{l}\text{a hat is red} \\ \text{a hat is made of felt}\end{array}\right)$) is getting on a bus ⇒

(7) a man (wh- a man is wearing a hat $\left(\begin{array}{l}\text{wh- a hat is red} \\ \text{wh- a hat is made of felt}\end{array}\right)$) is getting on a bus ⇒

(8) a man (who is wearing a hat $\left(\begin{array}{l}\text{which is red} \\ \text{which is made of felt}\end{array}\right)$) is getting on a bus ⇒

(9) a man (wearing a hat $\left(\begin{array}{l}\text{red} \\ \text{made of felt}\end{array}\right)$) is getting on a bus ⇒

(10) a man (wearing a red   hat) is getting on a bus ⇒
                        made of felt

(11) a man (wearing a red hat) is getting on a bus ⇒
                  felt

(12) a man (wearing a red felt hat) is getting on a bus ⇒

(13) a man wearing a red felt hat is getting on a bus.

Notice that at certain stages of the progression from (6) to (13) some underlying structure is lost: 'a man is wearing a hat' ⇒ 'who is wearing a hat' ⇒

'wearing a hat.' Such loss of structure accounts for the frequent ambiguity of surface structures. The sentence

(14) He goes to a small boys' school.

may have as its deep structure

(14a1) He goes to a school.
(14a2) The school is small.
(14a3) The school is for boys.

or

(14b1) He goes to a school.
(14b2) The school is for boys.
(14b3) The boys are small.

RECURSION

Recursion means literally 'the act of running back through,' and such running back through is an extremely significant characteristic of all natural languages. The grammars of natural languages have built-in recursive devices that permit the generation of an *infinite* number of sentences according to a *finite* set of rules. If natural languages did not have such devices, either the number of sentences a grammar could produce would be severely limited, or the number of grammatical rules would be infinite and thus unlearnable by a native speaker of the language. The effect would be the same in both cases. The grammar on page 138 contains no recursive mechanism, so that the number of strings it can produce may be quickly exhausted. But consider the following:

(1) $A \rightarrow B\widehat{\ }C$
(2) $C \rightarrow D(e)$
(3) $D \rightarrow E \begin{Bmatrix} F \\ B \end{Bmatrix}$
(4) $B \rightarrow b\widehat{\ }d(A)$

Note that in rule (4) *A* occurs as an option in the expansion or rewriting of B. Now, every time we choose this option we are sent back to rule (1) and the whole generative procedure begins again. In other words, we have set up the possibility of a loop which will carry us around and around through the grammatical rules as long as we keep choosing *A* in rule (4). We get out of the loop by not choosing *A* in rule (4). The following tree diagram illustrates the process:

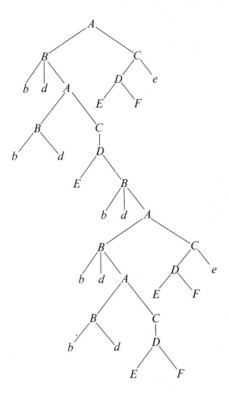

The terminal string here represented is:

b⌢d⌢b⌢d⌢E⌢b⌢d⌢b⌢d⌢b⌢d⌢E⌢F⌢E⌢F⌢e⌢E⌢F⌢e.

EXERCISES

1. Using the preceding grammatical rules write tree diagrams for *15* different terminal strings.
2. Write a simple recursive grammar of your own and produce *10* different terminal strings with it.

4.20 A Grammatical Model for Modern English

The grammatical model for Modern English presented below is just that—
a model, in the sense that it is a miniature representation of a *real* grammar.
The inventory of the lexicon is extremely small, and the rules of the base
and transformational components are relatively simple. Nevertheless, it will
serve to introduce you to a certain strategy of grammars.

BASE COMPONENT

Categorial subcomponent

1. S → (Q) (Neg) (Emph) NP⌢Aux⌢VP
2. VP → MV (Adv)
3. MV → V($\begin{Bmatrix} \text{Pred} \\ \text{NP} \end{Bmatrix}$)(PP)
4. PP → Prep⌢NP
5. Pred → $\begin{Bmatrix} \text{Adv} \\ \text{Adj} \\ \text{Pred Nom} \end{Bmatrix}$
6. Pred Nom → NP
7. NP → np (S)
8. np → $\begin{Bmatrix} \text{np} \ /\_\_ \text{S} \\ [+\text{pro}] \\ \text{Det⌢N⌢No (S)} \end{Bmatrix}$
9. Det → $\begin{Bmatrix} \text{a} \\ \text{np⌢poss} \end{Bmatrix}$
10. N → CS
    a. N → [+N, −V, +Det__No(S)]
    b. [+Det__No(S)] → [±common]
    c. [+common] → [±count]
    d. [+count] → [±animate]
    e. [−common] → [±animate]
    f. [+animate] → [±human]
    g. [−count] → [±abstract]
11. No → $\begin{Bmatrix} [\pm\text{pl}]/[+\text{count}] \\ [-\text{pl}] \end{Bmatrix}$
12. V → CS

a. $V \rightarrow [+V, -N, -Adj, +\alpha \widehat{\ } Aux \_\_ (Det \widehat{\ } \beta)$

b. $[+\alpha \widehat{\ } Aux \_\_ (Det \widehat{\ } \beta)] \rightarrow$

$$
[+\alpha \widehat{\ } Aux \_\_ \begin{bmatrix} \# \\ NP \\ Pred \\ Adj \\ (NP)\ (Prep)\ np \widehat{\ } S \\ \quad\quad\quad\quad \underset{[+pro]}{|} \\ np \widehat{\ } S \widehat{\ } of \widehat{\ } NP \\ \quad \underset{[+pro]}{|} \end{bmatrix}
$$

13. $Adj \rightarrow [+Adj, -N, -V, +\alpha \ldots \_\_]$
14. $Aux \rightarrow Aux_1\ (Aux_2)$
15. $Aux_1 \rightarrow T(M)$
16. $Aux_2 \rightarrow (have\text{-}en)\ (be\text{-}ing)$
17. $T \rightarrow \begin{Bmatrix} Pres \\ Pas \end{Bmatrix}$
18. $Adv \rightarrow \begin{Bmatrix} Adv_{time} \\ Adv_{place} \\ Adv_{manner} \end{Bmatrix}$

Lexicon

1. [+prep]: on, in, to, for, of, at, from, up
2. [+Adv$_{time}$]: now, then, yesterday, tomorrow
3. [+Adv$_{place}$]: here, there, home, downtown
4. [+Adv$_{manner}$]: thoroughly, quickly, slowly, carefully
5. [+M]: can, may, will, must, ought to
6. [+N, −V, +Det__No(S)]:
   a. [+common, +count, +human]: boy, shepherd, man, teacher, student, wife, girl
   b. [+common, +count, +animate, −human]: horse, sheep, flock, fly, bird, dog, fish
   c. [+common, +count, −animate]: field, tree, hill, chair, desk, house, car, lamp
   d. [+common, −count, −abstract]: milk, gas, water, salt, sugar, coal
   e. [+common, −count, +abstract]: truth, beauty, honesty, sincerity, justice
   f. [−common, +animate]: John, Betty, Mrs. Smith, Sister Sheila, Dr. Jones

g. [−common, −animate]: New York, China, Europe, Lake Erie, St. Louis, Trafalgar Square, Westminster Abbey

7. [+V, −N, −Adj, +α⌢Aux__(Det⌢β)]
   a. [+[+human] Aux __ #]: talk
   b. [+[−abstract] Aux __ #]: disappear
   c. [+[+human] Aux__(Det [+common, ±count, −animate, −abstract])]: write
   d. [+[+animate] Aux__(Det [±common, ±count, ±animate, −abstract])]: watch
   e. [+[+human] Aux__NP]: admire, love, believe, demand, require
   f. [+[+N] Aux __ Det [+animate]: frighten
   g. [+[+N, −abstract] Aux__Adj]: look, feel, smell, be, seem, appear
   h. [+[+N, −abstract] Aux__Pred Nom]: look like, be, seem, become, feel like, seem like, smell like
   i. [+[+N] Aux__Adv]: be
      [−manner]
   j. [+[+human] Aux__np⌢S]: prefer, believe, love
      [+pro]
   k. [+[+human] Aux__NP⌢of⌢np⌢S]: remind, convince, persuade
      [+pro]
   l. [+[+human] Aux__NP⌢with⌢np⌢S]: tempt
      [+pro]
   m. [+[+human] Aux__np⌢S⌢of⌢NP]: demand, require
      [+pro]

8. [+Adj, −V, −N, +α . . . __]:
   a. [+[±common, ±count, −abstract] . . . __]: red, green, black, heavy, light, dirty, clean, ugly, beautiful, wet, dry, old, awful
   b. [+[+animate] . . . __]: tall, short, sick, healthy, dead, alive, tired, sleepy, smart, stupid, clever
   c. [+[+human] . . . __]: cheerful, happy, morose, sullen, ambitious, lazy, guilty, shy, reverent

Deriving Underlying Strings

Armed with such a base component one can derive a considerable number and variety of underlying strings that would receive a semantic interpretation before being fed into the transformational component. We will not attempt an exhaustive display of the possibilities, but will illustrate a few of these in detail and suggest others.

A. 1. NP^Aux^VP

  2. NP^Aux^MV^Adv

  3. NP^Aux^V^NP^PP^Adv

  4. NP^Aux^V^NP^Prep^NP^Adv

  5. Does not apply
  6. Does not apply

  7. np^Aux^V^np^Prep^np^Adv

  8. Det^N^No^S^Aux^V^Det^N^No^Prep^Det^N^No^Adv

  9. a^N^No^S^Aux^V^np^poss^N^No^Prep^a^N^No^Adv

   [NOTE: the choice of *np poss* in rule 9 will require looping back to rule 8 for the expansion of *np*.]

 10. a^N^No^S^Aux^V^a^N^No^poss^N^No^Prep^a^N^No^Adv

      | | | |

   [+common]   [+common] [+common] [+common]

      | | | |

   [+count]   [+count] [+count]   [+count]

      | | | |

   [+human]   [+human] [+animate] [−animate]

                      |

                 [−human]

 11. a^N^[−pl]^S^Aux^V^a^N^[−pl]^poss^N^[+pl]^

    | | |

  [+etc.]   [+etc.]   [+etc.]

  Prep^a^N^[−pl]^Adv

       |

    [+etc.]

 12. The results of this rule do not appear as a new line in the derivation.

 13. Nor do these.

 14. a^N^[−pl]^S^Aux₁^V^a^N^[−pl]^poss^N^[+pl]^

    | | |

  [+etc.]   [+etc.]   [+etc.]

  Prep^a^N^[−pl]^Adv

       |

    [+etc.]

 15. a^N^[−pl]^S^T^V^a^N^[−pl]^poss^N^[+pl]^Prep^

    | | |

  [+etc.]   [+etc.]   [+etc.]

  a^N^[−pl]^Adv

    |

  [+etc.]

 16. Does not apply.

17. a⌢N⌢[−pl]⌢S⌢pas⌢V⌢a⌢N⌢[−pl]⌢poss⌢N⌢[+pl]⌢
      | | |
   [+etc.]   [+etc.]   [+etc.]
   Prep⌢a⌢N⌢[−pl]⌢Adv
          |
       [+etc.]

18. a⌢N⌢[−pl]⌢S⌢pas⌢V⌢a⌢N⌢[−pl]⌢poss⌢N⌢[+pl]⌢
     |
 [+common]   [+common] [+common]
     | | |
  [+count]   [+count]   [+count]
     | | |
  [+human]   [+human] [+animate]
                                 |
                             [−human]
   Prep⌢a⌢N⌢[−pl]⌢Adv$_{time}$
          |
   [+common]
       |
    [+count]
      |
  [−animate]

With the subcategorization complete, we move to the *lexicon:*

1. Select *from.*
2. Select *yesterday.*
3. No selection.
4. No selection.
5. No selection.
6. Select (a) *boy,* (a) *shepherd,* (b) *sheep,* (c) *hill* in that order.
7. Select (d) *watch.*

The terminal string now looks like this:

a⌢boy⌢[−pl]⌢S⌢Pas⌢watch⌢a⌢shepherd⌢[−pl]⌢Poss⌢sheep⌢[+pl]⌢from⌢
a⌢hill⌢[−pl]⌢yesterday.

And the phrase marker is shown on page 149.

A.

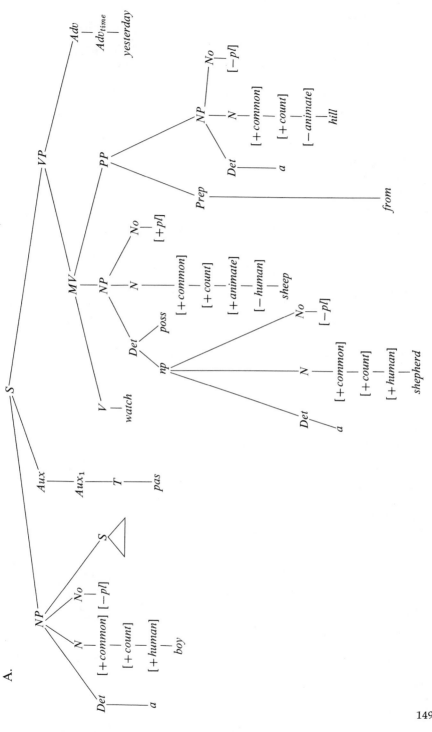

Since from base rule 7 the optional *S* was selected, we can run through the grammatical and lexical rules again thus producing another terminal string:

B. 1. NP^Aux^VP
    2. NP^Aux^MV
    3. NP^Aux^V^Pred
    4. Does not apply.
    5. NP^Aux^V^Adj
    6. Does not apply.
    7. np^Aux^V^Adj
    8. Det^N^No^Aux^V^Adj
    9. a^N^No^Aux^V^Adj
    10. a^N^No^Aux^V^Adj
        |
     [+common]
        |
     [+count]
        |
     [+human]
    11. a^N^[−pl]^Aux^V^Adj
        |
     [+common]
        |
     [+count]
        |
     [+human]
    14. a^N^[−pl]^Aux₁^V^Adj
        |
     [+common]
        |
     [+count]
        |
     [+human]
    15. a^N^[−pl]^T^V^Adj
        |
     [+common]
        |
     [+count]
        |
     [+human]
    16. Does not apply.

17. a⌒N⌒[−pl]⌒Pres⌒V⌒Adj
    |
  [+common]
     |
   [+count]
     |
   [+human]
18. Does not apply.

From the lexicon:

1. No selection.
2. No selection.
3. No selection.
4. No selection.
5. No selection.
6. Select (a) *boy.*
7. Select (g) *be.*
8. Select (c) *lazy.*

So that the new terminal string will be:

a⌒boy⌒[−pl]⌒Pres⌒be⌒lazy

The complete output of the base component will, then, be this:

a⌒boy⌒[−pl] (a⌒boy⌒[−pl]⌒Pres⌒be⌒lazy) Pas⌒watch⌒a⌒shepherd⌒[−pl]⌒
Poss⌒sheep⌒[pl]⌒from⌒a⌒hill⌒[−pl]⌒yesterday

The tree diagram on page 152 shows the grammatical relationships between the two underlying strings.

Clearly the first 18 rules of the base component will provide for many additional types of underlying strings. We suggest just a few of these in the abbreviated phrase markers diagramed on pages 153 and 154. The one on page 153 underlies such sentences as:

(1) John required Betty to be here.
(2) John required of Betty that she be here.
(3) It was required of Betty (by John) that she be here.
(4) That she be here was required of Betty by John.
(5) John required that Betty be here.

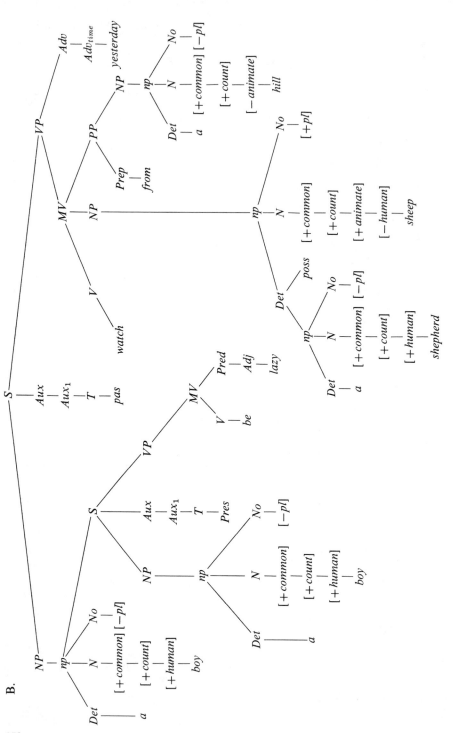

B.

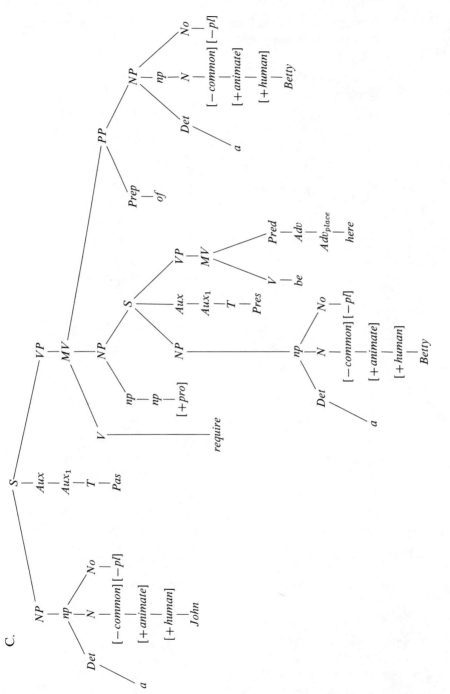

C.

The precise form which each of the sentences (1)–(5) takes is stipulated by rules of the transformational component.

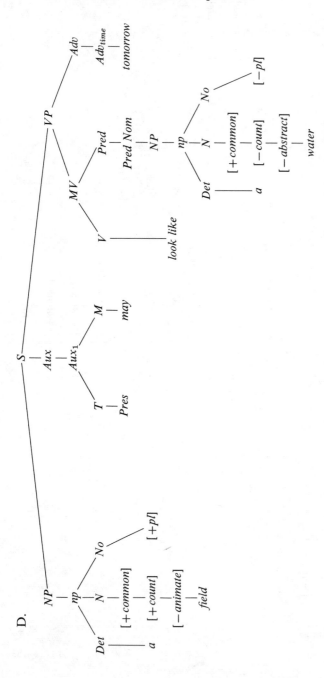

The phrase marker on page 154 underlies the sentence:

(1) Fields may look like water tomorrow.

EXERCISES

1. Using the rules given in the base component, write out the derivations for *three* differ-ent underlying terminal strings. Represent each of these derivations in a tree diagram.
2. Construct tree diagrams for *five* additional underlying strings.
3. Will the rules of the base generate strings which will ultimately prove to be non-English sentences? If so, what modifications of the rules are necessary?

TRANSFORMATIONAL COMPONENT

Transformation rules map the strings of grammatical elements derived from the base component into sentences—spoken, written, or both. Here we will concern ourselves with two general types of transformations: (1) *syntactic transformations*, which may add to, subtract from, or reorder the elements in a string; (2) *morphographemic transformations*, which assign the appropriate written shapes to the grammatical elements and combinations of grammatical elements in a string. If the grammar included a phonological component, this would assign sets of phonetic features to each symbol in the string thus giving an explicit characterization of the sound of that utterance in the spoken language.

SYNTACTIC TRANSFORMATIONS

Consider now the form of the string of grammatical elements derived above from the base:

a⌢boy⌢[−pl] (a⌢boy⌢[−pl⌢Pres⌢be⌢lazy) Pas⌢watch⌢a⌢shepherd⌢[−pl⌢ Poss⌢sheep⌢[pl⌢from⌢a⌢hill⌢[−pl⌢yesterday

One would immediately be inclined to comment on the repetition of the string *a*⌢*boy*⌢[−*pl*], and go on to suggest that any such repetition of nominal elements requires the pronominalization of one of them—taking the form, in this case, of a relative pronoun. In other words, our English grammar pro-vides an obligatory transformation that converts *a*⌢*boy*⌢[−*pl*] (*a*⌢*boy*⌢[−*pl*]) into *a*⌢*boy*⌢[−*pl*] (*who*). Another way of putting it is to say that the first instance of *a boy* [−*pl*] erases the second and substitutes *who.* Ultimately, this transformation would yield the construction *a boy who is lazy.* Suppose, however, we wish the final output to be *a lazy boy.* Two further transformational operations will have to be performed: (1) subtract or *delete who* and *is;* (2) *permute* the resulting order *a boy lazy* to *a lazy boy.*

These transformations may be specified in the following forms:

(1) T_{Rel}: X − NP (NP¹ˆAuxˆVP¹) Y $\Rightarrow$
         [+αₙ]

     X − NP (wh-ˆAuxˆVP¹) Y
         [+αₙ]

   where: NP¹ˆAuxˆVP¹ is dominated by an *S* which is dominated by *NP.*
      NP = NP¹
      [+αₙ] = the set of syntactic features characterizing the *N* of *NP¹.*

(2) T_{Adj}:

   (a) X − DetˆNˆNo (whˆAuxˆbeˆAdj) Y $\Rightarrow$
        X − DetˆNˆNoˆAdjˆY
   (b) X − DetˆNˆNoˆAdjˆY $\Rightarrow$
        X − DetˆAdjˆNˆNoˆY

Application of these transformation rules will yield *derived phrase markers* that look like these (only the pertinent segments of the phrase markers are represented in detail):

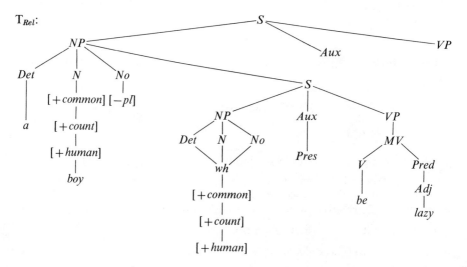

T_{Adj}:

(a)

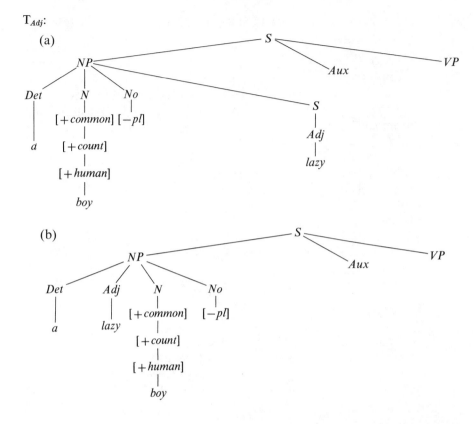

(b)

Like relative pronouns, personal pronouns are introduced transformationally by the mechanism of erasure and substitution wherever identity exists. When one converts 'John fell off John's bicycle' to 'John fell off his bicycle,' he expresses the opinion that since the second 'John' is identical to the first, it may be represented by the third person singular masculine pronoun. More formally, the rule may appear this way:

$$T_{Pro}: \quad X - Det\,\widehat{\,}N_1\,\widehat{\,}No - Y - Det\,\widehat{\,}N_2\,\widehat{\,}No - Z \Rightarrow$$
$$[+\alpha] \qquad\qquad\quad [+\alpha]$$
$$X - Det\,\widehat{\,}N\,\widehat{\,}No - Y - Pro\,\widehat{\,}No - Z$$
$$[+\alpha] \qquad\qquad [+\alpha]$$

where: $N_1 = N_2$

$[+\alpha]$ = The set of features characterizing N.

Morphographemic rules will then assign the appropriate written form of the pronoun.

The first rule of the grammar permits certain options; for example, one might choose the string, $Q^\frown NP^\frown Aux^\frown VP$, or $Neg^\frown NP^\frown Aux^\frown VP$, or $Emph^\frown NP^\frown Aux^\frown VP$, or $Q^\frown Neg^\frown NP^\frown Aux^\frown VP$, and so on. Choice of any one of these optional symbols will trigger an appropriate syntactic transformation: choice of Q a question transformation, choice of Neg a negative transformation, and choice of *Emph* an emphasis transformation. The question transformation may be formulated as follows:

$$T_Q: Q^\frown NP^\frown T \begin{Bmatrix} M \\ \text{have} \\ \text{be} \end{Bmatrix} X \Rightarrow T \begin{Bmatrix} M \\ \text{have} \\ \text{be} \end{Bmatrix} NP^\frown X$$

Thus, a string

(1) $Q^\frown a^\frown boy^\frown [-pl]^\frown Pres^\frown be^\frown lazy \Rightarrow Pres^\frown be^\frown a^\frown boy^\frown [-pl]^\frown lazy$ (underlying 'Is a boy lazy?').

A string

(2) $Q^\frown a^\frown boy^\frown [-pl]^\frown Pas^\frown may^\frown have^\frown en^\frown go \Rightarrow Pas^\frown may^\frown a^\frown boy^\frown [-pl]^\frown have^\frown en^\frown go$ (underlying 'Might a boy have gone?').

Suppose, however, a string contains *no* occurrence of *M, have,* or *be:*

(3) $Q^\frown a^\frown boy^\frown [-pl]^\frown Pas^\frown go$

In this event T_Q will not operate. Before they can be transformed into questions such strings must be supplied with the form *do,* the function of which is to carry the tense marker. We therefore need a rule that inserts *do* in the appropriate place:

$T_Q:$ (a) $Q^\frown NP^\frown T^\frown X \Rightarrow Q^\frown NP^\frown T^\frown do^\frown X$
where: $X \neq M, have, be$

Before we proceed, it is important to note additional circumstances requiring the introduction of *do;* namely, the desire for emphasis or negation. The emphatic form of 'John goes to work every day' is 'John *does* go to work every day'; of 'Bill lost the race yesterday,' 'Bill *did* lose the race yesterday.' The negative forms of these two positive statements are 'John doesn't go to work every day' and 'Bill didn't lose the race yesterday.' *Do,* then, must be introduced in both types of sentences to carry emphasis and negation markers and, secondarily, tense markers. We may formulate the following rule:

$$T_{Do}: \begin{Bmatrix} Q \\ Emph \\ Neg \end{Bmatrix} NP\widehat{\ }T\widehat{\ }X \Rightarrow \begin{Bmatrix} Q \\ Emph \\ Neg \end{Bmatrix} NP\widehat{\ }T\widehat{\ }do\widehat{\ }X$$

where: $X \neq M$, *have, be*

The earlier T_Q will now appear as:

$$T_Q: Q\widehat{\ }NP\widehat{\ }T\widehat{\ }Z\widehat{\ }X \Rightarrow T\widehat{\ }Z\widehat{\ }NP\widehat{\ }X$$

And we may add emphasis and negation transformations:

$$T_{Emph}: Emph\widehat{\ }NP\widehat{\ }T\widehat{\ }Z\widehat{\ }X \Rightarrow NP\widehat{\ }T\widehat{\ }\acute{Z}\widehat{\ }X$$
$$T_{Neg}: Neg\widehat{\ }NP\widehat{\ }T\widehat{\ }Z\widehat{\ }X \Rightarrow NP\widehat{\ }T\widehat{\ }Z\widehat{\ }not\widehat{\ }X$$

where: $Z = M$, *have, be,* or *do.*

Earlier, it was suggested that the rules of the base component would provide a number of various types of underlying strings, and a few of these were illustrated. One such was the string:

a$\widehat{\ }$John$\widehat{\ }$[−pl]$\widehat{\ }$Pas$\widehat{\ }$require$\widehat{\ }$np$\widehat{\ }$a$\widehat{\ }$Betty$\widehat{\ }$[−pl]$\widehat{\ }$Pres$\widehat{\ }$be$\widehat{\ }$here$\widehat{\ }$of$\widehat{\ }$a$\widehat{\ }$

$$[+\text{pro}]$$

Betty$\widehat{\ }$[−pl]

And we indicated that such a string underlies such sentences as

(1) John required Betty to be here.
(2) John required of Betty that she be here.
(3) It was required of Betty that she be here.
(4) That she be here was required of Betty.
(5) John required that Betty be here.
(6) Betty was required to be here by John.

Clearly, a number of very specific syntactic transformation rules are required to transform the string in question into the six English sentences we have cited. We make no attempt to reproduce these here, since our primary concern in this chapter lies elsewhere. The student who wishes more detailed information on transformational rules for English should examine the appropriate references at the end of this section.

At this point we will illustrate only one further transformation rule, one that will readjust the positions of various manifestations of *Aux* relative to each other and to *V*. From the rules of the base component any one of the phrase markers on page 160 may be derived.

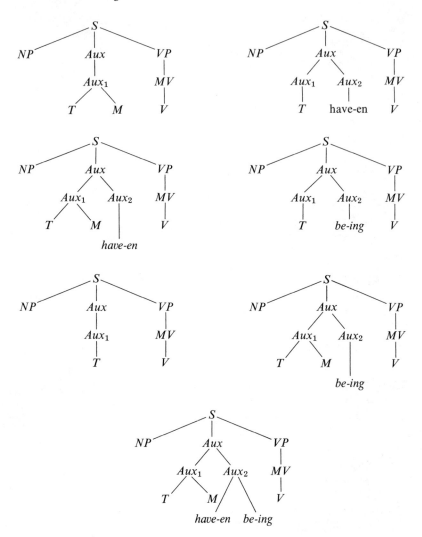

The auxiliary transformation rule takes the following form:

T_{Aux}: X − af⌢v − Y ⇒ X − v⌢af − Y
where: af = *T, -en, -ing*
      v = *V, have, be, M, do*

NOTE: This rule may apply *once only* to any given string.

The effect of this rule is shown in the derived phrase marker on page 161 so

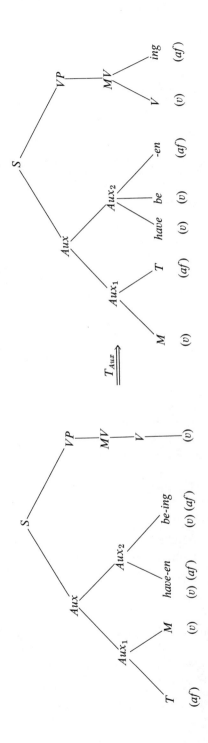

that any string, say:

(1)   NP^Pres^may^have-en^be-ing^study ⇒
(1a) NP^may^Pres^have^be-en^study-ing

which will ultimately convert to:

(1b) (the boy) may have been studying.

As a result of T$_{Aux}$, the string

(2)   a^lazy^boy^[−pl]^*Pas*^*watch*^a^shepherd^[−pl]^Poss^sheep^
      [pl]^from^a^hill^[−pl]^yesterday ⇒
(2a) a^lazy^boy^[−pl]^*watch*^*Pas*^a^shepherd^[−pl]^Poss^sheep^
      [pl]^from^a^hill^[−pl]^yesterday.

Morphographemic Transformations[1]

Morphographemic transformation rules have been defined as those "which assign the appropriate written shapes to the grammatical elements and combinations of grammatical elements in a string." In other words, such rules assign a written interpretation to the string. The preceding string (2), for instance, requires an interpretation of *boy*^[−pl], *watch*^*Pas*, *shepherd*^[−pl]^*Poss*, *sheep*^[+pl], *hill*^[−pl]. Of course, your own internalized grammar will at once provide the proper written forms:

(1) boy^[−pl] ⇒ boy
(2) watch^Pas ⇒ watched
(3) shepherd^[−pl]^Poss ⇒ shepherd's
(4) sheep^[+pl] ⇒ sheep
(5) hill^[−pl] ⇒ hill

These interpretations are the result of certain generalizations about the written form of grammatical elements in English that we have either induced or been taught. The singular form of an overwhelming number of English nouns is expressed by the rule:

[1] Additional rules for Modern English will be found in Appendix I.

(a) $N_x \hat{\ } [-pl] \Rightarrow N_x$

where x stands for the large subclass that includes such items as *boy, man, tree, car, bicycle, house, skirt, ear, pin, market, stock,* and so forth. A small number of borrowed nouns have retained, at least in formal writing, singular and plural forms that are characteristic of the grammatical system of the language from which they have been borrowed. Thus, the rules of English grammar must accommodate these special forms:

(b_1) $N_y \hat{\ } [-pl] \Rightarrow N_y \hat{\ } a$ (*alumna*)
(b_2) $N_z \hat{\ } [-pl] \Rightarrow N_z \hat{\ } on$ (*criterion*)
(b_3) $N_w \hat{\ } [-pl] \Rightarrow N_w \hat{\ } um$ (*datum*)

The forms of the plural are more varied in English than are forms of the singular and so require more rules:

(c) $\begin{bmatrix} N_{x1} \\ N_{x2} \end{bmatrix} [+pl] \Rightarrow \begin{bmatrix} N_{x1} \hat{\ } s \\ N_{x2} \hat{\ } es \end{bmatrix}$

where: N_{x2} = all nouns of class x ending in *-tch, -sh, -ss, -ch.*
N_{x1} = all others of class x.

We then have a number of subclasses of nouns, not only borrowed, but native, many of which contain just one member. A large number of very special rules are needed to provide the proper plural forms for these:

(d) $\begin{bmatrix} man \\ goose \\ sheep \\ mouse \\ child \\ foot \end{bmatrix} [+pl] \Rightarrow \begin{bmatrix} men \\ geese \\ sheep \\ mice \\ children \\ feet \end{bmatrix}$

On the preceding pages we have attempted to describe and illustrate the structure and operation of a model grammar for Modern English. The intent has been to provide the reader with a conception of the model, rather than to provide all of the mechanical details that would insure that the model will "work"; that is, that it will actually produce grammatical English sentences and no ungrammatical ones. Most of the rules will, in fact, work, but some will not work properly because they lack certain details of specification.

Unfortunately, we do not yet know enough about the ways in which grammars work to be able to write infallible rules. Nevertheless, it is only in the attempt to write and to understand carefully formulated grammatical descriptions that one really comes to grips with the nature of grammar.

SPECIAL LINGUISTIC TERMS

grammar
grammatical
ungrammatical
syntactic component
semantic component
phonological component
base component
categorial subcomponent
lexicon
deep structure
surface structure
transformational component
derivation
terminal and nonterminal strings
derived string
phrase marker
derived phrase marker
recursion
syntactic transformation
morphographemic transformation
erasure
vowel replacement

FOR ADDITIONAL REFERENCE

Bach, Emmon. "The Order of Elements in a Transformational Grammar of German," *Language* 38:263–69 (1962).
————. *An Introduction to Transformational Grammars.* New York, 1964.
Chomsky, Noam. *Syntactic Structures.* The Hague, 1957.
————. *Aspects of the Theory of Syntax.* M.I.T., 1965.
Dinneen, Francis P. *An Introduction to General Linguistics,* Chapter XII. New York, 1967.

Fillmore, C. J. *Indirect Object Constructions in English and the Ordering of Transformations.* Ohio State Research Foundation, Project of Syntactical Analysis, Report 1. Columbus, 1962.

———. "The Position of Embedding Transformations in a Grammar," *Word* 19:208–31 (1963).

Fodor, J. A., and J. J. Katz (eds). *The Structure of Language: Readings in the Philosophy of Language.* Englewood Cliffs, N. J., 1964.

Katz, J. J., and Paul M. Postal. *An Integrated Theory of Linguistic Descriptions.* M.I.T., 1964.

Klima, E. S. "Negation in English." *In* Fodor and Katz, 1964.

Koutsoudas, A. *Writing Transformational Grammars: An Introduction.* New York, 1966.

Lees, Robert B. *The Grammar of English Nominalizations.* Bloomington, 1960.

———. "A Multiply Ambiguous Adjectival Construction in English," *Language* 36:207–21 (1960).

———. "Grammatical Analysis of the English Comparative Construction," *Word* 17:171–85 (1961).

Postal, Paul M. *Constituent Structure: A Study of Contemporary Models of Syntactic Description.* Bloomington, 1964.

Roberts, Paul. *Modern Grammar.* New York, 1968.

Rosenbaum, Peter S. *The Grammar of English Predicate Complement Constructions.* M.I.T., 1967.

Smith, Carlota S. "A Class of Complex Modifiers in English," *Language* 37:342–65 (1961).

———. "Determiners and Relative Clauses in a Generative Grammar of English," *Language* 40:37–52 (1964).

Thomas, Owen. *Transformational Grammar and the Teacher of English.* New York, 1965.

EXERCISES

1. Using the rules of the base component, construct tree diagrams that represent the deep structure of each of the following sentences:

   a. Girls may have written to Mrs. Smith.
   b. A black dog was frightening a tired bird.
   c. John tempted Betty with a beautiful house.
   d. Do teachers require honesty?
   e. Dr. Jones' wife looked happy yesterday.
   f. Sister Sheila must have disappeared in an old car.
   g. Did John convince Dr. Jones of his sincerity?
   h. New York *isn't* dirty.
   i. Salt doesn't smell like sugar.
   j. Can John believe that Mrs. Smith is guilty?

2. Suggest ways in which the following common English constructions might be accommodated in a generative-transformational grammar.

   a. Bill tackled the quarterback before he could throw the ball.
   b. Connie is taller than Janice.
   c. Shut the door!
   d. What time does the plane leave?
   e. A bird watcher saw a red-winged blackbird.
   f. My wife loves to dance.
   g. Students are too honest to cheat on exams.
   h. Whatever you do, don't light a match.
   i. Mrs. Smith's singing of the national anthem left something to be desired.
   j. Both of the two very heavy red jackets were lost.

4.30   A Grammatical Model for Old English

In discussing the Old English specimen presented in section 1.20, we commented on a number of the features of Old English grammar that distinguish it from Modern English grammar. We noted in particular that Old English nouns, verbs, adjectives, adverbs, demonstratives, and some other word classes show a much greater diversity of formal characteristics than do their counterparts in Modern English. We noted, too, that such properties are of much greater significance in specifying the nature of grammatical relations which hold between and among lexical items in a sentence than they are in Modern English. Certain noun forms, for example, signal the relation 'subject of verb,' others 'object of verb,' still others 'indirect object of verb.' In addition, we pointed out that nouns have *grammatical* gender, being more or less arbitrarily assigned to masculine, feminine, and neuter classes. We noted certain characteristic features of *agreement* in number, gender, and grammatical relationship among demonstratives, adjectives, and nouns. And we commented on some differences in word-order patterns between Old and Modern English. Such differences will be reflected formally in the kinds of grammatical rules we will present for Old English.

But while we are concerned to represent *grammatical differences* between Old and Modern English, we should not ignore the fact that the two forms of English show a considerable amount of *similarity*. As a matter of fact, one of the more interesting emphases of modern linguistic research has been on the search for language universals. The human apparatus does, after all, function in just about the same way in every part of the globe. There is no reason to think that the emotional and conceptual mechanisms of a native of Kenya are any different from those of a native of New York City. The outward, observable manifestations of emotion and conceptualization will differ according to numerous factors of cultural dominance; but the set of neurological subsystems that stimulate and structure overt behavior are essentially the same. Since this is so, it is not unreasonable to suppose that the underlying deep structures of different languages are in reality very much alike and that the differences we observe are those of surface structure, accounted for, essentially, by a different set of mappings in the transformational component and a different set of interpretations generated by the semantic and phonological components. Let us attempt to illustrate this matter with an example from English language history.[2]

In his paper "The Case for Case" (in *Universals in Linguistic Theory*, eds. Emmon Bach and Robert T. Harms. Holt, Rinehart and Winston, 1968), Charles J. Fillmore suggests that ". . . the grammatical notion 'case' deserves a place in the base component in the grammar of every language." (p. 2). And he constructs a base component in which all noun phrases are introduced without regard to the surface order in which they occur, but only in terms of the roles they play in respect to the verb: "The sentence in its basic structure consists of a verb and one or more noun phrases, each associated with the verb in its particular case relationship." (p. 41). Once having accepted this base form for simple sentences, general rules can be provided to generate surface structures and to account for the types of elements that participate in these surface structures. For English, Fillmore assumes what he calls an "unmarked" or "preferred" subject choice:

> If there is an A [Agentive noun], it becomes the subject; otherwise, if there is an I [Instrumental noun], it becomes the subject; otherwise the subject is O [Objective noun] (p. 60).

The first rewrite rule in his base is

$$S \rightarrow M \hat{\ } P$$

where M is a "modality constituent" (tense, negative, etc.) and P is the proposition (a "tenseless set of relationships involving verbs and nouns") (p. 44).

Mrs. Hammer compares three translations of Exodus 20:11.

---

[2] For the grammatical analysis and rules that follow I am indebted to a seminar paper by my student, Mrs. Katherine Hammer, "Case Grammar for the Study of Different Stages of Language," University of Iowa, 1968.

Old English, *Wulfstan's* Homilies:

On six dagum wæron geworhte heofonas and eorðan, sunne and mona, sæ and fixas, and ealle þa ðe on him syndon (Albert S. Cook, ed. *Anglo-Saxon Biblical Quotations*. New York, 1903. P. 46).

Middle English, Wycliffite Bible:

Sex forsoð day god made heuen & erþ, the see & all þingis þat ben in hem (Conrad Lindberg, ed. *Ms. Bodley 959*, Vol 1. Stockholm, 1959. P. 127).

Modern English, The Dartmouth Bible:

For six days the Lord made heaven and earth, the sea and all that is in them (Roy B. Chamberlain and Herman Feldman, eds. *The Dartmouth Bible*. Boston, 1965. P. 100).

The Old English sentence has the following underlying strings:

(1) On⌢dagum⌢S⌢wæron⌢geworhte⌢heofonas
(2–6) the same structure for *eorðan, sunne, mona, sæ,* and *fixas.*
(7) On⌢dagum⌢S⌢wæron⌢geworhte⌢ealle⌢þa⌢S
(8) Dagas⌢wæron⌢six
(9) Ealle⌢þa⌢wæron⌢on⌢him

The Middle English sentence has the following:

(1) Forsoð⌢day⌢S⌢god⌢made⌢heuen
(2) Forsoð⌢day⌢S⌢god⌢made⌢erþ
(3) Forsoð⌢day⌢S⌢god⌢made⌢the⌢see
(4) Forsoð⌢day⌢S⌢god⌢made⌢all⌢þingis⌢S
(5) Day⌢ben⌢sex
(6) All⌢þingis⌢ben⌢in⌢hem

And the Modern English sentence:

(1) For⌢days⌢S⌢the⌢Lord⌢made⌢heaven
(2) For⌢days⌢S⌢the⌢Lord⌢made⌢earth

(3) For⌢days⌢S⌢the⌢Lord⌢made⌢the⌢sea
(4) For⌢days⌢S⌢the⌢Lord⌢made⌢all⌢S
(5) The⌢days⌢were⌢six
(6) All⌢was⌢in⌢them

The *cases* necessary for the structures to be described are these:

A. The Agentive (A): the case of "the perceived instigator of the action identified by the verb, typically animate."
B. The Factitive (F): the case of "the object or being resulting from the action or state identified by the verb, or understood as a part of the meaning of the verb."
C. The Locative (L): the case "which identifies the location or spatial orientation of the state or action identified by the verb."
D. The Objective (O): the case of "anything representable by a noun whose role in the action or state identified by the verb is identified by the semantic interpretation of the verb; conceivably the concept should be limited to things which are affected by the action or state identified by the verb."
E. The Temporal (T): a case that Fillmore suggests may be considered to be a component of the modality constituent. It is involved with the chronological orientation of the state or action identified by the verb.
(See Fillmore, pp. 44–47.)

The first three rules of the base will now look like this:

1. $S \rightarrow M⌢P$
2. $M \rightarrow$ (T) Tense
3. $P \rightarrow V \begin{Bmatrix} O(L) \\ (A)F \end{Bmatrix}$

Professor Fillmore proposes that all cases be rewritten as $K⌢NP$, K being replaced later by some kind of case marker, for example, an inflectional ending or a preposition, or both (p. 60). The lexicon will assign to N and V such features as will insure their proper position in a given string.

Mrs. Hammer writes these base rules to accommodate all three of the above passages:

(1) $S \rightarrow M⌢P$
(2) $M \rightarrow$ (D) (T) Tense
(3) $P \rightarrow V \begin{Bmatrix} O(L) \\ (A)F \end{Bmatrix}$

(4) Tense → $\begin{Bmatrix} \text{Pres} \\ \text{Pas} \end{Bmatrix}$

(5) V → $\begin{Bmatrix} \varnothing\ /\_\ \text{OL} \\ \text{Adj}\ /\_\ \text{O}\ \# \\ \text{TV} \end{Bmatrix}$

(6–10) O, L, T, A, F → K⌢NP

(11) NP → (Det) N⌢No (S)

(12) No → $\begin{Bmatrix} \text{sg} \\ \text{pl} \end{Bmatrix}$

The lexical rules needed for each historical stage are these:

Old English	*Middle English*	*Modern English*
(1) N → $\begin{Bmatrix} m \\ w_m \\ w_f \\ s \end{Bmatrix}$	(1) N → $\begin{Bmatrix} n \\ \text{Pro} \end{Bmatrix}$	(1) Det → all, the
(2) W_f → $\begin{Bmatrix} f_1 \\ f_2 \end{Bmatrix}$	(2) n → god, heuen, erþ, see, þing	(2) N → $\begin{Bmatrix} \varnothing/\text{all}\ \_\_\_ \\ n \\ \text{Pro} \end{Bmatrix}$
(3) TV → gewyrcan	(3) Pro → h-	(3) n → day, Lord, heaven, earth, sea
(4) Det → eall-	(4) D → forsoð	(4) Pro → th-
(5) m → heofon-, sæ-, fix-, dag-	(5) Det → all, the	(5) TV → make
(6) w_m → mon-	(6) Adj → sex	(6) Adj → six
(7) f_1 → sunn-	(7) TV → make	
(8) f_2 → eor-		
(9) s → þ-, h-		
(10) Adj → six		

where: m = masculine
w_m = weak masculine
w_f = weak feminine
s = subclass of noun

We may now compare some of the underlying phrase markers (see page 171) produced by these rules.

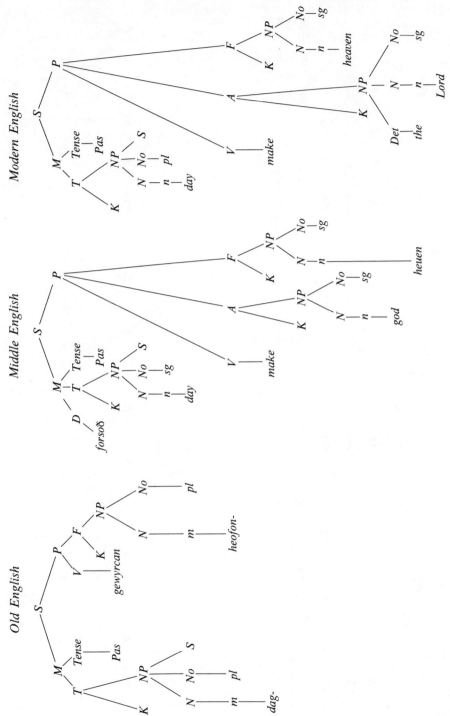

Old English

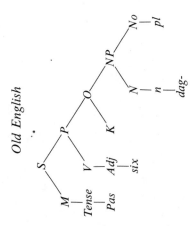

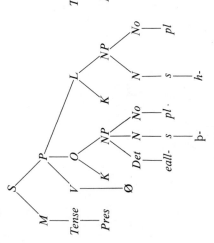

Middle English

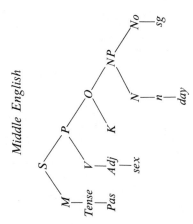

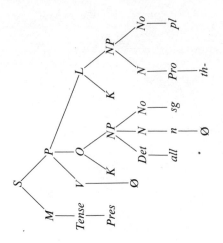

Modern English

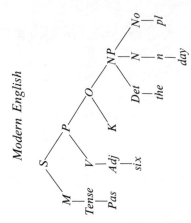

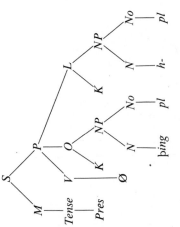

Additional phrase markers of these same types will be needed, differing only in their factitive nouns (for example, *eorð-, sunn-, mon-, sæ-, fix-* for Old English) and in the fact that one marker for each stage will contain an embedded sentence (which will ultimately become a relative clause).

The two additional types of markers are shown on page 172.

The phrase markers that have been produced represent the deep structure of the passages in question. The reader will note that the phrase markers of a given type are strikingly similar from one stage of the language to another. The absence of *A* from the first type of Old English phrase marker is accounted for by the fact that the Old English sentence is passive, while the other two are active. In the underlying Old English structure, *A* would be specified. Apart from this, the differences among markers are chiefly lexical.

Differences in the surface structure of the three sentences will be accounted for by differences in the syntactic and morphographemic transformations that characterize each stage of the language. We will not attempt to take the reader step by step through each different set of transformation rules, but rather will compare certain portions of the transformation sections in order to show how the final outputs are arrived at.

Before we discuss differences among the three transformational components we should mention some similarities. All three surface structures, for instance, require a conjoining transformation that conjoins any two or more noun phrases by *and* when the rest of their strings are identical. The operation of this transformation on the underlying strings of each sentence would have the following results:

(1) *Old English*

K^dag-^pl (Pas^six^K^dag-^pl) Pas^gewyrcan^K^heofon-^pl^and^K^eorð-^sg^and^K^sunn-^sg^and^K^mon-^sg^and^K^sæ-^sg^and^K^fix-^pl^and^K^eall-^þ-^pl (Pres^Ø^K^eall-^þ-^pl^K^h-^pl)

(2) *Middle English*

Forsoð^K^day^sg (Pas^sex^K^day^sg) Pas^make^K^god^sg^K^heuen^sg^and^K^erþ^sg^and^K^the^see^sg^and^K^all^þing-^pl (Pres^Ø^K^þing-^pl^K^h-^pl)

(3) *Modern English*

K^day^pl (Pas^six^K^day^pl) Pas^make^K^the^Lord^sg^K^heaven^sg^and^K^earth^sg^and^K^the^sea^sg^and^K^all^Ø^sg (Pres^Ø^K^all^Ø^sg^K^th-^pl)

Further, each component will have a T_{Rel} rule the outputs of which will be these:

(1) *Old English*

K^dag-^pl^þe^Pas^six^Pas^gewyrcan^K^heofon-^pl^and^K^eorð-^sg^
and^K^sunn-^sg^and^K^mon-^sg^and^K^sæ-^sg^and^K^fix-^pl^and^
K^eall-^þ-^pl^þe^Pres^Ø^K^h-^pl

(2) *Middle English*

Forsoð^K^day^sg^þat^Pas^sex^Pas^make^K^god^sg^K^heuen^sg^
and^K^erþ^sg^and^K^the^see^sg^and^K^all^þing^pl^þat^Pres^Ø^
K^h-^pl

(3) *Modern English*

K^day^pl^*that*^Pas^six^Pas^make^K^the^Lord^sg^K^heaven^sg^and^
K^earth^sg^and^K^the^sea^sg^and^K^all^Ø^sg^*that*^Pres^Ø^K^
th-^pl

The chief differences, among these sentences at least, are to be found in the rules that replace K and in the morphographemic rules that assign appropriate letter shapes. Compare the following K- replacement rules:

(1) *Old English*

$$K \Rightarrow \begin{bmatrix} \emptyset / \begin{Bmatrix} F \\ O \end{Bmatrix} < K^{\frown}NP \\ on / \begin{Bmatrix} L \\ T \end{Bmatrix} < K^{\frown}NP \end{bmatrix}$$

where: $\leq$ is to be read "dominates."

On^six^dag-^pl^Pas^gewyrcan^Ø^heofon-^pl^and^Ø^eorð-^sg^and^
Ø^sunn-^sg^and^Ø^mon-^sg^and^Ø^sæ-^sg^and^Ø^fix-^pl^and^Ø^
eall-^þ-^pl^þe^Pres^Ø^*on*^h-^pl

(2) *Middle English*

$$K \Rightarrow \begin{Bmatrix} by / A < K^{\frown}NP \\ \emptyset / \begin{Bmatrix} T \\ F \\ O \end{Bmatrix} < K^{\frown}NP \\ in / L < K^{\frown}NP \end{Bmatrix}$$

Forsoð^Ø^sex^day^sg^Pas^make^*by*^god^sg^Ø^heuen^sg^and^Ø^erþ^
sg^and^Ø^the^see^sg^and^Ø^all^þing^pl^þat^Pres^*in*^h-^pl

(3) *Modern English*

$$K \Rightarrow \begin{cases} by/A < K^\frown NP \\ for/T < K^\frown NP \\ \emptyset / \begin{Bmatrix} F \\ O \end{Bmatrix} < K^\frown NP \\ in/L < K^\frown NP \end{cases}$$

For^six^day^pl^Pas^make^*by*^the^Lord^sg^Ø^heaven^sg^and^Ø^
earth^sg^and^Ø^the^sea^sg^and^Ø^all^Ø^sg^that^Pres^Ø^*in*^th-^pl

Notice that for both Middle and Modern English *by* has replaced *K* where
A dominates *K*^NP. A transformation rule will move *A* to subject position
and delete *by*:

#M^V^*by*^NP^X ⇒ #NP^M^V^X

The resulting string for Middle English is:

Forsoð^Ø^sex^day^sg^god^sg^Pas^make^Ø^heuen^sg^and^Ø^erþ^sg^
and^Ø^the^see^sg^and^Ø^all^þing^pl^þat^Pres^Ø^*in*^h-^pl

and for Modern English:

For^six^day^pl^the^Lord^sg^Pas^make^Ø^heaven^sg^and^Ø^earth^
sg^and^Ø^the^sea^sg^and^Ø^all^Ø^sg^that^Pres^be^*in*^th-^pl

Additional syntactic and morphographemic rules peculiar to each stage of the
language will provide for the necessary agreement between subject noun and
verb, the appropriate written shapes for singular and plural, for past and
present, and for the pronouns, and for the introduction of the *be* verb in Old
and Middle English. Final derived strings from such rules would be the
following:

(1) *Old English*
on^six^dag-^um^wær-^on^geworhte^Ø^heofon-^as^and^Ø^eorð-^an^
and^Ø^sunn-^e^and^Ø^mon-^a^and^Ø^sæ-^Ø^and^Ø^fix-^as^and^Ø^
ealle^þa^ðe^synd-^on^on^h-^im

(2) *Middle English*

Forsoð ^Ø^ sex ^day ^Ø^ god ^Ø^ made ^Ø^ heuen ^Ø^ and ^Ø^ erþ ^Ø^ and^
Ø^ the ^see ^Ø^ and ^Ø^ all ^þing- ^is ^þat ^ben ^in ^h- ^em

(3) *Modern English*

For ^six ^day- ^s ^the ^Lord ^Ø^ made ^Ø^ heaven ^Ø^ and ^Ø^ earth ^Ø^ and^
Ø^ the ^sea ^Ø^ and ^Ø^ all ^Ø^ Ø^ that ^is ^in ^th- ^em

To summarize, a "universal" set of subcategorization rules was presented; for each language stage a set of lexical rules appropriate to that stage was given; and for each language stage a set of transformational rules was provided, some of which were "universal," that is, applicable to all three stages, some of which were peculiar to a given stage. One of the advantages of this approach in writing rules for different languages or for different stages of the same language is that the language universal section of the grammar is clearly distinguished from the language specific section. Furthermore, the very fact of such clear differentiation emphasizes the notion that language universals *do exist*. On the other hand, universality is achieved at the price of a rather high level of abstraction; and the higher the level of abstraction the less information we have about the phenomenon in question. One may refine differences out of existence: *All living things have a generative capacity.* The statement is true; it is also self-evident and therefore trivial. It tells us little about the world of living things. *Sentences in all languages contain something which may be called a verb and something else which may be called a noun and which stands in a certain relation to that verb.* One supposes that the statement is true; but it tells us little about language.

There are, then, as with most important questions, two sides to the coin. An understanding of "tree-ness" is only arrived at through the process of abstracting from specific trees those characteristics that all trees have in common. An understanding of "language-ness" is arrived at by abstracting from specific languages those characteristics that all languages have in common. But too high a level of abstraction leads to disarray, and disarray to a failure to understand or to characterize properly either "tree-ness" or "language-ness."

As far as economy of description is concerned, it seems to this writer that it makes little difference whether one has a small number of, for the most part, unordered rules in a base that attempts to express the universality of language and a very large number of language specific transformations, or a larger and more specific set of base rules and a smaller number of language specific transformations. But this comment immediately raises the question "What is meant by economy of description?" as well as the question "How does economy of description relate to validity of description?" Professor Chomsky has dealt with such questions at considerable length and with considerable insight. We can do no more here than call them to the reader's attention.

The base for the Old English grammar presented below tends to be language specific in character, although the overall pattern of rules shows considerable similarity to that given above for Modern English. We do not make use of Fillmore's theory of case (as we did not in the Modern English grammar), but rather treat case in the traditional way, that is, as an inflectional category signaling certain grammatical relationships among sentence elements.

Some Old English Paradigms

Nouns

As we have mentioned, Old English noun stems are classified as *masculine, feminine,* and *neuter,* and each of these gender types are subclassified according to the phonemic construction of the stem and the form of the inflection attached to it. In addition, they are further classified as *strong* or *weak* according as the stem *originally* ended in a vowel or a consonant. In large part, this latter classification is based on reconstruction since the pre-Old English history of the phonemic structure of noun stems tended to obscure the distinction. We will illustrate here only a few of the traditional noun stem types.

A. Strong Masculine

stan 'stone'
mearh 'horse'

	singular		plural	
nominative				
and accusative	stan	mearh	stanas	mearas
genitive	stanes	meares	stana	meara
dative	stane	meare	stanum	mearum

B. Strong Neuter

word 'word'
heafod 'head'

	singular		plural	
nominative				
and accusative	word	heafod	word	heafodu
genitive	wordes	heafdes	worda	heafda
dative	worde	heafde	wordum	heafdum

C. Strong Feminine

gief 'gift'
sawl- 'soul'

	singular			*plural*	
nominative	giefu sawol	*nominative*			
accusative,		*and accusative*		giefa, -e	sawla, -e
genitive		*genitive*		giefa, -ena	sawla
and dative	giefe sawle	*dative*		giefum	sawlum

D. Weak Masculine, Feminine, Neuter

gum- 'man' (masc)
tung- 'tongue' (fem)
eag- 'eye' (neut)

	singular		*plural*
nominative	guma, tunge, eage	*nominative*	
accusative	guman, tungan, eage	*and accusative*	guman, tungan, eagan
genitive		*genitive*	gumena, tungena, eagena
and dative	guman, tungan, eagan	*dative*	gumum, tungum, eagum

We have cited 6 different types of stems each of which participates in 2 numbers and 4 cases. A language that showed *maximal* distinctiveness would have 96 different formal characteristics under such circumstances; that is, each stem type would have 16 different forms. A language that showed clear distinctions in stem type, in case, and in number, but in which case markings are the same for both singular and plural, would have 48 different forms, each stem type having 8 different forms. A language that showed clear distinctions in stem type but in which all 6 stem types are similarly marked for case and number would have 12 different forms. How many *different* forms do you find for the 6 stem types above? On the basis of your count, what comments might you make on the usefulness or validity of the traditional classification?

The Old English evidence indicates that over a very long period of time prior to the earliest Old English records formal distinction among stem types and cases was gradually being lost. And this process of loss continues into the Middle English period. Since case markers are devices for signaling grammatical relationships within an utterance, it is clear that when such markers lose their distinctive character they lose their capacity to signal these relationships. Given the isolated form *stane,* we know that the grammatical relationship signaled is *dative,* whatever this happens to imply in Old English. But given the isolated form *giefe,* we cannot tell whether the relationship signaled is *genitive, dative,* or *accusative.* It is just this kind of equivocation that required English to employ more fully devices *other than* case markers to signal the grammatical relationships of nouns.

Verbs

There were two large classes of verb types in Old English, *strong* verbs and *weak* verbs. The terms *strong* and *weak* may not have been particularly happy choices, but since they are the terms by which these two classes have been traditionally denominated, we use them here. The two classes may be illustrated by the Modern English verbs *drive* and *learn.* You may be more familiar with the terms *irregular* and *regular* commonly applied to these two, but the notions of regularity and irregularity are quite misleading here. There was nothing irregular about the Old English strong verb. The point is that only a few verbs of the strong class have remained in that class, so that these appear to be irregularly formed in comparison with the great bulk of weak verbs.

The present, past, and past participle forms of *drive* are indicated by changes in the quality or quantity of its vowel nucleus: *drive* /drayv/, *drove* /drowv/, and *driven* /drivən/; while the past and past participle forms of *learn* are indicated by the addition of *-ed* (/əd/, /d/, or /t/): *learn* /lərn/, *learned* /lərnd/, and *has learned* /hæz lərnd/. The difference between these two verb classes is a difference in the grammatical devices used to signal present tense, past tense, and past participle. The Germanic languages share the grammatical device of vowel change with other members of the Indo-European language family. Compare, for instance, the Greek series πείθω (*peithō*), πέποιθα (*pepoitha*), ἔπιθον (*epithon*), a verb one of whose meanings is "to persuade." The addition of a *dental consonant* suffix to indicate past tense was, however, an *innovation* of the Germanic languages, and does not have a counterpart in other Indo-European languages.

In Old English, the class of strong verbs had seven subclasses, each defined by the nature of the vowel occurring in the present infinitive, the past tense singular, third person, the past tense plural, third person, and the past participle:

	infinitive	*third singular past*	*third plural past*	*past participle*	*meaning*
first	drifan	draf	drifon	drifen	to drive
second	smeocan	smeac	smucon	smocen	to smoke
third	climban	clamb	clumbon	clumben	to climb
	helpan	healp	hulpon	holpen	to help
fourth	teran	tær	tæron	toren	to tear
fifth	cnedan	cnæd	cnædon	cneden	to knead
sixth	bacan	boc	bocon	bacen	to bake
seventh	beatan	beot	beoton	beaten	to beat

These verbs have been deliberately chosen so as to suggest the fact that Old English strong verbs have undergone considerable variety of development since the tenth century. The forms *drive/drove/driven* give evidence of first class strong verb membership. But in the standard dialects both second class *smeocan* and third class *climban* have become weak: *climb/climbed, smoke/smoked.* The past tense or past participle *clumb* is now considered dialectal and usually vulgar. Third class *helpan* has become weak. Fourth class *teran* has remained strong, but the vowel of the past participle now occurs for the past tense as well: *tear/tore/torn.* Sixth class *bacan* has become weak, while seventh class *beatan,* although retaining its strong membership, employs the same stem vowel in all of its occurrences: "You beat him every day," "You beat him yesterday," "You have beaten him a number of times." The variety of development is typical of Old English strong verbs and has resulted in a large redistribution of their class membership in Modern English.

Old English weak verbs are traditionally divided into three subclasses on the basis of certain historical criteria that need not concern us here. Modern English *answer, learn,* and *fill* derive from the first class of weak verbs; *hate, hope,* and *love* from the second class; *have, live,* and *say* from the third class.

The Old English verb shows certain formal features that convey the following grammatical information: present and past *tense;* indicative, subjunctive, and imperative *mood;* first, second, and third *person;* and singular and plural *number.* It could be either *transitive* or *intransitive,* and it could occur with various kinds of auxiliary constructions. Both strong and weak verb conjugations are illustrated below.

A. Strong, Class I

Infinitive: *drifan* /dri·fɑn/

Present

Indicative: *singular*   *plural*
1. *drife* /dri·fe/ ⎫
2. *drifst* /dri·fst/ ⎬   *drifað* /dri·fɑθ/
3. *drifð* /dri·fθ/ ⎭

Subjunctive:
    1–3. *drife* /dri·fe/   *drifen* /dri·fen/

Imperative:
      drif /dri·f/   *drifað* /dri·faθ/

    Participle: *drifende* /dri·fende/

Past

    Indicative: *singular*   *plural*

      1 & 3. *draf* /drɑ·f/ ⎫

      2.   *drife* /drife/ ⎬   *drifon* /drifon/

    Subjunctive:

      1–3. *drife* /drife/   *drifen* /drifen/

    Participle: *gedrifen* /yedrifen/

B. Weak, Class II

    Infinitive: *lufian*

    Present

    Indicative: *singular*   *plural*

      1. *lufie* ⎫

      2. *lufast* ⎬   *lufiað*

      3. *lufa* ⎭

    Subjunctive:

      1–3. *lufie*   *lufien*

    Imperative:

        lufa   *lufiað*

    Participle: *lufiende*

    Past

    Indicative: *singular*   *plural*

      1., 3. *lufode* ⎫

      2.   *lufodest* ⎬   *lufodon*

    Subjunctive:

      1–3. *lufode*   *lufoden*

    Participle: *gelufod*

Although we will in general continue the practice of concerning ourselves with the graphemic rather than the phonemic shape of grammatical forms, we have given the phonemic forms of the verb *drifan* in order to point out that certain differentiations are made in pronunciation that are not always represented in the writing system. For example, the written forms of the past indicative, second person singular; the past subjunctive first, second, and third person singular; the present subjunctive, first, second, and third person singular; and the present indicative, first person singular, may have identical written shapes. The first two sets of forms, however, contain a *short* stem vowel, while the latter two have a *long* stem vowel. The present subjunctive plurals are similarly distinguished from the past subjunctive plurals. In the case of *lufian,* on the other hand, the vowel is short throughout the conjugation.

Adjectives in Old English show a number of grammatical differences from Modern English adjectives. First of all, they are declinable and must agree in gender, number, and case with the nouns they modify. You may be familiar with similar interaction between adjectives and nouns from other languages. In Latin, the masculine singular, nominative structure for "the good boy" is *bonus puer;* feminine "the good girl" is *bona puella;* neuter "the good gift" is *bonum dōnum.* In the genitive case, the forms would be *bonī puerī, bonae puellae,* and *bonī donī.* In the second place, most Old English adjectives have both a *strong* and a *weak* declension, each of which has its own set of case, gender, and number markings. Adjectives following a demonstrative or a possessive pronoun are declined according to the weak declension; elsewhere, they are declined strong. Below we show the forms of both declensions for the adjective *blind.*

	Strong			*Weak*		
			singular			
	masculine	*neuter*	*feminine*	*masculine*	*neuter*	*feminine*
nominative	blind	blind	blind	blinda	blinde	blinde
accusative	blinde	blind	blinde	blindan	blinde	blindan
genitive	blindes	blindes	blindre	blindan	———→	
dative	blindum	blindum	blindre	blindan	———→	
instrumental	blinde	blinde				

	Strong			*Weak*		
			plural			
	masculine	*neuter*	*feminine*	*masculine*	*neuter*	*feminine*
nominative, *accusative*	blinde	blind	blinda, -e	blindan	———→	
genitive	blindra	———————→		blindra, -ena	———→	
dative	blindum	———————→		blindum	———→	

Note the considerable amount of *nondistinctiveness,* especially in the weak declension. Since these forms provide such a relatively small amount of grammatical information, it is not surprising that the agreement feature between adjectives and nouns quickly disappears in Middle English.

Demonstratives

The simple demonstrative in Old English had these forms:

	masculine	*singular* *neuter*	*feminine*	*plural* *all genders*
nominative	se	þæt	sio, -eo	þa
accusative	þone	þæt	þa´	þa
genitive	þæs	þæs	þære	þæra
dative	þæm	þæm	þære	þæm
instrumental		þy, þon		

What is sometimes called the compound demonstrative or the *deictic* demonstrative arose from the attachment of an emphatic *-si* particle to the simple demonstrative. In Old Norse inscriptions one finds the emphatic demonstrative forms *sa-si, þat-si, su-si*. At an early stage in the development of this emphatic demonstrative only the first element (the single demonstrative) was inflected, but at a later time the second element underwent inflectional changes as well. In Old English the emphatic demonstrative frequently occurs to single out some part of a series: *on þysum geare for se micla here þe we gefyrn ymbe spræcon* 'in this year [within a chronicle of years] went the large army which we earlier about spoke.' The modern distinction between the more and less proximate *this* 'near'/*that* 'far' began to develop only in late Old English. The deictic demonstrative was declined as follows:

	masculine	*singular* *neuter*	*feminine*	*plural* *all genders*
nominative	þes	þis	þeos	þas
accusative	þisne	þis	þas	þas
genitive	þisses	þisses	þisse	þissa
dative	þissum	þissum	þisse	þissum
instrumental	þys	þys		

Personal Pronouns

The Old English personal pronoun system shows *three persons, three numbers* in the first and second persons and *two numbers* in the third person, *three genders* in the third person, and *four cases*.

	singular	First dual	plural
nominative	ic	wit (we two)	we
accusative	mec, me	uncit, unc	usic, us
genitive	min	uncer	ure, user
dative	me	unc	us

	singular	Second dual	plural
nominative	þu	git (you two)	ge
accusative	þec, þe	incit, inc	eowic, eow
genitive	þin	incer	eower
dative	þe	inc	eow

	masculine	Third singular neuter	feminine
nominative	he	hit	heo
accusative	hine	hit	hie
genitive	his	his	hire
dative	him	him	hire

	plural all genders
nominative *and accusative*	hie
genitive	heora, hiera
dative	him

Base Component

Categorial Subcomponent

1. $S \rightarrow$ (Q) (Neg) $\begin{Bmatrix} NP \\ \emptyset \end{Bmatrix}$ VP$\widehat{}$Aux

2. $VP \rightarrow$ (Adv) MV

3. $MV \rightarrow$ (PP) $\left(\begin{Bmatrix} Pred \\ NP \ (NP) \end{Bmatrix} \right)$ V

4. $Pred \rightarrow \begin{Bmatrix} Adj \\ Adv \\ Pred\ Nom \end{Bmatrix}$

5. $Pred\ Nom \rightarrow NP$

6. $Adv \rightarrow \begin{Bmatrix} PP \\ adv \end{Bmatrix}$

7. $PP \rightarrow prep\widehat{\ }NP$

8. $NP \rightarrow Det\widehat{\ }N\widehat{\ }Agr\ (S)$

9. $Det \rightarrow (Dem)\ (NP)$

10. $Aux \rightarrow (Aux_2)\ Aux_1$

11. $Aux_1 \rightarrow (Inf - M)\ CS/V\ (Aux_2)$ —
   a. $[+Aux_1] \rightarrow [+[\pm Pres],\ [\pm Ind]]$
   b. $[\pm Pres] \rightarrow [\pm Pres]$
      $\quad\ |\qquad\qquad |$
      $[-Ind]\quad\ [\pm Sub]$
   c. $[+Pres] \rightarrow [+Pres]$
      $\quad\ |\qquad\qquad |$
      $[-Sub]\quad\ [+Imp]$

12. $Aux_2 \rightarrow \left\{\begin{matrix} -en & \left\{\begin{matrix} habb/NP\widehat{\ }NP\widehat{\ }V\ \_ \\ wes \end{matrix}\right\} \\ -ende\widehat{\ }beo \end{matrix}\right\}^3$

13. $prep \rightarrow \left\{\begin{matrix} prep_1 \\ prep_2 \end{matrix}\right\}$

14. $Dem \rightarrow \left\{\begin{matrix} dem \\ \emptyset \end{matrix}\right\}$

15. $Agr \rightarrow CS/N\ \_$
   a. $[+Agr] \rightarrow [+[\pm masc],\ [\pm pl],\ [+Ca],\ [+pers]]$
   b. $[-masc] \rightarrow [\pm neut]$
   c. $[-neut] \rightarrow [+fem]$
   d. $[+pers/N\ \_] \rightarrow [+3]$

16. $N \rightarrow CS/Det\ \_\ Agr$
   a. $[+N] \rightarrow [\pm s]$
   b. $[-s] \rightarrow [\pm w]$
   c. $[-w] \rightarrow [+I]$
   d. $[\pm s] \rightarrow [\pm animate]$
   e. $[+animate] \rightarrow [\pm human]$

17. $V \rightarrow CS/\left[\begin{matrix} NP \\ \emptyset \end{matrix}\right]\left[\begin{matrix} \left\{\begin{matrix} Pred \\ NP\ (NP) \end{matrix}\right\} \\ NP \end{matrix}\right]\ \_$

18. $adv \rightarrow \left\{\begin{matrix} adv_{pl} \\ adv_t \\ adv_m \end{matrix}\right\}$

---

[3] As a matter of fact, the auxiliary *habban* does occasionally occur with a small subset of intransitive verbs, chiefly those of *motion;* however, this rule expresses the normal situation. For this analysis of *Aux* and for the order of elements in rules 1 and 3, with some slight modifications, we are indebted to Elizabeth Closs, "Diachronic Syntax and Generative Grammar," *Language* 41:402–415 (1965).

Lexicon

1. a. $[+\text{prep}_1]$ → fore, geond, in, ofer, on, ongean, þurh, wið, ymbe.
   b. $[+\text{prep}_2]$ → æfter, ær, æt, bi, betweonan, butan, fram, mid, of, to.
2. $[+\text{dem}]$ → þ-.
3. $[+\text{Adj}]$ → god, lytel, micel, yfel, earm, heard, leof, glæd, bliðe, cene, rice, geong, heah, lang, sceort, strang.
4. a. $[+\text{adv}_{pl}]$ → her, þær, utan, neah, feorr, suþan, æftan.
   b. $[+\text{adv}_t]$ → tidum, geardagum, oft, sona, þa.
   c. $[+\text{adv}_m]$ → soþe, bliþe, arfæstlice, eaþe, yfle, geþyldum.
5. $[+\text{N}, +\text{Det} \_\_ \text{Agr}]$
   a. $[+\text{N}, +\text{masc}]$ → cyning, æðeling, fæder, dryhten hyrd.
      $[+\text{s}]$
      $[+\text{human}]$
   b. $[+\text{N}, +\text{masc}]$ → mearh, fugol.
      $[+\text{s}]$
      $[+\text{animate}]$
      $[-\text{human}]$
   c. $[+\text{N}, +\text{masc}]$ → stan, hlaf, heofon, hyrd.
      $[+\text{s}]$
      $[-\text{animate}]$
   d. $[+\text{N}, +\text{neut}]$ → scip, brim, land, sweord, cneo, wæter, heafod.
      $[+\text{s}]$
      $[-\text{animate}]$
   e. $[+\text{N}, +\text{neut}]$ → bearn, folc.
      $[+\text{s}]$
      $[+\text{human}]$
   f. $[+\text{N}, +\text{neut}]$ → sceap, feoh.
      $[+\text{s}]$
      $[+\text{animate}]$
      $[-\text{human}]$
   g. $[+\text{N}, +\text{fem}]$ → cwen, bryd.
      $[+\text{s}]$
      $[+\text{human}]$

h. [+N, +fem] → glof, brycg, eaxl, ecg, rod, sorg, duguð, sawol,
   [+s]   myht, nyd, tid, wyrd.
   [−animate]

i. [+N, +masc] → gum-, ban-, cnap-, mon-, witeg-, gefer-.
   [+w]
   [+human]

j. [+N, +masc] → dogg-, fol-, har-, ass-.
   [+w]
   [+animate]
   [−human]

k. [+N, +neut] → eag-, ear-.
   [+w]
   [−animate]

l. [+N, +fem] → tung-, burn-, ceac-, cupp-, fold-, wæcc-, þrot-,
   [+w]   eorþ-.
   [−animate]

m. [+N, +fem] → nædr-, duc-, moþþ-, yc-.
   [+w]
   [+animate]
   [−human]

n. [+N, +masc] → man(n), wifman.
   [+I]
   [+human]

o. [+N, +masc] → fot, toþ.
   [+I]
   [−animate]

p. [+N, +fem] → gos, lus, mus, cu, gat
   [+I]
   [+animate]
   [−human]

6. [+V, +{ #NP (X) }—]
         { #Ø^NP }

   a. [+V, +Ø^NP__] → lyst-, þinc-, spow-.
   b. [+V, +#NP^NP__] → [±s]

   (i) [+s] → [+1 . . . 7]
      [+1] → bid-, grip-, hrin-, sniþ-, teo-.
      [+2] → bruc-, cleof-, neot-, dreog-, ceos-.
      [+3] → help-, beorg-, bind-, drinc-, weorp-.
      [+4] → ber-, stel-, ter-, nim-.
      [+5] → brec-, wef-, gief-, seo-.
      [+6] → bac-, wasc-, scac-, sle-.
      [+7] → heald-, cnaw-, ræd-, fo-.
   (ii) [−s] → [+1 . . . 3]
      [+1] → wen-, dem-, benæm-, answeri-, lær-.
      [+2] → wundri-, asci-, fæstni-, hati-.
      [+3] → habb-, secg-, hycg-.
 c. [+V, + #NP^NP^NP__] → [±s]
   (i) [+s] → [+1 . . . 7]
      [+3] → oðþring-.
      [+5] → bidd-, gief-.
   (ii) [−s] → [+1 . . . 3]
      [+1] → forwyrn-, lett-, sell-.
      [+2] → geþanci-.
 d. [+V, + #NP__] → [±s]
   (i) [+s] → [+1 . . . 7]
      [+1] → belif-, aris-, besmit-, gewit-, glid-.
      [+2] → creop-, dreop-, fleot-, greot-, fleog-.
      [+3] → rinn-, spring-, sinc-, hweorf-, steorf-.
      [+4] → cum-.
      [+5] → swef-, licg-, gefeo-.
      [+6] → far-, wad-, stand-, hliehh-.
      [+7] → gang-, weax-, blaw-, hleap-.
   (ii) [−s] → [+1 . . . 3]
      [+1] → swæt-, fys-, wræþ-, hlynn-, agylt-.
      [+2] → acealdi-, lati-, waci-, wergi-.
      [+3] → libb-.
 e. [+V, + #NP^Pred__] → beo-.
7. M → cunn-, mæg-, mot-, sceal-, will-.

Some comments on these categorial and lexical rules are in order. Rule 1 permits the selection of *Ø* rather than *NP* in order to provide the structure for certain *impersonal verbs* that occur in Old English without a subject: *ælcum menn þuhte* 'it seemed to each man.' Notice that rule 3 provides for the possible generation of a string *NP^NP^NP^V^Aux*, where the first *NP* constitutes the subject, the second and third *NP*'s double objects as in the following:

(1) adl oþþe yldo oþþe ecghete fægum fromweardum feorh oðþringe.
    'disease or age or swordhate the fated enterprising ones of life deprive.'

In this case we have conjoined subjects, *adl, yldo,* and *ecghete;* a dative object, *fægum fromweardum;* and an accusative object, *feorh.*

(2) þæt þa Deniscan him ne meahton þæs ripes forwiernan.
'That the Danes them might not the harvest keep from.'

Here, *Deniscan* is the subject, *him* a dative object, and *þæs ripes* a genitive object.

Rule 6 c. of the lexicon provides for the selection of appropriate verbs for such double object structures. Later rules will assign specific cases to these object *NP*'s according to the type of verb selected from the lexicon.

The departure in rules 1, 3, 10–12, from the order of these elements in Modern English is motivated by differences in Old English word-order patterns. We accept Professor Closs's arguments that the order presented here is the most economical (see footnote 3 above). The symbol *Agr* in rule 8 is attached to *N* and is later expanded in rule 15 into sets of features that characterize *N*. These are in part *agreement* features some of which must in the transformation section of the grammar be attached to *Dem, Adj, V,* and *Pro.* The expansion of Aux_2 in rule 12 should be compared with the expansion of this symbol in the Modern English model. In Old English *habb-* plus past participle occurs with *transitive* verbs to express perfective aspect: *þu hafast helle bereafod* 'you have despoiled hell'; *wes-* plus past participle occurs with intransitive verbs: *Hit ys nu geworden* 'It has now happened.' Further, the rule indicates another important difference between Old and Modern English, namely that such Modern English constructions as 'Bill has been working' do not occur in Old English. In short, perfect and progressive auxiliaries do not occur in the same string.

Rule 16 shows *N* to be a complex symbol containing features characteristic of the *strong* declension, the *weak* declension, or the *irregular* declension.

Rule 5 of the lexicon specifies the nouns that occur according as they are marked for gender, for animate, nonanimate, and so on, and for membership in a particular declension. These features must be carried into the transformational component where the noun will be assigned its proper shape.

Rule 6 provides a list of verbs specified according to frame features (impersonal verbs, intransitives, transitives with one object, transitives with two objects) and strong or weak subclassifications.

Some Phrase Markers

The diagrams on pages 190–195 are intended to represent only a few of the possible underlying phrase markers that the base component may generate.

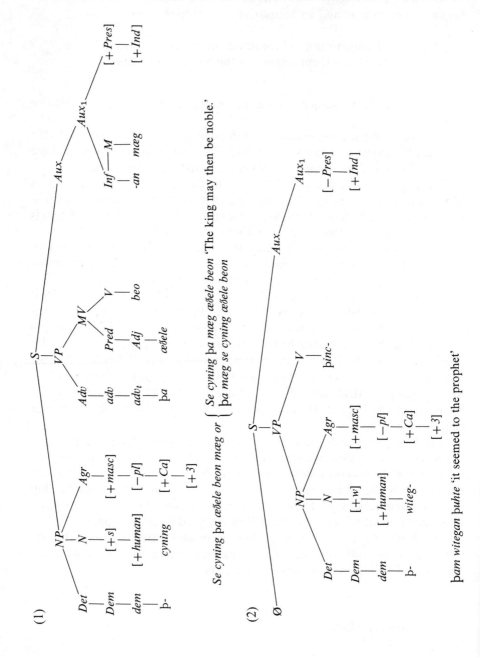

(1)

Se cyning þa mæg æðele beon mæg or { Se cyning þa mæg æðele beon 'The king may then be noble.'
                                      { þa mæg se cyning æðele beon

(2)

þam witegan þuhte 'it seemed to the prophet'

(3)

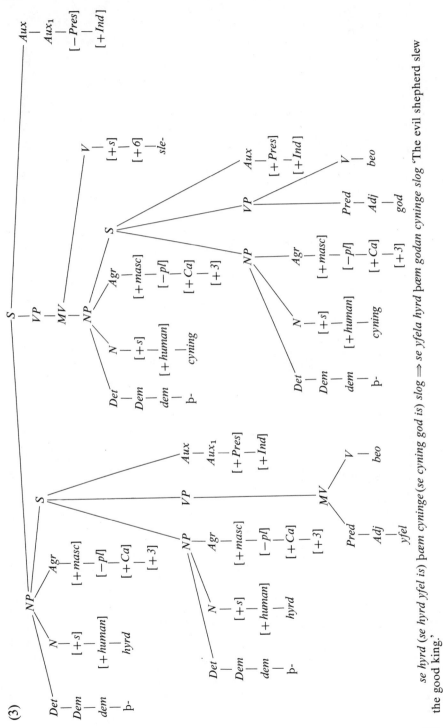

se hyrd (se hyrd yfel is) þæm cyninge (se cyning god is) slog ⇒ se yfela hyrd þæm godan cyninge slog 'The evil shepherd slew the good king.'

191

(4)

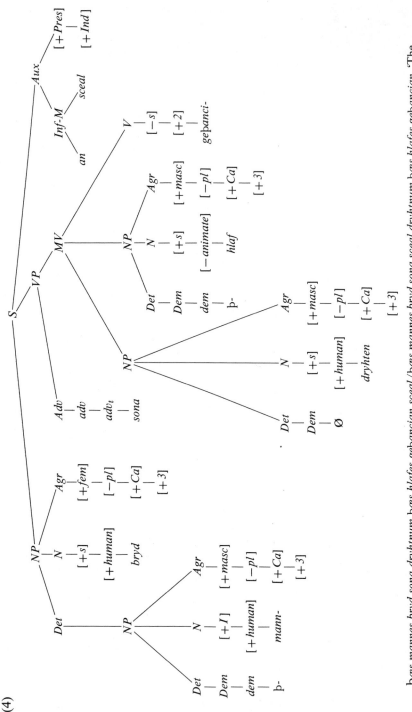

þæs mannes bryd sona dryhtnum þæs hlafes gebancian sceal / þæs mannes bryd sona sceal dryhtnum þæs hlafes gebancian. 'The man's bride soon the lord for the bread will thank.'

(5)

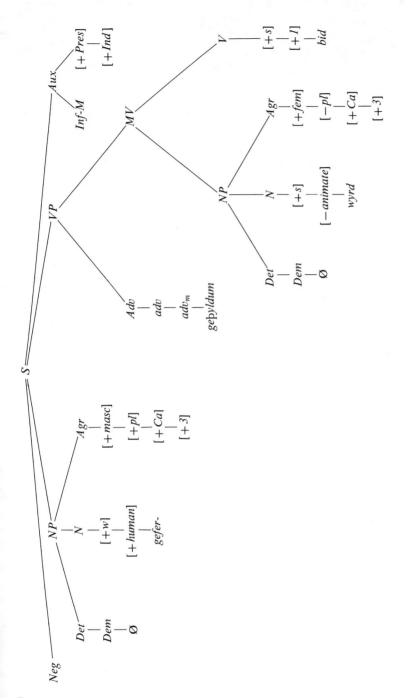

The negative transformation will convert the positive sentence *Geferan gebyldum wyrde bidan scealdon* to *(Ne) geferan gebyldum ne sceoldon wyrde bidan.* 'Companions patiently fate shall await.' 'Companions patiently shall not fate await.'

193

(6)

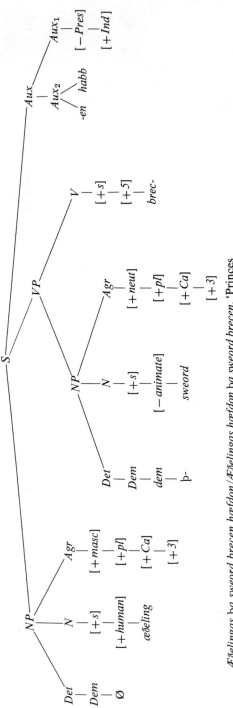

Æðelingas þa sweord brecen hæfdon/Æðelingas hæfdon þa sweord brecen. 'Princes had broken the swords.'

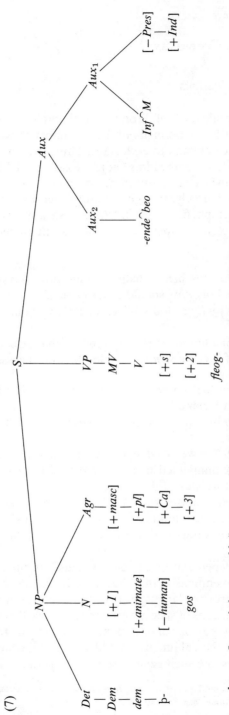

(7)

þa ges fleogende beon sceolde/þa ges sceolde fleogende beon. 'The geese should be flying.'

TRANSFORMATIONAL COMPONENT[4]

Syntactic Transformations

In illustrating the application of Professor Fillmore's "case grammar" to various stages of English, we pointed out that a number of syntactic transformation rules would be common to each stage. This is true of certain types of conjoining, relative clause embedding, adjectivization, and pronominalization. Differences in surface structure from one stage of the language to another will be expressed largely, though not altogether, by low-level morphophonemic or morphographemic rules. In Old English, a special problem exists in connection with certain types of embedding situations. Consider the following sentences:

(1) Hit nan wundor nys þæt se halga cyning untrumnysse *gehæle*. 'It is no wonder that the holy king should heal sickness.'

(2) Ic ræde þe þæt þu *lufie* God soðlice. 'I advise you that you should love God truly.'

(3) He heht hine þæt he *cume*. 'He ordered him that he come.'

(4) Nis nidbeþearf þæt we *sien* idelhende. 'It is not necessary that we be empty-handed.'

(5) Se preost cwæð þæt an wer *wære* on Irelande. 'The priest said that there was a man in Ireland.'

(6) þa acsode man hine hwylcne cræft he *cuðe*. 'Then someone asked him what skill he knew.'

(7) God bebead us ðæt we ne *æton*, ne we ðæt treow ne *hrepedon* ði læs ðe we *swelton*. 'God commanded us that we should not eat, nor should we touch that tree lest we should die.'

(8) He asende ða eft ut ane culfran, ðæt heo *sceawode* gyf ða wætera ða gyt *geswicon* ofer ðære eorðan bradnysse. 'He send then also out a dove, that she might see if the waters had abated over the broadness of the earth.'

The verbs in the dependent or embedded clauses in the above sentences have been italicized to emphasize that they are all *subjunctive*. It is characteristic of many Indo-European languages that they express unrealized or hypothetical situations by means of special verb forms. Notice that in the examples given above certain types of conditions are expressed in the independent clauses that occasion the subjunctive mood in the embedded clauses. It is not difficult to make some such general statement as this: "The subjunctive

---

[4] We present here only some types of *syntactic transformations*. For a detailed specification of *morphographemic transformations* see Appendix II.

mood in dependent clauses occurs after certain verbs of commanding, saying, desiring, asking; after expressions of necessity, conjecture, appropriateness, hypothetical comparison or condition; after certain time conjunctions, in expressions of purpose, concession, result, and the like." It is somewhat more difficult to formulate precise rules that will automatically generate the subjunctive under appropriate conditions.

One possible way of treating this problem is the following.
(1) Rules 8 and 9 of the subcategory rules are revised in accordance with rules 7 and 8 of the Modern English grammar (which should probably be done anyway). Thus,

8. $NP \rightarrow np(S)$

9. $np \rightarrow \begin{pmatrix} np/\_\_S \\ \quad | \\ [+pro] \\ Det\widehat{\ }N\widehat{\ }Agr(S) \end{pmatrix}$

(2) We introduce a syntactic transformation rule that assigns a feature $[+Sub]$ to certain occurrences of S:

$$T_{Sub}: \begin{bmatrix} for\widehat{\ }np\widehat{\ }S \\ \quad | \\ [+pro] \\ np\widehat{\ }S\ (X)\ V_y \\ \quad | \\ [+pro] \end{bmatrix} \Rightarrow \begin{bmatrix} for\widehat{\ }NP\ \widehat{\ }\ S \\ \quad | \qquad | \\ [+pro]\ [+Sub] \\ np\ \widehat{\ }\ S\ (X)\ V_y \\ \quad | \qquad | \\ [+pro]\ [+Sub] \end{bmatrix}$$

where: V_y = hat-, will-, wilni-, acsi-, þync-, þenc-, cweð-, et al.

Later morphographemic rules will provide the proper shape for np:
$$[+pro]$$

(1) $for\widehat{\ }\ np\ \widehat{\ }\ S \Rightarrow (for) \begin{Bmatrix} ðæm \\ ðy \\ ðæt \end{Bmatrix} (ðe)\ S$
$\qquad\quad | \qquad\quad |$
$\qquad [+pro]\,[+Sub]$

which will account for the structure of certain clauses of *result, purpose,* and *cause.*

(2) $np\ \widehat{\ }\ S\ (X)\ V_y \Rightarrow ðæt\widehat{\ }S\ (X)\ V_y$
$\quad\ |\qquad |$
$[+pro]\,[+Sub] \qquad\quad [+Sub]$

The subjunctive also occurs in certain embedded clauses expressing future or hypothetical time: *Gespræc þa se goda ... ær he on bed stige* 'Spoke then the noble one ... before he to bed went (should go).' *Gebad wintra torn ær he on weg hwurfe* 'He endured the suffering of many winters before he on his way went (died).' We will treat such constructions as embedded relatives:

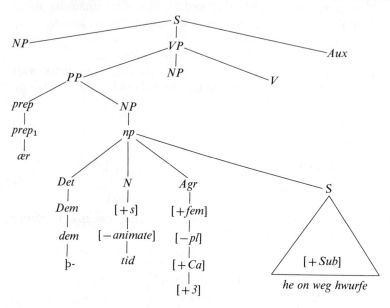

The subjunctive in the temporal clause would be generated by the following rule:

$$T_{Sub}: \quad X \,\widehat{}\, ær \,\widehat{}\, np \,\widehat{}\, Y \Rightarrow X \,\widehat{}\, ær \,\widehat{}\, np \,\widehat{}\, Y$$
$$\qquad\qquad\quad V \qquad\qquad\qquad\quad V$$
$$\qquad\qquad\quad S \qquad\qquad\qquad\quad S$$
$$\qquad\qquad\qquad\qquad\qquad\qquad\quad [+Sub]$$

where: np = 'np dominates S.'
$$\qquad\; V$$
$$\qquad\; S$$

We will not attempt to represent all of the details of this temporal clause transformation, but intend merely to suggest the manner in which [+Sub] is assigned. We assume something like the following progression:

... ær þære tide (þære tide he on weg hwurfe) ⟹
... ær þære tide (þære he on weg hwurfe) ⟹
... ær (þære he on weg hwurfe) ⟹
... ær (he on weg hwurfe) ⟹
... ær he on weg hwurfe.

The question transformation for Old English differs from that for Modern English chiefly in the fact that *do* is not required as a tense carrier for those strings that do not contain *M, be* or *have*. Note the following:

(1) Come ðu hider ær tide us to þreagenne? 'Come you hither before times us to torment?'
(2) Wille ge beon beswungen on leornunge? 'Will you be whipped for the sake of learning?'
(3) Andswarast ðu swa þam bisceope? 'Do you thus answer the bishop?'
(4) Cweðe ge sceolun ðæs brydguman cnihtas wepan ða hwile ðe se brydguma mid hym byþ? 'Think you shall the bridegroom's friends weep while the bridegroom is with them?'
(5) Mage gyt drincan ðone calic ðe ic to drincenne hæbbe? 'Are you two able to drink the cup which I have to drink?'
(6) Mot ic him forgyfan? 'Must I him forgive?'
(7) Ongyte ge ealle ðas þing? 'Understand you all those things?'
(8) Eower lareow ne gylt he gafol? 'Your master, does he not pay taxes?'
(9) Wilt þu fon sumne hwæl? 'Will you catch a whale?'

In some instances an interrogative particle *hu* (Modern *how*) heads the string, not as a *manner* adverbial but simply as an interrogative signal:

(10) Hu ne forlæt he ða nigon and hund nigontig on ðam muntum? 'Will he not leave the ninety and nine on the mountain?'
(11) Hu ne doþ hæðene swa? 'Do not the heathen likewise?'

It appears that in some conjoined questions the characteristic permutation of *NP* subject and *Aux* or *V* affects only the first of the conjoined strings:

(12) Ne understande ge gyt, ne ge ne geþenceaþ ðæra fif hlafa and fif þusend manna? 'Do you not yet understand, nor do you not remember the five loaves and five thousand people?'

The following rule will provide the appropriate order for questions:

$$T_Q: Q\widehat{\ }NP(X)\ Y\ \# \Rightarrow (hu)\ Y\widehat{\ }NP(X)\ \#$$
where: $Y = \begin{cases} M \\ habb\text{-} \\ wes\text{-} \\ beo\text{-} \\ V \end{cases} \begin{matrix} [\pm Pres] \\ [\pm Ind] \end{matrix}$

The underlying and derived phrase markers on pages 200–201 illustrate the operation of T_Q.

(1)

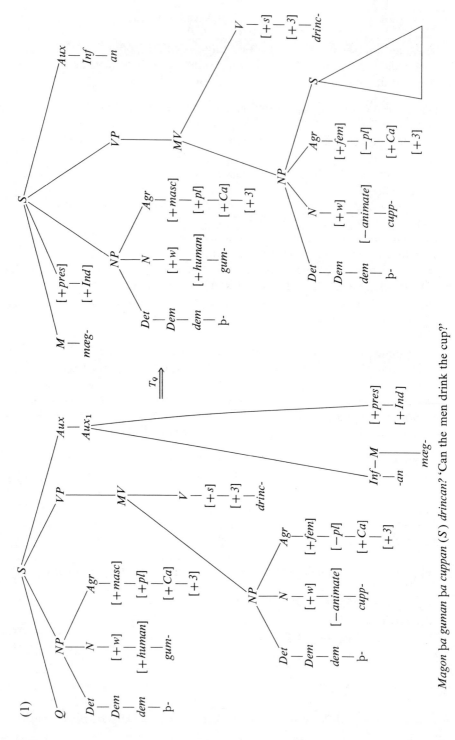

Magon þa guman þa cuppan (S) drincan? 'Can the men drink the cup?'

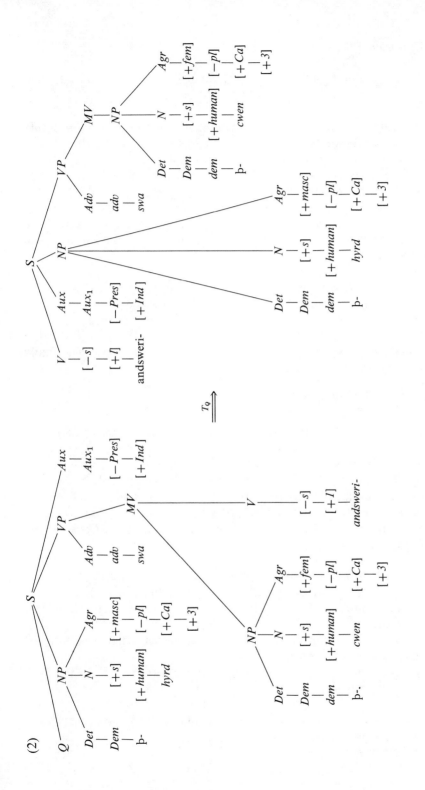

(2)

$T_Q \Longrightarrow$

Andswerede se hyrd swa þære cwene? 'Did the shepherd thus answer the woman?'

As in the case of T_Q, Old English T_{Neg} does *not* require the introduction of an empty form (*do*) to carry the obligatory features of *Aux:*

(1) Behealdaþ heofonan fuglas, forðam ðe hig *ne sawaþ, ne hig ne ripaþ, ne hig ne gadriaþ* on berne. 'Behold the fowls of heaven, for they do not sow, nor do they reap, nor do they gather into barns.'
(2) Soþ ic secge eow, *ne gemette* ic swa mycelne geleafan on Israhel. 'Truly I say to you, I have not found such great faith in Israel.'

Sentence (1) illustrates another aspect of Old English negation, namely, the frequent occurrence of multiple negatives (*ne hig ne* ripaþ, and so on). And the following:

(3) Hi *ne* namon *n*ane ele. 'They did not take (not) any oil.'
(4) *N*is *n*ænig swa snotor. 'There isn't (not) any so wise.'
(5) *Ne* hit *n*æfre *ne* gewurðe. '*Nor* it *not* ever *not* may happen.'

The basic negative transformation is quite uncomplex. We will simply introduce the negative particle *ne* before *V*:

$$T_{Neg}: \quad \text{Neg} \hat{\ } X \hat{\ } V \hat{\ } Y \Rightarrow X \hat{\ } \text{ne} \hat{\ } V \hat{\ } Y$$

This rule will have the effect of converting *Æðelingas þa sweord brecen hæfdon* 'Princes had broken the swords' to *Æðelingas þa sweord ne brecen hæfdon* 'Princes had not broken the swords.' However, the order of elements in the Old English negative sentence is at least very unusual, if not downright ungrammatical. Certain Old English adverbs together with the negative particle generally require permutation to the *head* of the construction, and they carry with them either *V* or *M* or appropriate elements of *Aux₂*. Consider the following examples:

(1) þa ferde to him Hierosolim—waru, and eal Iudea þeod. 'Then went out to him Jerusalem, and all the people of Judea.'
(2) þa andswarode se Hælend him and cwæþ. 'Then answered Jesus him and said.'
(3) þa wæs se Hælend gelæd fram Gaste on westen. 'Then was Jesus led away from the Spirit into a desert.'
(4) þa gebrohte se deofol hine on ða halgan ceastre. 'Then led the devil him into the holy city.'

This order, however, is not invariable, particularly when another adverbial occurs in the string:

(5) þa deofla soþlice hyne bædon. 'Then the devils truly him besought.'
(6) þa hyrdas witodlice flugon. 'Then the herdsmen indeed fled.'
(7) Hi þa sona forleton hyra nett and hyra fæder, and him fyligdon. 'They then immediately left their nets and their father and followed him.'

The interpretation of þa as the adverb *then* or as the conjunction *when* takes place in the base component. Once the transformation of þa (*adv*) moves it to the head of a string, the conjunction *may* be confused with the adverb where sentences (5) and (6) are compared with (8):

(8) þa se Hælend eode wið ða Galileiscan sæ. 'When Jesus walked along the Sea of Galilee.'

But for the most part, the two *are* distinguishable in the surface structure. þa, conjunction, is introduced at the head of an embedded clause by a T_{Rel}, and the order of the underlying string, $NP \frown VP \frown Aux$, is preserved. On the other hand, this order is disarranged by T_{adv}, so that compared with (8),

(9) þa eode se Hælend wið ða Galileiscan sæ

is to be interpreted '*Then* walked Jesus along the Sea of Galilee.'

Of additional interest is the fact that along with þa 'then,' þær 'there' may also undergo T_{adv_x}. You will note in the following that when þa and þær both occur in a clause, þær retains its untransformed position, but when it occurs without þa, the transformation applies:

(10) þa com þær ren, and mycele flod, and þær bleowun windas, and ahruron on ðæt hus. 'Then came *there* rain, and great floods, and *there* blew winds, and beat upon that house.'
(11) þær wæs soþlice unfeorran swyna heord manegra manna læswiende. '*There* was, indeed, not far off a herd of many hogs feeding.'
(12) And ðær wearþ geworden mice eorðbifung. 'And *there* occurred a great earthquake.'

It would be tempting to say that what we are observing here is the beginning of the now common "anticipatory *there*" construction ('there's a gentleman at the door'), if it were not for the fact that such a construction occurs in other Germanic languages as well as English. Even so, there can be little doubt that T_{adv_x} contributed to the development of anticipatory *there* and the word order which characterizes the construction. In Old English anticipatory þa/þær constructions existed along side such constructions as the following:

(13) Eornostlice seofon gebroðru wæron. 'And truly seven brothers were.'

At any rate, we assume that an Old English grammar requires at least an optional transformation which moves certain adverbs and the negative particle to the head of the string with attendant word-order modifications. Before we write such a T-rule, however, it is necessary to consider certain other features of word order. In general Old English syntax requires that where a string contains no conjoined or embedded strings, the last auxiliary verb in the string is permuted to a position somewhere before *MV*. For example:

(1)   Se cyning æðele beon mæg ⟹
(1a) Se cyning mæg æðele beon ⟹
(1b) Mæg se cyning æðele beon.

(2)   þa ges fleogende beon sceolde ⟹
(2a) þa ges sceolde fleogende beon ⟹
(2b) Sceolde þa ges fleogende beon.

(3)   Æðelingas þa sweord brecen hæfdon ⟹
(3a) Æðelingas hæfdon þa sweord brecen ⟹
(3b) Hæfdon æðelingas þa sweord brecen.

We can provide for such word order by the following rule:

$$T_{Aux}: \# \, NP \, (X) \, MV \, (Z) \, Y \, \# \Rightarrow \# \begin{Bmatrix} NP \, (X) \, Y^\frown MV \, (Z) \\ Y^\frown NP \, (X) \, MV \, (Z) \end{Bmatrix} \#$$

where: $Y = \begin{Bmatrix} M \\ habb\text{-} \\ wes\text{-} \\ beo \end{Bmatrix} \begin{matrix} [\pm Pres] \\ | \\ [\pm Ind] \end{matrix}$

A string *þa ges þa fleogende beon sceolde* produced by the base will have a (simplified) phrase marker:

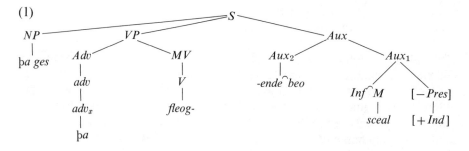

(1)

which by T_{Aux} will be transformed into either

(2)

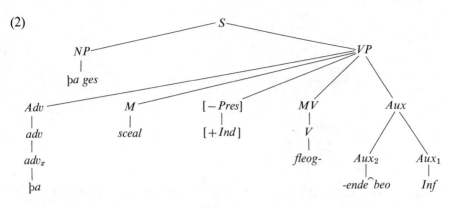

þa ges þa sceolde fleogende beon.

or

(3)

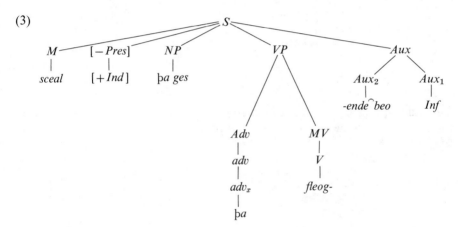

Sceolde þa ges þa fleogende beon.

The output of T$_{Aux}$ will be the input for the next rule:

T$_{adv_x}$:

    i. $\# \text{ NP}^\frown\text{adv}_x \begin{bmatrix} \text{Y (Z) V}^\frown\text{W} \\ \text{(Z) V}^\frown\text{Aux} \end{bmatrix} \# \Rightarrow$

    $\# \text{ adv}_x \begin{bmatrix} \text{Y}^\frown\text{NP (Z) V}^\frown\text{W} \\ \text{V}^\frown\text{Aux}^\frown\text{NP (Z)} \end{bmatrix} \#$

    ii. $\# \text{ Y}^\frown\text{NP}^\frown\text{adv}_x{}^\frown\text{Z} \# \Rightarrow \# \text{ adv}_x{}^\frown\text{Y}^\frown\text{NP}^\frown\text{Z} \#$

    where: Y = as above; W $\neq$ Y.

Phrase marker (2) above will be transformed by T$_{adv_x}$ i. into:

(4)

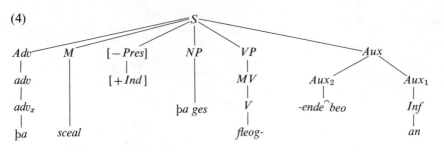

þa sceolde þa ges fleogende beon.

T_{adv_x} ii. will transform phrase marker (3) into a marker identical to (4). We will now rewrite T_{Neg} as follows:

T_{Neg}:   # Neg (X) Y (Z) # $\Rightarrow$ # (X) ne⌢Y (Z) #

where: $Y = \begin{Bmatrix} M \\ habb- \\ wes- \\ beo- \\ V \end{Bmatrix} \begin{matrix} [\pm Pres] \\ \mid \\ [\pm Ind] \end{matrix}$

$\quad X \neq Y$

This rule will have the effect of inserting the negative particle *ne* in front of the first verbal element in the string. Applied to (4) above, the output would be:

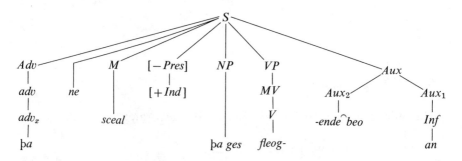

Consider now the problem of the imperative construction. In rule 11, $[+Aux_1]$ is expanded in c. to $[+\underset{\mid}{\underset{[+Imp]}{Pres}}]$. Rule 16 then presents us with a set of choices in the expansion of *N*. But if we choose anything but the feature [+human] for *N*, having already chosen [+Imp] in rule 11, the generation of our sentence will be blocked since only [+human] *N*'s can co-occur with [+Imp] (assuming that when a dog responds properly to 'come here!' he is responding to sets of vocal stimuli other than syntactic pattern). One means of solving the problem is to introduce into rule 16 a context restriction which will require that having chosen [+Imp] in rule 11, we will have to choose [+human] in the proper frame in rule 16. For example,

16. d. $[\pm s] \rightarrow \begin{cases} [+\text{animate}, +\text{human}]/\# \text{ Det } \_\_ \ldots [+\text{Imp}] \# \\ [\pm \text{animate}] \end{cases}$

Furthermore, rule 11 will create other problems. Specifically, it permits a string $X^\frown V^\frown Aux_2^\frown Inf - M^\frown [+Imp]$ which is impossible in Old English. That is to say, we cannot permit Aux_2 or $Inf - M$ to occur with [+Imp]. We *could* let the base generate such unwanted strings and then delete them by transformation, but in the long run this would be uneconomical. Another solution seems to be to add further context restrictions to rule 11:

11. b. $\begin{matrix} [\pm\text{Pres}] \\ | \\ [-\text{Ind}] \end{matrix} \rightarrow \begin{matrix} [\pm\text{Pres}] \\ | \\ [\pm\text{Sub}] \end{matrix}$

   c. $\begin{matrix} [\pm\text{Pres}] \\ | \\ [\pm\text{Sub}] \end{matrix} \rightarrow \begin{cases} \begin{matrix} [\pm\text{Pres}] \\ | \\ [+\text{Sub}] \end{matrix} \\ \\ \begin{matrix} [+\text{Pres}]/V \_\_ \# \\ | \\ [-\text{Sub}] \end{matrix} \end{cases}$

   d. $\begin{matrix} [+\text{Pres}] \\ | \\ [-\text{Sub}] \end{matrix} \rightarrow \begin{matrix} [+\text{Pres}] \\ | \\ [+\text{Imp}] \end{matrix}$

This set of rules permits the choice of [+Imp] only in those contexts where Aux_2 and/or $Inf - M$ do not occur.

A quite different approach to the imperative construction would be to generate an optional formative *Imp* in rule 1, just as we have generated an optional *Q* and an optional *Neg*. We would then be obliged to restrict the choices in rules 10 and 11:

10. $\text{Aux} \rightarrow \begin{pmatrix} Aux_2/X^\frown VP \_\_ \\ \text{where: } X \neq Imp \end{pmatrix} Aux_1$

11. $Aux_1 \rightarrow \begin{pmatrix} Inf - M/X^\frown VP \ (Aux_2) \_\_ \# \\ \text{where: } X \neq Imp \end{pmatrix} CS/V \ (Aux_2) \_\_ \#$

    a. $[+Aux_1] \rightarrow \begin{cases} [+\text{Pres}, +\text{Imp}]/Imp^\frown Y \_\_ \# \\ [\pm\text{Pres}, \pm\text{Ind}] \end{cases}$

These rules limit the choice of *Aux₂* and *Inf − M* to those strings that do *not* contain the formative *Imp,* and limit the choice of the *feature* [+Imp] to those strings that *do* contain it. Rule 16 would remain as revised above.

Regardless of which set of base rules for handling the imperative structure we decide on, certain syntactic transformations must apply. The base might produce the following (simplified) phrase marker:

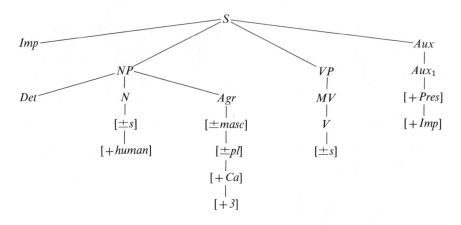

Consider now these examples of the Old English imperative:

(1) Hælaþ untrume, awecceaþ deade, clænsiaþ hreofle, drifaþ ut deoflu. 'Heal the sick, awaken the dead, cleanse the lepers, and drive out devils.'
(2) Asceacaþ ðæt dust of eowrum fotum. 'Shake the dust from your feet.'
(3) Gold-hordiaþ eow soþlice gold-hordas on heofenan. 'Therefore, hord up for yourselves gold-hords in heaven.'
(4) Lufiaþ eowre fynd. 'Love your enemies.'
(5) Eornustlice ne ondræde ge hig. 'Therefore, fear ye not them.'
(6) Cumaþ to me, ealle ðe swincaþ. 'Come to me, all who labor.'

First of all, choice of *Imp* (or [+Imp]) requires the permutation of *V* plus the appropriate *Aux* to a position preceding *NP*:

T_{Imp}:
        i. Imp⌢NP (X) V⌢Aux ⟹ V⌢Aux⌢NP (X)

Second, the occurrence of the feature [+Imp] will automatically generate a second person *Pro*-form to replace *NP*:

ii. $(X) V^\frown[+Imp]^\frown Det^\frown N^\frown Agr (Y) \Rightarrow$

$$[+\alpha]$$
$$[+3]$$

$(X) V^\frown[+Imp]^\frown Pro^\frown Agr (Y)$

$$[+\alpha]$$
$$[+2]$$

(where: $[+\alpha]$ = all of the features of *Agr* except $[+3]$.)

By T_{Imp} i., the preceding phrase marker will become:

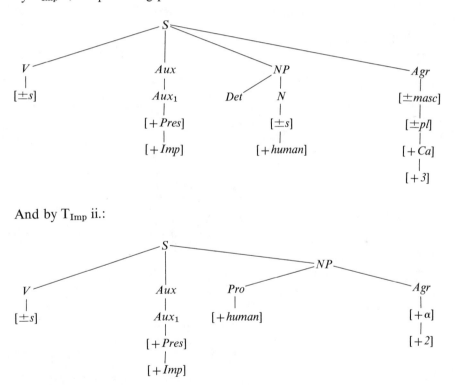

And by T_{Imp} ii.:

Since, as the examples indicate, the occurrence of *Pro* is optional, a later optional transformation (following T_{Agr}) will delete *NP*.

Finally, we will consider two low-level syntactic rules. The first assigns the proper specific case feature to the formative *Agr*.

T_{Ca}:

i. $X \widehat{\ } N_1 \widehat{\ } Agr \widehat{\ } N_2 \widehat{\ } Agr \widehat{\ } Y \Rightarrow X \widehat{\ } N_1 \widehat{\ } Agr \widehat{\ } N_2 \widehat{\ } Agr \widehat{\ } Y$

        $[+Ca]$ $[+Ca]$ $[+gen]$ $[+Ca]$

where: $N_1 <$ (is dominated by) Det

ii.

  a. $\# (X) Det \widehat{\ } N \widehat{\ } Agr \widehat{\ } Y \Rightarrow \# (X) Det \widehat{\ } N \widehat{\ } Agr \widehat{\ } Y$

                $[+Ca]$ $[+nom]$

where: $(X) \neq NP$

  b. $X \widehat{\ } Det \widehat{\ } N \widehat{\ } Agr \widehat{\ } Y \Rightarrow X \widehat{\ } Det \widehat{\ } N \widehat{\ } Agr \widehat{\ } Y$

              $[+Ca]$ $[+nom]$

where: $Det \widehat{\ } N \widehat{\ } Agr <$ Pred Nom

              $[+Ca]$

NOTE: This rule could have been omitted since $[+nom]$ will be carried along with other features in a later agreement rule.

iii. $X(Det \widehat{\ } N \widehat{\ } Agr) (Y) (Det \widehat{\ } N \widehat{\ } Agr) \begin{bmatrix} V_1 \\ V_2 \\ V_3 \end{bmatrix} Z \Rightarrow$

          $[+Ca]$ $[+Ca]$

$X (Det \widehat{\ } N \widehat{\ } Agr\ ) (Y) (Det \widehat{\ } N \widehat{\ } Agr\ ) \begin{bmatrix} V_1 \\ V_2 \\ V_3 \end{bmatrix} Z$

      $\begin{bmatrix} +acc \\ +dat \\ +dat \end{bmatrix}$ $\begin{bmatrix} +gen \\ +gen \\ +acc \end{bmatrix}$

where: $Det \widehat{\ } N \widehat{\ } Agr <$ MV

        $V_1 =$ bidd-, lett-, et al.

        $V_2 =$ forwyrn-, þanci-, gewani-, et al.

        $V_3 =$ gief-, oðþring-, sell-, et al.

NOTE: Old English, like a number of other Indo-European languages, contained transitive verbs some of which required two objects. Depending upon the type of semantic and syntactic relations involved, these objects had different cases, and different cases occurred with different verb subtypes. In the above rule it is the case that the first object is object of *person*, the second, object of *thing*. Thus, *bidd-* requires an accusative object of person and a genitive object of thing, *forwyrn-* a dative object of person and genitive object of thing, *gief-* a dative object of person and an accusative object of thing.

iv. $\text{X}^\frown\text{Det}^\frown\text{N}^\frown\underset{[+\text{Ca}]}{\text{Agr}}\ (\text{Y}) \begin{bmatrix} V_4 \\ V_5 \\ V_6 \end{bmatrix} \text{Z} \Rightarrow$

$\quad \text{X}^\frown\text{Det}^\frown\text{N}^\frown\underset{\begin{bmatrix}[+\text{gen}]\\ [+\text{dat}]\\ [+\text{acc}]\end{bmatrix}}{\text{Agr}}\ (\text{Y}) \begin{bmatrix} V_4 \\ V_5 \\ V_6 \end{bmatrix} \text{Z}$

where: $\text{Det}^\frown\text{N}^\frown\text{Agr} < \text{MV}, \nless \text{ (is not dominated by) Pred}$
$\qquad \text{Y} \neq \text{NP}$
$\qquad V_4 = \text{bid-, bruc-, help-, wen-, wundri-, et al.}$
$\qquad V_5 = \text{beorg-, dem-, andsweri-, et al.}$
$\qquad V_6 \neq V_4, V_5$

NOTE: Transitive verbs requiring a single object are classified according as their objects occur in the genitive, the dative, or the accusative cases. The latter subclass is by far the most numerous.

v. $\text{X} \begin{bmatrix} \text{prep}_1 \\ \text{prep}_2 \end{bmatrix} \text{Y}^\frown\underset{[+\text{Ca}]}{\text{Agr}}^\frown\text{Z} \Rightarrow \text{X} \begin{bmatrix} \text{prep}_1 \\ \text{prep}_2 \end{bmatrix} \text{Y} \overset{\text{Agr}}{\begin{bmatrix}[+\text{acc}]\\ [+\text{dat}]\end{bmatrix}} \text{Z}$

NOTE: Certain prepositions (see lexicon) require *accusative* case; others *dative* case.

Agreement rules in Old English must provide at least for the following: agreement (1) between noun subject and verb, (2) between noun subject and predicate noun, (3) between noun on the one hand and demonstrative and/or adjective on the other, (4) between noun and *Pro* substitute. This latter is automatic since the pronominalizing transformation will simply specify that $Det^\frown N^\frown Agr \Rightarrow Pro^\frown Agr$ (under certain syntactic conditions). The applicable features that characterize N and Agr will be retained on the right-hand side of the rule. Thus, any string

$$\text{Det}^\frown\text{N} \quad ^\frown \quad \text{Agr} \;\Rightarrow\; \text{Pro} \quad ^\frown \quad \text{Agr}$$

$$\begin{array}{cccc}
[+s] & [+\text{masc}] & [+\text{human}] & [+\text{masc}] \\
[+\text{human}] & [-\text{pl}] & & [-\text{pl}] \\
& [+\text{dat}] & & [+\text{dat}] \\
& [+3] & & [+3]
\end{array}$$

However, we will have to specify rules that assign agreement features in the cases of (1), (2), and (3).

T_{Agr}:

i. $(X) \; \text{\textcurrency}\,[+\text{Agr}]\,\text{\textcurrency} \; Y \; [\pm\text{Pres}] \; \text{\textcurrency}\,[+\text{Agr}]\,\text{\textcurrency} \; (Z) \Rightarrow$

$$\begin{array}{ccc}
\text{NP} & [\pm\text{Ind}] & \text{NP}
\end{array}$$

$(X) \; \text{\textcurrency}\,[+\text{Agr}]\,\text{\textcurrency} \; Y \; [\pm\text{Pres}] \; \text{\textcurrency}\,[+\text{Agr}]\,\text{\textcurrency} \; (Z)$

$$\begin{array}{ccc}
\text{NP} & [\pm\text{Ind}] & \text{NP} \\
& [+\text{Agr}] &
\end{array}$$

where: NP < S

$\text{\textcurrency}$ = one but not both elements so enclosed occurs.

$$Y = \left\{ \begin{array}{l} \text{M} \\ \text{wes-} \\ \text{habb-} \\ \text{beo-} \\ \text{V} \end{array} \right\}$$

This rule states that the agreement features of an *NP* dominated by *S* are attached to the *CS* of *Aux*$_1$. Only the relevant features of agreement, namely person and number, will be interpreted for the verb form in the morphographemic rules. Gender and case cannot be interpreted for verb forms.

ii. $(X) \, [+\text{Agr}] \, (Z) \, [+\text{Agr}] \, \text{beo}^\frown Y \Rightarrow$

$$\begin{array}{cc}
[+\alpha] & [+\beta] \\
\text{NP}_1 & \text{NP}_2
\end{array}$$

(X) [+Agr] (Z) [+Agr] beo⏜Y
$$\quad | \qquad\qquad |$$
$$\quad [+\alpha] \qquad\quad [+\alpha]$$
$$\quad NP_1 \qquad\qquad NP_2$$

where: $NP_1 < S$
$\qquad NP_2 < $ Pred Nom
$\qquad [+\alpha] = [\pm pl], [+Ca]$

Case and number features that characterize NP_1 are attached to NP_2.

iii. a. # Det⏜N⏜[+Agr] (X) Adj⏜Y # $\Rightarrow$
$$\qquad\qquad\quad | $$
$$\qquad\qquad\quad [+\alpha]$$
$$\quad \# \text{ Det⏜N⏜[+Agr] (X) Adj⏜[+Agr]⏜Y } \#$$
$$\qquad\qquad | \qquad\qquad\qquad |$$
$$\qquad\qquad [+\alpha] \qquad\qquad\quad [+\alpha]$$

where: Pred < MV

Adjective agreement is something of a problem. The adjective is introduced as an optional rewrite of *Pred* (see rule 4), and its agreement features
must be identical with those of the subject *NP*:

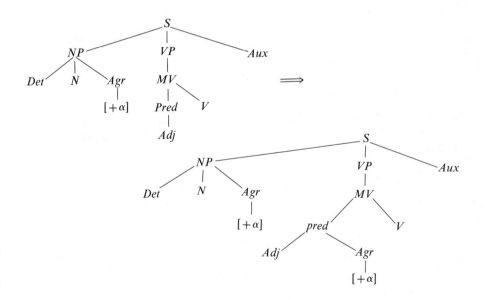

If the *S* in question is dominated by an *NP*, the *Ca* of its *N* may or may *not* be the same as that of the *N* of the dominating *NP*, for example,

1. The man⌢Agr (The man⌢Agr is good⌢Agr)

$$[+Ca] \qquad [+Ca] \qquad [+Ca]$$

$$[+Nom] \qquad [+Nom] \quad [+Nom]$$

went home.

2. I saw the man⌢Agr (The man⌢Agr is good⌢Agr)

$$[+Ca] \qquad [+Ca] \qquad [+Ca]$$

$$[+Acc] \qquad [+Nom] \quad [+Nom]$$

In 1, all three agreement features are characterized by *nominative* case. In 2, however, the object of the main sentence contains the case feature *accusative*, while the agreement features of the embedded sentence are characterized by *nominative* case. When *relativization* and *adjectivization* transformations have been performed, and *adjective* is now a constituent of the *NP* of the main sentence, case features for noun and adjective will be different:

3. I saw the man⌢Agr⌢good⌢Agr

$$[+Ca] \qquad [+Ca]$$

$$[+Acc] \quad [+Nom]$$

Therefore, we need an additional rule which will make the case features of *Agr* conform. We can, with the same rule, take care of agreement features for *dem:*

iv. X⌢dem⌢N⌢[+Agr] (Adj⌢[+Agr]) Y ⟹

$$[+\alpha] \qquad\qquad [\pm\alpha]$$

X⌢dem⌢[+Agr]⌢N⌢[+Agr] (Adj⌢[+Agr]) Y

$$[+\alpha] \qquad\quad [+\alpha] \qquad\qquad [+\alpha]$$

where: Pred < NP

Thus:

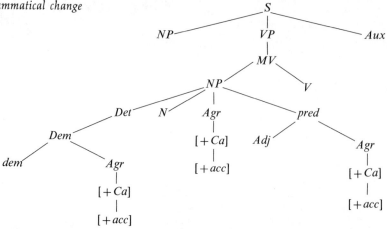

Consider the derived phrase marker on page 192. Applying T_{Ca} to this phrase marker we have these results:

(1) by T_{Ca} i.,

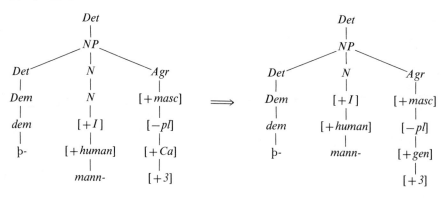

(2) by T_{Ca} ii.,

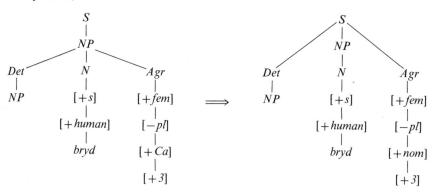

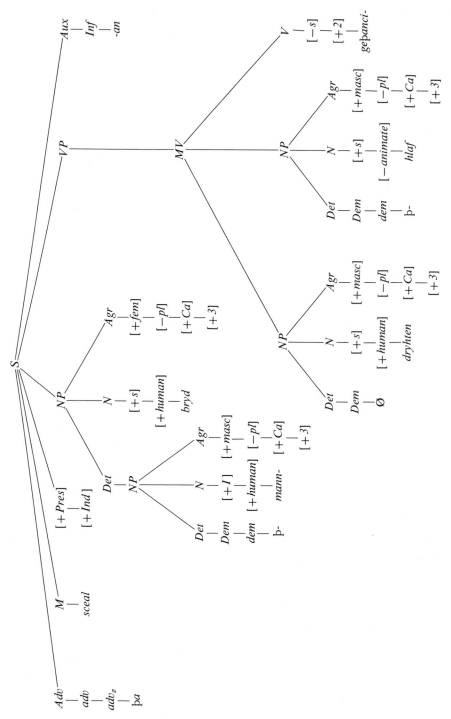

217

(3) by T_Ca iii.,

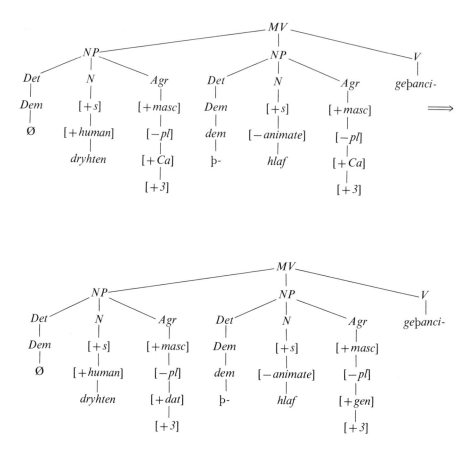

Case assignments have now been made for all *NP*'s in the phrase marker.

Application of T_Agr yields the results shown on pages 219–220. The string derived by case and agreement transformations would be this:

þa⌢sceal⌢[+Pres]⌢þ-⌢   Agr   ⌢   mann-   ⌢   Agr   ⌢   bryd   ⌢   Agr
              [+Ind]   [+masc]   [+I]   [+masc]   [+s]   [+fem]
              [−pl]   [−pl]   [+human]   [−pl]   [+human]   [−pl]
              [+3]   [+gen]   [+gen]   [+nom]
                          [+3]   [+3]   [+3]

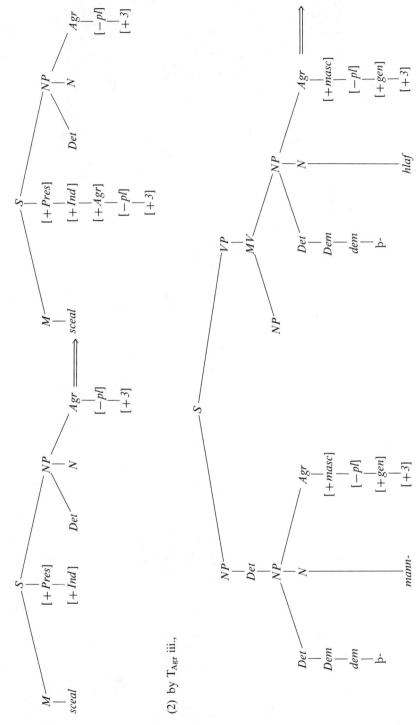

(1) by T_{Agr} i.,

(2) by T_{Agr} iii.,

219

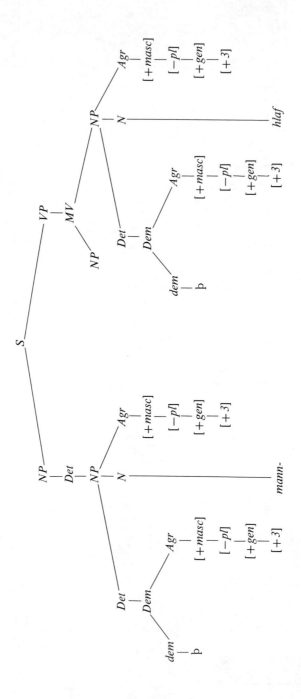

dryhten ⁀ Agr ⁀þ-⁀ Agr ⁀ hlaf ⁀ Agr ⁀geþanci⁀an

```
dryhten ^    Agr  ^þ-^  Agr   ^    hlaf   ^   Agr  ^geþanci^an
  |           |          |           |          |
[+s]      [+masc]    [+masc]       [+s]      [+masc]
  |           |          |           |          |
[+human]   [−pl]      [−pl]    [−animate]     [−pl]
            |          |                       |
          [+dat]     [+gen]                  [+gen]
            |          |                       |
          [+3]       [+3]                     [+3]
```

GLOSSARY

acealdi- to become cold
agylt- to offend, sin, do wrong
andsweri- to answer
arfæstlice piously
aris- to arise, get up, spring from, originate
asci- to ask, inquire, demand, call, summon, discover
ass- he-ass

æftan from behind, behind, in the rear
æfter along, behind, following, throughout, during, according to
ær before
æt near, by, in, on, upon, with, before, next to, into
æðeling nobleman, chief, prince

bac- to bake
ban- killer, slayer, murderer
bearn child, son, offspring, issue
belif- to be left over
benæm- to take away, deprive of, rob of
beo- be, exist, become, happen
beorg- to save, deliver, protect, defend, spare
ber- to carry, bring, take away, produce, endure, sustain
besmit- to soil, pollute, dishonor
betweonan between, among, amid
bi near, in, on, with, along, at, by, before, because of, through
bid- to stay, continue, live, remain, delay
bidd- to ask, entreat, pray, order, require
bind- to tie, bind, fasten, restrain
blaw- to blow, breathe

bliþe   joyfully, cheerfully, willingly, graciously
bliðe   joyous, cheerful, well-disposed
brec-   to break, shatter, burst, tear, injure, destroy
brim   surf, flood, sea, water
brycg   bridge
bryd   bride, young woman, betrothed
bruc-   to use, enjoy, possess, partake of
burn-   brook, stream
butan   out of, outside of, off, except, without, all but

ceac-   cheek, jawbone, jaw
cene-   bold, brave, fierce, powerful, clever
ceos-   to choose, seek out, decide, test, approve
cyning   king, ruler
cleof-   to cleave, split, separate
cnap-   child, youth, servant
cnaw-   to know, perceive, declare, acknowledge
cneo   knee
creop-   to creep, crawl
cum-   to come, arrive, assemble, approach, attain, go
cunn-   to know how to, have power to, be acquainted with
cupp-   cup
cwen   woman, wife, empress, queen, princess

dem-   to judge, determine, decide, decree, condemn
dogg-   dog
dreog-   to do, work, perform, conduct, take part in, endure, suffer, tolerate
dreop-   to drop, drip
dryhten   ruler, king, lord, prince
drinc-   to drink, engulf; to be entertained
duc-   duck
duguð   noble retainers, nobles, army, strength, excellence

eag-   eye
ear-   'ear' of corn
earm   poor, wretched, pitiful, miserable
eaþe   easy, smooth, agreeable
eaxl   shoulder
ecg   point, weapon, sword, battle-axe
eorþ-   ground, soil, earth, country, district

far-   to set forth, go, travel, suffer, happen
fæder   father
fæstni-   to fasten, fix, secure, confirm, betroth, secure for
feoh   cattle, herd, goods, property, riches
feorr   far, remote, distant, far away, further, besides
fys-   to impel, send, drive away, put to flight
fleog-   to flee, fly; to take flight
fleot-   to float, drift, flow, swim, sail
fo-   to take, grasp, seize, capture, receive, encounter
fol-   colt
folc   people, nation, tribe, troop, army
fold-   earth, ground, soil, land, region
fore   before, in the presence of, for the sake of, by reason of
forwyrn-   to hinder, prohibit, prevent, oppose, deny
fram   from, by, of, about, concerning, as a result of
fugol   bird, fowl

gang-   come, go, proceed, move, walk, depart, happen, occupy
geardagum   days of yore, former times, lifetime
gefeo-   to be glad, rejoice, exult
gefer-   companion, comrade
geond   throughout, through, over, up to, during
geong   young, youthful, recent, new, fresh
geþanci-   to thank
geþyldum   patiently
gewit-   to go, depart
gief-   to give, bestow, allot, devote, commit
glæd   bright, shining, brilliant, cheerful, joyous
glid-   to glide, slip
glof   glove
god   virtuous, desirable, valid, suitable, good
greot-   to cry, lament, weep
grip-   to assail, seek to hold, seize, take
gum-   man, lord, hero

habb-   possess, own, retain, cherish, esteem, obtain
har-   hare
hati-   to treat as an enemy; to hate
heafod   head, source, chief, leader
heah   tall, lofty, important, proud, esteemed
heald-   to hold, grasp, retain, inhabit, guard, defend, support

heard   harsh, severe, cruel, strong, intense, hardy, bold
help-   to help, support
heofon   sky, heaven
hycg-   to think, consider, meditate, study, determine
hyrd   herd, flock
hyrd-   shepherd, herdsman, guardian, keeper
hlaf   loaf, cake, bread, food
hleap-   to leap, run, go, jump, dance, spring
hliehh-   to laugh, laugh at, deride
hlynn-   to make a noise, shout, roar
hrin-   to touch, take hold of, reach, seize, strike
hweorf-   to turn, change, wonder about, turn back, turn from

in   into, upon, at, to, among, in, about, towards
yc-   toad, frog
yfel   bad, evil, wicked, wretched
yfle   evilly, wrongly, miserably
ymbe   around, about, at, upon, near, along, concerning

land   earth, territory, realm, province, property
lang   long, tall
lati-   to be slow, indolent; to linger, delay
lær-   to teach, instruct, advise, urge, preach
leof   dear, valued, pleasant, agreeable
lett-   to hinder, impede, delay, oppress
libb-   to live, experience, be, exist
licg-   to remain, be situated, lie down, yield, fail
lyst-   to please, cause pleasure or desire
lytel   little, unimportant, short, not much

mag-   to be able, have permission, avail, be strong
mann-   person, man, mankind, hero, servant
mearh   horse, steed
micel   great, intense, much, many
mid   with, in company with, through, by means of, among
myht   might, strength, power, authority, ability
mon-   moon
mot-   to be allowed, have opportunity to, be compelled to
moþþ-   moth

nædr-   adder, snake, serpent
neah   near, close to, according to

neot- to use, enjoy, employ
nim- take, undertake, accept, hold, catch, carry off, occupy, suffer, tolerate
nyd need

of from, out of, among, by, made of, belonging to
ofer beyond, above, upon, in, across, against, contrary to
oft often, frequently
on upon, onto, up to, in, within, during, at, about, according to
ongean towards, against, opposite to, in exchange for
oðþring- to deprive of

ræd- advise, persuade, consult, discuss, plot, read, guide
rice strong, powerful, great, rich
rinn- to run, flow, blend
rod cross, gallows

sawol soul, life, spirit
scac- to shake, move quickly, brandish, flee, glide
sceap sheep
sceort short, brief
scip ship
scul- to have to, be obliged to, must, ought to
secg- to say, speak, inform, declare, tell, explain
sell- to give, furnish, lend, give up, betray, hide
seo- to see, look, behold, observe, know, visit, experience
sinc- to sink, subside, become submerged
sle- to strike, beat, dash, break, rush, sting
sniþ- to cut, cut off, hew, slay, kill, reap
sona directly, immediately, at once
sorg sorrow, pain, grief, trouble, anxiety
soþe truly, accurately, rightly
spow- to succeed, thrive, profit, avail
spring- to jump, leap, burst forth, spread, grow
stan stone
stand- to occupy a place, remain, oppose, be present, stand
stel- to steal, rob
steorf- to die
strang strong, powerful, bold, brave, resolute, severe
suþan from the south
swæt- to sweat, labor, bleed, oppress
swef- to sleep, rest, slumber

sweord   sword

teo-   to pull, tug, draw, row, entice, educate, produce
ter-   to tear
tid   time, period, season, feast-day
tidum   at times, occasionally
to   to, into, according to, at, for

þ-   the, that
þa   then, at that time
þær   there, thither, yonder, where
þinc-   to appear, seem
þrot   throat
þurh   through, during, by means of, because of, for the sake of

utan   from outside, without

waci-   to be awake, keep awake, watch
wad-   to go, move, stride, advance
wasc-   to wash, cleanse
wæcc-   to watch
wæter   water, sea
weax-   to grow, increase, be fruitful, flourish
wef-   to weave, devise, arrange
wen-   to imagine, believe, think, expect, hope, wonder
weorp-   to throw, cast, expel, drive away, open
wergi-   to weary, exhaust
wifman-   woman
will-   to be willing; to wish, desire, be about to
witeg-   wise man, prophet, soothsayer
wið   by, near, against, beside, at, through, in return for
wyrd   fate, chance, fortune, destiny, providence
wræþ-   to anger, get angry, resist violently

EXERCISES

1. Using the rules of the base component, produce phrase markers underlying the following types of sentences:

   a. an impersonal verb construction.
   b. a transitive sentence with two objects.

c. a transitive sentence with one object.
d. an intransitive sentence.
e. a sentence containing *Aux₁* and *Aux₂*.
f. a sentence containing *Aux₂* and *CS* ([±Pres, ±Ind]).
g. a sentence containing *Pred*.
h. a sentence containing *PP*.
i. a sentence containing an embedded relative construction.
j. a transitive sentence containing a human *strong* subject noun and an inanimate *weak* object noun.

2. Add *Q* to the phrase markers underlying b, c, d, and e above, and using T$_Q$ construct new phrase markers showing the question transformation.
3. Add *Neg* and proceed as in 2.
4. Assign the appropriate case to nouns in your phrase markers for b, c, e, and h according to T$_{Ca}$.
5. Assign the appropriate agreement features to the appropriate verb form in b, c, d, e, f, and g according to T$_{Agr}$i.
6. Select from the lexicon a base form which fits the sets of features given below, and using the morphographemic rules in Appendix II, give that base form its proper final shape.

a. N $^\frown$[+masc]
   [+s]   [+pl]
           [+dat]

b. N $^\frown$[+fem]
   [+s]   [−pl]
           [+gen]

c. N $^\frown$[+neut]
   [+w]   [−pl]
           [+acc]

d. V $^\frown$[+Pres]
   [+s] [+Ind]
           [−pl]
           [+2]

e. V $^\frown$[+Pres]
   [+s] [+Sub]
           [−pl]

f. V $^\frown$[+Imp]
   [+s]   [+pl]

g. V $^\frown$[−Pres]
   [+s] [+Ind]
   [+2]   [−pl]
           [+2]

h. V $^\frown$[−Pres]
   [+s] [+Sub]
   [+1]   [+pl]

i. V $^\frown$−en
   [+s]
   [+5]

j. V $^\frown$[+Pres]
   [−s] [+Ind]
   [+1]   [+pl]

k. dem⌢ Agr   ⌢Adj⌢ Agr
       | |
    [+masc]   [+α]
     | (same features as for *dem*)
    [−pl]
     |
    [+acc]

l. dem⌢ Agr   ⌢Adj⌢ Agr
     | |
    [+fem]   [+α]
     |
    [−pl]
     |
    [+dat]

m. dem⌢ Agr   ⌢Adj⌢ Agr
     | |
    [+pl]   [+α]
     |
    [+gen]

n. Adj⌢ Agr
       |
    [+neut]
     |
    [−pl]
     |
    [+acc]

o. Adj⌢ Agr
       |
    [+fem]
     |
    [+pl]
     |
    [+nom]

SOME ADDITIONAL REMARKS ON OLD ENGLISH

Stem-vowel replacement in Old English nouns

A small class of nouns in Old English is characterized by the process of *stem-vowel replacement*. A number of these remain in Modern English as so-called "irregular" nouns: *foot/feet, man/men, goose/geese, mouse/mice,* and the like. The paradigm for Old English *fot* is as follows:

	singular	*plural*
nominative and accusative	fot	fet
genitive	fotes	fota
dative	fet	fotum

The altered vowel of the dative singular and nominative-accusative plural is the result of *vowel harmony,* more specifically *i-umlaut.* What this means is that at some earlier point in the development of Old English case and number forms, the dative singular and the nominative-accusative plural were indicated by an inflectional element containing a high, front, spread vowel. One may postulate for the nominative plural a form **foti.* In the course of time, the mid, *back, rounded* vowel of the stem was modified by the inflec-

---

* An asterisk before a phrase or sentence indicates that the construction is ungrammatical.

tional vowel to a mid, *front, spread* vowel. At some pre-Old English stage of development we might expect to find the form **feti*. In such a hypothetical form the inflectional ending is now a *redundant* grammatical signal, for its function has been taken over by the altered stem vowel. By the time of our earliest Old English records the inflectional element has been lost, leaving only stem-vowel replacement to signal grammatical function.

A number of nouns belonging to this class in Old English have since shifted into the much larger class of -(*e*)*s* plurals: Old English *boc* (sg)/*bec* (pl) ⇒ Modern English *book/books;* Old English *cu* (sg)/*cy* (pl) ⇒ Modern English *cow/cows* (the poetic-archaic *kine* goes back to an Old English genitive plural *cyna*); Old English *gat* (sg)/*gæt/get* (pl) ⇒ Modern English *goat/goats.* Such innovations in class membership are called *analogic change,* a process by which a given structure is reshaped to conform to a second structure whose frequency of occurrence is ordinarily much higher than that of the first.

More on case functions

The genitive case in Old English expressed a wide variety of grammatical relationships.

(1) subjective relationship: *Grendles* [gen] *dæda* 'Grendel's deeds.'
(2) possessive relationship: *ne wæs þæt forma sið þæt he Hroþgares* [gen] *ham gesohte* 'nor was that the first time that he Hrothgar's home sought.'
(3) defining relationship: *ða of wealle geseah weard Scildinga* [gen] 'then from the wall he saw the guardian of the Scyldings. . . .'
(4) partitive relationship: *He com mid feower hunde scipa* [gen] 'He came with four hundred [of] ships.'
(5) adverbial relationship: *dæges ond nihtes* 'by day and by night'; *wordes oððe dæde* 'by word or deed.'

In addition to the relationships indicated in the model Old English grammar, the dative case frequently specified these:

(1) instrumentality: *hondum* [dat] *gebroden* 'with/by hands woven (hand-woven)'; *wundum werig* 'with wounds weary.'
(2) accompaniment: *Ond þa geascode he þone cyning lytle werode* [dat] 'And then he discovered the king with a little band of retainers.'
(3) adverbial: *se þe of flanbogan fyrenum* [dat] *sceote* 'he who with bow-arrow criminally shoots'; *scop hwilum* [dat] *sang hador on Heorote* 'the scop at times sang clear-voiced in Heorot.'

Special uses of the past participle and the infinitive

In the verb phrase a form of agreement sometimes occurred that is quite strange to Modern English. The verb *habb-* 'to have, hold, possess' could occur not as an auxiliary but as a *full* verb followed by a past participle. In such cases the participle, which was declinable, agreed with the object of *habb-: oþþe hie hine* [acc] *ofslægenne* [acc] *hæfdon* 'until they held him slain.' So, too, the present participle: *ac he gefeng hraðe forman siðe slæpendne* [acc] *rinc* 'but he seized quickly at the first opportunity a sleeping warrior.' Such agreement was by no means consistently adhered to in Old English and quickly fell into disuse since the grammatical information it provided was unnecessary.

The Old English infinitive was also declinable: *do hit us to witanne* [acc] 'make it us to know,' in which the infinitive agrees with the accusative *us*. The infinitive was sometimes used to express the passive: *Heht þa eorla hleo eahta mearas fæted hleore on flet teon* [Inf] 'Then the protector of earls commanded eight horses with gold-decorated bridles to be led into the hall.' The Old English infinitive often occurred where Modern English would require a present participle: *He com secean* [Inf] 'He came seeking'; *geseah blacne leoman . . . scinan* [Inf] 'he saw a bright light . . . shining.'

The comparative particle

The comparative particle *than* must originally have been a temporal adverb (Old English *þonne, þanne*) expressing a sequential time relationship. That this was so can be seen in the development of the expression *rather than,* as 'I would rather eat than sleep.' Old English *raðe* (or *hraðe*) was a time adverb meaning 'quickly,' 'hastily,' 'promptly,' 'immediately,' 'soon.': *ac he gefeng hraðe forman siðe slæpendne rinc* 'but he seized quickly at the first opportunity a sleeping warrior.' In an early stage of development of comparative constructions the implication must have been that one activity was performed 'sooner,' and *then* another activity performed later. So that an early Old English construction comparable to our 'I would rather eat than sleep' would have implied that 'I will eat first and sleep later' or 'I will eat first, *then* sleep.' Notice that the adverb *soon* continues to be used in comparative constructions with *than* with a clear time implication: 'I would sooner die than be dishonest.' Notice, too, the semantically equivalent sentence 'I would die *before* I would be dishonest.' By the time of recorded Old English, the structure of temporal comparisons with *þanne, þonne* had been extended to non-temporal situations. However, the fact that temporal implications clung to the comparative particle long after this extension had taken place undoubtedly accounts in large part for the fact that the forms *than* and *then* are not consistently distinguished in comparative constructions until the early Modern English period. In an early Middle English work, *The Poema Morale* (c. 1170), we find in the first line, "Ich æm elder þen ich wes a wintre and a lore," but in the second, "Ic wælde more þanne ic dude, mi wit ah to ben more." Some two hundred years later in *Sir Gawayn & þe Grene Knyȝt* is found: "As growe grene as þe gres and grener hit semed, þen grene aumayl on gold glowande bryȝter," and "If he hem stowned vpon fyrst, stiller were þanne Alle þe heredmen in halle."

The changing character of Old English

We conclude our consideration of Old English by commenting briefly on the extent to which the grammatical devices of periphrasis and word order were already operative. As the inflectional system became less efficacious, the systems of periphrasis and word order became much more significant; and as these systems assumed an ever-increasing role in defining grammatical relationships, the inflectional system deteriorated even more. As a result of this circular process the grammatical character of the language was completely reshaped. How does one account for this change? The truth of the matter is that one does not—at least, not in any very precise way. There were undoubtedly a great many contributing factors, both linguistic and cultural, operating on the language from prehistoric times. One of the most frequently cited is the Germanic accent shift. To illustrate, in the parent language, Indo-European, the inflectional syllable in some word classes and in some forms of these classes received the primary stress accent, and this system of accent was maintained in the non-Germanic daughter languages. Thus, Sanskrit has the following distribution of the accent in the principal parts of the verb:

vártāmi   vavárta   vavrtimá   vartāná

In pre-Germanic, for the same verb we expect the following:

*wérθan   wárθi   wurðumí   wurðaná

But in the earliest recorded Germanic language, Gothic, we find:

wáirþan   wárþ   waúrþum   waúrþans

and in Old English:

weórþan   weárþ   wúrdon   wórden

What has happened is that the principle accent has, in the Germanic languages, shifted from inflectional syllable to root syllable, presumably weakening the articulation of the inflectional element. No doubt this Germanic innovation does account for a certain amount of change in the character of the Germanic inflectional system. It does not account for the fact that this system has deteriorated to a much greater degree in English than it has in any of the other Germanic languages. To explain this fact, it is probably necessary to look to the cultural milieu of the Germanic tribes in Britain, their contact with non-Germanic speaking peoples, and especially to the effects of the Scandinavian and Norman invasions on the development of English. We will not pursue the question here.

It is already apparent in late Old English that certain grammatical functions were not being adequately signaled by the inflectional system alone, so that periphrasis and word order were more and more being called upon to make up the deficiency. The prepositional system was fairly well developed and was assuming some of the functions of case markings. For instance, with the accusative: *Se wuldorcyning on middangeard com* 'the glory-king *to* earth came'; *Hi ymb þeodenstol* [acc] *þringaþ* 'They about the hord-stool throng'; *þa tacna þe he worhte ofer þa untruman* [acc] *men* 'the tokens (marvels) that he wrought *over* the infirm men.' With the dative: *Him* [dat] *on bearme* [dat] *læg madma mænigo* '(for) him *on* breast (on his breast) (they) put of treasures many (many treasures)'; *Wulfgar maþelode to his winedrihtne* [dat] 'Wulfgar spoke *to* his friend-lord'; *erede mid horsum* [dat] 'plowed *with* horses'; *him* [dat] *cenlice wið feaht mid lytlum werode* [dat] 'him boldly against he fought with a small band.' In this last sentence we should call particular attention to the positions occupied by *wið* and *mid. Mid* occupies the expected prenominal position, while *wið* not only does not precede the noun, but is separated from it by the adverb *cenlice.* Such a position is not at all uncommon in Old English: *ond þa gatu him* [dat] *to belocen hæfdon* 'and the gates him against locked (they) had'; *oþ him mara fultum to com* 'until them more help to came.' What we observe here is a kind of 'embedded' history of the post Indo-European prepositional system. You will notice that in the examples above, the preposition is 'preposed' before the verb, rather than before the noun. The suggestion is that at some point in their prehistory what we now call prepositions in a prenoun position were particles attached to verbs, their function being to alter in some way the force or meaning of the verb. In other words, they were adverbial particles. These gradually become detachable, and in transitive situations begin to assume an ambiguous syntactic relationship, being in part related to their verbs, in part related to the noun objects of the verbs. This ambiguous relationship seems still to be maintained in the examples of *wið* and *to* above, and from the point of view of one kind of grammatical model characterizes certain Modern English constructions. Consider the interesting ambiguity in the following: "He is working on the stage," which may be considered an answer either to the question, "What is he working on?" or the question "Where is he working?" A number of these particles have, of course, taken up a prenoun position and are considered to be more immediately related to the noun than to the verb, thus constituting what we consider a prepositional phrase.

In addition to the development of an extremely complex prepositional system, the refinement and stabilization of word-order patterns constitutes one of the most significant aspects of the history of English syntax. In Chapter 1 we noted some of the differences between the syntax of Alfred's time and that of Modern English. Some additional illustrations may be useful here.

(1) *Her hæþne men ærest on Sceapige ofer winter sætun.* 'Here (in this year) heathen men first in Sheppey during winter settled.' The basic order pattern here is *NP VP*, the order in the *VP* being *Adv MV*. All adverbial modifiers precede the verb.

(2) *Ond þa Deniscan ahton wælstowe gewald.* 'And the Danes gained the slaughter place's (battlefield's) mastery.' The order is what we would expect in Modern English: *NP Aux V NP*.

(3) *þa gemette hie Aeþelwulf aldorman on Englafelda, ond him þær wiþ gefeaht ond sige nam.* 'Then met them Aethelwolf the alderman on Englefield, and them there against fought and victory took.' Notice particularly the position of the verb in the first clause as contrasted with the verbs in the conjoined clauses.

(4) *Ond Hæstenes wif ond his suna twegen mon brohte to þæm cyninge; ond he hie him eft ageaf.* 'And Hesten's wife and his two sons someone brought to the king; and he them (to) him back gave.'

These sentences demonstrate the considerable flexibility of Old English word-order patterns. But this flexibility was dependent upon a reasonably efficient inflectional system, and we have already commented upon the extent to which this system had been losing its effectiveness during the Old English period. Note that in sentence (3) only the verb forms, which are both singular, indicate the proper subject of the sentence. Both the form *Aethelwulf* and the form *hie* could be either *nominative* or *accusative;* therefore, they provide no information about their grammatical relationships in the sentence. One can envision a number of situations in which the determination of subject and object of the verb, apart from word-order signals, would depend entirely on the interpretation of context. During the time when flexible word order was combined with a rapid deterioration of inflectional efficacy the grammatical system of Old English was extremely unstable. And instability requires change. The working out of extensive changes in the English grammatical system took place for the most part during the four hundred years or so which we call the Middle English period. It is to this period that we now turn our attention.

5. Grammatical change continued

Introduction

We have now discussed at some length two model grammars, one for Modern English and one for Old English. These represent, obviously, opposite ends of our historical spectrum. In this section our primary concern will be to plot the course of certain of the grammatical developments that led from one model to the other. We will be less concerned here than previously with the presentation of a grammatical model, although we will suggest ways in which the Old English rules must be modified to account for late Middle English grammatical structures.

5.10 Some Morphographemic Changes[1]

Noun Forms

During the four hundred years between the end of the tenth and the end of the fourteenth centuries, a number of changes took place in the character of the English noun. Grammatical gender, for instance, was lost in the North of England soon after the tenth century, in the Midlands by the end of the eleventh, and in the South during the twelfth and thirteenth centuries. In the dialect of Kent there are signs of its persistence as late as the middle of the fourteenth century. Because of the highly synthetic character of the Old English inflectional system, one cannot really speak of the loss of grammatical gender apart from the loss of certain other distinctive features that in the Old English grammar characterize agreement (*Agr*). Consider, for example, the Old and Middle English paradigms for the strong masculine and feminine nouns *end-* and *tal-*:

	Old English				*Middle English*	
	singular	*plural*			*singular*	*plural*
nominative,				*nominative,*		
accusative	ende	endas		*accusative,*		
genitive	endes	enda		*dative*	ende	endes
dative	ende	endum		*genitive*	endes	endes
nominative	talu	tala		*nominative,*		
accusative	tale	tala		*accusative,*		
genitive	tale	tala, -ena		*dative*	tale	tales
dative	tale	talum		*genitive*	tales	tales

In Old English the two noun types are differentiated in the *nominative singular,* the *genitive singular,* the *nominative-accusative plural,* and in one variant of the *genitive plural* of *tal-*. In Middle English there is no differentiation at all. And in part this loss of distinction between masculine and feminine nouns is the result of a leveling of case distinction. Not only is there no reason to speak of grammatical gender distinction in Middle English, there is no reason to speak of four cases either.

Verb Forms

Throughout the Middle English period and on into early Modern English, a considerable amount of migration of verbs from strong to weak and from one

---

[1] See Appendix III for rules specifying some morphographemic transformations for Middle English nouns, verbs, and personal pronouns.

class of strong verbs to another took place. Old English first class strong verb *scinan* has the normal strong development *shoon* for the past tense in Chaucer, but along side this strong form occurs the weak form *shynede*. With the development of alternate forms for the past tense comes a tendency toward syntactic differentiation, so that in Modern English the old strong form is intransitive, 'The sun shone yesterday,' while the new weak form is transitive, 'He shined his shoes yesterday.' Old English first class strong *sican* 'to sigh' had developed a weak past *siʒte* by the fourteenth century. Old English second class strong *creopan, creap* (third singular past), *crupon* (third plural past), *cropen* (past participle) had become in Chaucer *crepe, crepte* (third singular past *weak*), *crepten* (third plural past *weak*), *cropen* (strong)/*crepte* (weak). Chaucer has the strong forms *clymbe, clamb/clomb, clamben/clomben,* but weak past forms occurred elsewhere before the fifteenth century. One manuscript of *Cursor Mundi* has *He clamb mont synai* (early fourteenth century); a somewhat later manuscript has *He clymed on mont synay.* For the Old English third class strong verb *cearf* (third singular past), Chaucer has *karf,* but Sir Thomas Malory in the next century has both strong *carf* and weak *kerved.* Old English *beornan, bearn, burnon, burnen* occurs in Chaucer *brenne, brente, brenden/ybrent,* the weak past and past participle borrowed from, or influenced by, Old Norse *brenda.* The modern stem *burn* does not appear before the middle of the fifteenth century.

Occasionally, the opposite tendency, weak to strong, occurs. For instance, Old English weak *werian, werede, weredon, wered* remains weak in Chaucer, but becomes strong during the fifteenth century by analogy with *bear* and *tear.* Thus, Modern English has *wear, wore, worn.* When a small boy says, "I weared my raincoat yesterday," he is etymologically quite correct. Old English weak *cwacian* is in Chaucer *quake,* present, strong *quook/quoke* in the past, and weak participle *quaked.* The strong forms appear to arise by analogy with strong *forsake* and *shake.*

It is sometimes the case that both strong and weak forms of a given verb exist in Old English (although these may be slightly differentiated in meaning), and that in Middle English the two forms coalesce. So Chaucer has *wake, wook* (strong) beside *waked* (weak), *waken* (strong) beside *waked* (weak) from the sixth class of strong verbs *wacan, woc, wocon, wacen,* and the second class of weak verbs *wacian, wacode,* and so forth. Old English had a seventh class strong verb *hon, heng, hengon, hongen* beside weak *hangian.* Chaucer has *hange/honge, heng/hanged, hengen/hanged,* clearly a confusion of the two verbs, not only in the past tense forms, but in the stem vowels as well. The modern differentiation in meaning between *hang/hung* and *hang/hanged* is a later development.

Two points suggest themselves here. One is the indecision that occurs regarding the choice of grammatical devices one of which has ceased to be *productive.* A productive device is one by means of which new formations can be constructed. If a new verb *fim* enters the language, we immediately construct a past tense *fimmed*, not a past tense *fam*, since stem-vowel replacement is not a productive grammatical device in English. Stem-vowel replacement, whether in the case of noun stems or verb stems, had ceased to be a productive grammatical device long before our earliest Old English records, and the inventory of lexical fossils which exemplify this device has gradually become smaller and smaller. The grammatical rules that account for these fossils are very special indeed, and in a very important sense are ancillary to the grammatical system as a whole. The fact that the learning of such rules by a native speaker of the language is more often than not a matter of rote certainly seems to indicate their auxiliary character. Furthermore, the number and kind of such auxiliary subsystems give us important clues to the history of grammatical change in a given language.

The second point is purely pedagogical, and perhaps so obvious that it need not be labored. The development of the English verb system makes manifest the fact that recourse to language history as a basis for making assertions about grammatical purity or "correctness" may be very disappointing indeed. The past tense *shook* is not correct just because *shake* originally belonged to the sixth class of Old English strong verbs; nor is substandard *shaked* incorrect because it is not a strong form. On such a basis we would have to say that the boy's *weared* is correct for the past tense of *wear*, and that *climbed* is incorrect. The form *shook* is "correct" only because it is accepted as such by a certain class of native English speakers; the form *weared* is not "correct" because it is not so accepted by this same class. Historical considerations are almost totally irrelevant.

Personal Pronoun Forms

The personal pronoun forms for late Southeast Midland Middle English were these:[2]

	First person	
	singular	*plural*
nominative	i(ch)	we
common	me	us
genitive	mi(ne)	our(e(s))

---

[2] For the detailed rules that derive various dialectal forms for different stages of Middle English and commentary on these rules, see Appendix III. C.

Second person

	singular	plural
nominative	thou (ye)	ye
common	thee	you
genitive	thi(ne)	your(e(s))

Third person

singular

	masculine	feminine	neuter
nominative	he (ha, a)	s(c)he	(h)it
common	him	hir	him
genitive	his	hir(e(s))	his

plural

nominative	þei
common	hem
genitive	hir(e(s))

Additional changes in the shape of the English personal pronoun system took place between the end of the Middle English period and the end of the early Modern English period. In the late sixteenth century we find *thee* occurring as a *subject* form in the place of *thou,* a practice still adhered to by the Quakers. As the rules indicate, the originally plural *ye* already occurred in Middle English as the singular pronoun of respectful address in the subject; by the fifteenth century it is also being used under the same circumstances in the object. During the fourteenth century the object plural form *you* commonly replaces both *thou* and *thee,* and may also be found for the subject plural *ye.* By the fifteenth century there is considerable confusion in the use of the two forms, *ye* occurring as object, or as both subject and object, *you* occurring as subject, or as both subject and object. Nevertheless, some writers were careful to maintain the distinction *ye,* subject/*you,* object as late as the seventeenth century. By the end of the seventeenth century *ye* had disappeared in the standard language.

The neuter singular genitive forms *(h)it* and *his* continue to be used until the end of the sixteenth century, when they are gradually replaced by *its,* the *-s* presumably being added on analogy with *his.*

In Chapter 1 we commented briefly on the reflexive form *hamsylf* in Trevisa's text. In Old English, the declinable form *self* was frequently added to personal pronouns for emphasis and was declined with the pronoun: *ic selfa, mec selfne, min selfes, me selfum,* and the like. Even more emphatic was the repetition of the personal pronoun in the dative case: *ic me selfa, we us selfe.* In Middle English, during the thirteenth century, we find *self* considered as a noun and preceded typically by the *genitive* form of the pronoun, espe-cially in the first and second persons singular. Thus *mi self* and *thi self* exist along side of the older dative construction *me self* and *the self*. This practice is extended to the plural giving the alternants *oure/us self/selven* and *your/you self/selven*. It is not surprising, then, to find in Wycliffe such phrases as "so ӡe deme ӡousilf," "but ӡyue ӡe ӡousilf," "but also we vssilf," "and not plese to vssilf." The gentive forms *his self* and *their self* developed somewhat later and were comparatively short-lived in standard English. The object case forms *himself* and *themself* were predominant by the end of the fifteenth century, and not long after were the unique forms. In the nonstandard dia-lects, however, the genitive forms continued to be used. And where it cannot be shown that the forms *hisself* and *theirselves* in Modern nonstandard speech and writing are the result of inheritance, it is probably a safe assumption that they occur by analogy with genitive forms of the first and second persons. The *-s* plural of *-selves* became current in the sixteenth century and has, of course, remained.

DEMONSTRATIVE FORMS

The development of the Modern English definite article, and of the more and less proximate demonstratives *this* and *that* is of interest from both a formal and a functional point of view. Further, the manner in which formal and functional developments are interdependent is of importance to our understanding of the operation of grammatical change. We will express these developments in the following rules and then comment on some of their implications. For the sake of this analysis we will reexpand Old English [+dem] into þ₁- and þ₂-, where þ₂- is the deictic stem.

$$(1) \quad \text{þ}_1\text{-} \quad \text{Agr} \quad \text{ME} \quad \Rightarrow \quad \text{þe}$$

$$\begin{cases} [+\text{masc}] \\ [+\text{fem}] \end{cases} [+\text{13th cent}]$$

$$[-\text{pl}]$$

$$[+\text{nom}]$$

$$(2) \quad \text{þ}_1\text{-} \quad \text{Agr} \quad \text{ME} \quad \Rightarrow \quad \begin{cases} \text{þat} \\ \text{þet} \end{cases}$$

$$[+\text{neut}][+\text{13th cent}]$$

$$[-\text{pl}]$$

$$\begin{cases} [+\text{nom}] \\ [+\text{acc}] \end{cases}$$

(3)a. þ₁-⌢ Agr $\begin{bmatrix} \text{North} \\ \text{Elsewhere} \end{bmatrix}$ ME ⇒ $\begin{bmatrix} \text{þa} \\ \text{þo} \end{bmatrix}$
       | |
    $\left\{ \begin{matrix} [+\text{nom}] \\ [+\text{acc}] \end{matrix} \right\}$ [+12th cent]

        |
     [+pl]

b. $\begin{bmatrix} \text{þa⌢North⌢ME} \\ \quad | \\ \quad [+13\text{th cent}] \\ \text{þo⌢Elsewhere⌢ME} \\ \quad | \\ \quad [+15\text{th cent}] \end{bmatrix}$ ⇒ $\begin{bmatrix} \text{þas} \\ \\ \text{þos} \end{bmatrix}$

(4)a. þ₂-⌢ Agr ⌢North⌢ ME ⇒ þis
        | |
    [+neut]   [+12th cent]

    $\left\{ \begin{matrix} [+\text{nom}] \\ [+\text{acc}] \end{matrix} \right\}$

       |
     [−pl]

b. þ₂-⌢ Agr $\left\{ \begin{matrix} \text{Midlands} \\ \text{South} \end{matrix} \right\}$ ME ⇒ þes
        | |
    [+masc]   [+12th cent]

    [+nom]

     |
    [−pl]

c. þ₂-⌢ Agr $\left\{ \begin{matrix} \text{Midlands} \\ \text{Southern} \end{matrix} \right\}$ ME ⇒ þis
        | |
    [+neut]   [+13th cent]

    $\left\{ \begin{matrix} [+\text{nom}] \\ [+\text{acc}] \end{matrix} \right\}$

       |
     [−pl]

d. $\begin{bmatrix} \text{þes} \\ \text{þis} \end{bmatrix}$ [+pl] $\left\{ \begin{matrix} \text{Midlands} \\ \text{Southern} \end{matrix} \right\}$ ME ⇒ $\begin{bmatrix} \left\{ \begin{matrix} \text{þese} \\ \text{these} \end{matrix} \right\} \\ \left\{ \begin{matrix} \text{þise} \\ \text{thise} \end{matrix} \right\} \end{bmatrix}$
                         |
                    [+13th cent]

(5)a. þ₂-⌢ Agr ⌢Kent⌢ ME ⇒ þas
        | |
    [+pl]   [+13th cent]

b. þas⌢Kent⌢ME ⇏ $\left\{ \begin{matrix} \text{þese} \\ \text{these} \end{matrix} \right\}$
           |
    [+14th cent]

where: ⇏ = 'is replaced by.'

(6) X-⌒Agr⌒North⌒ME   ⇒ $\left\{ \begin{array}{l} \text{þir} \\ \text{þeir} \\ \text{thir} \\ \text{their} \end{array} \right\}$
      | |
   [+pl]   [+14th cent]

where: X = an undetermined stem.

Middle English þe, Modern *the*, stems from the Old English masculine or feminine nominative singular historical demonstrative (1). Middle English þat, Modern less proximate *that*, stems from the Old English neuter nominative-accusative singular (2). Two dialectal forms þa and þo arise in the twelfth century from the historical demonstrative nominative-accusative plural (3)a., which in the thirteenth century became þas in the North and þos elsewhere (3)b. The proximate form þis arises in the North in the twelfth century from the deictic demonstrative neuter nominative-accusative singular (4)a. Singular þes and þis develop in the Midlands and South from masculine and neuter singulars respectively (4)b., c. From these, plurals þese and þise are formed in the latter thirteenth century (4)d. In the thirteenth century in Kent a plural þas develops that is replaced by þese in the fourteenth (5)a., b. Plural forms of the proximate demonstrative þir, þeir, of undetermined origin, appear in the North in the fourteenth century (6).

Clearly, the development of Modern English *the, this, these, that,* and *those* depended to a large extent on the loss of gender and case distinctions in the Old English demonstrative system. As case and gender differentiation becomes less and less functional, forms in the demonstrative paradigms become available to express new grammatical functions. Thus, the masculine and feminine nominative singular forms of þ$_1$- coalesce and develop a grammatical function distinct from that of the nominative-accusative neuter. The Old English two-way contrast between þ$_1$- and þ$_2$- becomes a three-way contrast of quite a different type: *definite* contrasts with *spatial,* and *near* contrasts with *less near.*

5.20 *Some Syntactic Changes*

WORD ORDER

There is no simple way to describe the word-order patterns of the Middle English period that were eventually to stabilize into the order of arrangement that now characterizes Modern English. There are, for one thing, a great many variables to be taken into account: the character of the clause, whether independent or dependent; the number and kind of sentence adverbials; the nature of the auxiliary; the character of the sentence, whether transitive or intransitive; the semantic load of the noun phrases that occur as well as that of the verb; the nature of the discourse, whether prose or poetry; the style, whether formal or informal, expository, dramatic, lyric, and the like; the changing character of interrogative, negative, and imperative sentences. And, of course, there is the perennial difficulty—that of drawing general conclusions about a given historical period of a language on the basis of, for the most part, relatively sophisticated literary texts in which stylistic effects play an important role.

We have commented on the considerable flexibility of word order patterns characteristic of Old English, and the inflectional system that made this flexibility possible. The Middle English period was one of transition where we find traces both of the old inflectional system and of the old word-order flexibility. It should be no surprise, then, to discover that for the outsider Middle English syntax presents a somewhat confusing picture. Even so, some fairly definite patterns of development begin to take shape. Walerian Swieczkowski (*Word Order Patterning in Middle English,* The Hague, 1962) has examined in detail the word-order patterns of two Middle English texts, *Middle English Sermons,* ed. W. O. Ross (London, 1940) and *The Vision of William Concerning Piers the Plowman, In Three Parallel Texts,* ed. W. W. Skeat (Oxford, 1886). We make no attempt to estimate the extent to which Professor Swieczkowski's statistics typify the general late Middle English situation, but merely let them stand as being at least suggestive of Middle English syntactic trends.

For all three versions of *Piers Plowman* the order *subject-predicate* ($NP\widehat{\ }VP$) shows 77.6 percent occurrences as against 22.4 percent *predicate-subject* ($VP\widehat{\ }NP$) occurrences. The *Sermons* show 89 percent *subject-predicate* occurrences compared with 11 percent *predicate-subject* occurrences. Professor Swieczkowski then shows that the relative frequency of *predicate-subject* order is higher when the construction is preceded by a preposed element such as a verb modifier, an object, or a dependent clause, while the relative frequency of the *subject-predicate* order is proportionally lower under these conditions. For example, the A version of *Piers Plowman* contains 1004 examples of *subject-predicate* order out of a possible 1332, or 75.5 percent. Of this percentage 54.6 percent occur in constructions containing *no* preposed element; 20.7 percent occur in constructions *containing* a preposed element. The same text contains a total of 328 instances of *predicate-subject* order, or 24.5 percent of the total 1332. Of this percentage, only 2.1 percent occur in constructions containing *no* preposed element, while 22.6 percent occur in constructions *containing* a preposed element.

What these statistics seem to say is this: that although the order *subject-predicate (NP^VP)* is clearly dominant, there is a strong disposition to keep the elements of the predicate together, so that if one element of the verb phrase is optionally shifted to the head of the construction it will *tend* to take the rest of the verb phrase with it:

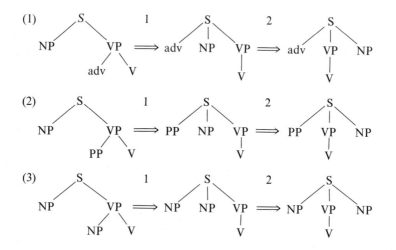

Neither of the transformations is obligatory, but if the first occurs, the second is highly predictable. The degree of predictability will vary depending upon the nature of the preposed element. For instance, the second transformation in (3) is more highly predictable than that of (1) and (2), the notion being that noun-objects are felt to be more closely tied to their verbs than are adverbial modifiers.

Of 1621 transitive sentences in the A version of *Piers Plowman,* over 60 percent occur in structures that show the order *subject-verb (NP^V)*. Approximately 83 percent of these show the object following the verb, *subject-verb-object (NP_1^V^NP_2)*; about 16 percent show the order *subject-object-verb (NP_1^NP_2^V)*; and about 1 percent show the order *object-subject-verb (NP_2^NP_1^V)*.

We have indicated the inadvisability of generalizing on the basis of Swieczkowski's statistics. For the texts he has studied, at least, it seems to be the case that for both transitive and intransitive sentences the order *subject-verb* clearly predominates in the late fourteenth century, as does the order *subject-verb-object.* Apparently, too, at this stage in the development of word-order patterns, such order is not, as it was to some extent in Old

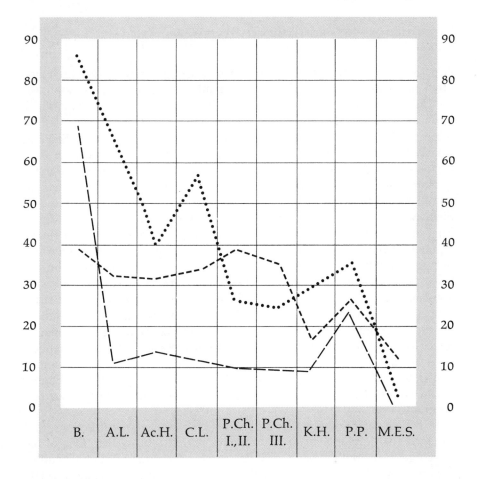

(*Table LXXX from Walerian Swieczkowski,* Word Order Patterning in Middle English, *Mouton & Co., 1962. Reproduced by permission.*)

English, contingent upon whether a given sentence is or is not embedded in another.

On the basis of his own studies and those of other scholars Professor Swieczkowski constructs the following graph showing the decrease of *predicate-subject* occurrences (- . - . - .), *final predicate* (*verb*) occurrences in *main clauses* (- - - -), and *final predicate* (verb) occurrences in *subordinate* (embedded) clauses (. . . .), from *Beowulf* through the *Middle English Sermons* (A. L., *Alfred's Laws;* Ae. H., *Aelfric's Homilies;* C. L., *Cnut's Laws;* P. Ch., *Peterborough Chronicles;* K. H., *King Horn;* P. P., *Piers Plowman*). The graph speaks for itself and needs no further comment.

Extension of the Prepositional System

A period of grammatical transition such as the one now under discussion often poses difficulties for the modern reader. Consider Chaucer's phrase, "she falleth him to fote." The construction harks back to Old English in which *him* was a dative singular. It is to be construed something like 'she falls in respect to him at foot,' or, in Modern English, 'she falls at his feet.' Since by Chaucer's time the dative and accusative singular of the masculine third person pronoun had fallen together, the grammatical function of *him* in the quotation is not immediately clear. This is not to say, of course, that the phrase would have confused Chaucer's contemporaries, since its status for them would have been idiomatic. But for nonnative speakers of Middle English such expressions may cause difficulty; they have neither a clearly differentiated case system nor a fully developed periphrastic system on which to base an analysis. A somewhat different use of the dative occurs in the sentence "what thing him were best to do." To modern ears it sounds somewhat non-English. As yet the periphrasis 'for him' is not demanded by the structure, and the dative implications of the form *him* are expected to establish the proper grammatical relationship with the rest of the utterance. But since the dative is not formally differentiated from the accusative, these implications are not clear. The nonexpression of anticipatory *it,* a very common omission in Middle English, simply adds to the confusion. Modern English would express the same idea in such a construction as 'what thing *it* were best *for* him to do.'

It is just such potentially indecisive grammatical constructions that hastened the development of an extensive periphrastic system. One of the most significant replacements of inflection by periphrasis is the *of-*genitive construction. The *of* equivalent of the inflectional genitive goes back to late Old English, where it usually signifies the notion 'out of.' It is not, however, until the twelfth century that it begins to occur as a regular possessive formation. The early thirteenth-century version of the poet Laȝamon's *Brut,* Laȝamon A, has *for mines drihtenes luve* 'for my lord's love,' while the second version a half century later, Laȝamon B, has *for love of mine drihte* 'for love of my lord.' In an unpublished dissertation (University of Michigan, 1931) R. Thomas tabulated a comparative percentage of occurrences of the inflectional and periphrastic genitive, based on a selection of Old and Middle English prose texts from the ninth to the fourteenth century. We reproduce this table on page 247.

It seems clear from this table that beginning in the thirteenth century the periphrastic construction enjoys considerable popularity, and that by the fourteenth its frequency approximates what one would expect in Modern English.

Period	Inflectional genitive (*in percent*)	Periphrastic genitive (*in percent*)
9th century (end)–10th century	99.5	0.5
Later 10th–beginning of 11th century	99.0	1.0
11th century	98.0	1.2
12th century	93.7	6.3
13th century (first half)	68.6	31.4
14th century	15.6	84.4

Scholars have not been all of one mind in accounting for the rapid spread of the *of*-periphrasis. Some have attributed it to the fact that Old English *of,* with the meaning 'from,' suggested more forcefully than the inflected form of the noun could the notions both of separation and origin. Others ascribe the popularity of the periphrasis to the influence of the French construction with *de.* Old English had an inflectional genitive of *definition,* as in *Egypta* (gen) *folc* 'Egypt's people.' The early Middle English counterpart of this can be seen in *Romess kineriche* 'Rome's kingdom' (or 'kingdom of Rome'). By the early twelfth century one finds the *of* construction in such phrases as *se burh of Lincolne* 'the town of Lincoln' and þ*one eorldom of Flandres* 'the earldom of Flanders.' In French, the corresponding construction occurs in *mon ostel est en mila vile de Paris.*

Whatever the contribution of French (or Latin) prepositional constructions to the development of like constructions in Middle English, there is no doubt that the seeds of periphrasis were already present in Old English. As grammatical functions ceased to be signaled by distinctive case forms, it was natural that the prepositional system should be extended to perform these functions. During the Middle English period the extension took place in a number of ways. Consider, for example, the preposition *be, bi* 'by.' In Old English it indicated (chiefly) space relationship, as in þ*a sume dæge rad se cyng up bi þære eæ* 'then one day the king rode up along the river,' or þ*e him big stodon* 'who stood next to him.' But it *could* be used in the sense of 'concerning' or 'in respect to' as *loca nu be þære sunnan ond eac be oðrum tunglum* 'look (consider) now concerning the sun and also concerning other heavenly bodies,' and 'according to,' *Aeghwilc gylt be hys gebyrdum* 'Each payed according to his descent (birth).' In Middle English, *by* comes to indicate, often as the result of metaphor, additional types of relationships. Just how extensive was this development can be seen by the treatment of *bi* in the *Middle English Dictionary* (eds., Hans Kurath and Sherman M. Kuhn, University of Michigan Press), where some ten pages of double columns are given over to this preposition and its various functions. Here we cite just a few of these.

1. Location, position, direction: *His heer was by his erys full round yshorn; Alle þe burnez so bolde þat hym by stoden; A shipman was ther, wonynge fer by weste.*
2. Association: *y neure ne þoʒte Bi Rymenhild for to ligge.*
3. Goal/object of an action: *thus hit fareþ by suche folke þat folwen here owene wil.*
4. Time: *It was a King bi olde dawene þat wel leude on godes lawe.*
5. Agent: *Bi us he sende word þe, þat he wule to þisse londe.*
6. Means: *Holy men & religiouse þat ben nouʒt defoulid by touchynge of wymmen; sche . . . yifth me nought to live by.*
7. Reference: *If I be absent in body . . . by spirit I am with ʒou.*
8. Comparison: *For hyt was darke, þat þay myght not well know Thomas by anoþer; a Kynges herte semeth by hyrs a wrecche.*
9. Number: *They fledden Euerichon . . . be On And be On.*
10. Amount/degree: *Parisshe prestes . . . teche Alle manere men to amenden by here myʒte.*

Translation:

1. His hair was next his ears cut quite round; All the knights so bold that stood beside him; A shipman there was, dwelling far to the west.
2. I never thought to lie by Rimenhild.
3. Thus it happens to such folk as follow their own will.
4. There was a king in olden days that believed entirely in God's law.
5. By us he sends you word that he will [come] to this land.
6. Holy and religious men that have not been defiled by touching women (or, by being touched by women); she gives me nothing to live by (not, here, motivation, but nourishment).
7. If I am absent in body . . . I am with you in spirit.
8. For it was dark, so that they couldn't tell Thomas from any of the others; a king's heart seems, in comparison with hers, a wretched thing.
9. They fled, everyone . . . one after the other.
10. Parish priests . . . teach all manner of men to amend (their lives) with all their might.

A number of *by* constructions occurred in Middle English (and still occur) that were direct translations of French phrases with *par: by aventure, by chance, by heart, by right, by force, by name.*

Other native English prepositions developed additional functions during the Middle English period in much the same way and to much the same extent. While they were doing so, new prepositional formations were appearing, some in imitation of French, others the result of *functional change* from adverb to preposition. *During* appears as a preposition in the fourteenth century, presumably in imitation of French *durant; save* in the sense 'except' is from Old French *sauf; maugre* from Old French *malgre* meaning 'in spite of'; *around* from French *ronde; according to* from Old French *accordant a. Behind, beneath, beside, out* appear in Old English as adverbs, but develop as prepositions during the Middle English period. There are instances in which an Old English form occurring as both adverb and preposition splits into two distinct forms, one of which assumes the adverbial and one the prepositional function. Old English *ongegn* 'again' was such a form. At the end of the Old English period the genitive *aʒeines* occurs almost exclusively as a preposition, and in the fourteenth century an *inorganic -t* is attached, giving Modern English *against.* The reflex of the uninflected form, *again,* assumed the role of adverb.

It is difficult to overemphasize the importance to Modern English structure of the prepositional development discussed above.

CHANGES IN THE NATURE OF *AUX*

The reader will perhaps recall these rules from the Old English model:

1. $S \rightarrow (Q) (Neg) \begin{Bmatrix} NP \\ \varnothing \end{Bmatrix} VP^\frown Aux$

10. $Aux \rightarrow (Aux_2)Aux_1$

11. $Aux_1 \rightarrow (Inf\text{-}M) \; CS/V(Aux_2) \text{\_\_\_}$
    a. $[+Aux_1] \rightarrow [+[\pm Pres], [\pm Ind]]$
    b. $[\pm Pres] \rightarrow [\pm Pres]$
       $\quad | \qquad\qquad |$
       $[-Ind] \qquad [\pm Sub]$
    c. $[+Pres] \rightarrow [+Pres]$
       $\quad | \qquad\qquad |$
       $[-Sub] \qquad [+Imp]$

12. $Aux_2 \begin{Bmatrix} \text{-en} \begin{Bmatrix} \text{habb-} & /NP^\frown NP^\frown V \\ \text{wes-} \end{Bmatrix} \\ \text{-ende}^\frown \text{beo} \end{Bmatrix}$

Professor Closs, in the article cited in Chapter 4 (fn. 3), points out that by the thirteenth century the order that characterizes Modern English, *Aux^VP,* is "favored" over that order which appears in rule 1.

By the end of the Middle English period important changes had taken place in *Aux₂.* The auxiliary *have* now occurs in both transitive and intransitive constructions:

(1) ʒe *habbeþ* þene world ivlowen. 'ye have flown the world.'
(2) hit is ney vif ʒer þat we *abbeþ* ylived in such vice.
    'it is nearly five years that we have lived in such vice.'

On the other hand, throughout the period the occurrence of *be + past participle* was more and more being limited to intransitive verbs of *motion:*

(1) at nyght *was* come into that hostelrye/wel nyne and twenty in a compaignye. 'at night had come into that hostelry, / well nine and twenty in a company.'

(2) min herte is growen into ston. 'My heart has turned to stone.'

The wider distribution of *have* and the more restricted distribution of *be* with the past participle at the end of the Middle English period may in part be accounted for by the direction of the *passive* development. Old English passives were formed with the auxiliaries *wes-, beo-,* and *weorð-.* By early Middle English *wes-* and *beo-* had coalesced in *be,* leaving two auxiliaries for the passive. By the twelfth century it is clear that *wurth-* (the reflex of *weorð-*) is rapidly losing ground to *be.* Tauno F. Mustanoja (*Syntax*) points out that whereas instances of *wurthe* are common in those sections of the *Peterborough Chronicle* written near the end of the eleventh century, they are quite rare in those sections written in the first half of the twelfth. There are notable exceptions, of course (Mustanoja cites examples of *wurthe* in *Laȝamon B*), but it seems to be the case that *wurthe* is no longer used as a passive auxiliary by the end of the fourteenth century. This means that *be* now occurs uniquely in this function. As the functional load of *be* increases in one direction, it decreases in another direction; and this decrease is abetted by the distributional spread of *have.* Of course, it is not possible to say whether *wurthe* lost ground to *be* because *be* was losing ground to *have,* or whether *have* gained ground on *be* because *be* was gaining ground on *wurthe.* The best we can say is that changes in the nature of one construction undoubtedly influenced changes in the nature of the other.

By the close of the Middle English period the mutual exclusion of *have + past participle* and *be + present participle* as indicated by rule (12) no longer obtains. Although it is clear that the combination of the two constructions does not become popular until the early Modern English period, it did in fact occur in Middle English. *Cursor Mundi* has, for instance, þof *he three dais had fastand bene* 'though he had been fasting for three days,' and Chaucer has *we han ben waitynge al this fourtenyght* 'we have been waiting all this fortnight.' The use of *have + be + past participle* (that is, a passive construction) begins to occur in the thirteenth century, and is common throughout the fourteenth:

(1) Engelond haþ ibe inome and iwerred ilome. 'England has been captured and made war upon frequently.'

(2) how ofte tyme hath it yknowen be, the tresoun that to wommen hath ben do. 'how often times has it been made known, the treason that has been done to women.'

We should perhaps comment here on the development of the present participle form during the Middle English period. Old English *-ende* survives in early Middle English as *-ind(e)* in the Southwest Midlands and the South, *-and(e)* (probably influenced by Old Norse *-ande*) in the North, and *-end(e)* elsewhere. By the end of the twelfth century, however, these forms are gradually being replaced by *-i/yng(e)*. What, precisely, were the reasons for this replacement has been the subject of much debate. The weakening of stress on inflectional endings led to some phonological confusion between various nonfinite forms of the verb, and between these and the *verbal noun*. This latter was marked in late Old English by *-ung/-ing* as in *leornung* 'learning,' *earnung* 'merit,' *wilnung* 'desire,' *þrowung* 'suffering,' and *ræding* 'lesson.' In Old English such parallel constructions as *he wæs feohtende* (with *beo* + *ende*) and *he wæs on feohtinge* (with *prep* + NP) may have contributed to the adoption of the *-ing* inflection for the participle. The fact that the inflected infinitive often took the forms *-inde/-ende,* that is, a form identical with that of the early participle marker, and the participle sometimes assumed a form *-an/-en* (the loss of the final *-d* presumably the result of weakened stress) identical with the form of the infinitive, certainly added to the confusion. At any rate, the *-ing* form is found along side the *-inde* form by the thirteenth century: *ne goinde ne ridingge* 'nor walking nor riding.' Reflexes of the *on* + *verbal noun* construction are preserved in Modern English in a few archaisms such as 'a-hunting we will go,' Old English *gyrstan dæg ic wæs on huntunge* 'yesterday I was a-hunting.' Middle English *thanne may he yit a-begging go* shows that the reduction of *on* to *a* had already occurred.

Periphrastic aspect forms with *be* + *ing* occurred in Old English, especially in prose, and very possibly under the influence of a similar Latin construction, *docens erat* 'was teaching' (compare with Old English *wæs lærende*). In early Middle English this construction occurs with great variation in frequency from one dialect to another. It is quite common in the North, occasional in the West Midlands, and practically nonexistent elsewhere. Before the end of the period, however, it is firmly established in all dialects. In addition to the Latin influence, the Old French construction *est chantant* 'is singing' contributed to the popularity of the English periphrasis in late Middle English. In both Old and Middle English the periphrastic construction often seems to be used to indicate a *durative* aspect, although there are clearly instances in which the phrase has no such implications, in which its force seems to be solely one of emphasis.

Development of the Do-Periphrasis[3]

One of the most important, and certainly one of the most interesting, periphrastic constructions in Modern English is the *do-periphrasis.* On page 159 (T_{Do}) we show the introduction of *do* by syntactic transformation; this *do* is, of course, historically related to the Modern English full verb *do.* Both go back to Old English *don* (*gedon*) which had two senses (1) 'to do, perform, accomplish' and (2) 'to make, cause.' The Old English construction *do hit us to witanne* 'make us to know it' seems to have been strongly influenced by the Latin constructions *facere* + *Inf* and *facere* + *ut,* 'to cause, make to do something' and 'to cause, make that (in order that) someone do something': *faciam uos fieri piscatores hominum* 'I will make you to be fishers of men.' An Old English gloss of the Latin would be, *ic do þæt gyt beoþ manna fisceras,* 'I cause that you two be fishers of men.'

The causative construction with *do* occurs in early Middle English in varying degrees in various dialects along side of causative constructions with the verbs *let, make,* and *ger.* But in Middle English the *do* causative begins to split into two somewhat different constructions, one in which the subject of the infinitive is expressed, and one in which it is not: (a) *þair siluer he tok . . . And to þair ine dit it be borne* 'there he took silver . . . and caused it to be carried therein'; *þai gert hym bere it with envy* 'they made him bear it with envy'; *þe ueond hit makede me to don* 'the fiend made me do it'; (b) *He dude writes sende* 'He caused to send writs'; *þai gert seke him in þat sesoune* 'they caused to seek him in that season.' Presumably, the (b) type of construction results from an optional deletion of the subject of the embedded sentence: 'He caused something – someone sent writs ⇒ He caused – someone sent writs ⇒ He caused – someone to send writs ⇒ He caused – to send writs.'

Important for our purposes is the fact that the (b) type construction becomes equivocal; it may be *causative* or it may be purely *periphrastic.* Professor Ellegård points out that in the texts he has examined only a handful of (b) type instances are unambiguously causative, and that even genuine ambiguity is rare. As an example of the latter he cites this sentence: *þo he þat writ dude rede* which he thinks may be interpreted either 'then he that wrote read (did read),' or 'then he that wrote caused to read.' The occurrence of either the (a) or the (b) type of construction is to some extent a matter of dialectal variance. In eastern texts the (b) type is rare in the thirteenth century, begins to gain ground in the fourteenth, and is quite common in the fifteenth. In the eastern poetic texts, Ellegård finds in the thirteenth century 4 instances of (b) against 66 of (a); in the fourteenth century 15 clear instances of (b)

[3] I am indebted here to Alvar Ellegård's excellent study, *The Auxiliary Do: The Establishment and Regulation of its Use in English* (Stockholm, 1953).

periphrastic, 164 of (b) *equivocal,* and 58 of (a); in the fifteenth, 253 of (b) *peri-phrastic,* 124 of (b) *equivocal,* and 16 of (a). On the other hand, Western poetic texts indicate that type (a) is rare, while type (b) is both frequent and for the most part periphrastic. In thirteenth century verse, 57 instances of (b) peri-phrastic occur, 39 of (b) equivocal, and 9 of (a); in the fourteenth, 32 of (b) periphrastic, 28 of (b) equivocal, and 6 of (a); in the fifteenth, 53 of (b) peri-phrastic, 21 of (b) equivocal, and 7 of (a).

The question now arises, "What kind of grammatical rules should be postulated for the introduction into the grammar of types (a) and (b) *do* constructions?" In early Middle English type (a) constructions continue to result, in the east and presumably the west too, from the introduction of a full verb causative *do* in a matrix sentence, followed by an embedding transformation that embeds a constituent sentence as object of the causative verb: *And dide hem grete oþes swere* 'and caused them to swear great oaths.'

1. And dide sum þynge
2. þei grete oþes swore

$\Rightarrow$ And dide — þei grete oþes swore $\Rightarrow$
And dide — hem grete oþes swore $\Rightarrow$
And dide — hem grete oþes swere

Do we wish to say, further, that the type (b) causatives, especially in the eastern texts where they were most common, still result from a deletion of the subject of the constituent sentence? This is possible; however, it is my opinion that the type (b) causative *do* comes to function as a modal auxiliary, with no necessary sense of a deleted subject of the MV: *i shal do slon hem baþe* 'I shall cause to slay them both.' For thirteenth-century eastern texts we need only introduce *do* as an *M* and as a *V*:

A. *Eastern*
   Subcategory Rules
   1. $S \rightarrow NP\widehat{\ }Aux\widehat{\ }VP$
   2. $VP \rightarrow MV(Adv)$
   3. $MV \rightarrow V \left(\left\{ \begin{matrix} Pred \\ NP \end{matrix} \right\} \right)$
   4. $NP \rightarrow np(S)$
   5. $np \rightarrow \left\{ \begin{matrix} np\ /\underline{\ \ }S \\ [+Pro] \\ Det\widehat{\ }N\widehat{\ }No(S) \end{matrix} \right\}$
   6. $Aux \rightarrow Aux_1 (Aux_2)$
   7. $Aux_1 \rightarrow T(M)$

Lexicon
1. [+M]: do (type (b) *causative*), et al.
2. [+[+animate] Aux __ np^S]: do (type (a)), et al.
   |
   [+Pro]

Western texts, however, show periphrastic *do,* auxiliary causative *do,* and type (a) *do* causative, although this latter is rare:

B. *Western*

Subcategory Rules
1. S → NP Aux VP
2. VP → MV(Adv)
3. MV → V $\left(\left\{ \begin{matrix} \text{Pred} \\ \text{NP} \end{matrix} \right\} \right)$
4. NP → np(S)
5. np → $\left\{ \begin{matrix} \text{np } /\underline{\quad}\text{ S} \\ | \\ [+\text{Pro}] \\ \text{Det}^\frown\text{N}^\frown\text{No (S)} \end{matrix} \right\}$
6. Aux → Aux$_1$ (Aux$_2$)
7. Aux$_1$ → T(M)
8. Aux$_2$ (have-en) ($\left\{ \begin{matrix} \text{be-ing} \\ \text{do } (periphrastic) \end{matrix} \right\}$)

Lexicon
1. [+M]: do (type (b) *causative*), et al.
2. [+[+animate] Aux __ np^S]: do (type (a)), et al.
   |
   [+Pro]

Since both type (a) *do* and type (b) causative *do* disappear from western texts, a later grammar would remove both from lexical rules 1 and 2.

What is not shown in these rules is the relative frequency of occurrence of the various types in eastern and western texts. In the west, type (a) *do* is replaced at a fairly early date by *let* and *make,* later by *cause,* leaving only type (b) *periphrastic* and *causative do* to compete with each other as in subcategory rule 8 and lexical rule 1. As we have already pointed out, it is sometimes difficult to know which of these has been selected: *he liet fette a bed . . . and dude strepe þis Maide naked* 'he had a bed fetched . . . and had this maid stripped naked,' or 'he had a bed fetched . . . and stripped (did strip) this maid naked.' The two translations do not, obviously, mean the same thing, but in the larger context of the utterance either one is perfectly acceptable.

Equivocal *do* is paralleled by French expressions with the verb *faire* at a time when French influence in England and on English poets was considerable. In Robert Manning's translation of Wace's *Brut*, for instance, one finds: *Berfreys dide make to gyue assaut*, translating *Berfrez fist e perreres faire; A coroune of gold he dyde hym make*, translating *corone d'or se fist cist faire*. There seems no doubt but that the popularity of the French expression, especially in contexts where it could clearly be taken as periphrastic, contributed materially to the spread of periphrastic *do*.

Another significant factor in the spread of periphrastic *do* was its exploitation by poets as a convenience in meter and rhyme. Not only could it be used to fill out the metrical pattern of a poetic line, but it could also be used to place a rhyme word in rhyming position:

(a) was non þat hauede þe hern panne
  so hard, þat he ne *dede* to cusshe
  and al to shiuere, and al to frusshe.
(b) wyþ man lyknesse þe fend *dide* take
  in þat likness þe folk *dide* make
(c) Our fredom þat day for ever toke þe leue
  For Harald it went away, his falshed *did* vs greue.

Ellegård finds a great deal of evidence to indicate that the *do*-periphrasis is very frequent in the poetry of eastern writers in the early fourteenth century, but that it scarcely occurs at all in eastern prose where causative *do* remains strong. As one might expect, periphrastic *do* gains momentum during the fourteenth century in the east, and instances of its use in prose begin to occur around the turn of the century. This momentum is due in part to the fact that type (a) *causative do* was gradually being replaced by *make* and *cause*, thus mitigating the possibility of conflict between it and periphrastic *do*. By the end of the fifteenth century the *do*-periphrasis is widely current in prose texts. As a matter of fact, it becomes a mark of high style among the educated, at times overdone to the point of pedantry and pretentiousness. Its use is illustrated in the following: *In faith, my lorde dyd quyte hym als curageousely as ever I wist man do* 'In faith, my lord did acquit himself as courageously as ever I knew a man to do'; *Englyschmen, whenne thei dyd fyrst inhabyde this lond* 'Englishmen, when they did first inhabit this land'; *wheche lettyr I hawe rede and do whell undyrstonde* 'which letter I have read and do well understand.'

An interesting consequence of the spread of periphrastic *do* into dialects in which causative *do* had a traditionally high frequency was the construction *did do: And the kynge dide do make this dragon in all the hast he might* 'And the king caused to make this dragon in all the haste he might'; *Charlys dyd do syng a masse solempny* 'Charles did cause to sing a solemn mass'; *two messengers he dyde do call* 'two messengers he did cause to (be) call(ed).' Ellegård thinks that this construction results from the fact that a number of eastern writers, among them the printer and translator Caxton, observing the rapid spread of periphrastic *do* and wishing both to be fashionable and to retain a causative *do*, combined the two as illustrated. Rules for eastern texts will now look like those given above for western texts except that type (a) causative *do* in lexical rule 2 has been replaced by *make* or *cause*.

As in Modern English, *do* occurs as a *pro-verb* in both Old and Middle English. Note the following:

Modern English
(1) Jack played football in college and so *did* Bill.
(2) Jack played football in college, *didn't* he?
(3) Professor Smith is going to teach the class, isn't he? He may *do* (British).
(4) He didn't teach yesterday, *did* he?

Old English
(1) he gefor eac on þæm ilcan tune þe his fæder dyde.
    'he went also into that same town which his father did
    (where his father had gone).'

Middle English
(1) I have him knawen and sal do ever.
    'I have known him and will continue to know him.'
(2) For als a man pusonde of a swete morcell takes venom þat slase his body, sa dose a synful wreche . . . destrues his sawle.
    'For just as a man poisoned by a sweet morsel takes venom that slays his body, so does a sinful wretch . . . destroy his soul.'
(3) and it schal drawe rust þere of . . . and so doþe vche goode man & womman takeþ rust of sin.

The last two Middle English sentences illustrate a rather interesting stylistic practice. The pro-verb occurs in the second clause to reflect the meaning of the full verb in the first clause, but lest the reader forget what that meaning is, a second full verb is introduced later in still a third clause. Note that both pro-verb and full verb in the third clause are *finite*. The clause that follows the pro-verb provides an expansion of or further commentary on the meaning of the second clause:

(4) Take good hede to þes pore faitours, how þei schewen here siknesses and here defautes . . . riʒt so scholde men and wommen do mekeliche tofore God, schewen here defautes and here synnes.
    'Take good heed of these poor beggars [who feign sickness], how they show their sickness and their wounds . . . even so should men and women do meekly before God, show their faults and their sins.'

(5) þan chase he out of his owne religion certeyn men to ber þe birden of
gouernauns with him lich as Moyses ded . . . he assigned certeyn men
to have gouernauns vndyr him and alle þe grete causes he wold re-
dresse himself. Thus ded our maystir; he chase men of sufficient
lettirrur.

'Then chose he out of his own religion certain men to bear the burden
of government with him just as Moses did . . . he assigned certain men
to have authority under him and all the most important causes he
would redress himself. Thus did our master; he chose men of sufficient
wisdom.'

The pro-verb *do* in all stages of the language is introduced by transformation. In general this will involve introducing the pro-verb into constructions
containing a repeated verb form, assigning to it the agreement morpheme,
and then deleting the repeated verb. Obviously, however, the Middle English
sentences (2) and (3) show complexities that are not quite so readily managed.
Sentence (2), for instance, may be derived in the following way:

(2)
a.1. a man (a morsel (a morsel is sweet) poisons a man) takes venom
(venom slays his body).
a.2. a man (a morsel (which is sweet) poisons a man) takes venom (that
slays his body).
a.3. a man (a sweet morsel poisons a man) takes venom (that slays his
body).
a.4. a man (a man is poisoned by a sweet morsel) takes venom (that slays
his body).
a.5. a man (poisoned by a sweet morsel) takes venom (that slays his body).
a.6. just às̑ a man poisoned by a sweet morsel takes venom that slays his
body.

b.1. a wretch (sin poisons a wretch) (a wretch takes venom) destroys his
soul.
b.2. a wretch (a wretch is poisoned by sin) (a wretch takes venom) destroys
his soul.
b.3. a wretch (who is poisoned by sin) (who takes venom) destroys his soul.
b.4. a wretch (poisoned by sin) (takes venom) destroys his soul.
b.5. a (poisoned by sin) wretch (takes venom) destroys his soul.
b.6. a (sinful) wretch (takes venom) destroys his soul.
b.7. *so*̑ a sinful wretch (does) destroys his soul.
b.8. sȏ does̑ a sinful wretch destroys his soul.

The analysis suggested by the set of b. strings accounts for the fact that *do*
and *destroy* in the surface structure are both finite verbs, and makes it clear

that *do* here is not simply periphrastic *do*. The pro-verb substitutes for the predication "takes venom," while *destroys* occurs in a separate clause.

The regulation of periphrastic *do* from the fifteenth century on is intimately associated with other grammatical developments. One of these was a change in the position of lightly stressed adverbs. In Middle English, anteposition (before *MV*) was much less frequent than it is today, the adverb regularly occurring in postposition. Increasingly, however, from the end of the fourteenth century the lightly stressed adverbs, including *not,* were placed before the verb; and concomitant with this increase was an increase in the use of the *do*-periphrasis in declarative affirmative sentences. This was especially true of those adverbs for which postposition had traditionally been required. When placed before the verb, the resulting construction was apparently felt to be awkward and esthetically unsatisfying; therefore, *do* was introduced to mitigate this awkwardness: *and the people did sore encrece.* As a matter of fact, however, this practice ultimately contributed to the decline of *do* in affirmative declarative constructions, since once the adverb was established in anteposition, *do* was no longer required and gradually disappeared.

We should note here that some adverbs may also occur at the head of the sentence: *and neuer aftir they fought; and neuere ye dide so grete folye.* For whatever reason, there was a rapid transition during the sixteenth century from the order *subject⁀verb* to the order *verb⁀subject* in such constructions. But since by this time inversion was becoming obsolete in other circumstances, the *do*-periphrasis was introduced to bring adverb-headed constructions in line with general practice. Thus in Modern English, *Never have I seen such a mess* is grammatical, while *Never I have seen such a mess* is ungrammatical; *Never did she feel at home here,* though a construction that seems to be going out of style, is grammatical, while *Never she felt at home here* is certainly not. Notice too that when two negative sentences are conjoined by *nor* in Modern English, the second must undergo not only a transformation that deletes the negative particle in the second sentence, but also an inversion (permutation) transformation:

(1) I do not like him ⎫
(2) I do not like her ⎭ ⟹ I do not like him-nor-I do not like her ⟹
                         I do not like him-nor-I do like her ⟹
                         I do not like him-nor-do I like her

In negative declarative sentences *do* was retained. We have discussed aspects of negation in Old English. In early Middle English the negative particle *ne* is introduced by similar transformation rules, the details of which we will omit here: *west þu þat ich ne singe?* 'know you that I (do) not sing?' *þere ne was ratoun . . . þat dorst have ybounden þe belle* 'there wasn't a rat . . . that dared to have bound the bell.' This *ne* was commonly procliticized to a following auxiliary: *nas* (*ne was/has*), *nam* (*ne am*), *nere* (*ne were*), *nil* (*ne wil*). Thus, *Hym thoughte his dreem nas but a vanitee* 'it seemed to him his dream wasn't but a vanity'; *noot* (*ne woot*) *I nat why* 'not know I not why.' Occasionally, *ne* was encliticized: *no more In* (*I ne*) *can* 'no more I not can.' Before the thirteenth century an intensified negative *ne . . . noht* had been introduced: *I ne seye noght; me ne schendest tu nawt; þu nart noʒt to non oþer þinge; that he ne wol nat suffre it heled be.* The intensification of negation by repetition of negative forms is by no means an uncommon feature of languages, and Middle English exemplifies profusely such strong negation. So in Chaucer, we find: *he nevere yet no vileynye ne sayde/In al his lyf unto no maner wight; no wyn ne drank she, neither whit ne reed; that ther nas no man in no regioun.*

It seems quite clear from the tendency toward proclitic and enclitic *ne* in Middle English that this particle was unstressed, and that the intensifier *noht*, if not strongly stressed, was at least given moderate emphasis. This notion is further substantiated by the fact that *ne* has disappeared from the language, while *noht* (*not*) has become the chief mark of negation. Now, once *ne* has disappeared, or is in free variation with zero, *noht* occurs as the negative adverb *following MV*. When *noht* is carried to a syntactic position *before MV* along with other adverbs, in such *potential* sentences as, **But fayth always not signifieth a life,* the structure is again considered awkward and *do* is introduced to mitigate the effects of what was thought to be an inversion: *But fayth doth not always signifye a life.* And here it has remained.

In the case of a small number of verbs whose frequency of occurrence with *not* was very high, the postposition without *do* was retained long after periphrastic *do* had been well established. Such negated verbs are *care not, doubt not, mistake not, know not.* Even today, these expressions are likely to sound less strange to us than, say, *study not, work not, read not, smell not, drive not,* and so on: "I know not what course others may take. . . ."

We have noted in another connection the rapid decline of what is usually called inversion of word-order patterns during the Middle English period. This decline does not result simply from the development of a stylistic preference, but is closely associated with the loss of inflection, that is, the loss of morphological signals to indicate grammatical relationships. With this loss comes a confusion that can only be resolved by other means. The sentence, *Saw Jack Bill* is ambiguous; it can mean either 'Jack saw Bill,' or 'Bill saw Jack.' Inversion, then, tended more and more to be studiously avoided toward the end of the Middle English period. We have already seen that the introduction of periphrastic *do* into negative declarative sentences softens the effect of the negative-adverb inversion. In affirmative sentences inversion was much more frequent with $V\#$ than with $V\frown NP$, since there was little chance of confusion here. Conversely, inversion with $V\frown NP$ was much more readily accepted when *M* or *do* were present in the construction, for then the order would be *object* $\begin{Bmatrix} M \\ do \end{Bmatrix}$ *subject* $\frown$ *verb: this do I affect.*

---

* An asterisk before a phrase or sentence indicates that the construction is ungrammatical.

In affirmative declarative unemphatic sentences inversion serves no grammatical function, and was abandoned in the early Modern English period except under rather specialized stylistic conditions. There was little reason for it in colloquial speech. And with the abandonment of inversion went the abandonment of the *do*-periphrasis in such sentences. In the seventeenth century the use of *do* came to be regarded as a mark of florid and indeed inexpert style, and though it can still be found today in bad poetry, for all intents and purposes modern practices were reached by the end of the seventeenth century.

But inversion was the unique grammatical mark of the *yes/no* interrogative; therefore, it could not be abandoned here. The resulting awkwardness, especially in the case of $V \! \frown \! NP$ where the verb had to precede both subject and object, could be lessened by the use of *do*. Professor Ellegård shows that by 1600 the *do* periphrasis occurs in 80 percent of $V \! \frown \! NP$ questions, 55 percent of $V \#$ questions; by 1700 the percentages have increased to 100 percent and 85 percent, respectively. In those instances where an object or adverbial is questioned, the percentage of *do* forms lags behind, presumably because its inclusion did not seem quite so vital:

(1) how worschipen þei and techen oþere to worchipe here gostli fadris?
(2) hou visiten þei men in prison?
(3) What power han þan worldly prelatis to make so many wickid lawes?
(4) Why reason ye, because ye have no bread?
(5) How many baskets full of fragments took ye up?

But also,

(6) Why doth this generation seek after a sign?

Note the contrasting practice in the following:

(7) Whom do men say that I am?

and two verses later,

(8) But whom say ye that I am?

In both negative and interrogative constructions there were certain verbs that resisted co-occurrence with periphrastic *do*. In Modern English, for instance, the constructions *you dare not go, you need not go, I haven't a cent on me* (but probably not *I have not a cent on me*), *I think not* (when *do* occurs, *so* must also occur: *I don't think so*) are quite grammatical in the standard language, though practically nonexistent in nonstandard American varieties.

This usage testifies to the fact that *do* was incorporated very slowly in such constructions. Similarly, though less apparent in present day standard English, a number of verbs like *say, feel, think, hear, come, go, see, call, care* persisted in interrogative sentences without *do*. Some of these occur in what Ellegård calls "enclitic questions": *And who would you visit there, say you? What surprise think you must they be in?* One thinks immediately of the Modern English formulaic greeting, *How goes it?* It is of some interest that the question with *do* has quite a different significance, *How does it go?*

In the older stages of the language, the *imperative* was signaled in part by inflection, in part by word order: *synga þu næfre ma* 'sing you never more.' With loss of inflection, and when the subject was expressed, inversion of subject and verb was the only device for signaling imperative: *Desyre thou not great fame; Love ye youre enemys.* Apparently the distaste for inverted word order contributed to the spread of periphrastic *do* in the imperative during the sixteenth century:

(1) Rather, O God! do thou have mercy on us.
(2) Would you laugh at that? why do ye laugh at it, then.
(3) Therfore doe Thou fulfill what Thou dost appoint.
(4) do you answer that question yourself.
(5) Nay, doe but looke on his hand.

Notice that the syntax of the imperative construction when the subject is expressed, with or without *do,* is precisely like that of the interrogative. The distinguishing feature, of course, is intonation. But the *do*-periphrasis seems to have spread into the imperative the more readily under the influence of the interrogative.

It is of some interest to note the way in which periphrastic *do* is treated by some of the nineteenth-century school grammars. Lindley Murray in his *An English Grammar* (3d ed., 1816) gives the following paradigm for the imperative mood:

Singular	Plural
1. Let me have.	1. Let us have.
2. Have, *or* have thou, *or* do thou have.	2. Have, *or* have ye, *or* do ye *or* you have.
3. Let him have.	3. Let them have.

George Spencer in *An English Grammar on Synthetical Principles* (New York, 1852) cites the imperative this way:

Singular	Plural
2. Love (you) *or* do (you) love. Love (thou) *or* do (thou) love.	2. Love (you) *or* do (you) love. Love (ye) *or* do (ye) love.

W. H. Wells' *A Grammar of the English Language* (New York, 1849) does not give the *do* option for the imperative:

Singular, See, *or* See you / See thou   Plural, See, *or* See you / See ye

but it reserves *do* for emphatic imperative. Of additional interest is his treatment of the interrogative and the negative:

Present, Hear I? *or* Do I hear?
Past,   Heard I? *or* Did I hear?

About the negative he comments: "A verb is conjugated negatively by introducing the adverb *not* in connection with it; as, *I know not; I do not know.* . . ."

The point is that at least as late as the mid-ninteenth century the school grammars were still citing *do* as an option in the imperative. It is difficult to know, however, to what extent this optional *do* was influenced by a somewhat different construction inherited from Old English, namely, the use of full verb *do* in the imperative followed by another imperative verb; for example, *do, make a disturbance!* should be interpreted 'do this (*or* something); make a disturbance!' and is akin to Modern English *go ahead, make a disturbance!* Modern English *do tell* and *do go on* are derived from the same source, and are *not* petrified phrases containing a periphrastic *do*.

It has seemed useful to dwell thus long on the *do*-periphrasis for several reasons. As we pointed out at the start of the discussion, this is an interesting and important construction. More than that, however, its history, as we have tried to suggest it, is extremely complex, its course being determined by a wide variety of factors. For whatever prior historical reason, we have a semantic differentiation in Old English between *do* causative and *do* noncausative; and the semantic differentiation reflects a grammatical one. Somewhere at work here is the influence of Latin constructions, an influence that is itself the result of various nonlinguistic historical conditions. In Middle English, the *do* development seems to be based upon a dialectal situation characterized by a preference on the part of a given dialect area for one word or set of words to express causation rather than for another word or set of words. There is again the influence of foreign grammatical constructions, itself the result of a series of sociocultural "accidents." Further, changes at work in other parts of the grammatical system affect the spread of periphrastic *do*, as do certain developments in poetic technique.

We have seen that any attempt to chart the history of *do* must concern itself with the history of other grammatical features: with the development of the interrogative construction, the negative, the imperative, and others.

Grammatical change, just as phonological change, must always be considered in terms of a system, or a set of systems; it is not only of little value, but it is well nigh impossible to trace the history of a given feature apart from the history of the whole system. And just as it can be extremely frustrating to try to assign reasons for a given phonological change in the history of a language, so too there are certain motivations for grammatical change that we may never be able to specify, either in linguistic or psychological terms.

FURTHER EXTENSION OF M

During the Old English period a number of periphrastic constructions in the verb phrase developed in competition with the inflectional subjunctive. This mood begins to be signaled by a number of auxiliaries: *sculan* 'must, ought to,' *willan* 'desire, intend,' *magan* 'may,' *moton* 'can, may, be allowed,' *burfan* 'need,' *hatan* 'call, name, order,' and others. The situation here is not unlike that which occasioned the extension of the prepositional system. As the inflectional subjunctive deteriorates, the periphrastic subjunctive becomes more and more necessary to the expression of modality. Mustanoja points out that by the fifteenth century the periphrastic subjunctive outnumbers the inflectional by nine to one. Inflectional constructions like *Cryst it me forbede* (Sub) '*may* Christ forbid it me,' and *als longe as owre lyf lasteth, lyve* (Sub) *we togideres* 'as long as our life lasts, *let* us live together' give way to periphrasis as in *now prift and pedom mote pou have, my leve swete barn* 'now prosperity and good fortune may you have, my dear sweet child,' and *now lat us stynte of Custance but a throwe* 'now let us stop (talking) of Constance for a time.'

Some of the Old English auxiliaries, such as *burfan* and *uton* 'let us,' were lost in Middle English, but the inventory of auxiliaries was greatly increased during this period by verbs and verb phrases that had not previously filled this role: *be about to, choose to, deign to, have to, keep, let, need, owe, purpose, could, seem, think,* and others. It was during Middle English times, too, that the reflexes of Old English *sculan* and *willan* underwent a shift in their auxiliary function. As we noted above, these two were at one time used to indicate *obligation* and *volition* respectively, but gradually they assume the additional function of marking future tense. The Old English verb had no future tense. Future time was generally implied by the context, the verb being in the present tense: *ic arise and ic fare to minum fæder* 'I will arise and I will go to my father.' This practice continued in Middle English: *although it be soure to suffre, pere cometh swete after,* where the idea of futurity is conveyed by the adverb. But the use of *shall* and *will* to mark futurity gains ground rapidly. Both were natural candidates for the role since *obligation* and *volition* suggest something yet to be done as in 'I ought to go' and 'I intend to go.' Consider this Old English sentence: *þonne sceolon beon gesamnode ealle ða menn ðe swyftoste hors habbað on þæm londe* 'then shall be summoned together all the men who the swiftest horses have in the land.' The force of *sceolon* here seems to be *both* obligation and futurity.

In early Middle English *shall* occurs much more frequently to indicate future than does *will*. When *will* begins to compete with *shall* as a future indicator later in the period, its use is characteristically more popular than formal. F. A. Blackburn, in *The English Future: Its Origin and Development*, finds that in fourteenth-century popular poems *shall* and *will* are about equally common, while in more formal "literary" works, *shall* is four times as frequent. Throughout their long history the use of *shall* and *will* in certain kinds of contexts and with certain persons of the pronoun has been complicated by the retention of modal overtones. In the course of time, *shall* attached itself to the first person as future indicator, *will* to the second and third persons. When this co-occurrence is reversed, modal implications are prominent. For years, in recent history, English teachers have struggled manfully to teach their students the proper use of the two, for the most part with little success. The reason for failure is obvious—most native speakers of English find little need for the distinction.

In Middle English, *shall, will,* and *may* occur in their past tense forms more commonly in subjunctive than in indicative expressions: *allas, that evere sholde fallen swich a cas* 'alas, that such a thing should ever happen'; *and prayed her to han good fame/And that she nolde [ne wolde] doon hem no shame* 'and prayed her to have good reputation, and that she would not do them (bring them) any shame'; *ʒiff þatt tu mihhtest lufenn Godd swa þatt itt wære himm cweme* 'if that you might love God so that it would be pleasing to him.'

In Old and early Middle English the verb *cunnan,* modern *can,* meant 'to know' or 'to know how to': *þa ondswarode he, ond cwæð, "Ne con ic noht singan"* 'then answered he, and said, "Not can (know) I not (how to) sing."' In this example it would seem quite appropriate to translate *con* by modern *can,* but in the following this is not the case: *swa þonne þis monna lif to medmiclum fæce ætywe; hwæt þær foregange, oððe hwæt þær eftfylge, we ne cunnun* 'so then this life of men appears but a little time; what has gone before, or what will follow after, we do not know.' There is no question here of translating *cunnun* by modern *can.* Similarly, Chaucer has, *she koude muche of wandrynge by the weye* 'she knew much of wandering along the way.' But in the course of the Middle English period this *verb* becomes an *auxiliary* with the senses of ability and possibility: *Alle þis loke þat þou write/As wele as þou kanst it dite* 'All this see that you write/As well as you can it endite'; *Ne was non so wise in al his lond/þe kude undon þis dremes bond* 'nor was there anyone so wise in all his land/Who could undo this dream's knot'; *a mayden ... so yung þat sho ne couthe gon on fote* 'a maiden ... so young that she couldn't go on foot.' It is relatively easy to analyze the grammatical mechanism involved in the shift of *cunnan* from *verb* to *auxiliary*. For one thing, it was to some extent already in competition with Old English *cnaw-an* 'to know.' Further, its frequent occurrence as a constituent in the construction *transitive verb + infinitive object,* as in *ne con ic noht singan* ('I do not know to sing' or 'I do not know singing' or 'I do not know how to sing') establishes it in a grammatical context that parallels the construction *Aux͡ V.* The pressure of other verbs with closely similar meanings, like, *cnawan,* then forces it into the class *M.*

5.30   *Conclusion*

On the preceding pages we have presented in some detail two grammatical models, one for Modern English and one for Old English. In so doing we have tried to show wherein the two models are similar and wherein they are different in terms of the types of rules necessary to account for grammatical sentences in each stage of the language. In general we have noted that to the extent some universality may be found in these different stages, it is to be found in the structure of the base component, while critical differences tend to show themselves in the transformation component of the grammar. Furthermore, some of the more obvious differences show up in the respective morphographemic rules. These differences, however, have frequently been generated in preceding sections of the grammar. The loss of the [+Sub] and [+Imp] features from Aux_1 reduces the number of morphographemic specifications for the verb, just as the loss of certain case and gender features reduces the number of morphographemic specifications for the noun. The reduced application of the agreement transformation obviates the necessity for morphographemic rules for adjective, infinitive, participle, and *dem*$_1$ (*the*), while greatly reducing the rules for *dem*$_2$ (*this, that*).

At the same time, the loss of such features is paralleled by the necessity for increased specifications in other parts of the grammatical system. The rules for generating *Aux* are somewhat more complex in Modern English than they were in Old English. In addition, the lexical inventory for *M* has been considerably increased with a concomitant increase in the rules for semantic interpretation of *M*. In this treatment of grammatical change there has been no attempt to specify the mechanism of the semantic component for the simple reason that despite recent investigations it is still not clear how it works. Nevertheless, it should be obvious that an expansion of the modality system must be accompanied by a greater number of semantic rules which interpret that system. At the same time, a similar thing can be said about the expansion of the prepositional system. Two considerations that our respective grammars fail to take account of are important here. One is the increase in interpretive rules; the other has to do with frequency of occurrence. Subcategorization rule 3 for Modern and for Old English is the following:

$$
\text{3.} \quad \textit{Old English} \qquad\qquad\qquad \textit{Modern English}
$$

$$
\text{3.} \quad \text{MV} \rightarrow \text{(PP)} \left(\left\{ \begin{array}{c} \text{Pred} \\ \text{NP(NP)} \end{array} \right\} \right) \text{V} \qquad\qquad \text{MV} \rightarrow \text{V} \left(\left\{ \begin{array}{c} \text{Pred} \\ \text{NP} \end{array} \right\} \right) \text{(PP)}
$$

Now although the implication is there, it is not immediately apparent that optional (PP) is chosen much more frequently in Modern English than it is in Old English. To anyone who knows Old and Modern English this fact is implied by the Old English option *NP(NP)* which is not present in Modern English.

In the light of this fact, the generalization to be made here is that any consideration of grammatical change should concern itself not only with structural changes in the system, but also with the changing nature of the distribution (see changes in class membership of strong and weak verbs) and frequency of a given structure. The point is equally valid for changes in the phonological and semantic systems.

Perhaps the major point that one would wish to make in a chapter such as this is that grammatical change, like phonological change, comes about, in large measure at least, as a result of instability in the system. And instability in a communication system may manifest itself both in terms of excessive redundancy and lack of redundancy. Where word-order systems are extremely flexible and inflectional systems no longer express discrete grammatical functions, redundancy is missing and confusion in the interpretation of the message results. Where there is too much redundancy, there is too little economy—and economy of effort is an important characteristic of human behavior. Redundancies that contribute nothing to interpretation (which is to say that they do not even provide an effective *secondary* mechanism on which interpretation can be based) tend to be lost. It is, of course, a truism that living languages are always changing, and this implies that they are always in a state of instability. But there are degrees of instability. That degree of instability which characterized English during the tenth and eleventh centuries was severe enough to require far-reaching changes in both phonological and grammatical systems. The lines of grammatical development and their direction were established during the Middle English period, and further developed during the early Modern English period.

We have made no attempt to construct model grammars for some stage of Middle and early Modern English. Not that these would not have been desirable. Still, there is always a point at which too close attention to the trees prevents one's view of the forest. It has seemed best in the section on Middle English to try to suggest some of the broader outlines of grammatical development together with some detail, since this is the period of transition from Old to Modern English, rather than to obscure these outlines by the kind of precision that grammatical models require.

5.40   Special Linguistic Terms

accusative	inorganic
agentive	instrumental
agreement	locative
analogic change	nominative
causative	objective
dative	productive
deictic	pro-verb
durative	redundant
factitive	stem-vowel replacement
functional change	strong conjugation
genitive	strong declension
imperative	verbal noun
impersonal construction	vowel harmony
indicative	weak conjugation
inflectional	weak declension
innovation	

5.50   For Additional Reference

Abbott, O. L. "The Formal Subjunctive in Seventeenth-Century American English," *AS* 36:181–7 (1961).
————. "The Preterit and Past Participle of Strong Verbs in Seventeenth-Century American English," *AS* 32:31–42 (1957).
Alston, R. C. *An Introduction to Old English*. London, 1961.
Andrew, S. O. "Relative and Demonstrative Pronouns in Old English," *Language* 12:282–93 (1936).

————. *Syntax and Style in Old English.* Cambridge, 1940.

Bambos, Rudolph C. "Verb forms in -s and -th in Early Modern English," *JEGP* 46:183–7 (1947).

Bazell, C. E. "Six Questions of Old and Middle English Morphology," *Tolkien Studies,* 5.9:51–62.

Carlton, Charles. "Word Order of Noun Modifiers in Old English Prose," *JEGP* 62:778–83 (1963).

Closs, Elizabeth. "Diachronic Syntax and Generative Grammar," *Language* 41:402–15 (1965).

Dean, Christopher. "Chaucer's Use of Function Words with Substantives," *CJL* 9:67–74 (1964).

Einarsson, Stefan. "Functional Change in Early English," *MLN* 64:498–500. (1949).

Ellegård, Alvar. *The Auxiliary Do: The Establishment and Regulation of its Use in English.* Stockholm, 1953.

Forsstrom, G. *The Verb 'To Be' in Middle English.* Lund, 1948.

Friden, Georg. *Studies on the Tenses of the English Verb from Chaucer to Shakespeare.* Uppsala, 1948.

————. "On the Use of Auxiliaries to Form the Perfect and the Pluperfect in Late Middle English and Early Modern English," *Archiv.* 196:152–3 (1959).

Funke, Otto. "Some Remarks on Late Old English Word-Order with Special Reference to Aelfric and the Maldon Poem," *ES* 37:99–104 (1956).

Heltveit, Trygve. *Studies in English Demonstrative Pronouns.* Oslo, 1953.

Howren, Robert. "The Generation of Old English Weak Verbs," *Language* 43:674–85 (1967).

Jacobsson, B. *Inversion in English.* Uppsala, 1951.

Karlberg, Göran. *The English Interrogative Pronouns: A Study of their Syntactic History.* Stockholm, 1954.

Lee, Donald Woodward. *Functional Change in Early English.* Wisconsin, 1948.

Levin, Samuel R. "Negative Contraction: An Old and Middle English Dialect Criterion," *JEGP* 57:492–501 (1958).

————. "A Reclassification of the Old English Strong Verbs," *Language* 40:156–61 (1964).

Long, Mary McDonald. *The English Strong Verb from Chaucer to Caxton.* Wisconsin, 1944.

Marchand, Hans. "The Syntactical Change from Inflectional to Word Order System and Some Effects of this Change in Relation 'verb/object' in English, A Diachronic and Synchronic Interpretation," *Anglia* 70: 1:47–89 (1951).

Marckwardt, Albert H. "Verb Inflections in Late Old English," *Philologica* 6.8, 79–88.

Moore, Samuel. "Earliest Morphological Changes in Middle English," *Language* 4:238–66 (1928).

Mosse, Fernand. *A Handbook of Middle English.* Trans. James A. Walker. Baltimore, 1952.

Mustanoja, Tauno F. *A Middle English Syntax, Pt. 1: Parts of Speech.* Helsinki, 1960.

Nathan, Norman. "Pronouns of Address in the *Canterbury Tales*," *MS* 21:193–201 (1959).

Ohlander, Urban. "A Study on the Use of the Infinitive Sign in Middle English," *SN* 14:58–66 (1941–1942).

Quirk, Randolph. *The Concessive Relation in Old English Poetry.* New Haven, 1954.

Quirk, Randolph, and C. L. Wrenn. *An Old English Grammar.* New York, 1957.

Rantavaara, Irma. "On the Development of the Periphrastic Dative in Late Middle English Prose," *NM* 63:175–203 (1962).

Scherer, Philip. "Aspect in the Old English of the Corpus Christi MS," *Language* 34:245–51 (1958).

Shannon, Ann. *A Descriptive Syntax of the Parker Manuscript of the Anglo-Saxon Chronicle from 734 to 891.* The Hague, 1964.

Swieczkowski, Walerian. *Word Order Patterning in Middle English: A Quantitative Study Based on* Piers Plowman *and* Middle English Sermons. The Hague, 1962.

Vallins, G. H. *The Patterns of English.* London, 1956.

Wright, Joseph and Elizabeth Mary. *Old English Grammar.* 3d ed. London, 1925; repr. 1934.

————. *An Elementary Middle English Grammar.* 2d ed. London, 1928; repr. 1934.

————. *An Elementary Historical New English Grammar.* London, 1924.

Wyld, H. C. *A History of Modern Colloquial English.* 3d ed. Oxford, 1953.

5.60   Some Historical Projects

1. Using information provided by the *Oxford English Dictionary* and the *Middle English Dictionary,* trace the grammatical development and distribution from Old English to Modern English of any one of the following prepositions.

in	after
on	at
over	from
through	of
with	under
against	

2. Investigate the history of *who, whom, which, that* as *relatives.*

3. For the following verbs, what *past tense* and *past participle* forms were common during the Middle English period (1150–1500)? During the Early Modern English period (1500–1700)?

glide	shone
rise	help
slide	starve
choose	eat
creep	shape

4. Investigate the development of natural gender in English and the present means of expressing gender differences among living creatures.

5. Examine the history of such morphologically plural but semantically singular forms as *news, gallows, bellows, tidings, pants, scissors,* and the like.
6. Trace the grammatical and semantic history of the indefinite indicators *a/an, certain, some, any.*
7. Account for the development of the anticipatory *there* construction ('There is a man at the door').
8. A number of verbs in English may occur with a complement consisting of a noun plus infinitive construction: 'He *helped* us (to) *finish* the job,' 'Dad let me take the car,' 'The teacher made us read the assignment.' What other verbs do you think of that participate in this construction? Historically, what has been the practice in the use of the marked (*to*) or unmarked infinitive?
9. What can you find out about the history of the following constructions? 'He is certain to leave tomorrow'; 'He is certain of leaving tomorrow.' Are these sentences paraphrases of each other, or do they have different meanings? If the latter, how can you account for this difference?
10. Look up the origin and use of the *split* infinitive in English.
11. When do the following constructions begin to appear in English?

start (to) go(ing)	get going
begin (to) go(ing)	like (to) go(ing)
keep going	hate (to) go(ing)

6. Semantic change

Introduction

"What does this word mean?" In every culture questions about the meaning of a word are everyday occurrences; and they suggest some very significant differences between the language subsystems we have thus far considered, and the semantic system to which we now turn our attention. It is a rare occasion when a native speaker of a language poses questions about some segment of the phonological system, or about the kinds of grammatical devices that characterize his language. This is not surprising since these latter may be taken as "givens"; they are the automatic consequence of the language learning process. And the fact that these systems develop automatically is directly related to the fact that for the most part they are *closed* systems. And in the course of a lifetime the phonological and grammatical inventories of these systems will change very little. Concerning the lexicon, however, the situation is quite otherwise. While the vocabulary of a given speaker of a language is limited, consisting for most people of a few thousand words, the lexical inventory of the *whole* language is practically limitless. This fact has important ramifications for any account of semantic change.

Unlike the phonemic and grammatical inventories which are pretty much the same for all individuals within a given speech community, lexical inventories will vary quite radically from one speaker to another. Thus, the semantic system, which we will tentatively define here as *an interlocking series of meaning networks,* of one individual will differ from that of another. Obviously, there is a considerable overlap; otherwise, there would be no communication. But since each of us has a unique personality that is the product of a unique genetic history and a unique set of experiences, each of us has a somewhat unique semantic system.

Furthermore, our respective lexical inventories are in a constant state of change (if change can be considered a constant state). Every moment modifies experience, however imperceptibly, and every modification of experience modifies the interlocking series of meaning networks that constitute the semantic system. New words enter the vocabulary; old words take on new meanings to accommodate new situations; old meanings are shifted from one word to another; some meanings cease to have relevance; some old words are lost. And all this demands some reorientation of established meaning networks. One may imagine a huge railroad yard in which new sections of track are continually being added and old sections being removed, and in which new switches and the reorientation of old switches constantly modify the relationships between tracks.

Not long ago it was fashionable to accuse linguists of ignoring meaning and thus of ignoring the very essence of language. This accusation was not altogether just, resulting in part from a misunderstanding both of the linguist's goals and of his capabilities. Consider the differences suggested above (and these are by no means all) between the phonological and grammatical systems on the one hand and the semantic system on the other. The former, because they are closed, are amenable to analysis and description by the methods now available to the linguist. The latter, by its very openness, eludes characterization in any strictly formal way. That there is a semantic system and that there is a mechanism for interpreting that system is quite clear. What is not at all clear is precisely how to characterize the features of this system, and how to specify the way in which the interpreting mechanism works. Answers to some of the more searching questions about how the semantic component of language, and of a given language, should be formulated must eventually come not from the linguist alone, but from the linguist working with the psychologist, the philosopher, the anthropologist, the speech pathologist, and the neurologist. In the meantime, we must admit that we are not able at present to characterize in any precise way the structure of semantic systems and their relation to other subsystems of language; still, we must try to deal with the problem of meaning as best we can.

It is perhaps obvious that what has just been said is intimately tied to the question "*How* does this word mean?" It is an old question, having received considerable attention from philosophers, psychologists, philologists, linguists, semanticists, and literary critics since the days of Aristotle. The literature on the subject is so vast, the tentative answers so various, that no attempt at presentation or review can be made in this chapter. It must be sufficient for our purposes merely to present two or three of the models which purport to explain the mechanism of meaning, and to make some comment on these.

Charles E. Osgood ("The Nature and Measurement of Meaning," *Psychological Bulletin*, XLIX [1952], 197–237) places theories of meaning in three categories, each category being determined by the way in which a given theory responds to the question "Under what conditions does something which is not the object become a sign of that object?" According to one theoretical category, meanings are *mental* events, objects and signs are *physical* events. An idea is a core of meaning, a mental event that relates the two different physical events, object and sign. The word *table* evokes the idea of a table in the mind; the perception of a table evokes the same idea. Thus the word *table*, which is not the object, becomes a sign of that object when it evokes the *idea* associated with the object. Illustrating this mentalistic view of the nature of meaning is the by now famous triangle of C. K. Ogden and I. A. Richards (*The Meaning of Meaning*, 4th ed. [London, 1936], 11):

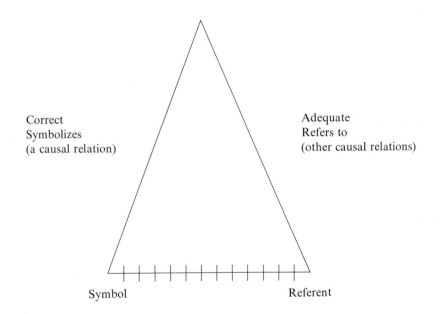

Thought or Reference

Correct
Symbolizes
(a causal relation)

Adequate
Refers to
(other causal relations)

Symbol

Referent

A second category suggests that an object is an unconditioned stimulus, that a sign is a conditioned stimulus, and that meaning is the result of the latter being substituted for the former. The notion here is that the sign (*s*) evokes the same response as the object (*S*):

$$S \diagdown \atop s \diagup \quad \longrightarrow R$$

A third theory, something of a modification of the second, takes meaning to be a "set" or "disposition" on the part of the organism to respond to the sign in a way that is somehow relevant to the object (see Charles Morris, "Foundations of the Theory of Signs," *International Encyclopedia of Unified Science,* eds. Otto Neurath, Rudolf Carnap, Charles Morris, Vol. 1, No. 2 [1938]). Signs achieve their meanings by eliciting responses that "take account of" the objects that they signify. Although the word *table* may elicit responses quite different from those elicited by the object to which it refers, and thus the sign is not a proper substitute for the object, still it produces in the organism a disposition to make *some* of the responses evoked by the object.

In the article referred to above, Professor Osgood presents his own theory of the behavioral process which he takes to define the nature of meaning. We paraphrase his argument. Stimulus objects evoke a complex pattern of reactions from the organism. When a stimulus which is not the object but which has previously been associated with it is presented without the object, it elicits some reduced portion of the total behavior elicited by the stimulus object. The discriminatory capacity of the organism tends to mediate in some way or another the reaction evoked by the sign of the object; this mediational response produces a certain degree of self-stimulation. Osgood illustrates the process this way (*The Measurement of Meaning,* Charles E. Osgood, George J. Suci, and Percy H. Tannenbaum, University of Illinois Press, 1961):

The stimulus object ($\dot{s}$), say a spider, elicits a complex pattern of behavior (R_t) that includes, for some people at least, a heavy load of autonomic fear. A part of this total response to the stimulus object, spider, becomes conditioned through association to the word *spider* ($\boxed{S}$). The mediating reaction (r_m) produces a distinctive pattern of self-stimulation (s_m) that in turn elicits different kinds of overt or covert behavior (R_x), perhaps an outward shudder,

a verbal response such as "Ugh!" an extra heart beat, a change in facial expression, and the like.

Interesting as these "models" of meaning may be, they all appear to fail in the same way; namely, that it is hard to see just what they have to do with language. For language is, quite clearly, *not* an inventory of signs and symbols. Given the two sentences:

(1) An exquisitely marked spider weaving its gossamer web in the morning sunlight is a thing of sheer beauty.
(2) The boy huddled in the dark recess of a cave watching horrified as a huge, black, hairy-legged spider crept closer and closer.

it seems obvious that an interpretation of the term *spider* will be quite different in the two sentences, and that this difference will be a reflection not only of the way in which all other terms in the sentences are interpreted, but also of the grammatical structures that permit these terms to be interpreted in such and such a way. It would seem, then, that any attempt to talk about sign behavior apart from grammatical behavior will simply lead us into a dead end. What we would like to have is some precise account of the interpretative mechanism which in its assignment of meaning to grammatical (and ungrammatical) utterances takes account of the relationship between sign behavior and grammatical structure.

Somewhat closer to the ideal suggested above are the statistical or probability models that have enjoyed currency in recent years. The mathematical complexity of such models prohibits any discussion of them here. Instead, we will quote Joshua Whatmough on the subject (*Language: A Modern Synthesis* [London, 1956]):

> . . . a reasoning mechanism based on the calculus of probability has been envisaged, and in principle no doubt could be designed, which would behave very much like the threshold control (sub- or superconsciousness) with which neurologists are familiar, and which has provoked the use of introspection with all its unconvincing assumptions and denials, in the attempt to discover how the human brain modifies verbal input to produce the often quite different, but still verbal, output that we find in the work of all creative thinkers, scientists, philosophers, artists and composers. We may think of two or more interlocked networks, corresponding to the nervous fibers and synopses of the brain, not only those which pro-present and handle information in the shape of discrete symbols, but those which control the information in relation to the intermediating probabilities to be associated with them. The interpretation of a concept in terms of the functioning of a mechanism of this kind, using statistical data, precisely as language itself does, comes very close to what is usually meant by 'thinking', even by 'invention' or 'discovery'. And this is far closer to the 'meaning of meaning' than anything hitherto suggested (pp. 77–78).

In recent years it has become increasingly clear that whatever boundary line may exist between semantics and syntax is very obscure indeed. A consideration of the notion *grammaticalness* will illustrate this point. Of the following sentences, we may say that (1) and (2) are fully grammatical, while (3) and (4) are in some way ungrammatical:

A. (1) John looked happy.
   (2) John found the ball.
   (3) John looked the ball.
   (4) John found happy.

Furthermore, of the following sentences we may say that (1) and (2) are at best very strange, apart from some highly imaginative context, while (3) and (4) are fully grammatical or quite "regular":

B. (1) Heavy weightless dreams awake riotously.
   (2) Horses may startle rain.
   (3) A scarecrow startled my horse.
   (4) Small weightless particles fell softly.

(See Noam Chomsky, *Aspects of the Theory of Syntax,* The M.I.T. Press [1965], 148–149).

Of set A, (3) and (4) are ungrammatical because they violate certain subcategory rules of the grammar, rules which classify verbs as *transitives* or *intransitives, pre-adjectival* or *pre-nominal,* and the like. Thus, the frame *John . . . the ball* does not allow the subcategory *pre-adjective,* and the frame *John . . . happy* does not allow the subcategory *transitive.*

Regarding set B, it is tempting to say that (1) and (2) simply do not make very good sense, rather than to say that they are ungrammatical. But notice that these sentences are not *uninterpretable;* there are certainly contexts in which they may be interpreted in some metaphorical way. And that *metaphorical way* involves at least the assignment of the syntactic feature [+animate] to the nouns *dreams* and *rain.* We will say that this feature is automatically assigned by the selectional constraints on the verbs *awake* and *startle.* The problem of "making sense" now arises because the grammar has previously assigned the feature [−animate] to these two nouns in order that such sentences as "Tell me your dream" may be produced where *Tell* is marked [+V, + __ NP[−animate]]. In order, then, to interpret sentence (1) of B, the feature [−animate] must be suspended temporarily by some mechanism that is an extension of our grammar. Put in a somewhat different way, this temporary suspension amounts to a violation of a certain type of sub-categorial rule of the grammar. In A, sentences (3) and (4) violate syntactic features that are specifiable in terms of frames. The type of rule involved here is called by Professor Chomsky a *strict subcategorization rule*. In B, sentences (1) and (2) temporarily suspend, or violate, or ignore, syntactic features that are specifiable in terms of such rules as:

dream, [+N, +common, +count, −animate, etc.].

These rules Chomsky calls *selectional rules*.

The relevance of what we have just been saying to semantic change may be illustrated in this way. The term *nickel* is currently polysemantic: it refers both to a mineral substance and to a coin made from that substance. Histori-cally, we know that the first meaning preceded the second, but an account of the change that states merely that the term *nickel* meaning 'a particular mineral substance' developed a secondary meaning, 'a coin having a particu-lar monetary value' is quite inadequate. For this sense change is closely tied to a change in syntactic features; thus *nickel,* [+N, +common, −count, −animate] develops in its secondary meaning the features *nickel,* [+N, +common, +count, −animate]. Furthermore, it is very likely the case that the change came about in a way specifiable in terms of syntactic transforma-tional rules:

(1) This coin is made out of nickel.
(2) It is a nickel coin.
(3) It is a nickel.

It is also apparent that the feature [+count] occasions a change in the frame rule; that is, *nickel* may now occur in the frame [a __], where formerly it could only occur in the frame [Ø __] (assuming that the definite article is introduced by transformation rule). *Nickel* now has two lexical entries:

(i) *nickel,* [+N, Ø __ , +common, −count, −animate]
(ii) *nickel,* [+N, a __ , +common, +count, −animate]

There is, of course, redundancy in the specification of the features [a __ , +count] and [Ø __ , −count]. The reader should note that it is the deletion transformation applied to (2) above that accounts for the transfer of the feature [a __ , +count] from *coin* to *nickel.*

6.10   The Semantic Component

In Chapter 4 (4.10) we noted that in addition to a syntactic and phonological component, a grammar contains a semantic component that interprets the structures generated by the base rules. The most elaborate model thus far proposed for a semantic component is that first outlined by Jerrold J. Katz and Jerry A. Fodor in "The Structure of a Semantic Theory," (*Language* 39:170–210 [1963]) and later expanded in Katz and Paul M. Postal *An Integrated Theory of Linguistic Descriptions* (M.I.T., 1964). In their view, the semantic component is a "projective device" consisting of two parts, *a dictionary* and *a set of projection rules*. The dictionary provides a meaning for each lexical item in the language, and does so in the following entry form:[1]

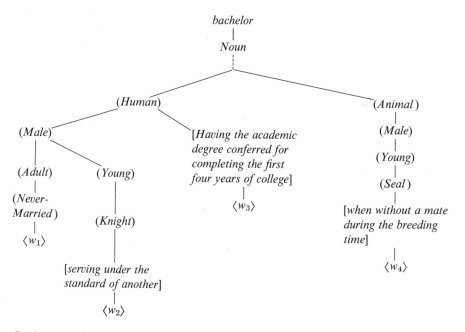

Such entry forms contain subsets of symbols each one of which provides a certain kind of information. In the diagram, unenclosed symbols are *syntactic markers,* parenthesized symbols are *semantic markers,* bracketed symbols are *distinguishers,* and those within angles are called *selection restrictions.* Syntactic markers differentiate the senses of a lexical item according to its morphological or syntactic class, or subclass; that is, according to whether it

[1] Diagram 2.7 from page 14 of *An Integrated Theory of Linguistic Descriptions,* Jerrold J. Katz and Paul M. Postal, copyright © 1964 The M.I.T. Press.

is a *noun, verb, adjective, preposition,* and so on. The dotted lines in the diagram provide for further subcategories of a given grammatical class (for example, [+count], [−animate] for nouns, and so on).[2] Semantic markers "express general semantic properties," while distinguishers differentiate the senses of a given lexical entry. A selection restriction is "a formally expressed necessary and sufficient condition" for a semantic reading of a given lexical item to combine with a semantic reading of some other lexical item with which it is syntactically conjoined. Although the semantic component will provide independent readings for the adjective *green* and the noun *truth,* there can be no derived reading for the combination *green truth* since the reading for *truth* fails to satisfy the selection restriction that characterizes *green.* According to Katz and Postal such a combination would be marked as *semantically anomolous.*

According to this format the dictionary entry for *nickel,* discussed above, would appear as follows:

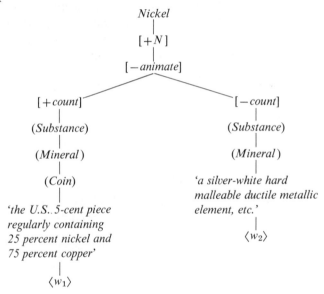

Katz and Postal point out that ". . . a necessary but not sufficient condition for a syntactically unambiguous sentence to be semantically ambiguous is that it contain at least one ambiguous lexical item (p. 15)." *Nickel* is such an item, so that the following is clearly ambiguous:

(1) A miner put the nickel in his pack.

---

[2] In the diagrams that follow we change these symbolic conventions slightly. We will use brackets [ ] for *syntactic markers,* parentheses ( ) for *semantic markers,* single quotes ' ' for *distinguishers,* and angles ⟨ ⟩ for *selection restrictions.*

There is nothing in sentence (1) to exclude either of the readings entered for *nickel*. However, in sentence (2) semantic readings of other lexical items in the sentence permit only *one* reading for *nickel*:

(2) A miner put the nickel in the coin-operated coffee machine.

Projection rules ". . . produce derived readings by combining the readings of lower-order constituents to form readings for higher-order constituents (Katz and Postal, p. 20)." Such rules operate on underlying phrase markers and produce readings for *S* that are unambiguous. Consider the underlying phrase markers for sentence (1) on pages 281 and 283 (these have been somewhat simplified).

The reader will notice at once that both a syntactic and a semantic incompatability exists between the *Det* (*a*) and the *N* feature [−count]. We could say that a low-level obligatory transformation deletes *a* before [−count], but this would mean deferring the operation of the projection rules that would give a derived reading for the *np* node of *MV* until this transformation rule has functioned. Furthermore, such a procedure would deny Katz and Postal's contention that projection rules operate on underlying rather than derived strings. We will have more to say on this point later. For the moment, we will impose an additional context restriction on the base rules that expand *Det:*

10a. Det → $\begin{Bmatrix} \text{A} \\ \text{np}^\frown\text{poss} \end{Bmatrix}$

10b. A → $\begin{Bmatrix} a/\_\_[+\text{count}] \\ \varnothing \end{Bmatrix}$

These rules must obviously occur *after* rule 10 which assigns syntactic features to *N*. The structure of the object *np* in the preceding phrase marker will be altered to:

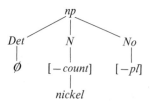

The projection rules will now provide derived readings starting with lowest-order constituents and working up the tree to *S*:

1. a − miner, Ø − nickel, his − pack

(1a)

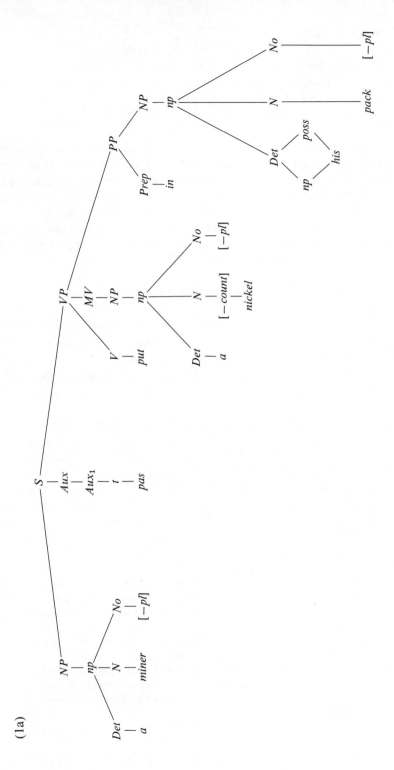

2. in — his⌢pack
3. put — Ø⌢nickel — in⌢his⌢pack
4. a⌢miner — put⌢Ø⌢nickel⌢in⌢his⌢pack
5. a⌢miner⌢put⌢Ø⌢nickel⌢in⌢his⌢pack

The ultimate derived reading for sentence (1b) provided by the projection rules will differ from that of (1a) just by the difference between the two readings for the lexical item *nickel.* The definite article transformation applied to either (1a) or (1b) produces a surface structure (1) in which the syntactic and semantic distinction between (1a) and (1b) has been neutralized.

In the case of sentences containing embeddings, the projection rules must operate first on those *S*'s that contain *no* embeddings, otherwise they are blocked. Consider the following sentence:

(1c) A miner who had finished work put nickel in his pack.

Before the leftmost *np* can be given a semantic reading, the *S* which it dominates must be given a reading since no reading for *a*⌢*miner*⌢*[−pl]*⌢*S* is possible. If the phrase marker for this *S* contains a node that dominates *another S,* then this latter must be assigned a semantic reading first, and so on. The projection rules must always begin with the lowest *S* in the phrase marker and work upward.

This, in brief, is the structure of the semantic component proposed by Katz and Postal and adopted in its essential parts by Chomsky (*Aspects*). However, we should point out that such a notion of the structure of the semantic mechanism has not proved acceptable to all linguists. One of the chief objectors to the assumption of a semantic component that is separate from and operates only to interpret the output of a syntactic component is James D. McCawley of the University of Chicago. In an article "Meaning and the Description of Languages" *Kotoba no uchu,* No. 9, 10, 11:1–27 (Tokyo, 1967), McCawley poses the following questions:

(1) Are semantic representations objects of a fundamentally different nature than syntactic representations or can syntactic and semantic representations more fruitfully be considered to be basically objects of the same type?

(2) Does the relationship between semantic representation and surface syntactic representation involve processes which are of two fundamentally different types and are organized into two separate systems, corresponding to what Chomsky called 'transformations' and 'semantic projection rules,' or is there in fact no such division of the processes which link the meaning of an utterance with its superficial form?

(p. 9)

(1b)

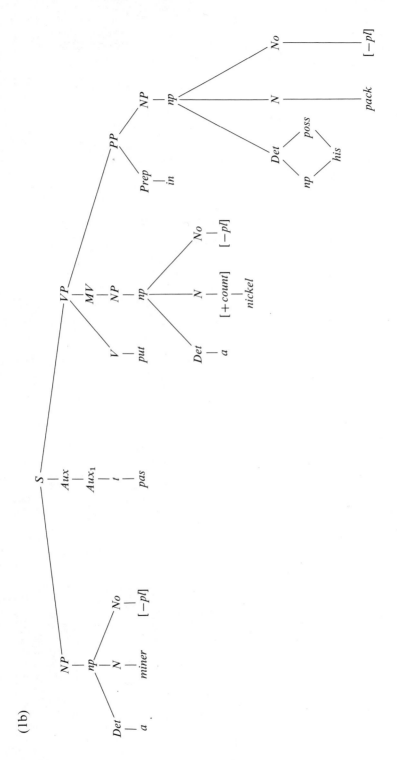

(1c)

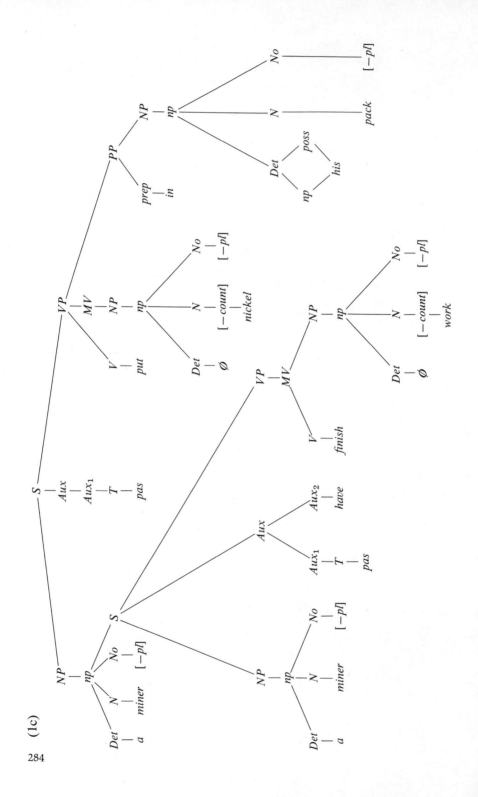

In answering these two questions, he first rejects the notion of "deep structure" in the Chomskian sense: "As an alternative to Chomsky's conception of linguistic structure, one could propose that in each language there is simply a single system of processes which convert the semantic representation of each sentence into its surface syntactic representation and that none of the intermediate stages in the conversion of semantic representation into surface syntactic representation is entitled to any special status such as that which Chomsky ascribes to 'deep structure' (p. 9)." Professor McCawley gives a number of examples designed to show that ambiguous surface structures cannot always be disambiguated simply by recourse to deep structure. He points out, for instance, concerning the sentence "Those men saw themselves in the mirror" (which can mean either 'each of the men saw himself in the mirror' or 'the entire group of men saw the entire group in the mirror'), that ". . . if *themselves* is derived from an underlying repetition of *those men,* there is no way in which the deep structures of the two meanings of *Those men saw themselves in the mirror* could differ from each other (p. 13)." He argues further that it is *not* the case that all lexical items are inserted into a sentence at a single point in the derivational history of that sentence, nor that these insertions all *precede* syntactic transformations. There are instances in which certain lexical items cannot be inserted until *after* all such transformations have been carried out. He concludes as follows:

> In summary, I believe that these considerations indicate that syntactic and semantic representations are objects of the same formal nature, namely ordered trees whose non-terminal nodes are labelled by syntactic category symbols, and that in each language there is a single system of transformations which convert semantic representations of sentences into their superficial form; these transformations include 'lexical transformations,' i.e., transformations which replace a portion of a tree by a lexical item. One may also draw the conclusion that syntax as a separate branch of linguistics simply does not exist: any generalizations about the way words can be combined in a language is merely the result of constraints on the ways in which semantic material may be combined and of the mechanisms which the language has for the conversion of semantic representations into the superficial forms of sentences (p. 25).

Elsewhere,[3] McCawley compares his own grammatical model (represented by B on the next page) with that of Chomsky (A):

---

[3] In a paper delivered at the University of Iowa *Language Colloquium,* December, 1968.

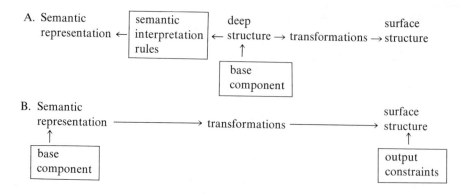

A. Semantic representation ← semantic interpretation rules ← deep structure → transformations → surface structure

base component

B. Semantic representation ⟶ transformations ⟶ surface structure

base component

output constraints

Clearly, there are important differences between these two models. In A, as we have seen, deep structure is generated by the base component; that structure then receives a semantic interpretation and a semantic representation. The result, which is still deep structure, is fed through the transformation rules the output of which is surface structure. Perhaps the most important point is that the transformations affect only syntactic structure and have no bearing on semantic interpretation. In B, there is nothing corresponding to deep structure. The base component provides a semantic representation which is then fed through a system of transformations that are both syntactic and lexical. The output is surface structure which is modified by a system of "output constraints." What this last appears to mean is this: Any output of the transformation component which a native speaker of the language would consider to be ungrammatical is blocked by the output constraints from appearing in the surface structure. To take only one of McCawley's examples: there is an acceptable passive sentence,

(1) Not many of the boys weren't examined by the doctor.

However, the active sentence from which (1) is derived by transformation

(2) The doctor didn't examine not many of the boys.

is unacceptable. It is important to note that in McCawley's scheme of things ungrammatical elements are neither deleted nor modified by the output constraints, but, as we have said, simply blocked from appearing as surface structure. In the case of our example, the phrase marker that describes the structure of (2) is transformed by the passive transformation into the phrase marker for (1) the final string of which is then permitted to appear as surface structure, while the final string of (2) is prevented from appearing as surface structure.

It seems to us that McCawley makes a very strong case against the notion that syntax and semantics may somehow be envisioned as separate subsystems of the grammar. Further, it is quite clear that it is not strictly the case that transformations do not introduce new lexical material; and this fact mitigates against any assumption that the semantic component operates only on the output of the base. It is also true that there are grammatical transformed structures, at least in English, which are derived from underlying ungrammatical structures. On the other hand, Professor McCawley's model as shown in B above is not without its difficulties. For one thing, he has nothing to say about the structure of the lexicon. For another, it is not at all clear precisely what is the mechanism of the interpretive device, nor how it provides derived semantic readings from syntactically combined lexical items, nor how it alters readings in lexical transformations. For a third, one is compelled to ask, what is the formal structure of the *output constraints?* Is this simply a list of exceptions to syntactic and lexical rules, or is it more than this? And if it is more than this, what more is it? Perhaps a more interesting question is this: Given the linguistic competence of a native speaker of a language, is it reasonable to suppose that his internalized grammar permits the generation of ungrammatical structures only to block them at the last moment? This seems highly unlikely.

Perhaps the model for the interpretive device which is actually to be found in the grammatical mechanism of a language speaker lies somewhere between that of Katz and Postal and that suggested by McCawley. What is certainly clear is that there yet remain a great many facets of the operation of the mind about which we know relatively little. And one of these is the way in which the mind handles meaning. Wherever relevant in the discussion of semantic change which follows, we will have in mind a semantic mechanism much like that proposed by Katz and Postal. Although it has its theoretical disadvantages, it has a number of redeeming features not the least of which is specificity.

6.20   *Semantic Change*

In dealing with semantic change we will need to be concerned both with the nature of lexical entries in the dictionary and the operation of projection rules. It seems reasonable to suppose that changes in the first will cause changes in the second. Specifically, change in a lexical entry may be characterized by changes in the syntactic markers, the semantic markers, the distinguishers, the selection restrictions, or any combination of these. For any given entry, new markers, distinguishers, or restrictions may be added, while old ones may be lost. In the case of *nickel,* a new syntactic marker [+count], a new semantic marker (coin), a new distinguisher, and a new selection restriction have all been added to the entry; at the same time, the features of the original entry are retained unchanged. One may expect to find situations in which features of the original entry have been lost altogether, and of course cases where the entry itself has either been lost without replacement or replaced by a new entry. In the latter case we will need to show the extent to which features characterizing the replaced entry have been transferred to the new entry.

Some General Considerations

We have pointed out that semantic change is much more obvious than either phonological or grammatical change. Since our experiences in the world and our attitudes toward these experiences are constantly changing, the semantic system by which we express our experiences and attitudes is in a perpetual state of instability. New developments in technologies, in social and political institutions and attitudes, in international relations, in the state of physical and chemical nature, in fashion, the arts, communication, sports—all these demand to be expressed in new ways.

Any one of us may at any time be responsible for a unique expression of an idea or situation. Hundreds of such innovations may occur daily, although only a very few will achieve some currency. Their adoption and spread will depend on many factors: the significance of the subject matter to a particular cultural group, the social situation in which an innovation occurs, the size and character of the audience, the status and prestige of the innovator, the aptness of the innovation, its emotional or psychological or esthetic effect, and so forth. The point is that we may actually observe a semantic change in the making, or be subjected to its effect shortly after it has occurred. Probably we have all had this experience. But how many of us have observed changes taking place in our phonemic or phonetic inventory, or have adopted a new grammatical device (in our native tongue) in the course of a lifetime? Changes of this latter sort are more akin to the chemical and physical changes which go on minute by minute, hour by hour, month by month, year by year, in the body structure. We know that such changes are taking place, but only the most precise scientific scrutiny will reveal them. Semantic changes, on the other hand, are somewhat more like changes in ladies' fashions: they tend to be abrupt and perfectly obvious; some of them become popular and are widely accepted, others are disfavored and rapidly disappear; their acceptance and spread depends in large part on the prestige both of the person who introduces them and those who are first to accept them. As in the case of ladies' fashions, once a trend is set fashions in words spread rapidly by an almost slavish imitation.

As one might expect, much of the interest that semanticists have shown in meaning change has centered around the classification of such changes. The classifications themselves may be classified. One of the oldest and perhaps most often cited methods of classifying types of semantic changes is the logical-rhetorical method by which changes are characterized as (1) genus to species, (2) species to genus, (3) species to species, and (4) analogical. Thus, one may say that the sense of Old English *meta* (Modern English *meat*) 'food' has been narrowed or particularized to a species of food in the course of its history. English *arrive* from French *arriver* from Latin *adripare* has undergone a widening of meaning from the sense 'to arrive from/by sea' to simply 'to arrive' whether from the sea, from the land, or from the air, whether by foot, bicycle, automobile, train, plane, canoe, spaceship, or whatever. A good explanation of the operation of analogy is provided by Gustaf Stern in *Meaning and Change of Meaning:*

> In ME, the adjective *light* acquired the meaning 'of small value, cheap.' ... The development can be clearly traced. The corresponding meaning of the adverb *lightly* is instanced once only, and it does not seem to have arisen through independent development of the adverb, but has probably been "borrowed" from the adjective. We have to assume that a speaker wishing to express the notion 'cheaply,' for some reason selects the stem *light*—, and, in accordance with the usual practice of forming adverbs, employs the word *lightly* (*Me buþ lihtliche a þing þet me luueþ lutel,* 'men buy cheaply a thing for which they care little.' *Ancren Riwle,* 392).
>
> Theoretically, the word *lightly* in this phrase may be explained in two ways. We can assume that the speaker, forming the *meaning* 'cheaply,' employs the well-known word *lightly* to express it, and feels at liberty to do so, because the new meaning of *lightly* corresponds to a current meaning of the adjective *light,* and he is accustomed to use cognate adjectives and adverbs in corresponding meanings. The process is one of group supplementation: the parallelism of meanings between *light* and *lightly* is completed with a missing member. We have the old word *lightly* used in a new sense.
>
> Secondly, we can assume that the adverb *lightly* in this context is a new coining, which the speaker makes on the basis of the adjective *light,* but without associating it with the previously—in other meanings—current adverb *lightly.* Genetically, we have then not the old word in a new meaning, but really a new word, although identical in form with the old word [a *homophonous* form]; a new word created through combinative analogy.

Stern then puts the question, "Which is the correct explanation?" and comments as follows:

I do not think it is unfair to counter this question with another: does it matter? For if we regard *lightly* as a new coining, we must assume (1) that the *speaker* who makes it and repeats it cannot in the long run avoid associating his *lightly* with the current word *lightly,* and thus apprehending them as the same word; and (2) that the *hearer* must at once apprehend *lightly* as being the current word, which, with the help of context, he is able to interpret in a new but perfectly natural manner, the new meaning corresponding to a familiar meaning of the adjective *light.* (212–213)

Stern's comments here call to mind the fact that semantic changes may be classified according to psychological or emotional states or processes that touch them off or enable them to be touched off. Stern himself refers to *intentional* and *unintentional* psychic processes as a means of characterizing certain types of change. His term *nomination,* for example, refers to an intentional "naming of a referent, new or old, with a name that has not previously been used for it" (282). The term *transfer,* on the other hand, refers to "a shift of meaning that may occur *unintentionally* and without the mediation of a peculiar verbal context" (342). Stern finds *nominations* to be the result of the speaker's conscious attempt to adapt speech to his purposes. The speaker may feel the need of increased possibilities of emotional relief and thus look for intensified expressions for emotionally charged situations. He may feel the need for, and pleasure in, creativity in language expression. He may wish his words to seem new, fresh, and expansive. He may be striving for a particular effect to be gained through some sort of semantic tension.

Such comments, of course, immediately take us into the realm of the *causes* of semantic change; and we should distinguish between *causes* and *conditions.* The latter define a semantic 'climate' that makes some part of the system amenable to change, and they tend to result from certain inherent characteristics of a semantic system, some of which we have already commented on. A number of semanticists cite the acquisition of language by a new generation as one universal condition of semantic change. We have referred above to the instability of semantic systems. Perhaps the term *fluid* would be appropriate here: semantic boundaries are difficult to delineate since fields of meaning tend to flow into one another. This tendency itself stems from the *polysemous* nature of the vocabulary. We have tried to show earlier the close connection between the syntactic and semantic systems. Clearly, changing states in the syntactic system provide conditions for change in some relevant part of the semantic system. Some illustrations of this were given in Chapter 5 (recall the development of *again* and *against*).

A further condition for potential semantic change is provided by the dual tendencies of *conservatism* and *innovation.* Old English *scipu* 'ship' has been retained in the language even though the nature of its reference has changed many times over. One would be hard put to find any similarity between a

Germanic 'ship' of the seventh century and a twentieth-century space 'ship,' other than that they are both means of transport. But so are donkeys and railroad cars. On the other hand, technical inventiveness frequently calls for a comparable lexical inventiveness. Such terms as *transonic, supersonic, hydromatic, phoneme, sonogram, skyscraper,* and *instamatic* and hundreds of other words expressing some result of technological development represent one type of semantic innovation.

Coming back to causes once again, the great French linguist Antoine Meillet was one of the first to deal with these in some systematic way. For him the causes of semantic change were of three types: (1) linguistic, (2) historical, and (3) social. The semantic differentiation of *again* and *against* results from a linguistic cause. In the same category belongs the strong negative sense of *but* which results in part from its earlier conjunction with the negative particle *ne.* An oft-cited instance of this kind of *linguistic contagion* is the negative connotations in French of *pas, rien, personne,* and other words that acquire a negative sense through their syntactic association with negative *ne.* An historical cause of sense change is illustrated by the word *ship* cited above, changes in referent being occasioned by the course of cultural-technological development. *[handwritten: LING. / HIST.]*

Social causes are those that usually result in a word being borrowed from one social group into another with consequent shift in reference. It seems to be the case that such sense changes are characterized by a shift from the particular to the general; that is, a term used by a small group to define some aspect of its social or professional interests is borrowed by the society at large to be used in a more general sense. For example, the term *feedback,* at one time used exclusively by communication systems engineers to refer to the return to the input of a machine or system some part of the output, has been borrowed by the general public and is now used in a somewhat broader and less technical sense to refer to a variety of self-stimulating situations. This type of change almost invariably involves a metaphoric transfer. Aircraft pilots have for years now been accustomed to landing their aircraft safely in bad weather by following a radio beam. They may be either 'on the beam,' or 'off the beam.' The phrase 'on the beam' has been borrowed by the general society and is used metaphorically of a person who is following a true course (itself a metaphor) toward some predetermined goal. The hippie movement has developed a number of terms, most of them already metaphors, which by further metaphoric transfer now have currency outside the movement itself. Perhaps the most obvious of these are the verbs *turn on* and *turn off.* Used by the hippies to indicate entrance into and emergence from a psychedelic state, they are now used by nonhippies to refer to any emotionally stimulating or, contrariwise, emotionally uninspiring, experience.

Sometimes the process of social borrowing may operate in a reverse fashion. The terms *program* and *programming*, which have been for a long time part of the general vocabulary, were borrowed by computer scientists to refer to highly technical sets of instructions fed into a digital computer. In this particular sense the terms were reborrowed by others outside the field of computer technology to refer to very detailed sets of instructions given to humans, as in programmed learning devices. They are now finding their way back into the vocabulary of the general populace where their considerably altered connotations exist alongside the connotations of the precomputer *program*. In fact, it may be that we need to consider the precomputer and postcomputer terms as quite separate words.

An analysis of the underlying factors that contribute to semantic change suggest a three-fold approach: (1) a consideration of the conditions which make such change possible; (2) a consideration of the types of causes responsible for innovation, either of sense or of symbol; (3) a consideration of the reasons for dissemination. We have commented briefly on the first two. Hans Sperber (*Einführung in die Bedeutungslehre*. Bonn, 1923) concerns himself primarily with the third. Once a change has been initiated by an individual or a small group of individuals, what sustains and nourishes it? How can we account for its gradual spread and acceptance? Sperber thinks that *emotive force* is responsible for sustaining the process of change and for providing the "fixative factor." If one is intensely interested in a given subject or has strong feelings about it, his language behavior will reflect this fact. When he talks about his subject he may find it necessary to borrow terms from other fields of interest in order that his expression may have the desired effect. Or, when speaking on a different subject, he may interlard his speech with terms transferred from the sphere in which he is most emotionally involved. Perhaps a mountaineer was responsible for first applying the term 'cliff-hanger' to an athletic contest the outcome of which seems to hang perpetually in the balance. This emotive force, this notion of dynamism, is incorporated by Sperber into something of a semantic 'law': "If at a certain time a complex of ideas is so strongly charged with feeling that it causes *one* word to extend its sphere and change its meaning, we may confidently expect that other words belonging to the same emotional complex will also shift their meaning" (translated by Professor W. E. Collinson in *MLR* 20:106).

SUBCATEGORIES OF SEMANTIC CHANGE

We have already commented upon and briefly illustrated the dual tendencies in language toward *conservatism* and *innovation*. These tendencies provide Stephen Ullmann (*The Principles of Semantics,* Chapter IV "Historical Semantics," Glasgow, 1951) with his first subcategories of semantic change. Like Stern, he assumes three modes of conservatism: (1) a factual or technical change in the referent, as in the example of *ship* above; (2) a change in our knowledge about the referent; (3) a change in our emotional reaction to a given term or its referent. Regarding (2), consider the phrase 'to split the atom.' In the event that we interpret *atom* in its classical Greek sense, the phrase means 'to split the unsplitable.' But our knowledge of atoms being what it is today—considerably more advanced than that of the ancient Greeks —the phrase does not seem to us self-contradictory. Regarding (3), it seems to this writer that over the past twenty years or so a considerable change has taken place in the general public's emotional reaction to *fallout* and its referent. Whether this change is to be explained by the saw "familiarity breeds contempt," or by some other psychological condition, the term and the terrifying environmental situation which it implies seem less charged with horror, panic, fear, and despair than they once were. Perhaps this is simply because for us the horror has not yet materialized; but note that an apparent mediation of such reactions has enabled the term to be transferred to contexts having no relation to atomic explosions. At present, the effects of almost any new and startling situation may be referred to as 'fallout.'

As one might anticipate, categorization of innovative changes is somewhat more complex. Again, Ullmann has three basic types: (a) transfers of names; (b) transfers of senses; and (c) composite changes. Types (a) and (b) are further subdivided according as the transfer is occasioned or facilitated by *similarity* or *contiguity*. For Ullmann, *contiguity* is a cover term for a variety of relations other than similarity. Name transfer may occur when similarity or contiguity exists between senses; that is, when there is some overlap between their semantic ranges. Consider the term *eye* in the following phrases:

(1) The eye of a man.
(2) The eye of a hurricane.
(3) The eye of a needle.

Presumably, some striking overlap exists between the semantic ranges of the animal organ, the center of a hurricane, and the small aperture at one end of a needle, although the overlap between (1) and (2), between (1) and (3), and between (2) and (3) is somewhat different. The semantic range of the animal organ includes at least the notion of *spherical, openness, smallness, and centeredness,* in addition to those that pertain to the function of sight. The *center* of a hurricane is comparatively *small, spherical, open* (in the sense of free of turbulence). The *opening* at one end of a needle is *small* and *spherical.* For both (2) and (3) the surface structure derives in the following way:

(3a) A needle has an aperture that is like an eye ⇒
(3b) A needle has an aperture like an eye ⇒
(3c) A needle has an eye-like aperture ⇒
(3d) A needle has an eye ⇒
(3) An eye of a needle.

Notice that in mapping the extension of the semantic range of *eye,* such definitions as (1) 'denotes the organ of sight in living creatures,' (2) 'used in reference to the small spherical opening at the blunt end of a needle,' and (3) 'may refer to the central, nonturbulent area of a hurricane or cyclone' are insufficient. It is necessary for the lexicon to take account as well of certain changes that have occurred in the syntactic features of *eye.* In particular, the feature of [+animate] characterizes *eye* (1), while [−animate] characterizes *eye* (2) and (3). We may put this in a different way. So long as the phrases 'eye of a needle' and 'eye of a hurricane' are felt to be metaphors, *eye* has retained the feature [+animate] in opposition to the feature [−animate] that characterizes the nouns *needle* and *hurricane.* Indeed, it is just this kind of ungrammaticality that accounts for metaphor. When the native speaker no longer perceives such phrases as metaphors, this fact is an indication that an opposition of features no longer exists. In the idiolect of the writer this is the case with *eye* (2) and (3).

Name transfers due to contiguity are often called *metonymic transfers,* the name of some aspect of a thing or a person becoming the name of the thing or person in question. The word *crown* extends its sphere of reference to include that of *monarch* and *monarchy; bar* includes court, tribunal, the profession of barristers and solicitors, and the like; *town* includes *townspeople, gown* includes those who are entitled to wear academic garb; *sail* includes in its reference all ships powered by sails; *steel* includes not only the material but objects made out of the material. Of a somewhat different order of contiguity are the referential extensions, or transfers, of such items as *main* and *private.* Their separate adjectival references, as in phrases like 'the main reason' and 'a private conversation,' have extended to the nominal references 'a principal sea' and 'a soldier of the lowest rank.'

As in the case of transfers of similarity, it is desirable to plot the course of these transfers in terms of transformational history:

(1) the attorney (the attorney was for the monarch (the monarch is wearing a crown)) prosecuted the case ⇒
(2) the attorney (who was for the monarch (who is wearing a crown)) prosecuted the case ⇒
(3) the attorney (for the monarch (wearing a crown)) prosecuted the case ⇒
(4) the attorney (for the wearing a crown monarch) prosecuted the case ⇒
(5) the attorney (for the crown-wearing monarch) prosecuted the case⇒
(6) the attorney (for the crown) prosecuted the case ⇒
(7) the attorney for the Crown prosecuted the case.

We account for our ability to interpret (7) on the basis of the recoverability of the underlying strings in (1) that are assigned an interpretation by the semantic component. The ensuing transformations do not effect this interpretation; they simply impose on the interpreter the burden of reconstructing underlying syntactic and semantic relationships. One of the ways he does this is *to assign a part of the syntactic and semantic features of deleted items to contiguous nondeleted items.* In a sense, this is the old "something understood" explanation of certain surface structures which has been subjected to some abuse in recent years by structural grammarians. Something is, in fact, "understood"; and what is understood is the underlying set of syntactic structures that result by transformation in the surface structure. In the preceding example, certain syntactic and semantic features belonging to the deleted item *monarch* are retained in the transformed structure attached to the contiguous item *crown*. The word *crown* now contains the semantic feature 'monarch' and the syntactic feature 'human.' The permanency of the attachment of these features to crown will depend on continuous reenforcement, which itself depends on the acceptability and interpretability of the surface structure early in its career. Apparently it is the case that once the semantic and syntactic features transferred to *crown* by transformational processes have become permanent fixtures (in other words the expression has ceased to be a metaphor), the transformational history ceases to be of any particular relevance to the language speaking community.

The process of metonymic transfer may be viewed somewhat differently. One may consider that as a result of constant syntactic and semantic conjunction between term A and term B (which is often the result of a physical conjunction between the referents of A and B) one or the other, or perhaps both, assumes a set of *satellite* features corresponding to the syntactic and semantic features of the other. The lexical entry for *crown*, for example, might be this:

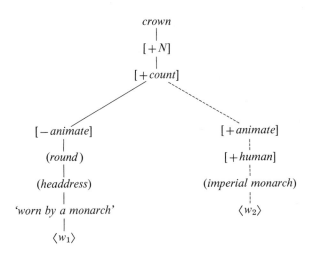

Consider now the sentence "The Crown will decide the issue." If there were no satellite features for *crown* the structure would be rejected as semantically anomalous since the selection restrictions $\langle w_1 \rangle$ for *crown* and $\langle w_x \rangle$ for *decide* are incompatible. However, in this case the $\langle w_x \rangle$ for *decide* will require the choice of the satellite features for *crown*. If this choice finds general acceptability among speakers of the language, satellite features become part of the standard entry form for crown; in other words, dotted lines in the diagram become solid. It is perhaps in this sense that we can say ". . . certain syntactic and semantic features belonging to the deleted item *monarch* are retained in the transformed structure attached to the contiguous item *crown*."[4]

Sense transfers may occur as a result of similarity between names. The history of *shamefast,* and *shamefaced* provides an interesting example of this type of transfer. In the course of a rather lengthy discussion of these words we will try to illustrate some other aspects of semantic change as well.

The noun and verb *shame* go back to Old English *sceamu* and *sceamian* respectively, cognate with Gothic *skaman sik* 'to be ashamed of' and Icelandic *skɛmm/skam/skami* 'shame, disgrace.' Some fairly early occurrences of *sceamu* and *sceamian* show a rather wide semantic range. In the eighth-century *Vespasian Psalter* the Mercian form *scome* glosses the Latin *verecundia* (46.16) 'bashfulness, shyness, modesty, shame,' *pudore* (70.13) 'modesty, decency, propriety, desire for approval,' *confusionem* (39.16) 'confusion, disorder, blush,' and *reverentia* (68.8) 'timidity, respect, regard, fear, awe, reverence.' The verb *scomien* glosses, among other things, the Latin *erubescant* 'they grow red, blush (with shame, modesty, and so on).' This latter, in which a physical manifestation of an emotion stands for the emotion, is of particular interest. The Latin term seems to have undergone a name transfer due to contiguity of senses. The point to be made here is that already in Old English times there was apparently an association between an emotion expressed by *sceamu* and a facial manifestation of that emotion.

Turning to the compounds, the earliest occurrence of *shamefast* recorded by the *Oxford English Dictionary* is found in Alfred's translation of Pope Gregory's *Cura Pastoralis* (c. 897), XXXI.204: "On oðre wisan sint to læronne ðe scamleasan, on oðre ða scamfæstan." The terms *scamleasan* and *scamfæstan* are clearly intended to be contrasted here, the first meaning 'loss of shame' or 'loss of the capacity to feel shame,' the second, 'fastened in shame' or 'fastened in the capacity to feel shame.' Loss of the capacity to feel shame results from a hardening of the heart, from a loss of innocence, and is thus sinful. One who is fastened in the capacity to feel shame retains the capacity

---

[4] There is some problem with the word *contiguous* here. When one speaks of name transfers due to contiguity he means contiguity of the *objects* referred to: a crown sits on a monarch's head. The grammatical expression of a physical contiguity ('The monarch wears a crown') may involve a contiguity of the lexical items used to refer to the physical objects where *contiguity* here means "within the same phrase marker" but not necessarily "next to each other."

to repent of his sinfulness and to attain virtue. The contrast then is between *guilt* and *innocence,* between *sinfulness* and *virtuousness.*

Some form of *shamefast* signifying 'bashful, modest, virtuous, shy, awkward, innocent' occurs throughout the Middle English period and on into Modern English:

c. 1200, Orm: ȝho wass wiss wiþþ alle shammfæsst, & daffte [mild], & sedeful [modest].
c. 1385, Chaucer: Ther nas no lak, but that he was agast to loue, & for to speke shamefast.
1590, Spenser: With chaunge of cheare the seeming simple Maid. Let fall her eyen, as shamefast to the earth.
1642, D. Rogers: Others out of bashfulnesse and shamefastnesse, loath to be troublesome.
1835, Motherwell: The rose with its sweet shamefast look.

At the same time, *shamefast* in the sense 'ashamed, abashed, full of shame' also occurred:

c. 1275, *Sinners Beware:* And þeos gedelynges [fellows] summe, Huenne heo to schrifte come, Heo beoþ schomeuast.
1388, Wycliffe: He schal hide the schamefast membris with pryuy lynnun clothis.
1634, Sir T. Herbert: With their hands couer their shamefast faces.

This appears to be the last date for *shamefast* in this sense. It is particularly interesting for it provides an example of an *actual* (rather than supposed) syntactic contiguity of the phonetically similar /-fæst/ and /fæysɨz/, a similarity that reenforces the relation between the emotion implied and the way in which the emotion is physically manifested.

The earliest instance of *shamefaced* is dated by the *Oxford English Dictionary* 1593, from R. Harvey. It occurs in the sense 'bashful, shy, modest':

Cordeil being euer modestly and maydenly shamefaced.

From the seventeenth century *shamefaced* and *shamefacedness* for *shamefast* and *shamefastness* occur in both senses:

1634, W. Cartwright: Her blush doth shed All o'r the bed Clear shamefac'd beames.
1608, *Pennyless Parliament:* Some Maidens shall blush more for Shame, than for shamefacedness.
1803, Wordsworth: The embarrassed look of shy distress, And maidenly shamefacedness.
1641, J. Trappe: Shee [the soul] stands off in a sinful shame fac'dnesse.
1896, Ian Maclaren: The minister . . . hears the shamefaced confession of some lassie whom love has led astray.

Our earlier quotation from the translation of Gregory's *Cura Pastoralis* illustrates the contrast in meaning between *shameless* and *shamefast*. We may suggest here that *shameless* is potentially ambiguous, both semantically and syntactically, if we consider that the compound is derived from two underlying grammatical structures: 'less (without) the capacity for shame,' thus 'without virtue,' and 'less (without) shame,' or 'less whatever causes shame,' thus 'virtuous.' The same may be said of *shamefast*. It may be derived either from the underlying structure 'fast in capacity to feel shame,' thus 'modest, bashful, virtuous,' or from 'fast in shame,' thus 'shameful, lacking in virtue.' That this is a valid description of the situation seems clear from the examples we have cited of the occurrence of both *shamefast* and *shamefaced* in the two opposing senses, and from the following occurrence of *shameless* which requires the interpretation 'less whatever causes shame,' thus 'innocent, virtuous':

1390, Gower: For hou so that the cause wende, The trouthe is schameless ate end, Bot what thing that is troutheless, It mai noght wel be schameless.

Shameful exhibits a semantic behavior very much like *shameless* and *shamefast*. It may derive from an underlying 'full of the capacity for shame,' thus, 'shamefast, modest, virtuous,' or from 'full of the quality of shame,' thus 'disgraceful, indecent, immodest.' The *Oxford English Dictionary's* first entry for *shameful* is the following:

c. 950, *Durham Ritual:* sceomfull [glosses Lat. *pudica*].

The Latin adjective *pudicus* means 'bashful, modest, chaste, pure, virtuous.' And the word continues to be used in this sense:

1300, *Cursor Mundi:* And þof sco scamful was, i-wiss, sco tint na contenance wit þis [and though she was modest, she lost no favors on this account].
c. 1375, *Sc. Legends Saints* (Magdalena): Nocht for-þi scho come eftir þame schamfully & gat in handis Cristis fete.
1625, Fletcher: For certain Sir, his bashfulness undo's him, for from his Cradle h' had a shameful face.
1638, Junius *Paint.* Ancients: It is fit we should endue children with shamefulnesse and desire of glorie.

In the sense 'disgracefully' *shameful(ly)* seems not to occur until the Middle English period:

1300, *Cursor Mundi:* Qua mar tas þan he bere might oþere he sal leue it wit-alle or schamfulli þar vnderstand.
1375, Barbour. *Bruce:* So schamfull that he vencust wes, That . . . He gaf thar his vardanry [custody, wardenry, command].

It should be clear at this point that the history of compounds with *shame* is both semantically and syntactically complex. As we have indicated, the root *shame* had in its earliest occurrences a fairly wide semantic range which contributed to ambiguity; that is, it could connote both desirable and undesirable characteristics. This is still the case today:

(1) It is to my enduring shame that I did not speak kindly to my father before he died.
(2) There goes a woman without shame.

In sentence (1) *shame* obviously implies something bad, while in (2) it may imply something good. The semantic ambiguity we have noted in the compounds *shamefast-shamefaced, shameless,* and *shameful* may be in part attributed to the ambiguities implicit in the semantic range of the root word. But we have also tried to show that the compounds are syntactically ambiguous as well, and that contrary interpretations are the result of different underlying grammatical structures. In Modern English these compounds have ceased to be ambiguous. For the writer at least, *shamefaced* (*shamefast* does not occur) means 'a face which reflects shame or embarrassment,' *shameless* means 'having no sense of shame,' and *shameful* means 'indecent, disgraceful.' It is worth noting that the three do not all share the same syntactic features; while *shamefaced* and *shameless* have a feature [+Human], *shameful* would seem to have a feature [−Animate].

The diagram on page 300 attempts to represent some of the information we have presented concerning *shamefast, shamefaced, shameful,* and *shameless.* Like most diagrams, however, it suggests a rigidity that does not exist and so should not be taken too seriously.

As an instance of sense transfer resulting from contiguity we may refer to certain modern constructions with *but.* Consider the following:

(1) He had but one son.
(2) There is but one God.
(3) He has but one dwelling.
(4) He sings but one mass a day.
(5) There were but few men as good as he was.
(6) For I was but seven years old.

Although none of the usual forms of the negative occur in these sentences, negation is certainly an implicit feature of each. Thus one might say:

(1a) He had no sons but (*except, apart from*) the one he had.
(2a) There are no gods but (*apart from, except*) God.
(3a) There were no men but (*except, apart from*) (a) few men as good as he was.

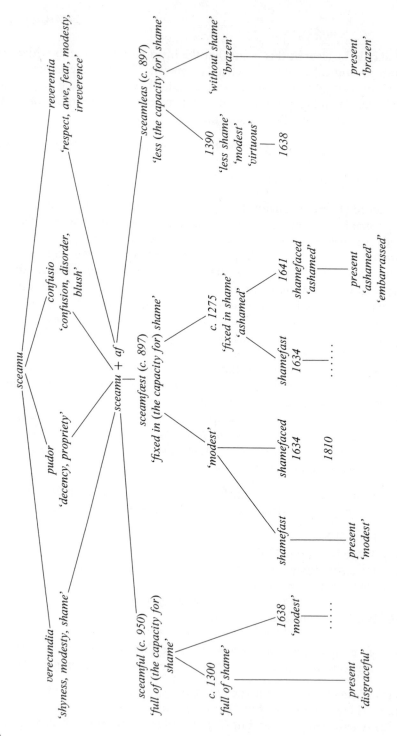

And these sentences seem to parallel the common utterance type:

(7) He has nothing but (*except, apart from*) money.
(8) She wore nothing but (*except, apart from*) a bathing suit.
(9) The thieves took nothing but (*except, apart from*) canceled checks.

In Old English and early Middle English sentences akin to (1)–(6) occurred with an overt negative marker:

(1b) c. 1200, Layamon's *Brut: N*efede he boten anne sune.
(2b) c. 1200, *St. Katherine:* þer *n*is buten an godd.
(3b) c. 1250, *Owl & Nightingale:* He naueþ bute one woning.
(4b) c. 1395, Chaucer, *Canterbury Tales:* He syngeth *nat* but o masse in a day.
(5b) c. 1470, Malory, *Works:* There was *none* but fewe so goodly a man as he was.
(6b) c. 1330, *Bevis:* For i *n*as boute seue winter old.

During the course of the Middle English and early Modern English period, the negative particle tends to disappear and the sense of negation is transferred to *but*. A later manuscript of Bevis, about 1500, has *was but* for the earlier *nas boute.*

As the term *composite transfer* suggests, it is often the case that a combination of factors is responsible for a semantic change. In discussing the transfer of *shamefast* to *shamefaced* we took special note of the sentence from Herbert, "With their hands couer their shamefast faces." We have no notion how frequent may have been the phrase "shamefast faces." But given the fact that the notion of blushing had been a part of the semantic range of *shame* from Old English times, the conjecture that the phrase may well have been quite common has some merit. If in fact this were the case, we would be inclined to say that the transfer in question was *composite;* both phonetic similarity and syntactic contiguity were involved.

SEMANTIC FIELDS AND RANGES

In commenting upon the various meanings of a word, we have used the term *semantic range.* It may be appropriate here to consider in some detail some of the notions of semantic or "linguistic" fields that have appealed to semanticists in recent years. Although not the first to see in such concepts a significant avenue of approach to semantic problems, Jost Trier (*Der deutsche Wortschatz im Sinnbezirk des Verstandes. Die Geschichte eines Sprachlichen Feldes,* Heidelberg, 1934) was one of the first scholars to direct extensive research along lines suggested by the notion of a *field.* His work on intellectual terms in Old and Middle High German gave him the idea of ". . . a closely knit and articulated lexical sphere where the significance of each unit was determined by its neighbors, with their semantic areas reciprocally limiting one another and dividing up and covering the whole sphere between them. Such an organically articulated section of the general vocabulary is termed a 'linguistic field' " (translated by Stephen Ullmann, p. 157).

The notion of what constitutes a linguistic field, or semantic field, or semantic range (depending on which term happens to strike the fancy of a particular author) will vary from one investigator to another, and to this writer at least it is not at all clear what mechanism is employed to define the limits of a field or a range. Suppose that for our purposes we use the term *range* to mean 'the range of meanings of a given term,' and the term *field* to mean 'the combined ranges of all those terms considered to apply to some specified area of human concern.' Thus, *wisdom, knowledge, learning, judgment, insight, discernment* will each have its own *semantic range* that enables us to differentiate one from another, while their combined semantic ranges constitute a semantic field. It is perfectly obvious that the range of one term will shade off into the range of a second, or third, or fourth, and so for each of the terms in a field. Some terms will seem more central, others more peripheral, to a field. Furthermore, terms from one identified field will shade off into other fields. Although we do not wish to deny that there may be "organically articulated section(s) of the general vocabulary," we are not at all sure what mechanical or automatic means exist for delimiting these sections.

Despite this drawback, Trier's work has proven to be both interesting and fruitful. One important result has been to disabuse linguists and semanticists alike of the notion that an atomistic view of semantic change provides us with any useful information about the nature of such change. The situation is partly analogous to that which obtained in our discussion of phonological and grammatical change. In a phonological system, the phonetic symbol [v] represents a subsystem of articulatory and acoustic features that bears a certain relationship to other subsystems of articulatory and acoustic features represented by other phonetic symbols within the phonological system. Suppose the system is that of Old English. When we talk about the change of Old English [v] to Middle English /v/, we are talking about a shifting pattern of relationships between subsystems, a shifting pattern that results in a realignment of those subsystems within the overall phonological system. Thus it is of very little consequence to set one's self the task of tracing the development of some Old English phone through a course of changes from the ninth century to the present, since such changes are meaningful only as they represent the realignments of subsystems of phonological features within the total phonological process of change. As far as grammatical change is concerned, you may recall that we attempted to discuss changes in the Old English inflectional system in relation to changes that were taking place in the periphrastic and word order systems, and we suggested that the change of one system in one direction was directly related to a change in another system in a different direction.

So too with semantic change. Each lexical item is defined by a class of syntactic and semantic features: *meat* [+ N, − animate, − count, + common, and so forth], (+ solid, + edible, + food, + animal tissue, and so on). This system of features stands in a certain relationship to the systems of features of other lexical items. In some cases, this relationship may be *exclusive;* this is to say, no feature, either syntactic or semantic, of one item is common to another item. One suspects that such a relation is rare. More commonly, lexical items will share some semantic or syntactic features, or both. The range of possible relationships, which, incidentally, define degrees of synonymy and antonymy, is very considerable. Any alteration in the syntactic-semantic feature system of a given lexical item may disturb the relational equilibrium between it and the feature system of some other item, and thus provide the potential for change in one or the other or both.

On the next few pages we will attempt to illustrate this matter of interrelated syntactic-semantic ranges and the semantic fields which these interrelationships tend to define. Consider the Modern English word *deer*. In Old English it appears in such contexts as the following:

(1) ðær him cwom to monigra cynn[a] deor, & wunedon mid hine (ninth century *Martyrology*).

There to him came 'deer' of many kinds, and they dwelt with him.

(2) Settun ða deadlican ðiowa ðinra mettas fuglum heofenes & flæsc haligra ðinra wildeorum eorðan (*Vespasian Psalter*).

They have placed the dead bodies of your servants as food for the fowls of heaven and the flesh of your holy ones for the wild 'deer' of the earth.

(3) God cwæþ eac swilce, læde seo eorþe forð cuce nitena on heora cinne, and creopende cinn and deor æfter heora hiwum: hit wæs þa swa geworden.

God spoke in this way, let the earth lead forth quick [living] creatures in their kind, and the creeping kind, and 'deer' after their fashion: it was then so performed (Aelfric, Translation *Heptateuch*).

(4) Is þæt deor pandher bi noman haten (OE *Bestiary;* Exeter Book).

(5) He wæs swyðe spedig man on þæm æhtum þe heora speda on beoð, þæt is on wildeorum. He hæfde þa gyt, ðahe þone cyninge sohte, tamra deora unbebohtra syx hund. þa deor hi hatað hranas; þara wæron syx stælhranas; ða beoð swyðe dyre mid Finnum, for ðæm hy foð þa wildan hranas mid. (Aelfred, *Orosius,* Ohthere & Wulfstan).

He was a very prosperous man in those possessions [ownings] which their wealth consisted in, that is, in wild 'deer.' He then yet had, when he sought out the king, six hundred unsold tame 'deer.' These deer he called "hranas" [reindeer]; of these six were decoy "hranas"; these are very valuable among the Finns, for they catch the wild 'hranas' with them.

The word *deor* occurs in a number of compounds in Old English:

(1) *deorcynn* 'race of animals'
(2) *deorfold* 'enclosure for animals'
(3) *deorfellen* 'animal skins'
(4) *deorfriþ* 'game preserve'
(5) *deorgeat* 'gate for animals'
(6) *deornett* 'hunting (animal) net'
(7) *deortun* 'animal park'
(8) *mere deor/sæ deor* 'sea monster'

The lexical entry for Old English *deor* will look something like this:

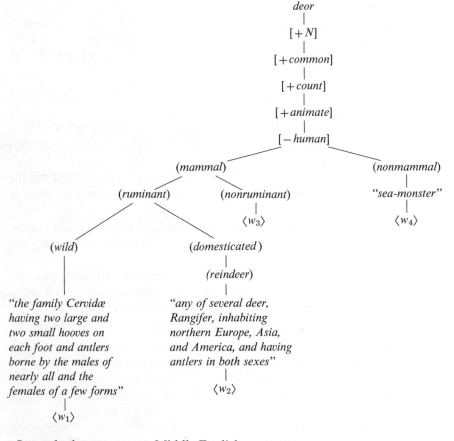

Let us look now at some Middle English contexts:

(1) Pais he makede men & dær (1135).
    He made peace for men and 'deer.'

(2) He [the fox] weneð to beon of duʒeð, baldest alre deoren (c. 1200).
   He thought to be one of the doughty ones, boldest of all 'deer.'
(3) Do we forði so doð ðis der [ant] (c. 1300).
   Let us therefore do as does this 'deer.'
(4) But sone he was besette/As deer [fish] is in a nette (c. 1350).
(5) Ratons & myse and soche smale dere . . . was hys mete (1500).
   Rats and mice and such small 'deer' . . . were his food.

It seems clear from these quotations that the semantic range of *deer* not only includes *animals* of various sizes and species (fox, rat, mouse), but also extends to *insects* and *fish*. In the following, the feature (wild) is emphasized:

(6) þe wurmes & te wilde deor þet o þis wald wunieð libbet efter þe lahe
   (c. 1225).
(7) God made wirme and wilde der (c. 1325).
(8) He koude hunte at wilde deer (c. 1390).
(9) We . . . hunted þe wilde dere (c. 1400).

The feature (domesticated) also continues into Middle English:

(10) þatt follc rideþþ onn a der þatt iss Dromeluss nemmned (c. 1200).

The attendant notions *sacrificial, clean, unclean,* and *apocalyptic,* although peripheral, obtain in Middle English:

(11) þeʒʒ . . . tokenn þiderr . . . off alle kinne cwike der, off clene & off
   unclene (c. 1200).
(12) He is let ut flegen, crepen, and gon, wið uten ilc seuend clene der &
   ðe he sacrede on an aucter (c. 1250).
(13) þatt deor . . . wass i mannes like /þatt deor . . . wass inn ærness like
   (c. 1200).

It is apparent from these contexts that on into the Middle English period the semantic range of *deer* was very broad indeed, including meanings that are now expressed by *deer, reindeer, animal, creature, beast, brute, insect, serpent, fish, monster,* and some others. Of some interest is the fact that to the best of the author's knowledge the word *deer,* unlike *animal, creature* and *beast,* has never included the feature [+human]. The significance of this will become clearer as we examine the semantic ranges of the latter three terms. The Middle English entry for *dere* will be something like the following:

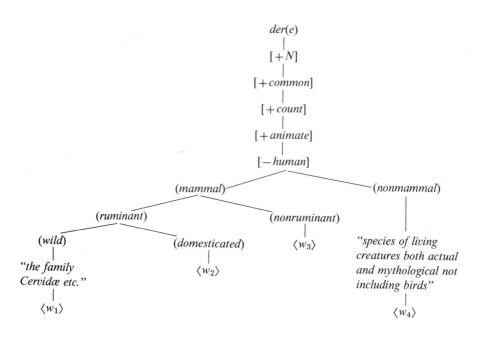

The chief difference between this entry and the preceding is in the fact that the distinguisher for (*nonmammal*) specifies the inclusion of a much wider variety of living creatures. Further, there is no distinguisher for the feature (domesticated).

An important aspect of the development of *deer* in Middle English is the considerable increase in contexts in which the semantic features (ruminant) and the distinguisher "The family Cervidæ, etc." obtains:

(1) no mihten heo deor iwinne, nouþer heort no hinde (c. 1200).
(2) He let þe parc of wodestoke, & der þer inne do (1297).
(3) þe blod hond [hound] . . . þe smul haþ wel of eurich best, of hare & ek of dure (c. 1325).
(4) [He] went . . . to purchase venysoun, for than the deir war in sesoun (1375).
(5) He shewed hym . . . parkes ful of wilde deer, Ther saw he hertes with hir hornes hye (c. 1395).
(6) There he chaced at the rede deare (c. 1470).
(7) a massebok covered with deres leþer (1415).

Some reason for this particularization is evident in the spread of the Old French word *beast*. The word begins to occur in Middle English texts early in the thirteenth century, gradually encroaching on more and more of the semantic territory formerly held by *deer:*

  (1) Dahet habbe þat ilke best þat fuleþ his owe nest (c. 1250).

  (2) þan sent drihtin a lite beist [locust] (c. 1300).

  (3) The bee . . . is a litel schort beste wiþ many feet (c. 1398).

  (4) The serpent . . . was moost wily of alle othere bestes (c. 1390).

  (5) Bestes . . . þat ben so inmevable . . . as schelle fische (1450).

  (6) The bee is a Passynge wrathfull beste (1500).

The semantic range encompassed here includes all living creatures but man. The following suggest a more limited range:

  (7) Ȝe . . . ne schulen habbe na beast bute cat (c. 1230).

  (8) þe worm dude is heste al so . . . foules duden is heste . . . bestes duden al so is heste (c. 1300).

  (9) The beestes and the briddes alle fledden for fere (c. 1385).

  (10) No lyues creature, Be it of fissh or bryd or beest or man (c. 1395).

  (11) þow I had as many hertys . . . as þer arn . . . fischys, fowelys, bestys, & leevys up-on treys (c. 1400).

The term *beast* also occurs with both the features (wild) and (domesticated):

  (12) þe heorte is a ful wilde beast (c. 1230).

  (13) Game of houndes he louede inou & of wilde best (c. 1325).

  (14) þe forest was . . . wiþ wilde bestes ysprad (c. 1330).

  (15) In reyn with wilde beestes walked he (c. 1375).

  (16) þere ne was . . . bere ne bor ne other best wilde (c. 1378).

  (17) þis cowherd comes on a time to kepen is bestes (1375).

  (18) The asse hatte asinus . . . as it were a beste to sitte vpon (1398).

  (19) Besteis in þat kingrike all, hors, asse, mule, ox, camell (1400).

  (20) þere he may hyre a hors or what beest þat he wil (1450).

  (21) Geve your ploughe beestes sufficyaunt mete (1500).

And it begins to take over that feature of *deer* which expressed the notion of fabulous creature, monster, apocalyptic creature:

  (22) þe mere-minnes [fabled sea-creatures; mermaids] . . . beoþ bestes of mochele ginne (c. 1300).

  (23) þus was þis witty best werwolf ferst maked (c. 1375).

(24) A certeyne beiste hauynge iiii feet and ii wynggis (c. 1425).

(25) Saynt Iohn telles vs yt yer is a maner of bestes yt ben cleped Grifons (1500).

(26) I siȝe a beest stiȝinge up of These, hauynge seuen heedes and ten hornes (1384).

(27) þe beest of which it is spokun, apocalipse xiije chapitre, schal leese oon of hise vij heedis, ffor bi þilk vij heedis men vnderstonden vij deedly synnys (c. 1475).

The encroaching pressure of the semantic range of *beast* forces an adjustment in the range of *deer,* narrowing this range more and more to the features (ruminant, hooved, antlered, with spotted young). Perhaps an additional element of pressure is to be found in the fact that the range of *beast* encompassed not only the lower animals, but man as well:

(28) A witteles best as y was born (c. 1330).

(29) For slayn is man right as another beest (c. 1385).

(30) Isider seiþ þat a man is a best Iliche to god (1398).

(31) Wyves been bestes very vnstable in ther desires (1449).

(32) Maners of Bestes er fyue, þat ys to wete: man, and volatille, ffyssh of þe water, þat gooþ on ffoure feet, & stirrys vpon wombe (1500).

(33) What thyng is a man? A dedlych best and resonable (c. 1450).

The feature [+human], not shared with *deer,* gives to the term a usefulness and perhaps a prestige that adds impetus to its replacement of many of the semantic features of *deer.* In addition, from the thirteenth century we also find *beast* being used to signify a brutish, cruel, or stupid person:

(34) Best is þe best-liche mon þet ne þencheð nout of God (c. 1250).

(35) Men of Crete, euermore lyeris, yuel beestis . . . this witnessing is trewe (c. 1384).

(36) Man wythouten knoulech of his maker es but a best (c. 1450).

(37) Hwet medschipe makeð þe, þu bittre baleful beast (c. 1210).

We give below the lexical entry for *beast* and as a subclass (1) the entry for *deer.*

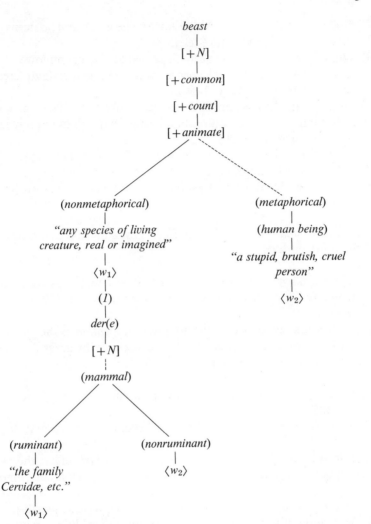

From the early fourteenth century, the term *creature,* with its semantic range, enters the field and must have played a part in reducing the range of Old English *deor.* Its earliest recorded reference seems to be to *anything created, animate* or *inanimate,* to the *created universe;* and these senses continue to characterize *creature* at least to the seventeenth century:

(1) Jhesu Crist . . . On me, þi schap, nouȝ haue merci . . . þi creature al so was i (c. 1300).

(2) Godes creatures sere . . . Als þe son and þe mone and þe sterns (1340).

(3) þe Cros is a cold Creature (c. 1390).

(4) What tyme þou perceyuest . . . þe wodde . . . or midowe . . . or þe felde sowen with dyuerse cornes, and suche maner fayre creatours, lifte vppe thyne herte (c. 1450).

(5) Sum creatur has beyng wythout vertu anymore, As ston & erth & sich thing. . . . Sum creatures han beyng, that lif han but felyng none, As trees, erbes (c. 1500).

(6) Fierce fire and iron . . . creatures of note for mercy-lacking vses (1595).

(7) His creature [creation] is grete, & ay shel be (c. 1400).

(8) For þi es godd, als sais scripture, nan elder þan his creature [creation] (c. 1300).

The sense *created universe,* as in (7) and (8), is gradually taken over by *creation* late in the fourteenth century:

(9) Thise . . . rokkes blake . . . semen rather a foul confusioun of werk than any fair creacioun of swich a parfit wys god (c. 1395).

It is of some interest that with the adoption of *creation* as the general term for the created universe, *creature* begins to occur with great frequency in contiguous relationship with some term for 'living':

(10) I am . . . with loue offended most That euere was any lyues creature (c. 1385).

(11) No lyues creature, Be it of fissh, or bryd, or beest, or man (c. 1395).

Note that in this last example the occurrence of *creature* affects the range of *beast* which is here limited to the features [+animate, −human] (mammal).

(12) In this world, no lyues creature Withouten loue is worth (c. 1385).

(13) Man and fende and aungelle . . . aftir þis lyfe sal lyf ay, And na qwik creature bot þai (c. 1400).

(14) His birth was shawed . . . by creatures . . . that haden beying, lif & felyng, As wilde bestis han (c. 1400).

'Living,' then, becomes one of the predominant semantic features of *creature.* That the term includes man is clear from the preceding, but more emphatically so from the following:

(15) Gret deol he hadde . . . þat he was a-morþred so, And swuch a creature ase he was in so lowe stude ido (c. 1300).

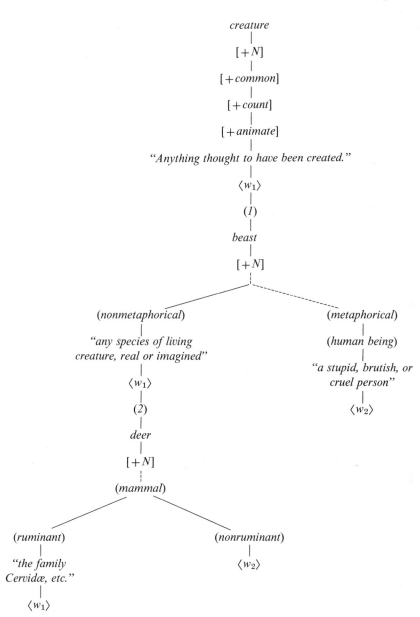

(16) Ʒe, goyng in to al the world, preche the gospel to ech creature (c. 1384).

(17) Every cristene creature shulde be kynde til other (c. 1378).

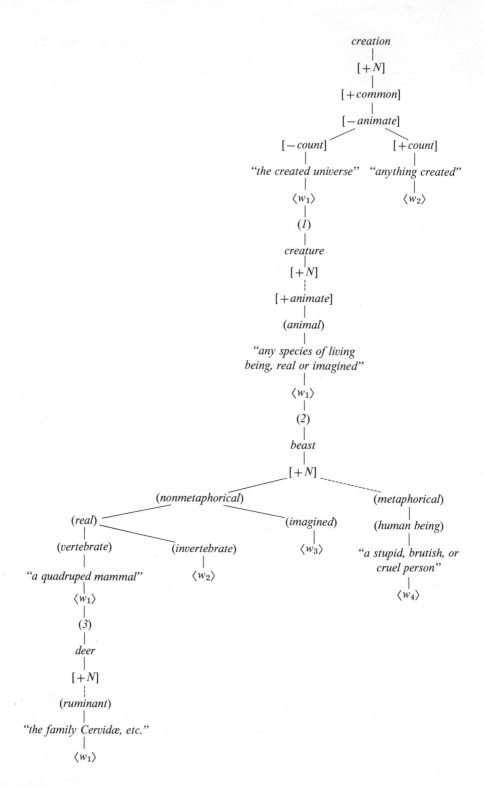

(18) Preche ȝe þe gospel to iche creature, þat is, to iche man (c. 1415).
(19) Hym thouht she was so faire a creature (c. 1421).
(20) On a nygth, as þis creature lay in his bedde wyth hir husbond (c. 1438).

In connection with the semantic field defined by the semantic ranges of *deer, beast,* and *creature,* we should mention the term *animal.* This word comes into the language much later than either *beast* or *creature,* its earliest recorded instances from the fourteenth century:

(1) þe vousour was anow[rn]ed al Of ich maner diuers animal (c. 1330).
(2) Al þat is comprehended of fleissh and of spiryte of lif, and so of body and of soule, is ycleped animal, a best, wheþur it be ayry as fowil, or wattry as fissh ... oþer erþy as bestes þat goþ on grounde ... as men and bestes wilde and tame (c. 1398).
(3) Quid est homo? A dedlych best and resonable, animal racionale (c. 1450).
(4) In foure elementes byn comprehendid thynges thre: animal, vegitable, and mynerall (c. 1490).

We may say that in late Middle English the terms *deer, beast, creature,* and *animal* with their semantic ranges constitute a semantic field. In attempting to account for the reduction and particularization of the range of *deer* during the course of this period, we have indicated the ways in which the ranges of the borrowed terms *beast, creature,* and *animal* have encroached on the range that seemed to characterize Old English and early Middle English *deer.* What interests us in considering semantic change is not so much the change in the semantic range of one term or another, but rather the shifting pattern of the feature relationships that alter the shape of the semantic field. These can be noted, in part at least, in the successive lexical entries we have included above. As feature relationships within a semantic field change, the selection restrictions and projection rules also change. In Modern English, for example, no derived reading is possible for such a construction as 'rats and mice and such small deer.' Although we would get a reading for 'wives are very unstable beasts,' it would be quite different from that derived from the Middle English sentence. The construction 'the cross is a cold creature' would probably be marked as anomalous in Modern English.

SEMANTIC PATHOLOGY

In the course of our discussion of language change, whether phonological, grammatical, or semantic, we have used the terms *stability, instability,* and *equilibrium.* The term *pathology* is often employed by linguists and semanticists "... for any condition disturbing the equilibrium of synchronous systems, interfering with the efficient working of the language mechanism, and calling for some 'curative' countermeasure" (Ullmann, *Principles,* p. 121). *Polysemantic overloads,* that is, two or more incompatible features of a given term each of which is susceptible to interpretation in the same semantic and grammatical context, constitute one variety of semantic pathology. We have seen that this has been the case with *shameful, shamefast,* and *shameless,* and that in the course of time *one* interpretation for each term has tended to become dominant. Another case in point is suggested by the pair *flower-flour,* which in Modern English constitutes homophonous forms (different words having the same phonemic shape). The present differentiation is clearly the result of a polysemantic overload. In Middle English, the word, spelled *flur, flor, flour, flower, floer, flowyr,* and other ways, occurs in the sense 'blossom, or flowering plant':

(1) Whit so eni lilie, brit so eni flour (c. 1275).
(2) Euerich herbe was ful of floures (c. 1290).
(3) Faire floures þei founde of fele maner hewes (c. 1375).
(4) Of alle the floures in the mede (c. 1375).
(5) Take flourys of Vyolet, boyle hem, presse hem, bray hem smal. Flowrys of Hawiorn.—In þe same maner as vyolet (c. 1450).

By a metaphoric transfer it comes to mean 'prize, victory':

(6) Is Edward ded? Of cristendome he ber þe flour (c. 1307).
(7) Now is þat schip þat bar þe flour Selden seȝe & Sone forȝete (c. 1390).
(8) Of many a cuntrey he was conqueroure And of chyualry that tyme bare the floure (c. 1450).

And then by further transfer, 'most excellent, the best of its kind':

(9) The flour of al the toun was there And of the Court also (c. 1391).
(10) Kynges, Dukes, on and oþer . . . of ȝonge Kniȝttes slouȝen þe floure (c. 1400).
(11) þare was þe flowre of chevallry (c. 1350).
(12) He is cleped the Floure of Doctouris (c. 1464).

From this latter sense comes the modern meaning of *flour:*

(1) Meriadok dede floure bring And strewed it bi tvene (c. 1330).
(2) He half a busshel of hir flour hath take And bad his wyf to knede it in a cake (c. 1390).

(3) The flour is goon, ther is na moore to telle; the bren, as I best kan, now moste I selle (c. 1395).
(4) Hit is worthy he ete bred of bran, þat wiþ floure his foo wil fede (c. 1419).

The semantic mechanism is not hard to follow; presumably, the best part of the wheat was referred to as the *flower,* which is eventually differentiated as *flour:*

(5) Zuych difference ase þer betuene þe . . . bren and flour of huete, betuene þe uelle [the good] and þe beste (c. 1340).

In statements of the following sort we seem to be on the verge of ambiguity:

(6) Creame . . . flos [flower] lactis [of milk]. Rightly so tearmed by the Latines, for it is the very flower of milke, as also butter is the flower of Creame (1599).

There is no good reason to think that *flour* and *flower* do not both develop metaphorical senses. The variants *flower, flour, flur, floure,* and so forth, *flower* as 'the best of something,' are applied to the notion 'the best of the wheat,' later differentiated as *flour,* which then by additional metaphoric transfer in reverse comes to mean 'the best of something.' In the following, for instance, is *flour(e)* to be considered a metaphorical use based on 'the best part of the plant, the blossom or flower' or on 'the best part of the wheat, the flour'?

(1) Engelond hiȝt of lond, floure of londes al aboute (1387).
(2) They sal haue the flour of il endyng (c. 1390).
(3) Buttre moysteþ bodyes þat he toucheþ, for buttre is þe flour of mylk (c. 1398).
(4) Of alle toures his was flour (c. 1425).

Clearly, there is no easy way to answer this question; it is a case of semantic pathology. This being so, a means is found in the spelling system whereby the meanings "flower" and "flour" can be distinguished. The differentiation does not occur overnight. The spelling *flower* for "flour" continues to occur at least as late as the early nineteenth century:

(1) Breade of fyne flowre of wheate . . . is slow of digestion (1533).
(2) . . . after they have been flower'd and fry'd (1725).
(3) We shaved and had our wigs flowered (1732).
(4) In a long voyage . . . flower will not keep (1809).

If one can rely on the *Oxford English Dictionary*, the spelling *flour* for "flower" does not continue quite so long. The latest entry given by this dictionary for this spelling is dated 1667:

(1) Als fresch as flouris that in May vp spredis (1508).
(2) Leif nor flour fynd could I none of rew (1500–1520).
(3) O flours That never will in other climate grow (1667).

Samuel Johnson's entry reflects the assumption that he is dealing with one word. He cites only the spelling *flower*, with the following glosses:

1. The part of a plant which contains the seeds.
2. An ornament; an establishment.
3. The prime; the flourishing part.
4. The edible part of Corn; the meal.
5. The most excellent or valuable part of anything.

At least for Johnson in the mid-eighteenth century the semantic load was not great enough to force a split into homophonous but graphemically distinct forms.

Coinciding with the differentiation in semantic features is, of course, a differentiation in syntactic features, chief of which is that between [+count] and [−count]. However, this latter is difficult to trace owing to the fact that throughout the Middle English period and on into early Modern English *singular, count, indefiniteness* could be marked either by *a(n)* or by ∅. Mustanoja comments as follows: "While the indefinite article becomes a regular feature in individualising function at an early date, its generalising (generic) use is by no means firmly established. In later ME the use of the indefinite article for purposes of generalisation shows a steady increase; yet some amount of wavering continues down to the end of the period. It is not until early Mod. E. that the principles now governing the use of the indefinite article are more consistently observed" (*Syntax,* p. 263). The citations given for *flower* by the *Middle English Dictionary* contain the marker *a(n)* only rarely:

(1) Houndystonge hathe a flour of purpill colour almoste like to comfery flour (c. 1373).
(2) þat heo ne schal fade as a flour (c. 1390).
(3) A somer flour . . . lesith his fayrnesse with a sodeyne shour (c. 1440).
(4) Out a þat braunch in nazareth A flowre xal blome (c. 1475).
(5) On þat helme stode a flour (c. 1330).

In the sense of 'prize, victory' citations show *flower* occurring only with a definite indicator. However, of some interest is the fact that in the further transferred sense of 'the best of a class' an overt marker before the noun is rare:

(1) þan was . . . Sir Amis . . . yholden flour & priis (c. 1300).
(2) Hym þat was . . . floure of poetes thorghout al breteyne (c. 1421).
(3) She was holden of alle queenes flour (c. 1386).
(4) þe noble tour, þat of alle toures of engelond is iholde flour (c. 1300).
(5) þere was flour of philosophie (c. 1450).
(6) He of pite was fruyt & flour (c. 1450).

As far as the singular article is concerned, then, the transfer during the Middle English period of the grammatical feature [+count] to the feature [−count] tends to be covert:

'flower' [N, +count] (a) [+count] → [±pl]
                      (b) [−pl] → [(det)]
'flour' [N, −count]   (a) [−count] → [−pl]
                      (b) [−pl] → [+Ø]

The cure for the semantic overload on *flower-flour* has been the development of homophonous forms distinguished by Modern English spelling practice. Another rather frequent cure in English history has been to divide the semantic features between formal doublets. Such has been the case with Modern English *ditch* and *dike*. These doublets stem from different inflectional forms of Old English *dic,* depending on the occurrence of a front or a back vowel in the inflectional ending. Thus, *ditch* is from Old English *dice, dices;* while *dike* is from *dica, dicum.* The latter with palato-velar stop is reenforced by the unpalatalized Icelandic *diki.* The two forms occur side by side throughout the Middle English period and on into Modern English, although the forms with stop consonant are somewhat more prevalent in the North and Northeast where Scandinavian influence was strongest. Both refer to an excavated trench used for fencing or marking a boundary:

(1) He lauez hys gyftez as water of dyche [rime: *chyche*] (c. 1378).
(2) A yeerd she hadde, enclosed al aboute With stikkes, and a drye dych withoute (c. 1390).
(3) John Blakall browtt . . . a dyker for to make yowr dykes . . . we wyst nott . . . whedyr ye wold have hytt sengyll dydge or [dobyll] dydge (c. 1475?). [Note both forms here.]
(4) Summe leye in dikes slenget (c. 1300).
(5) Sho [a female stork] wolde go vnto a dike at was beside þe place, & þer sho wolde wassh hur (c. 1450).

(6) þai wende he had bene dede with wogh; in to a dike þai him drogh (c. 1400).

From the meanings here suggested it is a simple step to that of a defensive ditch before a wall or about a fortified structure:

(1) An oþer Castel þe haue dich abuten & weater beo i þe dich (c. 1230).
(2) þe tauerne is a dich [F fosse] to þieves and þe dyeules castel uor to werri god an his halʒen (1340).
(3) þaye . . . Laddres to þe walle bere for al þe dupe deke [rime: *eke*] (c. 1380).
(4) The wallis in werre wikked to assoile With depe dikes and derk, doubull of water (c. 1450).

By virtue of the physical contiguity of a trench and the pile of dirt thrown out of it, both forms come to be used in the sense of a wall, especially a *defensive* wall:

(1) Sauer . . . dide make an ouerthwert dik [F fosse] Bitwyxte to sees . . . & þer on a pale wel ypoynt (c. 1338).
(2) There they rerid a dyche, and a febill castel vpon, of lardis and turues (c. 1500).
(3) The comyns brake down al the gardens . . . & all the dyches and hegys . . . The comyns of this Cite . . . brake vp the hegis & in diuers places cast downe the dyke (c. 1469).

The occurrence of *ditch* in the sense of an embankment of some kind persisted in the standard dialects into the nineteenth century. The *Oxford English Dictionary* cites a definition of the form from 1880, 'a fence, generally of earth.' However, in recent times the word seems to be restricted to the sense 'a long narrow excavation dug in the earth for defense, drainage, or irrigation.' On the other hand, *dike* seems to have been retained among some speakers of English in both senses:

(1) The Cheef capitaine Manneryng had his deathes wounde, and fell doune in the dike before the gate (1575).
(2) I wil laye sege to the rounde aboute and graue vp dykes agaynst ye (1535).
(3) The main Channel of an high swoln flood, In vain by Dikes and broken works withstood (1635–1656).
(4) Some rushy dyke to jump, or bank to climb (1821).
(5) *Dyke,* a natural lakelet, mere, or pond. . . . (1889).

Local names on the river Humber, as *Goole Dike* and *Doncaster Dike* for navigable channels, attest to the continuation of the sense 'watercourse.' Despite this fact, for a large segment of the English speaking population today *ditch* and *dike* have quite opposite references, the differentiation occurring by way of alleviating a potentially pathological situation.

It appears to be the case that polysemy is more likely to be tolerated without pathological disturbance when the various senses of a word refer to different spheres of thought or action. In the case of both *flower-flour* and *ditch-dike* the senses, as we have noted, were bound up in one sphere of activity—or at least very closely related spheres: for the first, 'the best of something'; for the second, 'the result of digging and piling up the loose dirt.' Consider now the case of *fair*. It occurs in at least the following contexts:

(1) He writes a very fair hand.
(2) She has a fair complexion.
(3) The weather report is for fair and warmer.
(4) This new car cost me a fair amount.
(5) The judge's decision was eminently fair.
(6) The wind was fair out of the Southwest.

In each case a different sphere, as defined by the context, is involved: legibility or elegance of handwriting; lightness of complexion; a bright, sunny, cloudless day; an ample amount of money; a just, impartial, unbiased decision; a promising or favorable wind. These senses, and more, characterized the word *fair* (from Old English *fæger*) in Middle English:

(1) Poetes clepin him [Mercury] god of fair spekyng [translates Latin *eloquentie*] (c. 1398).
(2) So fare perones, so bright of ble [complexion] (c. 1338).
(3) Cym þenne fæʒer wæder & brihte sunnæ (c. 1175).
(4) It is a ryght fayr porcioun [of the world] (c. 1380).
(5) A fayrere eleccioun neuere there was (c. 1410).
(6) Our Lord sent hem a fayr wynde þat broute hem owt of þat cuntre (c. 1438).

Apparently, the senses of *fair* have been considered to involve, for the most part, spheres of activity and thought that are carefully enough distinguished by the contexts which each sense requires that they do not get in each other's way. Thus this polysemantic condition has endured relatively little change since Middle English times.

In Chapter 2 we took some account of the extensive borrowing, especially from Scandinavian, French, and Latin, that has occurred in English as a result of certain critical social, political, and cultural events. And we noted that one of the effects of this borrowing was to create a considerable number of synonyms, or near synonyms (you will recall such groups as *happiness-felicity, cottage-hut, amity-friendship, cordial-hearty, fire-flame, pardon-forgive,* and the like). The question, however interesting, of what constitutes a synonym aside, the appearance of such pairs of lexical items in a language will frequently cause some disturbance in the semantic system. Consider, for example, the pair *ask* (native)-*demand* (borrowed). Old English *acsian* occurs with a number of senses: "ask, demand, summon, call, inquire, seek for, examine, observe, discover, hear of, announce." Most of these senses continue into Middle English with some variation in syntactic structure depending upon the sense:

A. (inquire)

$$x\widehat{\ }ask\ (NP) \qquad \left\{ \begin{array}{c} NP \\ | \\ [\pm animate] \\ np\widehat{\ }S \\ | \\ [+pro] \end{array} \right\}$$

$$\begin{array}{c} | \\ [+human] \\ | \\ [+dat] \end{array}$$

(1) Ic axie þe hwæt spryest þu? (c. 1000).
(2) ða acsode ðe bisceop hwa sceolde andswerian for his modor (c. 1038).
(3) þa axode petrus 'Hu ofte sceal ic forȝifæn' (c. 1135).
(4) He axeden aðelinges, wer leye þa kinges (c. 1225).
(5) Ich acsy þe a questioun (c. 1333).
(6) þeos eorles . . . seoððe axeden his grið (c. 1225).

B. (ask for, summon, call for, seek for)

$$x\widehat{\ }ask\ (NP) \qquad \left\{ \begin{array}{c} NP \\ PP \end{array} \right\}$$

$$\begin{array}{c} | \\ [+human] \end{array}$$

(1) He lette axien anan men þat cuðen hæuwen stan (c. 1200).
(2) The kynge asked his horse, and ther on lepte (c. 1450).
(3) Suyche a payne prikkede hym, he asked a confessour (c. 1450).
(4) A poore beggere . . . if he axe nat his mete, he dyeth for hunger (c. 1390).
(5) þe ancre . . . þet is axinde efter tiðinges (c. 1250).
(6) þey asked Brutes of conseill, what þey schold do for more vitail (c. 1338).
(7) The versifiour pullid of his hoode . . . and asked of two pens (c. 1500).

C. (ask about, inquire about)

x͡ask (NP)   PP
      |
  [+human]

(1) To Seint Albon huy comen and echsten after him þere (c. 1300).
(2) His wife . . . vnto [about] þat bride was askande (c. 1400).
(3) Vppon a day he axkid . . . of his ffader, and hough is moder was (c. 1450).

D. (demand, require)

x͡ask͡NP
    |
 [−animate]

(1) Iusticia . . . acseð riht of alle ure misdades, and dom (c. 1200).
(2) God wile acsi rekeninge ate daye of dome (1340).
(3) Whan tyme and place axeth (1340).
(4) To cleime and axe his rightful heritage (c. 1400).
(5) It will ask some time, yea and cunning too, to find it out (1623).
(6) To give a Milton birth ask'd ages more (1780).

By the beginning of the thirteenth century, a new structure begins to occur for sense A. (ask):

x͡ask͡   PP   ͡ np ͡S
          | |
  [+human] [+pro]

(1) þa escade Paul to mihhal, hwet þe alde mon were (c. 1225).
(2) þan oxed anon Sir Gij to þe barouns . . . 'what is he . . .?' (c. 1330).
(3) Heo aschede at Corineus, how heo so hardi were (1297).
(4) ych axede of an hebrewe . . . wat þe chyldrun seyde (c. 1475).

It does not seem unlikely that this construction developed among bilingual French and English speakers by analogy with French *demander à*. It begins to occur at a date considerably earlier than the occurrence of *demand* in English.

When *demand* begins to occur as an English verb early in the fifteenth century it is a close synonym with *ask*, having both the semantic features (inquire) and (require). Furthermore, with the feature (inquire) it shows the same grammatical structure:

(1) Bot I demaunde you, have ye envy to see vs and our ladies? (c. 1450).

(2) Cato makithe a question to . . . Scipion and Lilius, demaunding them why they . . . had wasted . . . theire inheritaunce (c. 1475).
(3) She demaunded him how he felte himself and how he ferde (c. 1457).
(4) They were demaunded why they departed (1568).
(5) Philip . . . being a long time prisoner . . . was demanded what upheld him all that time (1635).
(6) I wold demaunde a question, yf I shold not displease (1484).
(7) Had our Ancestors . . . been demanded these few questions (1643).

It is of some interest that the early occurrences of *demand* as an English verb do *not* pattern after French *demander à*. However, by the sixteenth century one finds the following:

(1) Quhen God sal rise to iudge, and quhen he sal demand at me quhat sal I answer (1588).
(2) The king receyued hym moche benyngly and demanded to hym som tydynges (c. 1500).
(3) Then the same Thomas demondid of the seide Hugh whether. . . . (c. 1458).

The question we would like to be able to answer is "Under which influence, the French or the English, did this construction develop?" Did the verb *demand,* having moved into the semantic range of the native *ask,* assume a syntactic characteristic which *ask* had itself borrowed from the native French *demander à,* or did later users of the English *demand* recall the original French construction and import it as a loan translation into their speech? The question cannot, it seems to this writer, be answered with certainty. There is evidence, however, that *demand* did come to be used in a construction borrowed from *ask* in the sense (ask for):

(1) I intreated Sir Richard Halkins to goe a shoare to the Governour and demand him for my Gold (1632).
(2) To free himself of it, he demanded [(inquire)] for a sword (1654).

If, as we think, *demand for* was modeled after *ask for,* there is also the possibility that the construction *demand at* was modeled after *ask at* which itself was modeled after *demander à.* If this is in fact the case, then we have the interesting situation in which a native word and a foreign word with essentially the same semantic features exist side by side in a community of bilingual speakers. The native word borrows certain syntactic features characteristic of the foreign word, the foreign word becomes anglicized and then reborrows certain syntactic features which now characterize the native synonym. And further, because of the synonymity, the borrowed word borrows additional *new* syntactic features from the native word.

The verb *ask* continued to be characterized by a feature (require) and the verb *demand* by a feature (inquire) at least until the eighteenth century. Indeed there are still a few contexts in which the two are more or less interchangeable: "The law asks/demands that you refrain from stealing." But for the most part *ask* is now characterized by the feature (inquire) and *demand* by the feature (require). The pathological situation involved here would seem to be in part a lack of economy in the system; that is, the existence side by side of two different terms with much the same semantic range; in part a rather critical psychological confusion; that is, a confusion over the authoritarian or nonauthoritarian features of the two terms which could materially affect communication between two parties; and the need to resolve this confusion—to be clear as to the speaker's attitude and intent. The authoritarian feature is removed from *ask* and becomes a primary feature of *demand.* Thus the distinction between the speaker's attitude in "I asked that the car be brought around" and "I demanded that the car be brought around" is now perfectly clear.

Consider, finally, one further case of synonymy—the trio *forgive, pardon,* and *excuse.* In Modern English, although all three may occur in identical syntactic structures with closely similar meanings ('God will excuse/forgive/pardon your sins'), each contains as part of its lexical entry a distinguisher that clearly differentiates the three, as well as unique syntactic characteristics. For example, it is probably the case that all three are marked by the semantic feature (release); but the distinguisher for each will characterize this feature differently. For *excuse,* the distinguisher will contain the notion 'extenuating circumstances'; for *forgive,* the notion 'without personal resentment or desire for revenge, a personal and subjective commitment'; for *pardon,* the notion 'free from penalty, an impersonal and generally objective commitment.' Further, *forgive* will probably be marked for somewhat stronger moral and religious overtones than the other two, while *pardon* will probably be marked for more formal-legal overtones. The difference among the three can be seen in the following:

(1) The governor excused the criminal.
(2) The governor forgave the criminal.
(3) The governor pardoned the criminal.

The word *forgive* is native English; the other two appear in Middle English as borrowings from French. In Old English the most frequent sense of *forgifan* is 'to give, grant, or provide'; the sense "forgive" is rare:

(1) God cwæþ þa, Efne, ic forgeaf eow eall gærs and wyrta sæd berende ofer eorðan.
'God then said, Eve, I will give you all grass and plants carrying seeds over the earth.'

(2) . . . wiððon þe him mon andlyfne forgeaf.
'. . . on condition that someone provide them with substance.'
(3) . . . ond hi him andlyfne ond are forgeafen for heora gewinne.
'. . . and they gave them substance and property (in payment) for their struggle.'

However by early Middle English times, the modern sense of *forgive* clearly dominates, undoubtedly as a result of the encroachment of *gifan* 'give' on the other senses of *forgifan:*

(1) þæt God sylf us forȝife ure synnæn (c. 1175).
(2) We forȝifæð þam ðe wið [against] us aȝyltæð (c. 1175).
(3) þu forȝeuest þam monne þe wið þe agulteð (c. 1225).
(4) God forsothe is holi . . . ne forȝyueth to ȝoure hidows [hideous] synnes (c. 1382).
(5) His synnes forȝoven to hym scholen be (c. 1410).
(6) Forȝeuyth me þat I have grevyd ȝow be þe wey (c. 1438).

Interestingly enough the development of this specialized sense is paralleled by a new sense of *forgive,* namely 'the abandonment of revenge, or legal action, or vengeful feeling':

(1) Ic forȝeue [abandon] min hating for þe luue of heuene king (c. 1225).
(2) Loke þat ȝe euere fforȝiue . . . of wraþþe toward eny man (c. 1280).
(3) Acorded we ben of þat dede, & forȝeuen al hatrede (c. 1300).
(4) God loueþ hem dere þat forȝyuen here wraþ (c. 1303).

The notion 'to excuse from payment of a debt or penalty,' that is, a *legal* feature of the term also develops:

(1) Rotbert of Normandig . . . forgeaf þa þreo þusend marc þe him seo cyng Heanrig be foreweard ælce geare gifan sceolde (c. 1121).
'Robert of Normandy . . . excused the three thousand marks which King Henry by agreement was supposed to pay him each year.'

(2) The lord of that seruaunt . . . forȝaue to hym the dette (c. 1384).
(3) He was Hongede and his Heuede smyten of . . . But at þe prayer of þe quene . . . his drawyng was forȝeuen him (1400).
(4) I forgife Bertyn my son all that he awes me (1459).

We might comment at this point on a rather interesting grammatical situation admirably illustrated by the verb *forgive.* Of the following sentences, it is generally acknowledged that the second is derived from the first by transformation:

(1) Bill gave some money to his girl friend.
(2) Bill gave his girl friend some money.

What, then, of this sentence:

(3) Bill forgave his girl friend her faults.

The sentence

(4) *Bill forgave her faults to his girl friend.

is clearly ungrammatical in Modern English. But it was *not* ungrammatical in Middle English if we are to believe what we read. Old English *forgifan* often required a person in the dative case and a thing in the accusative case. The dative relationship was frequently signaled in Middle English, and beyond, by the preposition *to*. Instances of this use are numerous in Middle English texts:

(1) Thi synnes ben forȝouun to thee (c. 1384).
(2) His synnes forȝoven to hym scholen be (c. 1410).
(3) Yef we voryeueþ to ham þet ous habbeþ mi[s] do (c. 1340).
(4) The lord of that seruaunt . . . forȝaue to hym the dette (c. 1384).

The derivation, therefore, of 'Bill forgave his girl friend her faults' from 'Bill forgave her faults to his girl friend' is historically justified, even though the underlying construction yields an ungrammatical sentence in Modern English. One suspects that this situation is by no means unusual. There are a great many constructions in Modern English that appear to be derived by syntactic transformation from some underlying string; yet, no grammatical underlying string can be found for these. What we are suggesting here is that the *grammatical* underlying string may be embedded somewhere in the history of the language, its persistence blocked by certain constraints which we are at a loss to explain. It may be, of course, that a change in the disposition of the semantic features of a word may be responsible for the blockage. In the case of *forgive,* it does not seem unreasonable to suppose that the loss of *to* is directly related to the loss of a sense of 'dativeness,' that is, 'target of an action of giving, granting, providing, and so on,' when these semantic features no longer obtain, as they do not in the later development of *forgive.* We submit here that it is just this kind of study of the interrelatedness of syntactic and semantic features that must be pursued in future if we are to have any significant notions about the nature of syntactic and semantic change.

The verb *excuse* is recorded as entering the semantic field as early as the first quarter of the thirteenth century, when it sometimes replaces Old English *werian* 'to protect, guard, ward off, defend, and so forth.' The notion here is that one's behavior may be *excused*, that is, *defended*, on the basis of some extenuating circumstance:

(1) The ydel man excuseth hym in wynter by cause of the grete coold (c. 1390).
(2) Thanne wole he ... deffenden or excusen his synne by vnstedefastnesse of his flessh (c. 1390).
(3) She beganne to excuse her[self], and saide that the serpent hadd counsailed her (c. 1450).
(4) So spake the Fiend, and with necessitie ... excus'd his devilish deeds (1667).

This has been one of the most persistent senses of *excuse.*

Closely related though different senses are those of 'exonerate' or 'vindicate' or 'acquit':

(1) The thef ... escusede Jhesu Cryst, And hym gelty gan ȝelde (c. 1315).
(2) Ilkon of hem excused hym that he was never ... assentyng to the dethe of the Duc of Gloucestre (1399).
(3) No mon is excusid here of consenting to þis synne (c. 1400).
(4) If þai [suspected lepers] ben hole men, þai schal be excused [Latin *absoluendi sunt*]. ... (c. 1425).
(5) To excuse him of the death of the archbishop Thomas (1577).

These senses of *excuse* are gradually taken over by the words given above as senses: *exonerate, vindicate* and *acquit*. Although the first two enter the semantic field after the Middle English period, the last is coextensive with *excuse.* It occurs in the following in the legal sense which continues to characterize it today:

(1) A man may acquyte hym self biforn god by penitence in this world and nat by Tresor (c. 1390).
(2) He to be beleved be his othe & ij or iij of his credible neyghbours with him sworne, & so to be acquitte (1442).
(3) Thomas ap Rees ... Hoel ap John David, were secretely ... arrayned, and then and there were thereof acquyted (1472–1475).

The other persistent sense of *excuse*, namely 'to exempt, free, or relieve from a task, duty, obligation, promise, penalty,' and the like, occurs frequently from the end of the fourteenth century on:

(1) I wol as now excuse thee of thy tale (c. 1390).
(2) Bot yf he haf resonable cause to be excused by (1409).
(3) Yf any of hem absente hym . . . but yf he have a resonable and notable cause to be excused (1433).
(4) To holde me escusyd of that y p[ro]mittyd you (1463).

Certain senses then, which earlier were a part of the semantic range of *forgive* are gradually preempted by the borrowed word *excuse* and cease to play primary roles as distinguishers for *forgive*. One syntactic manifestation of this semantic redeployment is the change from the structure *excused of* to *excused from*.

The formal, official, legalistic sense that tends to distinguish the verbs *pardon* and *forgive* is probably a result of the use of the noun *pardon* to refer to an official political or ecclesiastical indulgence and to the document that assured such indulgence:

(1) þe Pope ȝaf alle pardon þat þudere wolden gon (1290).
(2) De ceo que chartres de pardoun ont este si legierment grantees avent ces heures, des homicides, etc., (1328).
(3) þis bischop of Rome . . . stireþ men bi grete perdon to breke opynly Goddis hestis (c. 1380).
(4) His walet [lay] biforn hym in his lappe Bret ful of pardon comen from Rome al hoot (c. 1386).
(5) Your Letters of pardon under your grete seale (1450).
(6) Letters of privie Seale, of Pardon generall or speciall (1473).
(7) Their pardons, and other of their trumperye, hath bene bought and solde in Lambard strete (1542–1545).
(8) Offering to all such as were in the Iland a generall pardon in his Maiesties behalfe, if they woulde yeeld (1600).

It is worth noting that the noun *forgiveness* rarely occurs in this legalistic sense. I find only this unequivocal citation from the *Middle English Dictionary*:

(1) Mercye haþ þe lettres of forȝeuenesses and þe indulgences (c. 1400).

This noun occurs most frequently in connection with a more personal, subjective, and less formal act of pardon, either by God or by one's fellow man.

When the verb *pardon* enters the field in the early fifteenth century (later than the noun) and encroaches on the semantic range of *forgive,* a certain amount of semantic specialization for each term gradually results. The verb *pardon* assumes (or continues) as one of its *primary* semantic distinguishers the legalistic sense carried over from the noun. Whatever the degree to which this sense characterized *forgiveness* and *forgive,* it was quickly abandoned.

We should notice that the specialization of senses for *excuse, forgive,* and *pardon* by which they may now be distinguished tends to arise under circumstances of some moment: excusing culpable behavior because of extenuating circumstances, forgiving a religious offense, pardoning a crime against society. In more or less trivial circumstances any one of the three words may occur to suggest 'courteous forbearance of or allowance for some fault':

(1) To pardon me of my rude wrytyng (1509).
(2) I beseche you to pardon my boldnes (1526).
(3) I beg your pardon: you will not make one at ombre (1676)?
(4) Pardon me from dwelling so long on this sad theme (1795).
(5) Pardon my impatience (1684).
(6) I prey . . . every discret persone . . . to have my rewde endytyng for excused (c. 1391).
(7) Some tymes we excuse a fault and accuse the reporter (1553).
(8) Excuse my glove, Thomas (1775).
(9) The boldest heart may be excused a shudder (1857).
(10) That infernal (excuse me) coward and villain (1889).
(11) Thy frailtie and infirmer sex forgiv'n (1667).
(12) Dear Sir, forgive the Prejudice of Youth (1738).
(13) Forgive me if I remind you, that . . . (1828).
(14) An example so much better—forgive me to say—before her (1742).

It seems to be the case that the strong moral and religious senses which continue to characterize *forgive* inhibit its general use in situations that call for mild forbearance or purely formal apologies. Although I have no statistics to present, my impression is that an accidental collision between two persons on the sidewalk is much more likely to call forth either the responses "pardon me" or "excuse me" than it is the response "forgive me."

6.30   Conclusion

In this chapter we have done little more than scratch the surface in so far as various types and mechanisms of semantic change are concerned. It has not been the intent of the chapter to review the extensive contributions of semanticists in specifying conditions, causes, and kinds of semantic change, though of necessity we have made reference to some of these. The attempt has been rather to specify the nature of a semantic component and to locate its sphere of operation relative to the grammar of a language—in this case English. Some of the important questions are: "How are syntactic and semantic features that are assigned to a lexical item in the lexicon combined with other lexical items in a given structure to yield derived readings for that structure?" "What part does syntactic structure play in the assignment of syntactic features to a lexical item, and perhaps ultimately to the assignment to that item of semantic features?" As a corollary to this, "How do changes in syntactic structure effect changes in semantic features (see, for example, the syntactic and semantic development of *again* [adverb] and *against* [preposition])?" "What view of the relationship between syntax and semantics must one have in order to account for the synonymity of *hearty* and *cordial* in 'They gave us a hearty/cordial welcome' but the lack of it in 'He's a very cordial fellow' and 'He's a very hearty fellow.' " (NOTE: In this last the extent to which a semantic overlap between *hearty* and *hardy* is reenforced by what borders on a phonological identity.) "What part do syntactic transformations play in the operation of semantic change?" "How do additions and losses of lexical items in a semantic field create realignments in the syntactic and semantic features of these items, and ultimately changes in the projection rules that provide derived readings?"

We have provided no final answers to any of these questions. What we have tried to do is to suggest the directions from which the answers will ultimately come.

6.40   Special Linguistic Terms

composite transfer	polysemous
conservatism	projection rule
contiguity	selection restriction
derived reading	selectional rule
distinguisher	semantic anomaly
grammaticalness	semantic field
homophonous form	semantic marker
innovation	semantic pathology
linguistic contagion	semantic range
metonymic transfer	sense transfer
name transfer	similarity
output constraint	subcategorization rule
polysemantic overload	syntactic marker

6.50   *For Additional Reference*

Antal, László. "Meaning and its Change," *Linguistics* 6:14–28 (1964).

Bréal, Michel. *Semantics: Studies in the Science of Meaning*. Trans. Mrs. Henry Cust. London, 1900.

Carnap, Rudolf. *Introduction to Semantics*. Cambridge, 1942.

————. *Meaning and Necessity: A Study in Semantics and Modal Logic*. Chicago, 1956.

Chomsky, Noam. "Logical Syntax and Semantics: Their Linguistic Relevance," *Language* 31:36–45 (1955).

Copley, J. *Shift of Meaning*. London, 1961.

Culbert, Sidney S. "Perceptual Distortion Resulting from Semantic Transfer: A Study in Verbal Mediation," *SL* 8:77–81 (1954).

Estrich, Robert M., and Hans Sperber. *Three Keys to Language*. New York, 1952.

Firth, John R. "The Technique of Semantics," *TPS* 1935:37–72.

Garvin, Paul L. "A Descriptive Technique for the Treatment of Meaning," *Language* 34:1–32 (1958).

Householder, Fred W., Jr. "On the Uniqueness of Semantic Mapping," *Word* 18:173–85 (1962).

Katz, Jerrold J., and Jerry A. Fodor. "The Structure of a Semantic Theory," *Language* 39:170–210 (1963).

————, and Paul M. Postal. *An Integrated Theory of Linguistic Descriptions*. M.I.T., 1964.

Kroesch, Samuel. "Semantic Borrowing in Old English," *Klaeber Miscellany* [6.10] 50–72.

Langer, Suzanne. *Philosophy in a New Key*. New York (NAL) 1959.

Levin, Samuel R. "Aspects of Semantic and Grammatical Change," *Linguistics* 2:26–37 (1963).

McCawley, James D. "The Role of Semantics in a Grammar," in *Universals in Linguistic Theory* eds. Emmon Bach and Robert T. Harms. New York, 1968.

Menner, Robert J. "Multiple Meaning and Change of Meaning in English," *Language* 21:59–76 (1945).

Morris, Charles. *Signs, Language, and Behavior*. New York, 1946; repr. 1955.

Newman, Stanley S. "Semantic Problems in Grammatical Systems and Lexemes: a Search for Method," *Language in Culture* [33.13], 89–91.

Noyes, Gertrude E. "The Beginnings of the Study of Synonyms in England," *PMLA* 66:951–70 (1951).

Ogden, Charles K., and I. A. Richards. *The Meaning of Meaning*. 4th rev. ed. London, 1936.

Osgood, Charles, G. Suci, and P. Tannenbaum. *The Measurement of Meaning*. Urbana, 1957.

Robins, R. H. "A Problem in the Statement of Meanings," *Lingua* 3:121–137 (1952).

Rudskoyer, Arene. *Fair, Foul, Nice, Proper: A Contribution to the Study of Polysemy*. Stockholm, 1952.

Schibsbye, K. "The Grammatical Aspects of Semantics," *ES* 40:455–8 (1959).

Stern, Gustav. *Meaning and Change of Meaning, with Special Reference to the English Language*. Göteborg, 1931; repr. Bloomington, 1963.

Trier, Jost. *Der Deutsche Wortschatz im Sinnbezirk des Verstandes. Die Geschichte eines Sprachlichen Feldes*. Heidelberg, 1934.

Ullmann, Stephen. *The Principles of Semantics*. Glasgow, 1951.

————. "Descriptive Semantics and Linguistic Typology," *Word* 9:225–40 (1953).

————. *Semantics: An Introduction to the Science of Meaning*. New York, 1962.

Weinreich, U. "On the Semantic Structure of Language," in *Universals of Language,* ed. J. H. Greenberg. M.I.T., (1963).

Ziff, Paul. *Semantic Analysis*. Ithaca, 1960.

6.60   Exercises

1. The following two poems contain structures which have resulted from the suspension either of strict subcategorial rules or selectional rules. They are thus *ungrammatical* in the sense in which we have used this term. Identify the structures in question and the type of grammatical rule suspended. Can one obtain semantic readings for these structures? If so, how?

Fall in Corrales[5]
Richard Wilbur (1921–   )

Winter will be feasts and fires in the shut houses,
Lovers with hot mouths in their blanched bed,
Prayers and poems made, and all recourses
Against the world huge and dead:

Charms, all charms, as in stillness of plumb summer
The shut head lies down in bottomless grasses,
Willing that its thought be all heat and hum,
That it not dream the time passes.

Now as these light buildings of summer begin
To crumble, the air husky with blown tile,
It is as when in bald April the wind
Unhoused the spirit for a while:

Then there was no need by tales or drowsing
To make the thing that we were mothered by;
It was ourselves who melted in the mountains,
And the sun dove into every eye.

Our desires dwelt in the weather as fine as bomb-dust;
It was our sex that made the fountains yield;
Our flesh fought in the roots, and at last rested
Whole among cows in the risen field.

Now in its empty bed the truant river
Leaves but the perfect rumples of its flow;
The cottonwoods are spending gold like water;
Weeds in their light detachments go;

In a dry world more huge than rhyme or dreaming
We hear the sentences of straws and stones,
Stand in the wind and, bowing to this time,
Practise the candor of our bones.   1961

Fern Hill[6]
Dylan Thomas (1914–1953)

Now as I was young and easy under the apple boughs
About the lilting house and happy as the grass was green,
   The night above the dingle starry,
    Time let me hail and climb
   Golden in the heydays of his eyes,
And honored among wagons I was prince of the apple towns
And once below a time I lordly had the trees and leaves
     Trail with daisies and barley
   Down the rivers of the windfall light.

And as I was green and carefree, famous among the barns
About the happy yard and singing as the farm was home,
   In the sun that is young once only,
    Time let me play and be
   Golden in the mercy of his means,
And green and golden I was huntsman and herdsman, the calves
Sang to my horn, the foxes on the hills barked clear and cold,
     And the sabbath rang slowly
   In the pebbles of the holy streams.

All the sun long it was running, it was lovely, the hay
Fields high as the house, the tunes from the chimneys, it was air
   And playing, lovely and watery
      And fire green as grass.
   And nightly under the simple stars
As I rode to sleep the owls were bearing the farm away,
All the moon long I heard, blessed among stables, the night-jars
   Flying with the ricks, and the horses
      Flashing into the dark.

And then to awake, and the farm, like a wanderer white
With the dew, come back, the cock on his shoulder: it was all
   Shining, it was Adam and maiden,
      The sky gathered again
   And the sun grew round that very day.
So it must have been after the birth of the simple light
In the first, spinning place, the spellbound horses walking warm
   Out of the whinnying green stable
      On to the fields of praise.

And honored among foxes and pheasants by the gay house
Under the new made clouds and happy as the heart was long,
   In the sun born over and over,
      I ran my heedless ways,
   My wishes raced through the house high hay
And nothing I cared, at my sky blue trades, that time allows
In all his tuneful turning so few and such morning songs
   Before the children green and golden
      Follow him out of grace,

Nothing I cared, in the lamb white days, that time would take me
Up to the swallow thronged loft by the shadow of my hand,
   In the moon that is always rising,
      Nor that riding to sleep
   I should hear him fly with the high fields
And wake to the farm forever fled from the childless land.
Oh as I was young and easy in the mercy of his means,
      Time held me green and dying
   Though I sang in my chains like the sea.

2. A large number of Old English lexical items have either been lost to the language or have undergone considerable modification of their semantic ranges. Using the *Oxford English Dictionary* and the *Middle English Dictionary* trace the semantic and

distributional history of the following words, referring whenever possible to other lexical items, native or borrowed, which may have contributed to the course of their history.

wain	kith	wight
mere	chap	rime
lief	main	wode
erian	doom	shroud
wierd	snithan	housel

3. The following pairs of phonetically similar but semantically distinct words derive from a common etymon. Trace the semantic split involved, giving close attention wherever relevant to syntactic differentiation as well.

to-too	mettle-metal
of-off	travel-travail
through-thorough	posy-poesy
human-humane	tone-tune
urban-urbane	catch-chase
curtsy-courtesy	gentle-genteel

4. In either of the two dictionaries mentioned above find the earliest recorded instance of the following common metaphors. Attempt to find an underlying syntactic structure for each in which the body part is *not* used metaphorically. If you cannot find one, suggest one.

head of a pin	brow of a hill
eye of a needle	tooth of a saw
mouth of a river	neck of a bottle
foot of a mountain	tongue of a flame
hands of a clock	finger of land
arm of the law	shoulder of a road

5. Attempt to account for the historical modification of the semantic ranges of each item in the following groups in terms of the interaction of these items within a semantic field.

a. kill, slay, murder, assassinate, execute
b. crafty, skillful, artful, clever, cunning
c. hit, strike, smite, slay, punch, slap
d. honest, worthy, truthful, upright, sincere
e. loving, erotic, amorous, affectionate, venereal, lustful
f. pious, devout, sanctimonious, reverent, worshipful
g. cut, carve, slice, hew, shear

6. What sociopsychological phenomenon is illustrated by the following pairs. Look up the history of each word in the pair. Which words are borrowed, which are native? When did each borrowed word enter the language? What changes in meaning and social distribution have occurred to both members of the pair.

perspire-sweat	purloin-steal
insane-mad	urine-piss
lingerie-underwear	belly-abdomen
fib-lie	cunt-vagina
sin-transgression	copulate-fuck

Appendixes

Appendix I: Some Rules for Modern English

A number of rules are necessary to assign the appropriate written shape to English verb forms. For example, a large number of past tense forms may be assigned by the following rule:

(a) $V_{x1}\!\!\frown\!Pas \Rightarrow V_{x1}\!\!\frown\!d$

    where: V_{x1} = native English words which in the singular end in the grapheme sequence $\langle -Ce \rangle$ (*rope, dope, tape, rape, tame, bathe, dare, convince,* and so forth).

Another set of forms is assigned by the rule:

(b) $V_{x2}\!\!\frown\!Pas \Rightarrow V_{x2}\!\!\frown\!-C_{x2}\!\!\frown\!ed$

    where: (1) V_{x2} has the graphemic shape $\langle -VC \rangle$.
           (2) $-C_{x2}$ is a repetition of the final $\langle C \rangle$ in V_{x2} (*rap/rapped, stop/stopped, map/ mapped, bat/batted, hem/hemmed,* and so forth).

Still another set by the rule:

(c) $V_{x3}\!\!\frown\!Pas \Rightarrow V_{x3}\!\!\frown\!ed$

    where: $V_{x3} \neq V_{x1}/V_{x2}$ (*fear/feared, burn/burned, root/rooted, learn/learned, peel/peeled, watch/watched,* and so forth).

A relatively small number of verbs (some sixty) in English form their past tenses, and in some cases their past participles also, by replacing the vowel letter of the present tense with a different vowel letter: *swim/swam/swum, take/took, come/came, begin/began/begun, sing/sang/sung, tear/tore, hide/hid,* and so on. Still others make use both of the device of adding a dental consonant letter to the stem and that of replacement: *keep/kept, sleep/slept, feel/felt,* and so on. Each one of these "irregular" verbs must be subclassified and morphographemic rules written to provide the appropriate past tense and past participle letter shape (phonological rules would assign a phonetic interpretation). One such rule might appear this way:

(d) $V_{y\langle i \rangle}\begin{bmatrix} Pas \\ -en \end{bmatrix} \Rightarrow \begin{bmatrix} V_{y\langle a \rangle} \\ V_{y\langle u \rangle} \end{bmatrix}$

which may be interpreted to mean: 'all verbs of class y containing the grapheme $\langle i \rangle$ in the stem change that $\langle i \rangle$ to $\langle a \rangle$ in the past and to $\langle u \rangle$ in the past participle' (*begin/began/begun, swim/swam/ swum,* and so on). Another such rule might be:

(e) $V_{z\langle ee \rangle}\begin{Bmatrix} Pas \\ -en \end{Bmatrix} \Rightarrow V_{z\langle e \rangle}\!\!\frown\!t$

that is, 'all verbs of class z with $\langle ee \rangle$ in the stem change $\langle ee \rangle$ to $\langle e \rangle$ in the past *or* past participle, and add t (*sleep/slept, keep/kept,* and so on). The base component presented above requires a number of such morphographemic rules. We may, for instance, produce a string:

(1) $a\!\!\frown\!man\!\!\frown\![+pl]\!\!\frown\!Poss\!\!\frown\!shoe\,[+pl]$

A rule is required to assign the proper letter shape to possessive nouns, singular or plural:

(f_1) $N_x \begin{bmatrix} [+pl] \\ [-pl] \end{bmatrix}$ Poss $\Rightarrow N_x \begin{bmatrix} [+pl]^\frown \\ [-pl]^\frown \text{'s} \end{bmatrix}$

(f_2) $N_y^\frown [\pm pl]^\frown$ Poss $\Rightarrow N_y^\frown [\pm pl]$'s

Rule (f_1) will convert noun singulars and plurals of class x into $N_x^\frown [-pl]^\frown$'s and $N_x^\frown [+pl]^\frown$ ' respectively. Rules assigning singular and plural forms to this noun class will then apply, converting the strings to $N_x^\frown$'s and $N_x^\frown \begin{Bmatrix} s \\ es \end{Bmatrix}^\frown$ ' respectively. Thus,

boy$^\frown [-pl]^\frown$ Poss $\Rightarrow$
boy$^\frown [-pl]^\frown$'s $\Rightarrow$
boy$^\frown$'s
boy$^\frown [+pl]^\frown$ Poss
boy$^\frown [+pl]^\frown$ '
boy$^\frown$ s$^\frown$ '

Rule (f_2) will convert noun singulars and plurals of class y into $N_y^\frown [-pl]^\frown$'s and $N_y^\frown [+pl]^\frown$'s:

man$^\frown [-pl]^\frown$ Poss $\Rightarrow$
man$^\frown [-pl]^\frown$'s $\Rightarrow$
man$^\frown$'s
man$^\frown [+pl]^\frown$ Poss $\Rightarrow$
man$^\frown [+pl]^\frown$'s $\Rightarrow$
men$^\frown$'s

Number and possessive rules will then convert the string in (1) above to:

(1b) a$^\frown$ men$^\frown$'s$^\frown$ shoe$^\frown$ s

Clearly an additional rule that deletes *a* before noun plurals is necessary. Such a rule, however, must be more general than this since we will also have to delete *a* before all nouns specified for $\begin{Bmatrix} [-\text{count}] \\ [-\text{common}] \end{Bmatrix}$

(g) $a(X) \begin{Bmatrix} [+pl] \\ \begin{Bmatrix} [-\text{count}] \\ [-\text{common}] \end{Bmatrix} \end{Bmatrix} (Y) \Rightarrow (X) \begin{Bmatrix} [+pl] \\ \begin{Bmatrix} [-\text{count}] \\ [-\text{common}] \end{Bmatrix} \end{Bmatrix} (Y)$

where: (X) any form or set of forms which may intervene between *a* and $\begin{Bmatrix} [pl] \\ \begin{Bmatrix} [-\text{count}] \\ [-\text{common}] \end{Bmatrix} \end{Bmatrix}$

(Y) any form or set of forms which may follow.

In Chapter 4 both *relativization* and *pronominalization* transformations were given. Morphographemic rules are necessary to convert the symbols thus introduced into standard English forms:

(h)$_i$ X$^\frown$wh-$^\frown$No$^\frown$Poss$^\frown$Y $\Rightarrow$ X$^\frown$whose$^\frown$Y

$\quad$ [$\pm$animate]

[NOTE: For the author the sentence 'We visited the prison whose inmates were on strike last week' is fully grammatical. The sentence 'We visited the prison the inmates of which were on strike last week' is a rather cumbersome stylistic variant.]

(h)$_{ii}$ X$^\frown$wh-$^\frown$Y $\Rightarrow$ X $\begin{bmatrix} \text{who, that} \\ \text{which, that} \end{bmatrix}$ Y

$\quad \begin{bmatrix} [+\text{Human}] \\ [-\text{Human}] \end{bmatrix}$

$\qquad$ where: Y $\neq$ Poss

(i) i. #$^\frown$Pro$^\frown$[$-$pl]$^\frown$X $\Rightarrow$ # $\begin{bmatrix} \text{he} \\ \text{she} \end{bmatrix}$ X

$\qquad$ [$+$human]

$\qquad \begin{bmatrix} [+\text{male}] \\ [+\text{female}] \end{bmatrix}$

$\qquad$ where: X $\neq$ Poss

ii. (X) Pro$^\frown$[$-$pl]$^\frown$Poss$^\frown$NP(Y) $\Rightarrow$ (X) $\begin{bmatrix} \text{his} \\ \text{her} \end{bmatrix}$ NP(Y)

$\qquad$ [$+$human]

$\qquad \begin{bmatrix} [+\text{male}] \\ [+\text{female}] \end{bmatrix}$

iii. X $\begin{Bmatrix} \text{V} \\ \text{Prep} \end{Bmatrix}$ Pro$^\frown$[$-$pl] (Y) $\Rightarrow$ X $\begin{Bmatrix} \text{V} \\ \text{Prep} \end{Bmatrix} \begin{bmatrix} \text{him} \\ \text{her} \end{bmatrix}$ (Y)

$\qquad$ [$+$human]

$\qquad \begin{bmatrix} [+\text{male}] \\ [+\text{female}] \end{bmatrix}$

$\qquad$ where: Y $\neq$ Poss

iv. (X) Pro$^\frown$[$-$pl]$^\frown$Poss$^\frown$NP(Y) $\Rightarrow$ (X) its$^\frown$NP(Y)

$\qquad$ [$-$animate]

v. (X) Pro$^\frown$[$-$pl] (Y) $\Rightarrow$ (X) it (Y)

$\qquad$ [$-$animate]

$\qquad$ where: Y $\neq$ Poss

vi. #$^\frown$Pro$^\frown$[$+$pl]$^\frown$X $\Rightarrow$ #$^\frown$they$^\frown$X

$\qquad$ [$\pm$animate]

$\qquad$ where: X $\neq$ Poss

vii. (X) Pro$^\frown$[$+$pl]$^\frown$Poss$^\frown$NP(Y) $\Rightarrow$ (X) their$^\frown$NP(Y)

$\qquad$ [$\pm$animate]

viii. X $\begin{Bmatrix} V \\ Prep \end{Bmatrix}$ $\underset{[\pm\text{animate}]}{\text{Pro}\widehat{}[+\text{pl}]}$ (Y) X $\begin{Bmatrix} V \\ Prep \end{Bmatrix}$ them (Y)

where: Y ≠ Poss

Appendix II: Some Rules for Old English

These rules will provide the proper graphemic shapes characteristic of Old English grammatical elements—shapes like those cited in the paradigms on pages 177–184. We will not attempt an exhaustive inventory of such rules, but will simply suggest the form that they will take.

(1) T_N:

    A. i. $\underset{[+s]}{N} \begin{Bmatrix} [+\text{masc}] \\ [+\text{neut}] \end{Bmatrix} \Rightarrow N \begin{bmatrix} \text{-}\emptyset \\ \text{-es} \\ \text{-e} \end{bmatrix}$

              $\underset{[-\text{pl}]}{}$

              $\begin{bmatrix} \begin{Bmatrix} [+\text{nom}] \\ [+\text{acc}] \end{Bmatrix} \\ [+\text{gen}] \\ [+\text{dat}] \end{bmatrix}$

      ii. $\underset{[+s]}{N} \widehat{} \underset{[+\text{pl}]}{[+\text{masc}]} \Rightarrow N \begin{bmatrix} \text{-as} \\ \text{-a} \\ \text{-um} \end{bmatrix}$

              $\begin{bmatrix} \begin{Bmatrix} [+\text{nom}] \\ [+\text{acc}] \end{Bmatrix} \\ [+\text{gen}] \\ [+\text{dat}] \end{bmatrix}$

      iii. $\underset{[+s]}{N} \widehat{} \underset{[+\text{pl}]}{[+\text{neut}]} \Rightarrow N \begin{bmatrix} \text{-}\begin{Bmatrix} \emptyset \\ u \end{Bmatrix} \\ \text{-a} \\ \text{-um} \end{bmatrix}$

              $\begin{bmatrix} \begin{Bmatrix} [+\text{nom}] \\ [+\text{acc}] \end{Bmatrix} \\ [+\text{gen}] \\ [+\text{dat}] \end{bmatrix}$

    B. i. $\underset{[+s]}{N} \widehat{} \underset{[-\text{pl}]}{[+\text{fem}]} \Rightarrow N \begin{bmatrix} \text{-}\begin{Bmatrix} u \\ \emptyset \end{Bmatrix} \\ \text{-e} \end{bmatrix}$

              $\begin{bmatrix} [+\text{nom}] \\ \begin{Bmatrix} [+\text{acc}] \\ [+\text{gen}] \\ [+\text{dat}] \end{Bmatrix} \end{bmatrix}$

ii. $\text{N} \overset{\frown}{} [+\text{fem}] \Rightarrow \text{N} \begin{bmatrix} -\begin{Bmatrix} a \\ e \end{Bmatrix} \\ -\begin{Bmatrix} a \\ ena \end{Bmatrix} \\ -um \end{bmatrix}$

$\underset{[+\text{s}]}{|} \quad \underset{[+\text{pl}]}{|}$

$\begin{bmatrix} \begin{Bmatrix} [+\text{nom}] \\ [+\text{acc}] \end{Bmatrix} \\ [+\text{gen}] \\ [+\text{dat}] \end{bmatrix}$

C. i. $\text{N} \begin{bmatrix} [+\text{masc}] \\ \begin{Bmatrix} [+\text{neut}] \\ [+\text{fem}] \end{Bmatrix} \end{bmatrix} \Rightarrow \text{N} \begin{bmatrix} -a \\ -e \end{bmatrix}$

$\underset{[+\text{w}]}{|}$

$\underset{[-\text{pl}]}{|}$

$\underset{[+\text{nom}]}{|}$

ii. $\text{N} \begin{bmatrix} [+\text{neut}] \\ \begin{Bmatrix} [+\text{masc}] \\ [+\text{fem}] \end{Bmatrix} \end{bmatrix} \Rightarrow \text{N} \begin{bmatrix} -e \\ -an \end{bmatrix}$

$\underset{[+\text{w}]}{|}$

$\underset{[-\text{pl}]}{|}$

$\underset{[+\text{acc}]}{|}$

iii. $\text{N} \quad \begin{Bmatrix} [+\text{masc}] \\ [+\text{neut}] \\ [+\text{fem}] \end{Bmatrix} \Rightarrow \text{N} \overset{\frown}{} -an$

$\underset{[+\text{w}]}{|}$

$\underset{[-\text{pl}]}{|}$

$\begin{Bmatrix} [\text{gen}] \\ [\text{dat}] \end{Bmatrix}$

iv. $\text{N} \quad \begin{Bmatrix} [+\text{masc}] \\ [+\text{neut}] \\ [+\text{fem}] \end{Bmatrix} \Rightarrow \text{N} \begin{bmatrix} -an \\ -ena \\ -um \end{bmatrix}$

$\underset{[+\text{w}]}{|}$

$\underset{[+\text{pl}]}{|}$

$\begin{bmatrix} \begin{Bmatrix} [+\text{nom}] \\ [+\text{acc}] \end{Bmatrix} \\ [+\text{gen}] \\ [+\text{dat}] \end{bmatrix}$

(2) T_V:

A. i. $\text{V} \overset{\frown}{} [+\text{Pres}] \Rightarrow \text{V} \begin{bmatrix} -e \\ -st \\ -\delta \end{bmatrix}$

$\underset{[+\text{s}]}{|} \quad \underset{[+\text{Ind}]}{|}$

$\underset{[-\text{pl}]}{|}$

$\begin{bmatrix} [+1] \\ [+2] \\ [+3] \end{bmatrix}$

ii. V ⌐[+Pres] ⟹ V⌐-að
    | |
  [+s] [+Ind]
         |
       [+pl]

iii. V ⌐[+Pres] ⟹ V$\begin{bmatrix} \text{-e} \\ \text{-en} \end{bmatrix}$
    | |
  [+s] [+Sub]
         |
      $\begin{bmatrix} [-\text{pl}] \\ [+\text{pl}] \end{bmatrix}$

iv. V ⌐[+Imp] ⟹ V$\begin{bmatrix} \text{-Ø} \\ \text{-að} \end{bmatrix}$
   | |
 [+s] $\begin{bmatrix} [-\text{pl}] \\ [+\text{pl}] \end{bmatrix}$

v. V   ⌐[−Pres] ⟹ V⟨v⟩⌐Ø
   | | |
 [+s]   [+Ind]

$$\begin{bmatrix} +1 \\ +2 \\ +3 \\ +4 \\ +5 \\ +6 \\ +7 \end{bmatrix} \quad [-\text{pl}] \\ \left\{\begin{matrix}[+1]\\ [+3]\end{matrix}\right\} \quad \begin{bmatrix} \langle a \rangle \\ \langle ea \rangle \\ \langle a \rangle / \langle ea \rangle \\ \langle æ \rangle \\ \langle æ \rangle \\ \langle o \rangle \\ \langle e \rangle \end{bmatrix}$$

   where: ⟨v⟩ = stem vowel

vi. a. V ⌐ [−Pres] ⟹ V⟨v⟩
     | | |
   [+s]

$$\begin{bmatrix} +1 \\ +2 \\ +3 \\ +4 \\ +5 \\ +6 \\ +7 \end{bmatrix} \left\{\begin{matrix}[+\text{Ind}]\\ \left\{\begin{matrix}[-\text{pl}]\\ \begin{matrix}[+2]\\[+\text{pl}]\end{matrix}\end{matrix}\right\}\\ [+\text{Sub}]\\ [\pm\text{pl}]\end{matrix}\right\} \begin{bmatrix} \langle i \rangle \\ \langle u \rangle \\ \langle u \rangle \\ \langle æ \rangle \\ \langle æ \rangle \\ \langle o \rangle \\ \langle eo \rangle \end{bmatrix}$$

  b. V⟨v⟩ ⌐ [−Pres] ⟹ V⟨v⟩⌐−e
      | | |
   [+⟨α⟩] [+Ind] [+⟨α⟩]

$$[+\langle\alpha\rangle] \left\{\begin{matrix}[+\text{Ind}]\\ [+2]\\ [+\text{Sub}]\\ \left\{\begin{matrix}[+1]\\ [+2]\\ [+3]\end{matrix}\right\}\\ [-\text{pl}]\end{matrix}\right\} [+\langle\alpha\rangle]$$

c. $V\langle v\rangle \,\hat{}\, [-\text{Pres}] \Rightarrow V\langle v\rangle \,\hat{}\, \begin{bmatrix} -\text{on} \\ -\text{en} \end{bmatrix}$

   $\quad | \qquad\qquad\qquad | $
   $[+\langle\alpha\rangle] \begin{bmatrix}[+\text{Ind}]\\ [+\text{Sub}]\end{bmatrix} \quad [+\langle\alpha\rangle]$
   $\qquad\qquad |$
   $\qquad\quad [+\text{pl}]$

where: $[+\langle\alpha\rangle]$ = stem vowel features generated by vi.a.

NOTE: Rule vi.a. indicates the changes the stem vowel of the verb undergoes under the conditions specified; namely [−Pres], *either* indicative, singular, second person *and* any person in the plural, *or* subjunctive, singular or plural, any person. Rule vi.b. specifies the inflectional ending for [−Pres], singular, either indicative second person, or subjunctive first, second, or third persons. Rule vi.c. assigns the endings for [−Pres], indicative plural and subjunctive plural.

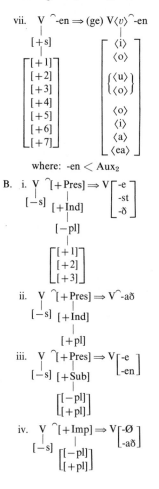

vii. $V \,\hat{}\, \text{-en} \Rightarrow (\text{ge})\, V\langle v\rangle \,\hat{}\, \text{-en}$

   $\;|$
   $[+\text{s}]$

   $\begin{bmatrix}[+1]\\ [+2]\\ [+3]\\ [+4]\\ [+5]\\ [+6]\\ [+7]\end{bmatrix} \qquad \begin{bmatrix}\langle i\rangle \\ \langle o\rangle \\ \left\{\begin{matrix}\langle u\rangle\\ \langle o\rangle\end{matrix}\right\} \\ \langle o\rangle \\ \langle i\rangle \\ \langle a\rangle \\ \langle ea\rangle \end{bmatrix}$

where: -en $<$ Aux$_2$

B.   i. $V \,\hat{}\, [+\text{Pres}] \Rightarrow V \begin{bmatrix} -e \\ -\text{st} \\ -\eth \end{bmatrix}$
   $\;|\qquad\quad |$
   $[-\text{s}]\; [+\text{Ind}]$
   $\qquad\qquad |$
   $\qquad\quad [-\text{pl}]$
   $\qquad\qquad |$
   $\qquad\quad \begin{bmatrix}[+1]\\ [+2]\\ [+3]\end{bmatrix}$

   ii. $V \,\hat{}\, [+\text{Pres}] \Rightarrow V \,\hat{}\, \text{-a}\eth$
   $\;|\qquad\quad |$
   $[-\text{s}]\; [+\text{Ind}]$
   $\qquad\qquad |$
   $\qquad\quad [+\text{pl}]$

   iii. $V \,\hat{}\, [+\text{Pres}] \Rightarrow V \begin{bmatrix} -e \\ -\text{en} \end{bmatrix}$
   $\;|\qquad\quad |$
   $[-\text{s}]\; [+\text{Sub}]$
   $\qquad\qquad |$
   $\qquad\quad \begin{bmatrix}[-\text{pl}]\\ [+\text{pl}]\end{bmatrix}$

   iv. $V \,\hat{}\, [+\text{Imp}] \Rightarrow V \begin{bmatrix} -\emptyset \\ -\text{a}\eth \end{bmatrix}$
   $\;|\qquad\quad |$
   $[-\text{s}]\; [-\text{pl}]$
   $\qquad\qquad \begin{bmatrix}[-\text{pl}]\\ [+\text{pl}]\end{bmatrix}$

v. $\underset{[-s]}{V} \widehat{\underset{[+Ind]}{[-Pres]}} \Rightarrow V\begin{bmatrix} -de \\ -dest \end{bmatrix}$

$$[-pl]$$

$$\begin{bmatrix} \left\{\begin{matrix} [+1] \\ [+3] \end{matrix}\right\} \\ [+2] \end{bmatrix}$$

vi. $\underset{[-s]}{V} \widehat{\underset{[+Ind]}{[-Pres]}} \Rightarrow \widehat{V}\text{-don}$

$$[+pl]$$

vii. $\underset{[-s]}{V} \widehat{\underset{[+Sub]}{[-Pres]}} \Rightarrow V\begin{bmatrix} -de \\ -den \end{bmatrix}$

$$\begin{bmatrix} [-pl] \\ [+pl] \end{bmatrix}$$

viii. $\underset{[-s]}{V} \widehat{}\text{-en} \Rightarrow \text{(ge)} \ \widehat{V}\text{-ed}$

where: -en $<$ Aux$_2$

Some comment on rules B.i.–viii. is necessary. Consider the weak verbs of class 1, *fremm-, neri-,* and *dem-,* and the weak verb of class 2, *lufi-*. Rules B.i.–viii. will produce the following forms:

B.i.:

fremme	neri	deme	lufie
*fremmst	*nerist	demst	*lufist
*fremmð	*nerið	demð	*lufið

B.ii.:

| fremmað | neriað | demað | lufiað |

B.iii.:

fremme	nerie	deme	lufie
fremmen	nerien	demen	lufien

B.iv.:

*fremm	*neri	dem	*lufi
fremmað	neriað	demað	lufiað

B.v.:

*fremmde	*neride	demde	*lufide
*fremmdest	*neridest	demdest	*lufidest

B.vi.:

| *fremmdon | *neridon | demdon | *lufidon |

B.vii.:

*fremmde	*neride	demde	*lufide
*fremmden	*neriden	demden	*lufiden

B.viii.:

| *gefremmed | *generied | gedemed | *gelufied |

The asterisked forms in the preceding list are ungrammatical. Notice that only the forms for *dem-* are grammatical throughout. There are cogent historical reasons for writing the B. rules as we have; however, we cannot pursue these reasons here.[1] For a subclass *x* of class 1 weak verbs and for class 2, additional rules must be written to convert the ungrammatical forms into grammatical ones.

B.ix.: $V<-C\begin{Bmatrix}C\\V\end{Bmatrix}\#>\,^\frown[+\text{Pres}] \Rightarrow V<-C\begin{bmatrix}-e\\-a\end{bmatrix}\#>$

$$\begin{matrix}[-s]\\[+1]\\[+a]\end{matrix} \qquad \begin{Bmatrix}[+\text{Ind}]\\\begin{Bmatrix}[+2]\\[+3]\end{Bmatrix}\\[-\text{pl}]\\[+\text{Imp}]\\[-\text{pl}]\end{Bmatrix}$$

where: C = any consonant grapheme
V = any vowel grapheme
$CC = C_1C_1$ (that is, a doubled consonant grapheme)
$CV = C\,^\frown i$

This rule will effect the following changes in the preceding ungrammatical forms:

Present, Indicative, second, singular: *fremest, nerest, lufast*
Present, Indicative, third, singular: *fremeð, nereð, lufað*
Imperative, singular: *freme, nere, lufa*

B.x.: $V<C\begin{Bmatrix}C\\V\end{Bmatrix}\#>\,^\frown \begin{Bmatrix}[-\text{Pres}]\\-\text{en}\end{Bmatrix} \Rightarrow V<C\begin{bmatrix}-e\\-o\end{bmatrix}\#>$

$$\begin{matrix}[-s]\\[+1]\\[+2]\end{matrix}$$

This rule will provide these forms for the nonpresent:

Indicative, first and second, singular: *fremede, nerede, lufode*
Indicative, second, singular: *fremedest, neredest, lufodest*
Indicative, first through third, plural: *fremedon, neredon, lufodon*
Subjunctive, first through third, singular: *fremede, nerede, lufode*
Subjunctive, first through third, plural: *fremeden, nereden, lufoden*
Past participle: *gefremeed, genereed, gelufoed*

B.xi.: $\text{ge}\,^\frown\text{x}\begin{bmatrix}e\\o\end{bmatrix}\text{-ed} \Rightarrow \text{ge}\,^\frown\text{x}\begin{bmatrix}e\\o\end{bmatrix}\text{-d}$

where: x = any sequence of consonants and vowels
-ed < Aux$_2$

[1] See Robert Howren, "The Generation of Old English Weak Verbs," *Language* 43:674–685 (1967).

As a result of B.xi.,

gefremeed $\Rightarrow$ gefremed
genereed $\Rightarrow$ genered
gelufoed $\Rightarrow$ gelufod[2]

(3) $T_{dem(Adj)}$:
A.

i. (X) dem⌢Agr (Adj⌢Agr) Y $\Rightarrow$

[+masc] [+masc]

[−pl] [−pl]

$$\begin{bmatrix} [+\text{nom}] \\ [+\text{acc}] \\ [+\text{gen}] \\ [+\text{dat}] \end{bmatrix} \begin{bmatrix} [+\text{nom}] \\ \begin{Bmatrix} [+\text{acc}] \\ [+\text{gen}] \\ [+\text{dat}] \end{Bmatrix} \end{bmatrix}$$

(X) dem $\begin{bmatrix} \text{-e} \\ \text{-one} \\ \text{-æs} \\ \text{-æm} \end{bmatrix}$ (Adj $\begin{bmatrix} \text{-a} \\ \text{-an} \end{bmatrix}$) Y

ii. (X) dem⌢Agr (Adj⌢Agr) Y $\Rightarrow$ *

[+neut] [+neut]

[−pl] [−pl]

$$\begin{bmatrix} \begin{Bmatrix} [+\text{nom}] \\ [+\text{acc}] \end{Bmatrix} \\ [+\text{gen}] \\ [+\text{dat}] \end{bmatrix} \begin{bmatrix} \begin{Bmatrix} [+\text{nom}] \\ [+\text{acc}] \end{Bmatrix} \\ \begin{Bmatrix} [+\text{gen}] \\ [+\text{dat}] \end{Bmatrix} \end{bmatrix}$$

(X) dem $\begin{bmatrix} \text{-æt} \\ \text{-æs} \\ \text{-æm} \end{bmatrix}$ (Adj $\begin{bmatrix} \text{-e} \\ \text{-an} \end{bmatrix}$) Y

---

[2] In rule B.viii. the inflectional form for the past participle is cited as *-ed*. This form is historically inaccurate, as Professor Howren has shown. He gives the form *-d.* Had we followed his analysis we would have had no need for rule B.xi since the past participle forms of *fremm-, neri-,* and *lufi-* would already be *gefremed, genered,* and *gelufod.* However, we would now have to account for the occurrence of *-e-* in *gedem-e-d,* in terms of a set of theme vowels that are historically justified and the reconstruction of which contributes not only to an accurate but also to an economical account of weak verb forms. We have not followed Professor Howren here for the simple reason that his account, while more accurate, is also more difficult for the beginning student.

iii. (X) dem⌢Agr   (Adj⌢Agr) Y ⟹
        | |
       [+fem]   [+fem]
        | |
       [−pl]   [−pl]

$$\text{(X) dem} \begin{bmatrix} [+\text{nom}] \\ [+\text{acc}] \\ \left\{ \begin{matrix} [+\text{gen}] \\ [+\text{dat}] \end{matrix} \right\} \end{bmatrix} \begin{bmatrix} [+\text{nom}] \\ \left\{ \begin{matrix} [+\text{acc}] \\ [+\text{gen}] \\ [+\text{dat}] \end{matrix} \right\} \end{bmatrix}$$

$$\text{(X) dem} \begin{bmatrix} \text{-eo} \\ \text{-a} \\ \text{-ære} \end{bmatrix} (\text{Adj} \begin{bmatrix} \text{-e} \\ \text{-an} \end{bmatrix}) \text{ Y}$$

iv. (X) dem⌢Agr   (Adj⌢Agr) Y ⟹
        | |
       [+pl]   [+pl]

$$\text{(X) dem} \begin{bmatrix} \left\{ \begin{matrix} [+\text{nom}] \\ [+\text{acc}] \end{matrix} \right\} \\ [+\text{gen}] \\ [+\text{dat}] \end{bmatrix} \begin{bmatrix} \left\{ \begin{matrix} [+\text{nom}] \\ [+\text{acc}] \end{matrix} \right\} \\ [+\text{gen}] \\ [+\text{dat}] \end{bmatrix}$$

$$\text{(X) dem} \begin{bmatrix} \text{-a} \\ \text{-ara} \\ \text{-æm} \end{bmatrix} (\text{Adj} \begin{bmatrix} \text{-an} \\ \text{-ra} \\ \text{-um} \end{bmatrix}) \text{ Y}$$

B.

i. (X) Adj⌢Agr⌢Y ⟹ (X) Adj $\begin{bmatrix} \text{-Ø} \\ \text{-es} \\ \text{-um} \end{bmatrix}$ Y
     |
  $\left\{ \begin{matrix} [+\text{masc}] \\ [+\text{neut}] \end{matrix} \right\}$
     |
   [−pl]
     |
 $\begin{bmatrix} [+\text{nom}] \\ [+\text{gen}] \\ [+\text{dat}] \end{bmatrix}$

ii. (X) Adj⌢Agr⌢Y ⟹ (X) Adj $\begin{bmatrix} \text{-ne} \\ \text{-Ø} \end{bmatrix}$ Y
     |
  $\begin{bmatrix} [+\text{masc}] \\ [+\text{neut}] \end{bmatrix}$
     |
   [−pl]
     |
  [+acc]

iii. (X) Adj⌢Agr⌢Y ⟹ (X) Adj $\begin{bmatrix} \text{-u} \\ \text{-e} \\ \text{-re} \end{bmatrix}$ Y
     |
   [+fem]
     |
   [−pl]
     |
 $\begin{bmatrix} [+\text{nom}] \\ [+\text{acc}] \\ \left\{ \begin{matrix} [+\text{gen}] \\ [+\text{dat}] \end{matrix} \right\} \end{bmatrix}$

iv. (X) Adj⌢Agr⌢Y ⟹ (X) Adj $\begin{bmatrix} \text{-e} \\ \text{-u} \\ \text{-a} \end{bmatrix}$ Y
   |
$\begin{bmatrix} [+\text{masc}] \\ [+\text{neut}] \\ [+\text{fem}] \end{bmatrix}$
   |
[+pl]
   |
$\left\{ \begin{matrix} [+\text{nom}] \\ [+\text{acc}] \end{matrix} \right\}$

v. (X) Adj⌢Agr⌢Y ⟹ (X) Adj $\begin{bmatrix} \text{-ra} \\ \text{-um} \end{bmatrix}$ Y
   |
$\left\{ \begin{matrix} [+\text{masc}] \\ [+\text{neut}] \\ [+\text{fem}] \end{matrix} \right\}$
   |
[+pl]
   |
$\begin{bmatrix} [+\text{gen}] \\ [+\text{dat}] \end{bmatrix}$

where: X ≠ dem

C.   (X) þ-⌢Agr⌢Y ⟹ (X) s-⌢Agr⌢Y
      | |
$\left\{ \begin{matrix} [+\text{masc}] \\ [+\text{fem}] \end{matrix} \right\}$ $[+\alpha]$
      |
[−pl]
      |
[+nom]

By way of illustration we will carry two strings that are outputs of the syntactic transformation rules just presented through the morphographemic rules just presented.

(1) þa⌢scul-⌐[+Pres]⌐þ-⌢   Agr   ⌢   mann-   ⌢   Agr   ⌢   bryd   ⌢   Agr   ⌢
        | | | |
     [+Ind]   [+masc]   [+I]   [+masc]   [+s]   [+fem]
        | | [+human] | [+human] |
     [−pl]   [−pl]   [−pl]   [−pl]
        | | | |
     [+3]   [+gen]   [+gen]   [+nom]
                            | | |
                         [+3]   [+3]   [+3]

   dryhten   ⌢   Agr   ⌢þ-   Agr   ⌢   hlaf   ⌢   Agr   ⌢geþanci-⌢-an[3]
      | | | | |
   [+s]   [+masc] [+masc]   [+s]   [+masc]
      | | | | |
[+human]   [−pl]   [−pl]   [−animate]   [−pl]
                  | | |
               [+dat]   [+gen]   [+gen]
                  | | |
               [+3]   [+3]   [+3]

[3] Both *scul-* and *mann-* belong to special subclasses which the rules do not take account of. We simply give the proper forms in the derivation.

By T_N (A.i., B.i.):

1a) þa⌢scul-⌉[+Pres]⌉þ-⌢   Agr   ⌢mann-⌢-es⌢bryd⌢Ø⌢dryhten⌢-e
                | |
             [+Ind]   [+masc]
                | |
             [−pl]   [−pl]
                | |
             [+3]   [+gen]
                                     |
                                  [+3]
      þ-⌢   Agr   ⌢hlaf⌢-es⌢geþanci⌢-an
              |
          [+masc]
              |
          [−pl]
              |
          [+gen]
              |
          [+3]

By T_V:

(1b) þa⌢sceal⌢Ø⌢þ-⌢   Agr   ⌢mann-⌢-es⌢bryd⌢Ø⌢dryhten⌢-e⌢þ-⌢   Agr   ⌢
                      | |
                  [+masc]   [+masc]
                      | |
                  [−pl]   [−pl]
                      | |
                  [+gen]   [+gen]
                      | |
                  [+3]   [+3]
      hlaf⌢-es⌢geþanci-⌢-an

By T_dem(Adj) (A.i.):

(1c) þa⌢sceal⌢Ø⌢þ-⌢-æs⌢mann-⌢-es⌢bryd⌢Ø⌢dryhten⌢-e⌢þ-⌢-æs⌢
      hlaf⌢-es⌢geþanci-⌢-an

   The one ungrammatical form in string (1c) is *dryhtene.* A very low-level, but general, rule will delete the second stem vowel, giving *dryhtne:*

þa sceal þæs mannes bryd dryhtne þæs hlafes geþancian.

(2) þ-⌢   Agr   ⌢yfel⌢   Agr   ⌢   hyrd   ⌢   Agr   ⌢þ-⌢   Agr   ⌢god⌢   Agr   ⌢   cyning   ⌢
          | | | | | | |
      [+masc]   [+masc]   [+s]   [+masc]   [+masc]   [+masc]   [+s]
          | | | | | | |
      [−pl]   [−pl]   [+human]   [−pl]   [−pl]   [−pl]   [+human]
          | | | | |
      [+nom]   [+nom]   [+nom]   [+dat]   [+dat]
          | | | | |
      [+3]   [+3]   [+3]   [+3]   [+3]

```
Agr    ⌒andsweri-⌒[−Pres]
 |          |           |
[+masc]   [−s]       [+Ind]
 |          |           |
[−pl]     [+2]        [−pl]
 |                      |
[+dat]                [+3]
 |
[+3]
```

By T$_N$ (A.i.):

(2a)
```
þ-⌒  Agr  ⌒yfel⌒  Agr  ⌒hyrd⌒Ø⌒þ-⌒  Agr  ⌒god⌒  Agr  ⌒cyning⌒-e⌒
      |          |                 |           |
   [+masc]    [+masc]           [+masc]     [+masc]
      |          |                 |           |
    [−pl]      [−pl]             [−pl]       [−pl]
      |          |                 |           |
   [+nom]     [+nom]            [+dat]      [+dat]
      |          |                 |           |
    [+3]       [+3]              [+3]        [+3]
```
```
andsweri-⌒[−Pres]
   |           |
 [−s]       [+Ind]
   |           |
 [+2]       [−pl]
               |
             [+3]
```

By T$_V$ (B.v.):

(2b)
```
þ-⌒  Agr  ⌒yfel⌒  Agr  ⌒hyrd⌒Ø⌒þ-⌒  Agr  ⌒god⌒  Agr  ⌒cyning⌒
      |          |                 |           |
   [+masc]    [+masc]           [+masc]     [+masc]
      |          |                 |           |
    [−pl]      [−pl]             [−pl]       [−pl]
      |          |                 |           |
   [+nom]     [+nom]            [+dat]      [+dat]
      |          |                 |           |
    [+3]       [+3]              [+3]        [+3]
```
-e⌒andsweri-⌒-de (which by B.x. becomes *andswero-⌒-de*)

By T$_{dem(Adj)}$ (A.i., ii.):

(2c) þ-⌒e⌒yfel⌒-a⌒hyrd⌒Ø⌒þ-⌒-æm⌒god⌒-an⌒cyning⌒-e⌒andswero-⌒-de

By T$_{dem(Adj)}$ (C):

(2d) s-⌒e⌒yfel⌒-a⌒hyrd⌒Ø⌒þ-⌒-æm⌒god⌒-an⌒cyning⌒-e⌒andswero-⌒-de

Se yfela hyrd þæm godan cyninge andswerode.

A. NOUNS

The following morphographemic rules show the breakdown in Middle English of the Old English gender and case distinctions:

$$(1)\quad \underset{[+s]}{\overset{N}{|}}\quad
\begin{Bmatrix} [+\text{masc}] \\ [+\text{neut}] \\ [+\text{fem}] \end{Bmatrix}
\underset{[-\text{pl}]}{\big|}
\begin{bmatrix} \begin{Bmatrix}[+\text{nom}] \\ [+\text{acc}]\end{Bmatrix} \\ [+\text{gen}] \\ [+\text{dat}] \end{bmatrix}
\quad \text{EME} \Rightarrow N
\begin{bmatrix} -\begin{Bmatrix}\varnothing \\ e\end{Bmatrix} \\ -(e)s \\ -\begin{Bmatrix}\varnothing \\ e\end{Bmatrix} \end{bmatrix}$$

$$(2)\quad \underset{[+s]}{\overset{N}{|}}\quad
\begin{Bmatrix} [+\text{masc}] \\ [+\text{neut}] \end{Bmatrix}
\underset{[+\text{pl}]}{\big|}
\begin{bmatrix} \begin{Bmatrix}[+\text{nom}] \\ [+\text{acc}]\end{Bmatrix} \\ [+\text{gen}] \\ [+\text{dat}] \end{bmatrix}
\quad \text{EME} \Rightarrow N
\begin{bmatrix} -(e)s \\ -e \\ -en \end{bmatrix}
\quad \text{LME} \Rightarrow N\text{^}-(e)s$$

Thus Old English *stan* becomes in early Middle English:

	singular	plural
nominative, accusative	ston(e)	stones
genitive	stones	stone
dative	ston(e)	stonen

In late Middle English the plural for all cases is simply *stones*.

$$(3)\quad \underset{[+s]}{\overset{N\ \text{^}}{|}}\ \underset{[+\text{pl}]}{\overset{[+\text{fem}]}{|}}\
\begin{Bmatrix} [+\text{nom}] \\ [+\text{acc}] \\ [+\text{gen}] \\ [+\text{dat}] \end{Bmatrix}
\begin{bmatrix} \text{North and Midlands} \\ \text{Kent and Southern} \end{bmatrix}
\Rightarrow N \begin{bmatrix} -(e)s \\ -(e)n \end{bmatrix}$$

Rule (3) indicates that relics of the Old English strong feminine declension have a common plural *-(e)s* in the Middle English dialects of the North and Midlands, but a common plural *-(e)n* in the dialects of Kent and Southern. This latter was disappearing by the end of the fourteenth century.

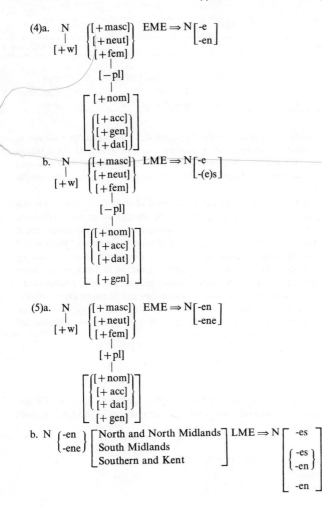

(4)a. N [+w] {[+masc] [+neut] [+fem]} EME ⇒ N[-e -en]
[−pl]
[[+nom] {[+acc] [+gen] [+dat]}]

b. N [+w] {[+masc] [+neut] [+fem]} LME ⇒ N[-e -(e)s]
[−pl]
[[{[+nom] [+acc] [+dat]}] [+gen]]

(5)a. N [+w] {[+masc] [+neut] [+fem]} EME ⇒ N[-en -ene]
[+pl]
[[{[+nom] [+acc] [+dat]}] [+gen]]

b. N {-en -ene} [North and North Midlands / South Midlands / Southern and Kent] LME ⇒ N [-es / {-es -en} / -en]

According to rules (4) and (5) Old English weak neuter *eag-* assumes the following inflectional forms in Middle English:

Early Middle English

	singular		plural
nominative	eʒe	*nominative,*	
accusative,		*accusative,*	
genitive,		*dative*	eʒen
dative	eʒen	*genitive*	eʒene

Late Middle English

	singular		plural (all cases)
nominative, accusative, dative genitive	eȝe eȝes	North and North Midlands South Midlands Southern and Kent	eȝes eȝes, eȝen eȝen

The -*s* plurals for the weak declension first appear in the Northern dialects by analogy with strong plurals. The South Midlands dialects continue to show variant -*s* and -*n* inflections until late in the fourteenth century. Chaucer, for instance, has both *asshen* and *asshes* 'ashes,' *been* and *bees* 'bees,' *toon* and *toos* 'toes.' In Southern and Kentish dialects the -*n* plural remained the unique form until the beginning of the fifteenth century.

These rules present only the broad outlines of the inflectional change that affected English nouns; they do not show many of the complexities that attended the change within certain dialects. To mention only one of these, analogy did not operate in just one direction in the development of the noun plural. In certain dialects, and over a certain period of time, some strong feminine and masculine declensions, which would normally have an -*(e)s* plural, developed an -*(e)n* plural by analogy with weak declension nouns. This practice was especially common in Southern and Kent where -*(e)n* plurals were even attached to Anglo-Norman nouns. One reads in an old Kentish sermon (c. 1250), "wanne hi to me clepieth ine hire sorgh*en*," 'when they call to me in their sorrows.' Old English *sorg*, a strong feminine, here assumes a weak plural. And from the *Life of Saint Juliana*, a Southern text with a few Midland characteristics of the early thirteenth century, "Biwepe ant bireowse ower sunn*en*," 'Weep for and repent of your sins.'

B. VERBS

Coalescence of inflectional forms goes on apace in Middle English, and as in the case of nouns dialect diversity increases. Below we provide rules for generating verb inflections in Middle English and some illustrative paradigms.

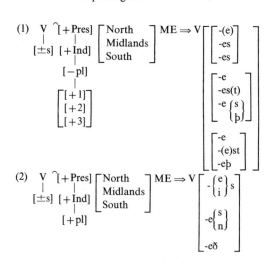

(3) $\begin{array}{cc} \text{V} & \widehat{}\ [+\text{Pres}] \\ | & | \\ [\pm\text{s}] & [+\text{Sub}] \\ & | \\ & \begin{bmatrix}[-\text{pl}]\\ [+\text{pl}]\end{bmatrix} \end{array}$ $\begin{bmatrix} \text{North} \\ \left\{\begin{array}{l}\text{Midlands}\\ \text{South}\end{array}\right\} \end{bmatrix}$ ME $\Rightarrow$ V $\begin{bmatrix} \begin{bmatrix}\text{-(e)}\\ \text{-(en)}\end{bmatrix} \\ \begin{bmatrix}\text{-e}\\ \text{-e(n)}\end{bmatrix} \end{bmatrix}$

(4) $\begin{array}{cc} \text{V} & [+\text{Imp}] \\ | & \\ [\pm\text{s}] & \begin{bmatrix}[-\text{pl}]\\ [+\text{pl}]\end{bmatrix} \end{array}$ $\begin{bmatrix} \text{North} \\ \left\{\begin{array}{l}\text{Midlands}\\ \text{South}\end{array}\right\} \end{bmatrix}$ ME $\Rightarrow$ V $\begin{bmatrix} \begin{bmatrix}\text{-Ø}\\ \text{-es}\end{bmatrix} \\ \begin{bmatrix}\text{-Ø}\\ \text{-eþ}\end{bmatrix} \end{bmatrix}$

Consider the Middle English strong verb *driv-* (Old English *drif-*), and the weak verbs *love-* (Old English *lufi-*) and *her-* (Old English *hier-*). Rule (1) will yield the following:

	North	
driv-(e)	love-(e)	her-(e)
driv-es	love-es	her-es
driv-es	love-es	her-es

	Midlands	
driv-e	love-e	her-e
driv-es(t)	love-es(t)	her-es(t)
driv-e$\left\{\begin{array}{l}\text{s}\\ \text{þ}\end{array}\right\}$	love-e$\left\{\begin{array}{l}\text{s}\\ \text{þ}\end{array}\right\}$	her-e$\left\{\begin{array}{l}\text{s}\\ \text{þ}\end{array}\right\}$

	South	
driv-e	love-e	her-e
driv-(e)st	love-(e)st	her-(e)st
driv-eþ	love-eþ	her-eþ

By rule (2):

	North	
driv-$\left\{\begin{array}{l}\text{e}\\ \text{i}\end{array}\right\}$s	love-$\left\{\begin{array}{l}\text{e}\\ \text{i}\end{array}\right\}$s	her-$\left\{\begin{array}{l}\text{e}\\ \text{i}\end{array}\right\}$s

	Midlands	
driv-e$\left\{\begin{array}{l}\text{s}\\ \text{n}\end{array}\right\}$	love-e$\left\{\begin{array}{l}\text{s}\\ \text{n}\end{array}\right\}$	her-e$\left\{\begin{array}{l}\text{s}\\ \text{n}\end{array}\right\}$

	South	
driv-eþ	love-eþ	her-eþ

By rule (3):

	North	
driv-(e)	love-(e)	her-(e)
driv-(en)	love-(en)	her-(en)

	Midlands/South	
driv-e	love-e	her-e
driv-e(n)	love-e(n)	her-e(n)

By rule (4):

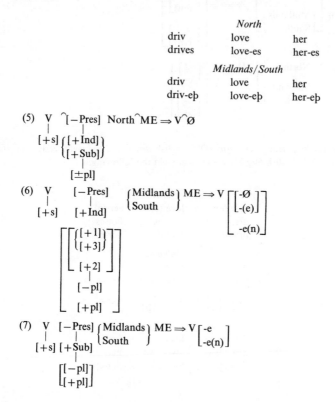

	North	
driv	love	her
drives	love-es	her-es

	Midlands/South	
driv	love	her
driv-eþ	love-eþ	her-eþ

According to rule (5) *driv-* would have Ø inflectional endings throughout the past tense paradigm in the North. With vowel replacement (which we do not deal with here) the standard Northern form would then be *draf.* Rule (6) gives the forms:

> drof
> drof-(e)/drov-(e)
> drof-e(n)/drov-e(n)

And rule (7) gives:

> drof-e/drov-e
> drof-e(n)/drov-e(n)

By rule (8) the weak verbs *love-* and *her-* will have but one form throughout the paradigm in the North: *love-d* and *her-d*.

(9) $\underset{[-s]}{\overset{V}{\mid}}$ $\begin{bmatrix} [-\text{Pres}] \\ \begin{bmatrix} [+\text{Ind}] \\ \begin{bmatrix} [+1] \\ [+3] \\ [+\text{Sub}] \end{bmatrix} \\ [-\text{pl}] \end{bmatrix} \end{bmatrix}$ $\left\{ \begin{matrix} \text{Midlands} \\ \text{South} \end{matrix} \right\}$ ME $\Rightarrow$ V⌢-de

(10) $\underset{[-s]}{\overset{V}{\mid}}$ $\begin{matrix} \overset{\frown}{[-\text{Pres}]} \\ [+\text{Ind}] \\ [-\text{pl}] \\ [+2] \end{matrix}$ $\left\{ \begin{matrix} \text{Midlands} \\ \text{South} \end{matrix} \right\}$ ME $\Rightarrow$ V⌢-dest

(11) $\underset{[-s]}{\overset{V}{\mid}}$ $\begin{matrix} \overset{\frown}{[-\text{Pres}]} \\ \left\{ \begin{matrix} [+\text{Ind}] \\ [+\text{Sub}] \end{matrix} \right\} \\ [+\text{pl}] \end{matrix}$ $\left\{ \begin{matrix} \text{Midlands} \\ \text{South} \end{matrix} \right\}$ ME $\Rightarrow$ V⌢-d(e(n))

Rule (9) yields the forms *love-de* and *her-de* for the past indicative, first and third, singular, and the subjunctive singular; rule (10) the forms *love-dest* and *her-dest;* rule (11) the variants *love-d, love-de, love-den* and *her-d, her-de, her-den*.

One morphographemic problem remains. For historical reasons we have cited the stem form *love-* in our consideration of weak verbs. Recall that the Old English stem form also ended in a vowel letter, *lufi-*. As a result, our rules for the present tense will generate an extra vowel letter for all verbs of the same class; for example, *love-eþ*. At least for late Middle English and for earlier Middle English in some dialects we would need a rule that deletes the final stem vowel of this verb class in all instances of present tense, something in the manner of the following:

$$T_{2\text{-stem-vowel deletion}}: \underset{\underset{[+x]}{[-s]}}{\overset{V}{\mid}} <\text{-}V\#> \overset{\frown}{} [+\text{Pres}] < \#V\text{-}> \Rightarrow$$

$$\underset{\underset{[+x]}{[-s]}}{\overset{V}{\mid}} <\text{-}\varnothing\#> \overset{\frown}{} [+\text{Pres}] < \#V\text{-}>$$

Notice that the alternative to this analysis is to posit double past tense forms for weak verbs:

lov-	*her-*
-ed(e)	-d(e)
-edest	-dest
-ed(e)	-d(e)
-ed(e(n))	-d(e(n))

Any attempt to account for the forms on the left runs into serious difficulties, primarily because it is counter-historical (compare the analysis of weak verbs in Appendix II).

C. PERSONAL PRONOUNS

(1) $[+\text{Pro}]$ $[-\text{pl}]$
$$\begin{bmatrix} [+\text{nom}] \\ \left\{ \begin{matrix} [+\text{acc}] \\ [+\text{dat}] \end{matrix} \right\} \\ [+1] \end{bmatrix}$$
$\begin{bmatrix} \text{North} \\ \left\{ \begin{matrix} \text{Midlands} \\ \text{South} \end{matrix} \right\} \end{bmatrix} \text{ME} \Rightarrow \begin{bmatrix} \left\{ \begin{matrix} \text{i(c)} \\ \text{ich} \end{matrix} \right\} \\ \text{me} \end{bmatrix}$

(2) $[+\text{Pro}]$ $[+\text{pl}]$ $\text{ME} \Rightarrow \begin{bmatrix} \text{we} \\ \text{us} \end{bmatrix}$
$$\begin{bmatrix} [+\text{nom}] \\ \left\{ \begin{matrix} [+\text{acc}] \\ [+\text{dat}] \end{matrix} \right\} \\ [+1] \end{bmatrix}$$

(3) $[+\text{Pro}]$ $[-\text{pl}]$ $\text{ME} \Rightarrow \begin{bmatrix} \left\{ \begin{matrix} \text{thou} \\ \text{ye} \end{matrix} \right\} \\ \text{thee} \end{bmatrix}$
$$\begin{bmatrix} [+\text{nom}] \\ \left\{ \begin{matrix} [+\text{acc}] \\ [+\text{dat}] \end{matrix} \right\} \\ [+2] \end{bmatrix}$$

NOTE: *ye* occurred to indicate respectful address.

(4) $[+\text{Pro}]$ $[+\text{pl}]$ $\Rightarrow \begin{bmatrix} \text{ye} \\ \text{you} \end{bmatrix}$
$$\begin{bmatrix} [+\text{nom}] \\ \left\{ \begin{matrix} [+\text{acc}] \\ [+\text{dat}] \end{matrix} \right\} \\ [+2] \end{bmatrix}$$

(5) $[+\text{Pro}]\,[+\text{masc}]\,\text{ME} \Rightarrow \begin{bmatrix} \left\{ \begin{matrix} \text{he} \\ \text{ha, a} \end{matrix} \right\} \\ \text{him} \end{bmatrix}$
$$\begin{bmatrix} [+\text{nom}] \\ [+\text{dat}] \\ [-\text{pl}] \\ [+3] \end{bmatrix}$$

NOTE: *ha, a* are unstressed variants.

(6) $[+\text{Pro}]\,[+\text{masc}]$
$$\begin{bmatrix} [+\text{acc}] \\ [-\text{pl}] \\ [+3] \end{bmatrix}$$
$\begin{bmatrix} \left\{ \begin{matrix} \text{North} \\ \text{Midlands} \end{matrix} \right\} \\ \text{South} \end{bmatrix} \text{ME} \Rightarrow \begin{bmatrix} \text{him} \\ \text{hine} \end{bmatrix}$

(7) $[+\text{Pro}]\ [+\text{neut}]\ \text{ME} \Rightarrow \left[\begin{matrix}\left\{\begin{matrix}\text{hit}\\\text{it}\end{matrix}\right\}\\\text{him}\end{matrix}\right]$

$\left[\begin{matrix}\left[\left\{\begin{matrix}[+\text{nom}]\\[+\text{acc}]\end{matrix}\right\}\right]\\[+\text{dat}]\end{matrix}\right]$

$[-\text{pl}]$

$[+3]$

NOTE: *it* is an unstressed variant.

(8) $[+\text{Pro}]\ [+\text{fem}]$ $\left[\begin{matrix}\left[\begin{matrix}\text{South Midlands}\\\text{South}\end{matrix}\right]\\\left[\begin{matrix}\text{West Midlands}\\\text{Southwest Midlands}\end{matrix}\right]\\\text{East Midlands}\\\left\{\begin{matrix}\text{North Midlands}\\\text{North}\end{matrix}\right\}\end{matrix}\right]$ $\text{EME} \Rightarrow$ $\left[\begin{matrix}\text{he}\\\left[\begin{matrix}\text{hue}\\\text{ho}\end{matrix}\right]\\\left\{\begin{matrix}\text{ʒhe}\\\text{ʒho}\end{matrix}\right\}\\\text{scho}\end{matrix}\right]$ $\text{LME} \Rightarrow$ $\left[\begin{matrix}\left[\begin{matrix}\text{sche}\\\text{he}\end{matrix}\right]\\\left[\begin{matrix}\text{sche}\\\text{ho}\end{matrix}\right]\\\text{sche}\\\text{scho}\end{matrix}\right]$

$[+\text{nom}]$

$[-\text{pl}]$

$[+3]$

(9) $[+\text{Pro}]\ [+\text{fem}]$ $\left[\begin{matrix}\text{Kent}\\\text{Elsewhere}\end{matrix}\right]\ \text{ME} \Rightarrow$ $\left[\begin{matrix}\text{hie}\\\left\{\begin{matrix}\text{hir(e)}\\\text{her(e)}\end{matrix}\right\}\end{matrix}\right]$

$\left\{\begin{matrix}[+\text{acc}]\\[+\text{dat}]\end{matrix}\right\}$

$[-\text{pl}]$

$[+3]$

(10)a. $[+\text{Pro}]\ [+\text{pl}]$ $\left[\begin{matrix}\text{North}\\\text{Elsewhere}\end{matrix}\right]$ $\underset{[+11\text{th cent}]}{\text{ME}} \Rightarrow$ $\left[\begin{matrix}\text{þei}\\\left\{\begin{matrix}\text{hi(e)}\\\text{he}\end{matrix}\right\}\end{matrix}\right]$

$[+\text{nom}]$

$[+3]$

b. $[+\text{Pro}]\ [+\alpha]$ $\left[\begin{matrix}\left\{\begin{matrix}\text{North}\\\text{East Midlands}\end{matrix}\right\}\\\text{Elsewhere}\end{matrix}\right]$ $\underset{[+12\text{th cent}]}{\text{ME}} \Rightarrow$ $\left[\begin{matrix}\text{þei}\\\left\{\begin{matrix}\text{hi}\\\text{he}\end{matrix}\right\}\end{matrix}\right]$

c. $[+\text{Pro}]\ [+\alpha]$ $\left[\begin{matrix}\left\{\begin{matrix}\text{North}\\\text{Midlands}\end{matrix}\right\}\\\text{South}\end{matrix}\right]$ $\underset{[+14\text{th cent}]}{\text{ME}} \Rightarrow$ $\left[\begin{matrix}\text{þei}\\\left\{\begin{matrix}\text{hi}\\\text{he}\end{matrix}\right\}\end{matrix}\right]$

d. $[+\text{Pro}]\ [+\alpha]$ $\underset{[+15\text{th cent}]}{\text{ME}} \Rightarrow \left\{\begin{matrix}\text{thei}\\\text{they}\end{matrix}\right\}$

(11)a. $[+\text{Pro}]\ [+\text{pl}]$ $\left[\begin{matrix}\left[\begin{matrix}\text{North}\\\text{Midlands}\end{matrix}\right]\\\text{South}\end{matrix}\right]$ $\underset{[+11\text{th cent}]}{\text{ME}} \Rightarrow$ $\left[\begin{matrix}\left[\begin{matrix}\left\{\begin{matrix}\text{þam}\\\text{þem}\\\text{þeim}\end{matrix}\right\}\\\left\{\begin{matrix}\text{ham}\\\text{hem}\end{matrix}\right\}\end{matrix}\right]\\\text{hi}\end{matrix}\right]$

$\left\{\begin{matrix}[+\text{acc}]\\[+\text{dat}]\end{matrix}\right\}$

$[+3]$

b. $[+\text{Pro}]\ [+\alpha]$ $\underset{[+15\text{th cent}]}{\text{ME}} \Rightarrow$ $\left\{\begin{matrix}\text{þem}\\\text{them}\end{matrix}\right\}$

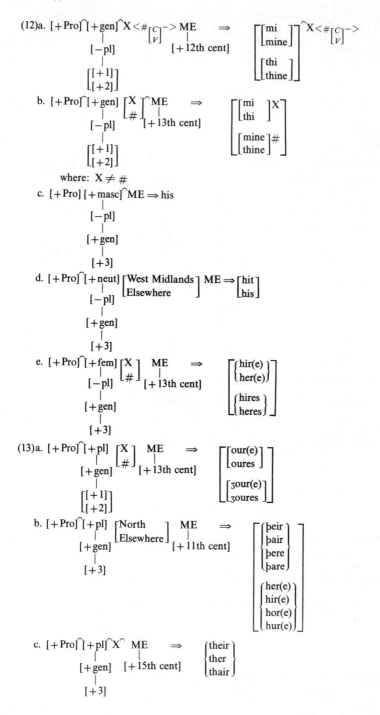

(12)a. $[+\text{Pro}]\frown[+\text{gen}]\frown X<\#_{[\begin{smallmatrix}C\\V\end{smallmatrix}]}->\text{ME} \Rightarrow \begin{bmatrix}\begin{bmatrix}\text{mi}\\\text{mine}\end{bmatrix}\\\begin{bmatrix}\text{thi}\\\text{thine}\end{bmatrix}\end{bmatrix}\frown X<\#_{[\begin{smallmatrix}C\\V\end{smallmatrix}]}->$

$\quad\quad\quad\quad\quad\quad |\quad\quad\quad\quad\quad\quad\quad\quad\quad |$
$\quad\quad\quad\quad\quad [-\text{pl}]\quad\quad\quad\quad\quad [+12\text{th cent}]$
$\quad\quad\quad\quad\quad\quad |$
$\quad\quad\quad\quad\quad\begin{bmatrix}[+1]\\ [+2]\end{bmatrix}$

b. $[+\text{Pro}]\frown[+\text{gen}]\begin{bmatrix}X\\ \#\end{bmatrix}\frown\text{ME} \Rightarrow \begin{bmatrix}\begin{bmatrix}\text{mi}\\\text{thi}\end{bmatrix}X\\ \begin{bmatrix}\text{mine}\\\text{thine}\end{bmatrix}\#\end{bmatrix}$

$\quad\quad\quad\quad\quad\quad |\quad\quad\quad\quad\quad [+13\text{th cent}]$
$\quad\quad\quad\quad\quad [-\text{pl}]$
$\quad\quad\quad\quad\quad\quad |$
$\quad\quad\quad\quad\quad\begin{bmatrix}[+1]\\ [+2]\end{bmatrix}$

where: $X \ne \#$

c. $[+\text{Pro}]\,[+\text{masc}]\frown\text{ME} \Rightarrow \text{his}$

$\quad\quad\quad\quad\quad |$
$\quad\quad\quad\quad [-\text{pl}]$
$\quad\quad\quad\quad\quad |$
$\quad\quad\quad\quad [+\text{gen}]$
$\quad\quad\quad\quad\quad |$
$\quad\quad\quad\quad [+3]$

d. $[+\text{Pro}]\frown[+\text{neut}]\begin{bmatrix}\text{West Midlands}\\\text{Elsewhere}\end{bmatrix}\text{ME} \Rightarrow \begin{bmatrix}\text{hit}\\\text{his}\end{bmatrix}$

$\quad\quad\quad\quad\quad\quad |$
$\quad\quad\quad\quad\quad [-\text{pl}]$
$\quad\quad\quad\quad\quad\quad |$
$\quad\quad\quad\quad\quad [+\text{gen}]$
$\quad\quad\quad\quad\quad\quad |$
$\quad\quad\quad\quad\quad [+3]$

e. $[+\text{Pro}]\frown[+\text{fem}]\begin{bmatrix}X\\ \#\end{bmatrix}\text{ME} \Rightarrow \begin{bmatrix}\left\{\begin{smallmatrix}\text{hir(e)}\\\text{her(e)}\end{smallmatrix}\right\}\\ \left\{\begin{smallmatrix}\text{hires}\\\text{heres}\end{smallmatrix}\right\}\end{bmatrix}$

$\quad\quad\quad\quad\quad\quad |\quad\quad\quad\quad\quad [+13\text{th cent}]$
$\quad\quad\quad\quad\quad [-\text{pl}]$
$\quad\quad\quad\quad\quad\quad |$
$\quad\quad\quad\quad\quad [+\text{gen}]$
$\quad\quad\quad\quad\quad\quad |$
$\quad\quad\quad\quad\quad [+3]$

(13)a. $[+\text{Pro}]\frown[+\text{pl}]\begin{bmatrix}X\\ \#\end{bmatrix}\text{ME} \Rightarrow \begin{bmatrix}\begin{bmatrix}\text{our(e)}\\\text{oures}\end{bmatrix}\\ \begin{bmatrix}\text{ȝour(e)}\\\text{ȝoures}\end{bmatrix}\end{bmatrix}$

$\quad\quad\quad\quad\quad\quad |\quad\quad\quad\quad\quad [+13\text{th cent}]$
$\quad\quad\quad\quad\quad [+\text{gen}]$
$\quad\quad\quad\quad\quad\quad |$
$\quad\quad\quad\quad\quad\begin{bmatrix}[+1]\\ [+2]\end{bmatrix}$

b. $[+\text{Pro}]\frown[+\text{pl}]\begin{bmatrix}\text{North}\\\text{Elsewhere}\end{bmatrix}\text{ME} \Rightarrow \begin{bmatrix}\left\{\begin{smallmatrix}\text{þeir}\\\text{þair}\\\text{þere}\\\text{þare}\end{smallmatrix}\right\}\\ \left\{\begin{smallmatrix}\text{her(e)}\\\text{hir(e)}\\\text{hor(e)}\\\text{hur(e)}\end{smallmatrix}\right\}\end{bmatrix}$

$\quad\quad\quad\quad\quad\quad |\quad\quad\quad\quad\quad [+11\text{th cent}]$
$\quad\quad\quad\quad\quad [+\text{gen}]$
$\quad\quad\quad\quad\quad\quad |$
$\quad\quad\quad\quad\quad [+3]$

c. $[+\text{Pro}]\frown[+\text{pl}]\frown X\frown\text{ME} \Rightarrow \left\{\begin{smallmatrix}\text{their}\\\text{ther}\\\text{thair}\end{smallmatrix}\right\}$

$\quad\quad\quad\quad\quad\quad |\quad\quad\quad\quad [+15\text{th cent}]$
$\quad\quad\quad\quad\quad [+\text{gen}]$
$\quad\quad\quad\quad\quad\quad |$
$\quad\quad\quad\quad\quad [+3]$

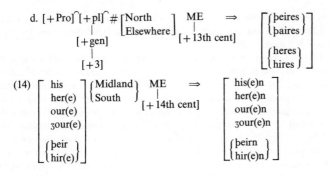

d. $[+\text{Pro}]\begin{bmatrix}+\text{pl}\end{bmatrix}\#\begin{bmatrix}\text{North}\\\text{Elsewhere}\end{bmatrix}\overset{\text{ME}}{\underset{[+13\text{th cent}]}{\Rightarrow}}\begin{bmatrix}\begin{Bmatrix}\text{þeires}\\\text{þaires}\end{Bmatrix}\\\begin{Bmatrix}\text{heres}\\\text{hires}\end{Bmatrix}\end{bmatrix}$

(14) $\begin{bmatrix}\text{his}\\\text{her(e)}\\\text{our(e)}\\\text{ʒour(e)}\\\begin{Bmatrix}\text{þeir}\\\text{hir(e)}\end{Bmatrix}\end{bmatrix}\begin{Bmatrix}\text{Midland}\\\text{South}\end{Bmatrix}\overset{\text{ME}}{\underset{[+14\text{th cent}]}{\Rightarrow}}\begin{bmatrix}\text{his(e)n}\\\text{her(e)n}\\\text{our(e)n}\\\text{ʒour(e)n}\\\begin{Bmatrix}\text{þeirn}\\\text{hir(e)n}\end{Bmatrix}\end{bmatrix}$

Some comment on the above rules is in order. Rule (1) indicates dialect differentiation in the first person singular nominative that comes about as a result of further Old English palatalization of the palatal stop /k/ in *ic* /ik/, which gave Midland and South /ič/. Rule (8) suggests the fairly considerable diversity in the feminine pronoun. Rules (10) and (11) and their subrules try to suggest the dialect situation regarding the spread of the borrowed Scandinavian forms for the third person plural. As the reader will note, these latter forms appear early in the north and gradually spread southward during the twelfth, thirteenth, and fourteenth centuries so that by the fifteenth century they are almost universal in the island. Rules (12), (13), and (14) show the development of genitive or possessive forms. Rules (12) a. and b. show that a differentiation in first and second singular forms occasioned by differences in phonological environment (12)a. is transferred to a syntactic environment (12)b. That is to say, *mi* and *thi* originally occur before items beginning with a consonant letter, *mine* and *thine* before items beginning with a vowel letter. In the thirteenth century, a noun phrase deletion rule permitted the occurrence of genitive noun or pronoun forms before *space* (#). *Mine* and *thine* were then assigned to this syntactic slot, while *mi* and *thi* were assigned to the slot before *noun phrase* ('this is my book'—'this is mine'). Rules (12)e., (13)a., and (13)d. show the assignment of the by now regular genitive *-(e)s* to pronouns ending in *-r(e)* occurring in disjunctive positions ('This book is *hers, ours, yours, theirs*'). Rule (14) indicates that in some dialects of the Midlands and the South competing disjunctive forms arose modeled on the *-n(e)* forms of the first and second person singular.

Appendix IV: Phonemic Transcriptions

A. PASSAGE FROM TREVISA

as hit is iknow huw meniy maneyr peypl büyθ in ðis iyloənd, ðeər büyθ alsoə ov soə meniy peypl loəngaəjez and tongez; noəðeleəs walšmen and skotez, ðat büyθ noxt imeled wiθ owðer naəsiownz, hoəldeθ weyl niy her fürst loəngaəj and speəč, bot yef skotez ðat weər som tiym konfederat and woned wiθ ðe piktez draw somwat after her speəč. bot ðe flemingez, ðat woneθ in ðe west siyd ov waəlez, habeθ ileft her straənj speəč and speəkeθ saksonliyč inuw. alsoə, englišmen, ðey hiy had fram ðe bigining θrey maneyr speəč, suwðeron, norðeron, and midel speəč, in ðe midel of ðe loənd, as hiy kowm ov θrey maneyr peypl ov germaənia, noəðeleəs, biy komikstiown and meling fürst wiθ daənez and afterward wiθ normanz, in meniy ðe kontray loəngaəj is apeyred, and som uwzeθ straənj wlafing, čitering, haring and garing, grisbiting. ðis apeyring ov ðe bürθtong is bikawz ov twey θingez. oən is, for čildern in skowl, ayeynez ðe uwsaəj and maneyr ov al owðer naəsiownz, büyθ kompeled for tow leəv her own loəngaəj and for tow konstriw her lesownz and her θingez a freynš, and habeθ süθ ðe normanz kowm fürst intow engeloənd. alsoə, jentilmen čildren büyθ itawxt for tow speək freynš fram tiym ðat a büyθ iroked in her kraədel, and koneθ speək and play wiθ a čiyld his bruč; and uploəndiš men wol liykne hamsilf tow jentilmen, and foəndeθ wiθ greət bisiynes for tow speək freynš for tow bey moər itoəld ov.

ðis maneyr was moč iuwzed towfoər ðe fürst moreyn, and is seθ somdeəl ičawnjed. for joəhan kornwal a mayster ov grameyr, čaynjed ðe loər in grameyrskowl and konstruksiown ov freynš intow engliš; and ričard penkrič lurned ðat maneyr teəčing ov him, and owðer men ov penkrič, soə ðat nuw, ðe yeər ov uwr loərd, a θuwsond θrey hondred fuwr skoər and fiyv, ov ðe sekund king ričard after ðe konkwest niyn, in al ðe grameyrskowlez of engeloənd čildern leəveθ frenš and konstriweθ and lurneθ an engliš, and habeθ ðeyrbiy avawntaəj in oən siyd and disavawntaəj in anowðer. her avawntaəj is, ðat a lurneθ her grameyr in las tiym ðan čildern weər iwoned tow dow; disavawntaəj is, ðat nuw čildern ov grameyrskowl koneθ noə moər frenš ðan kan her lift heyl, and ðat is harm for ham and a skol pas ðe seə and travayl in straənj loəndez, and in meniy kaəs alsoə. alsoə jentilmen habeθ nuw moč ileft for tow teəč her čildern frenš.

B. PASSAGE FROM BEDE

αnd θα· æfter θon θe se· here wæs hα·m hwərfende ond hi· hæfdon u·t α·mæ·rde ond to·stenkte θα· bi·gengαn θyses a·londes, θα· ongunnon hi· stičemæ·lum mo·d ond mægen nimαn; ond forθə·dαn of θα·m di·glum sto·wum θe hi· æ·r on behy·dde wæ·ron, ond alre α·nmo·dre yeθαfunge həfonri·čes fultumes him wæ·ron biddende, θæt hi· oθ forwyrd æ·ghwæ·r fordiligαde ne wæ·ron. wæs on θα· ti·d hərα heretogα ond lαttə·w ambro·sius hα·ten, o·θre nαmαn aureliα·nus. se· wæs go·d mαn ond yemetfæst, ro·mαnišes kynnes mαn. on θyses mαnnes ti·d mo·d ond mægen bryttαs onfe·ngon; ond he· hi· to· yefəxte forθyečy·gde ond him sije yehe·t; ond hi· a·č on θα·m yefəxte θurx godes fultum sije onfe·ngon. ond θα· of θæ·re ti·de hwi·lum bryttαs, hwi·lum eft saksαn sije yeslo·gαn oθ θæt ye·r ymbsetes θæ·re badonešαn du·ne, θα· hi· myčel wæl on αngelkynne yeslo·gαn, ymb fə·wer ond fə·wertig wintrα αngelkynnes kyme on brətone.

Selected Bibliography

A. HISTORY OF EARLY ENGLAND

Björkman, E. *Scandinavian Loan-Words in Middle English.* Halle, 1900–1902.
Collingwood, R. G. *Roman Britain.* New York, 1932.
Green, J. R. *Short History of the English People.* New York, 1899.
Haskins, Charles H. *The Normans in European History.* Boston, 1915.
Haverfield, E. *The Roman Occupation of Britain.* Oxford, 1924.
Hodgkin, R. H. *History of the Anglo-Saxons.* 2 vols. 3d ed. New York, 1953.
Jackson, Kenneth. *Language and History in Early Britain.* Edinburgh, 1953.
Kendricks, T. D. *A History of the Vikings.* New York, 1930.
Lambley, Kathleen. *The Teaching and Cultivation of the French Language in England during Tudor and Stuart Times, With an Introductory Chapter on the Preceding Period.* Manchester, 1920.
Leeds, E. Thurlow. *The Archaeology of the Anglo-Saxon Settlements.* Oxford, 1913.
Lindkvist, H. *Middle-English Place-Names of Scandinavian Origin,* Part I. Uppsala, 1912.
Plummer, C. *Life and Times of Alfred the Great.* Oxford, 1902.
Poole, Austin L. *From Domesday Book to Magna Carta 1087–1216.* Oxford, 1951.
Robinson, J. A. *The Times of St. Dunstan.* Oxford, 1923.
Stenton, F. M. *Anglo-Saxon England.* 2d ed. Oxford, 1947.
Trevelyan, G. M. *History of England.* New York, 1953.
Vising, Johan. *Anglo-Norman Language and Literature.* London, 1923.

B. HISTORY OF ENGLISH

Barfield, Owen. *History in English Words.* London, 1953; Grand Rapids, 1967.
Baugh, A. C. *A History of the English Language,* 2d ed. New York, 1957.
Bloomfield, Morton W., and Leonard Newmark. *A Linguistic Introduction to the History of English.* New York, 1963.
Brook, G. L. *A History of the English Language.* London, 1958.
Bryant, Margaret M. *Modern English and its Heritage.* 2d ed. New York, 1962.
Groom, Bernard. *A Short History of English Words.* London, 1934; repr. 1965.
Jespersen, Otto H. *Growth and Structure of the English Language.* 9th ed. Oxford, 1962.
Jones, R. F. *The Triumph of the English Language.* Stanford, 1953.
Peters, Robert A. *A Linguistic History of English.* Boston, 1968.
Potter, Simeon. *Our Language.* Harmondsworth, 1950.
Pyles, Thomas. *The Origins and Development of the English Language.* New York, 1964.
Robertson, Stuart, and Frederic G. Cassidy. *The Development of Modern English.* 2d ed. New York, 1954.
Wyld, Henry Cecil. *A Short History of English.* 3d ed. Revised. London, 1951.
———. *A History of Modern Colloquial English.* 3d ed. Oxford, 1953.

C. OLD ENGLISH

Alston, R. C. *An Introduction to Old English.* London, 1961.
Andrew, S. O. "Relative and Demonstrative Pronouns in Old English," *Language* 12:282–293 (1936).
———. *Syntax and Style in Old English.* Cambridge, 1940.
Bazell, C. E. "Six Questions of Old and Middle English Morphology," *Tolkien Studies* 5.9:51–62.
Brunner, K. "The Old English Vowel Phonemes," *English Studies* 34:247–251 (1953).

Campbell, A. *Old English Grammar*. Oxford, 1959.

Carlton, Charles. "Word Order of Noun Modifiers in Old English Prose," *Journal of English and Germanic Philology* 62:778–783 (1963).

Daunt, Marjorie. "Some Notes on Old English Phonology," *Transactions of the Philological Society* 1952:48–54. London, 1953.

Funke, Otto. "Some Remarks on Late Old English Word-Order with Special Reference to Aelfric and the Maldon Poem," *English Studies* 37:99–104 (1956).

Hockett, C. F. "The Stressed Syllabics of Old English," *Language* 35:575–597 (1959).

Howren, Robert. "The Generation of Old English Weak Verbs," *Language* 43:674–685 (1967).

Kuhn, Sherman M., and Randolph Quirk. "Some Recent Interpretations of Old English Digraph Spellings," *Language* 29:143–156 (1953).

Levin, Samuel R. "A Reclassification of the Old English Strong Verbs," *Language* 40:156–161 (1964).

Marckwardt, Albert H. "Verb Inflections in Late Old English," *Philologica* 6.8:79–88.

Moulton, W. G. "Stops and Spirants of Early Germanic," *Language* 30:1–42 (1954).

Quirk, Randolph. *The Concessive Relation in Old English Poetry*. New Haven, 1954.

————, and C. L. Wrenn. *An Old English Grammar*. New York, 1957.

Samuels, M. L. "The Study of Old English Phonology," *Transactions of the Philological Society* 1952:15–47. London, 1953.

Scherer, Philip. "Aspect in the Old English of the Corpus Christi MS," *Language* 34:245–251 (1958).

Shannon, Ann. *A Descriptive Syntax of the Parker Manuscript of the Anglo-Saxon Chronicle from 734 to 891*. The Hague, 1964.

Stockwell, R. P., and C. W. Barritt. "Some Old English Graphemic-Phonemic Correspondences," *Studies in Linguistics*, Occasional Papers, No. 4 (1951).

Wright, Joseph, and Elizabeth Mary. *Old English Grammar*. 3d ed. London, 1925; repr. 1934.

D. MIDDLE ENGLISH

Dean, Christopher. "Chaucer's Use of Function Words with Substantives," *Canadian Journal of Linguistics* 9:67–74 (1964).

Ellegård, Alvar. *The Auxiliary Do: The Establishment and Regulation of its Use in English*. Stockholm, 1953.

Forsstrom, G. *The Verb 'To Be' in Middle English*. Lund, 1948.

Friden, Georg. *Studies on the Tenses of the English Verb from Chaucer to Shakespeare*. Uppsala, 1948.

————. "On the Use of Auxiliaries to Form the Perfect and the Pluperfect in Late Middle English and Early Modern English," *Archiv.* 196:152–153 (1959).

Long, Mary McDonald. *The English Strong Verb from Chaucer to Caxton*. Wisconsin, 1944.

McLaughlin, John C. *A Graphemic-Phonemic Study of a Middle English Manuscript*. The Hague, 1963.

Moore, Samuel. "Earliest Morphological Changes in Middle English," *Language* 4:238–266 (1928).

————, Sanford B. Meech, and Harold Whitehall. "Middle English Dialect Characteristics and Dialect Boundaries," *Essays and Studies in English and Comparative Literature*, University of Michigan Publication, Language and Literature XIII, Ann Arbor, 1935:1–60.

Mossé, Fernand. *A Handbook of Middle English*. Trans. James A. Walker. Baltimore, 1952.

Mustanoja, Tanno F. *A Middle English Syntax*, Pt. 1: Parts of Speech. Helsinki, 1960.

Nathan, Norman. "Pronouns of Address in the Canterbury Tales," *Mediaeval Studies* 21:193–201 (1959).

Ohlander, Urban. "A Study on the Use of the Infinitive Sign in Middle English," *Studia Neophilologica* 14:58–66 (1941–1942).

Rantavaara, Irma. "On the Development of the Periphrastic Dative in Late Middle English Prose," *Neuphilologische Mitteilungen* 63:175–203 (1962).

Stockwell, Robert P. "The ME 'long close' and 'long open' Vowels," *Texas Studies in Literature and Language,* 4:530–538 (1961).

Swieczkowski, Wolerian. *Word Order Patterning in Middle English: A Quantitative Study Based on Piers Plowman and Middle English Sermons.* The Hague, 1962.

Wardale, E. E. *An Introduction to Middle English.* London, 1937.

Wright, Joseph, and Elizabeth Mary. *An Elementary Middle English Grammar.* 2d ed. Oxford, 1928.

E. EARLY MODERN ENGLISH

Abbott, O. L. "The Formal Subjunctive in Seventeenth-Century American English," *American Speech* 36:181–187 (1961).

————. "The Preterit and Past Participle of Strong Verbs in Seventeenth-Century American English," *American Speech* 32:31–42 (1957).

Bambas, Rudolph C. "Verb Forms in -s and -th in Early Modern English," *Journal of English and Germanic Philology* 46:183–187 (1947).

Brunner, Karl. "Expanded Verbal Forms in Early Modern English," *English Studies* 36:218–221 (1955).

Dobbie, Elliot. "On Early Modern English Pronunciation," *American Speech* 33:111–115 (1958).

Dobson, Eric J. *English Pronunciation, 1500–1700.* 2 vols. Oxford, 1957.

————. "Early Modern Standard English," *Transactions of the Philological Society* 1955:25–54 (1956).

Kökeritz, Helge. *Shakespeare's Pronunciation.* New Haven, 1953.

————. "Guy Miege's Pronunciation (1685)," *Language* 19:141–146 (1943).

Matthews, William. "Variant Pronunciations in the Seventeenth Century," *Journal of English and Germanic Philology* 37:189–206 (1938).

Price, Hereward T. "Grammar and the Compositor in the Sixteenth and Seventeenth Centuries," *Journal of English and Germanic Philology* 38:540–548 (1939).

Wright, Joseph, and Elizabeth Mary. *An Elementary Historical New English Grammar.* Oxford, 1924.

Zachrisson, R. E. *Pronunciation of English Vowels, 1400–1700.* Göteborg, 1913.

F. GENERAL LINGUISTIC THEORY AND METHODOLOGY

Antal, Lászlo. "Meaning and its Change," *Linguistics* 6:14–28 (1964).

Bach, Emmon. *An Introduction to Transformational Grammars.* New York, 1964.

Bolinger, Dwight. *Aspects of Language.* New York, 1968.

Bréal, Michel. *Semantics: Studies in the Science of Meaning.* Trans. Mrs. Henry Cust. London, 1900.

Carnop, Rudolf. *Meaning and Necessity: A Study in Semantics and Modal Logic.* Chicago, 1956.

Chomsky, Noam. *Syntactic Structures.* The Hague, 1957.

————. *Aspects of the Theory of Syntax.* M.I.T., 1965.

Closs, Elizabeth. "Diachronic Syntax and Generative Grammar," *Language* 41:402–415 (1965).

Dineen, Francis P. *An Introduction to General Linguistics.* New York, 1967.

Estrich, Robert M., and Hans Sperber. *Three Keys to Language.* New York, 1952.

Fillmore, C. J. "The Case for Case," in *Universals in Linguistic Theory,* eds. Emmon Bach and Robert T. Harms. New York, 1968.

Fodor, J. A., and J. J. Katz (eds.). *The Structure of Language: Readings in the Philosophy of Language.* Englewood Cliffs, N. J., 1964.

Garvin, Paul L. "A Descriptive Technique for the Treatment of Meaning," *Language* 34:1–32 (1958).

Gleason, H. A. *An Introduction to Descriptive Linguistics.* Revised ed. New York, 1961.

Heffner, Roe-Merrill. *General Phonetics.* Madison, 1949.

Hill, A. *Introduction to Linguistic Structures.* New York, 1958.

Hockett, C. F. *A Course in Linguistics.* New York, 1958.

Jones, David. *The Phoneme: Its Nature and Use.* Cambridge, 1950.

Katz, Jerrold J., and Jerry A. Fodor. "The Structure of a Semantic Theory," *Language* 39 : 170–210 (1963).

————, and Paul M. Postal. *An Integrated Theory of Linguistic Descriptions.* M.I.T., 1964.

Koutsoudas, A. *Writing Transformational Grammars: An Introduction.* New York, 1966.

Lees, Robert B. *The Grammar of English Nominalizations.* Bloomington, 1960.

Levin, Samuel R. "Aspects of Semantic and Grammatical Change," *Linguistics* 2 : 26–37 (1963).

McCawley, James D. "The Role of Semantics in a Grammar," in *Universals in Linguistic Theory,* eds. Emmon Bach and Robert T. Harms. New York, 1968.

Morris, Charles. *Signs, Language* and *Behavior.* New York, 1946; repr. 1955.

Osgood, Charles, G. Suci, and P. Tannenbaum. *The Measurement of Meaning.* Urbana, 1957.

Postal, Paul. *Constituent Structure: A Study of Contemporary Models of Syntactic Description.* Bloomington, 1964.

Rosenbaum, Peter S. *The Grammar of English Predicate Complement Constructions.* M.I.T., 1967.

Stern, Gustav. *Meaning and Change of Meaning, with Special Reference to the English Language.* Göteborg, 1931; repr. Bloomington, 1963.

Thomas, Owen. *Transformational Grammar and the Teacher of English.* New York, 1965.

Trier, Jost. *Der Deutsche Wortschatz im Sinnbezirk des Verstandes. Die Geschichte eines Sprachlichen Feldes.* Heidelberg, 1934.

Ullmann, Stephen. *Semantics: An Introduction to the Science of Meaning.*

Ziff, Paul. *Semantic Analysis.* Ithaca, 1960.

Index

A